Strategic Cyber Security Management

This textbook places cyber security management within an organizational and strategic framework, enabling students to develop their knowledge and skills for a future career. The reader will learn to:

- evaluate different types of cyber risk
- carry out a threat analysis and place cyber threats in order of severity
- formulate appropriate cyber security management policy
- establish an organization-specific intelligence framework and security culture
- devise and implement a cyber security awareness programme
- integrate cyber security within an organization's operating system

Learning objectives, chapter summaries and further reading in each chapter provide structure and routes to further in-depth research. Firm theoretical grounding is coupled with short problem-based case studies reflecting a range of organizations and perspectives, illustrating how the theory translates to practice, with each case study followed by a set of questions to encourage understanding and analysis. Non-technical and comprehensive, this textbook shows final year undergraduate students and postgraduate students of Cyber Security Management, as well as reflective practitioners, how to adopt a pro-active approach to the management of cyber security. Online resources include PowerPoint slides, an instructor's manual and a test bank of questions.

Peter Trim is a Senior Lecturer in Management at Birkbeck, University of London.

Yang-Im Lee is a Senior Lecturer in Marketing at Westminster Business School, University of Westminster.

Strategic Cyber Security Management

Peter Trim and Yang-Im Lee

Routledge
Taylor & Francis Group

LONDON AND NEW YORK

Cover image: © nadla / Getty Images

First published 2023
by Routledge
4 Park Square, Milton Park, Abingdon, Oxon OX14 4RN

and by Routledge
605 Third Avenue, New York, NY 10158

Routledge is an imprint of the Taylor & Francis Group, an informa business

British Library Cataloguing-in-Publication Data
A catalogue record for this book is available from the British Library

Library of Congress Cataloging-in-Publication Data
Names: Trim, Peter R. J., author. | Lee, Yang-Im, author.
Title: Strategic cyber security management / Peter Trim, Yang-Im Lee.
Description: 1 Edition. | New York, NY : Routledge, 2023. | Includes
bibliographical references and index.
Identifiers: LCCN 2022009512 (print) | LCCN 2022009513 (ebook) | ISBN
9781032154756 (hardback) | ISBN 9781032154763 (paperback) | ISBN
9781003244295 (ebook)
Subjects: LCSH: Business enterprises—Computer networks—Security measures.|
Computer security. | Computer crimes—Prevention. | Corporations—Security measures.
Classification: LCC HF5548.37.T745 2023 (print) | LCC HF5548.37 (ebook)|
DDC 658.4/78—dc23/eng/20220307
LC record available at https://lccn.loc.gov/2022009512
LC ebook record available at https://lccn.loc.gov/2022009513

ISBN: 978-1-032-15475-6 (hbk)
ISBN: 978-1-032-15476-3 (pbk)
ISBN: 978-1-003-24429-5 (ebk)

DOI: 10.4324/9781003244295

Typeset in Bembo
by codeMantra

Access the Support Material: www.routledge.com/9781032154763

To Richard

With much love and gratitude

Contents

Figures

Tables

Mini Cases

Extended Cases

Authors

Dr. Peter Trim is a Senior Lecturer in Management at Birkbeck, University of London, and holds degrees from NELP/CNAA (BSc), Cranfield (MSc and PhD), City University (MBA) and the University of Cambridge (MEd). Peter is a Fellow of the Higher Education Academy and the Royal Society of Arts, and was actively involved with the Information Assurance Advisory Council (IAAC) Academic Liaison Panel over a number of years. He has published over 50 academic articles in a range of journals, including *Industrial Marketing Management, European Journal of Marketing, Journal of Business & Industrial Marketing, Journal of Brand Management, Security Journal, International Journal of Intelligence and Counter Intelligence, Disaster Prevention and Management, Cross-Cultural Management: An International Journal, Journal of Business Continuity & Emergency Planning, Simulation & Gaming: An International Journal of Theory, Practice and Research, Big Data and Cognitive Computing, Journal of Global Scholars of Marketing Science: Bridging Asia and the World,* and *International Journal of Retail & Distribution Management.* Peter has produced a number of single authored, co-authored and edited books. He has co-authored with Yang-Im Lee, a book entitled *Cyber Security Management: A Governance, Risk and Compliance Framework* (Farnham: Gower Publishing); a co-authored book with David Upton, entitled *Cyber Security Culture: Counteracting Cyber Threats through Organizational Learning and Training* (Farnham: Gower Publishing); and co-edited a book with Jack Caravelli entitled *Strategizing Resilience and Reducing Vulnerability* (New York: Nova Science Publishers Inc.).

Peter has been the Chair of the UK Cyber Security Research Network and taken two delegations of UK cyber security experts to South Korea and hosted two cyber security South Korean delegations in the UK. He has with Professor Youm organized four UK and Korea cyber security workshops and co-edited two reports for government entitled *Korea-UK Initiatives in Cyber Security Research: Government, University and Industry Collaboration* (British Embassy Seoul: Republic of Korea); and *Korea-UK Collaboration in Cyber Security: From Issues and Challenges to Sustainable Partnership* (British Embassy Seoul: Republic of Korea). Prior to this, Peter contributed the Cyber Attacks section of the University College London report *Scientific Advice and Evidence in Emergencies,* which was edited by Professor McGuire and submitted to the House of Commons Science and Technology Committee as written evidence.

Peter has won a number of grants and been the Principal Investigator on two research projects: one was funded by the UK's Technology Strategy Board and the other was funded by the Technology Strategy Board and SEEDA (South East England Development Agency). In addition to this, he has been involved in a number of initiatives such as the Canada-UK Partnership for Knowledge Forum; the Law Enforcement and National Security Global Forum and *Increasing Cyber Security Provision in the UK and Korea: Identifying Market Opportunities for SME's*, which was funded by the UK's Department of Business Innovation & Skills and the Korean Government's Ministry of Science, ICT and Future Planning.

Dr. Yang-Im Lee is a Senior Lecturer in Marketing at Westminster Business School, University of Westminster, where she teaches marketing. Yang-Im has studied and worked in Korea, Japan and the UK. She undertook postgraduate studies at the School of Oriental and African Studies in London; and was awarded a scholarship by Stirling University to undertake a PhD at that institution. Yang-Im has worked for both Brunel University and Royal Holloway, University of London, and provided guest lectures at Birkbeck, University of London. She has published over 30 articles in a range of academic journals, including *Industrial Marketing Management, European Journal of Marketing, Journal of Business & Industrial Marketing, International Journal of Retail & Distribution Management, Journal of Brand Management, Simulation & Gaming: An International Journal of Theory, Practice and Research, Big Data and Cognitive Computing*, and also co-authored several books.

Yang-Im is a Fellow of the Higher Education Academy and the Royal Society of Arts and was involved in the iGRC Consortium three-year research project funded by the Technology Strategy Board and SEEDA. She also provided research input into the Technology Strategy Board Fast Track project undertaken by Peter Trim and David Upton entitled 'Develop proven software system to improve emergency response exercises, and extend it to develop robustness in critical information infrastructure'. Yang-Im has been a member of the UK-Korea Cyber Security Research Network and a Visiting Fellow at Birkbeck, University of London. She also provided support for the Information Assurance Advisory Council and was their Academic Liaison Panel Co-ordinator for a number of years.

Preface

Strategic Cyber Security Management has been written for a range of readers, including university students, reflective practitioners, government policy makers and those without prior knowledge of cyber security management. The purpose of the book is to place cyber security at the heart of security and ensure that a collectivist approach is adopted to cyber security management. Taking cognizance of the fact that staff in an organization work with staff based in a number of organizations, those that have a trading relationship with the organization, means that the collectivist/stakeholder approach can be placed in the context of a partnership arrangement. The logic of this is that an organization, whether it is a company or an institution or a charity, does not operate in isolation but in unison with a number of organizations through trade and various forms of interaction, at home and abroad. By placing cyber security management within a strategic context, the cyber security management decision-making process will be strengthened and cyber threats will be anticipated and result in cyber security awareness and appropriate cyber security countermeasures being implemented.

To assist the reader in their journey into strategic cyber security management, the book has been written from the perspective of helping the reader absorb the complexities involved so that they can navigate through the subject matter and place it in a management context. It is for this reason that risk management and strategic intelligence are given attention, and the role of the cyber security manager is given prominence. The reader will become aware that the cyber security manager is a key player within the senior management team and performs a well-defined set of tasks. One of which is to liaise with other senior managers in the organization and those based in external organizations, so that relevant data and information related to cyber attacks are shared. This being the case, the wider community will benefit and everybody will be adequately informed and well prepared to deal with all forms of cyber attack. The objective of the cyber security manager in terms of helping organizations throughout the supply chain and the marketing channel is to maintain their level of resilience. This will be made clear.

One of the advantages of the book is that it contains a set of mini cases and a set of extended cases, which will help the reader to link theory and practice. The questions posed will enable the reader to relate to the issues and think through the consequences from the perspective of a cyber security manager. This should result in various intellectual challenges and intellectual fulfilment. By incorporating various insights into the field of cyber security, it is hoped that university students in particular will identify a number of topics that can be undertaken in the form of a research project.

1 An Introduction to Strategic Cyber Security Management

1.1 Introduction

Strategic Cyber Security Management is written for a broad audience, including final-year undergraduate management students and postgraduate management students. In addition, researchers, who are studying aspects of cyber security and wish to know more about how cyber security is managed, will find the book highly informative as it covers a range of topics that are underpinned by social science theory. The reader will, therefore, be able to place cyber security management within a holistic and strategic context, and understand why a cyber security manager is considered to be part of the senior management team. In the process of deploying various concepts, frameworks and models, the reader will see how the cyber security manager can develop theoretical perspectives and approaches, which result in a deeper understanding of the cyber security management process.

Through the process of understanding how and why the various bodies of knowledge should be integrated, a holistic view of cyber security will be developed and placed at the centre of security. By placing themselves in the role of a cyber security manager, the reader will be able to link the separate but related bodies of knowledge, and derive their own interpretation of what cyber security management involves. The emphasis is, therefore, to place cyber security management within a strategic context so that the cyber security management decision-making process allows key individuals, such as the cyber security manager in unison with other senior managers, to identify and solve cyber security-related problems by devising and putting in place appropriate countermeasures that thwart cyber attacks. By accepting that cyber security is a shared responsibility, the cyber security manager can work with managers based in various organizations and ensure that a united approach is adopted to counteracting various forms of cyber attack. The advantage of viewing cyber security from a partnership arrangement perspective, which can be defined in various ways (e.g. vertical or horizontal or contractual basis), is that it allows a collectivist approach to cyber security to be adopted. A collectivist approach involves managers and their subordinates sharing information and undertaking certain tasks, in an equal and fair way, so that cyber security is viewed as a priority to those in the partnership arrangement who interpret events and provide a framework within which the various stakeholders can contribute to the process of eradicating organizational vulnerabilities.

As well as appealing to an academic audience, the book will also appeal to reflective practitioners that want to deepen their knowledge of the subject and broaden their view of how they can deal with various cyber security challenges that they are confronted

DOI: 10.4324/9781003244295-1

with. The data, theoretical insights, frameworks and interpretation provided throughout the book will allow the reader to develop their own view as to what cyber security management involves and how the cyber security manager can perform a valuable and unique role within an organization. The topics and subtopics are crafted in a way that helps the reader to link theory and practice, and at the same time deepen their knowledge and understanding of how the cyber security manager evaluates the technical aspects and considerations relating to cyber security alongside the human aspects, so that the overall complexity of the subject is made apparent.

Strategic Cyber Security Management has been written in such a way as to place emphasis on cyber security management knowledge enhancement and utilization. The objective of this is to help the reader understand why the cyber security manager plays a role in helping the organization to deal with a range of cyber threats. Throughout the book, the role of the cyber security manager is explained through the use of real world examples, which highlight the nature and form of cyber attacks that occur across industries. The evidence-based approach adds weight to the argument for the appointment of a cyber security manager, and what *Strategic Cyber Security Management* does is outline as to how management theory can be drawn on to provide cyber security solutions. The development of cyber security management knowledge and its utilization is very much associated with helping the reader gain a holistic view of cyber security and to better understand why a pro-active and collectivist approach to counteracting cyber attacks is needed.

1.2 Placing the Book in Context

The book contains this introductory chapter, which outlines what the chapters are composed of and makes reference to a navigational map. The intention is to provide a basis for the reader and people of various disciplines that have varying degrees of knowledge of cyber security from a management perspective, and to develop insights into how to make and implement decisions that counteract the actions of cyber criminals in real time. In the process, *Strategic Cyber Security Management* will help those that are not fully versed in the technical field associated with cyber security to better understand the technical issues and concerns, and to link management theory with the management of IT and information systems. The theoretical underpinning through case examples throughout the book enables the reader to develop specific insights into specific types of problem solution. The link between the cases and the questions, and the process by which a solution is derived, should enrich the learning experience and result in enhanced knowledge.

The mini cases and extended cases, which have been written to highlight specific situations and illustrate a range of issues and challenges, can be used for class discussion but also can be read by individuals who want to know more about the intricacies of cyber security management. The cases have been drawn from a number of sources and are to illustrate points of interest only. References are provided that enable the reader to develop deeper insights into the case material. It can be noted, therefore, that each case is defined in terms of learning aims and outcomes, and evidence of this lies in the type of questions posed at the end of each case. Each case has been written to highlight a specific problem(s) and is representative of a range of challenges confronting private and public sector organizations.

A further reading list is provided for each chapter and provides a platform from which the reader can develop more specific knowledge relating to a theme(s) identified in the case(s). It is hoped, therefore, that the reader will be encouraged to deepen their knowledge of certain aspects of cyber security management as they progress through the book. Again, the emphasis is placed on the role of the cyber security manager and how such a person can contribute to security and make the organization more resilient. With respect to the references provided, it should be possible for the reader to select appropriate background material and build up an all-round appreciation of how countermeasures can be put in place to deal with the cyber threats identified.

Strategic Cyber Security Management is distinct in the sense it contains reference to policies, systems and procedures that will enable university students, researchers and reflective practitioners, to understand the complexity associated with cyber security management and how the subject is evolving. The navigational map, Figure 1.1, illustrates how the reader is to be guided through the material, and how the main themes and topics are linked with the subtopics covered. The main objective of cyber security management and indeed the work of the cyber security manager is to put in place organizational structures that make an organization more resilient and enable managers to deal better with various forms of cyber attack. The learning objectives have been outlined and provided at the start of each chapter and a learning summary is provided at the end of each chapter. The cases contain a number of reflective questions, and it is hoped that the reader, when answering the questions posed, is able to undergo a period of self-reflection, and deepen their all-round knowledge of cyber security management. A key aspect of the self-reflection process is that the reader will challenge existing assumptions and gain confidence to devise cyber security management solutions as they progress through the book.

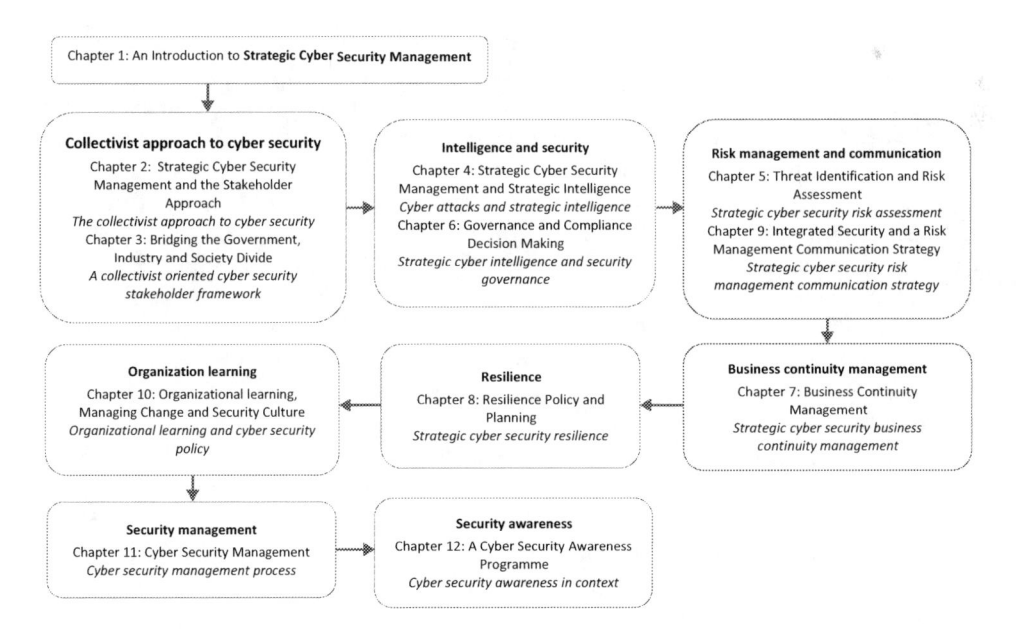

Figure 1.1 Navigational map: the linkage between the themes and topics of strategic cyber security management.

As regards non-management specialists, *Strategic Cyber Security Management* will be of interest to those that have a firm understanding of the technical aspects of cyber security but want to learn more about the management and human side of dealing with cyber security issues and challenges. By having a deeper appreciation of the motivations of people, in particular, an understanding of why certain individuals instigate a cyber attack and why individuals are motivated to counteract such attacks will help raise the profile of the cyber security manager and highlight further the need for cyber security management. Indeed, the readers will, as they progress through the book, develop a mindset in terms of identifying how cyber security management can be viewed as a shared responsibility as opposed to just the responsibility of an individual or group of individuals.

1.3 Adding to Management Knowledge

The greater the knowledge an individual possesses as regards cyber attacks and how and why they are launched on an organization should bode well in terms of them being able to anticipate events and work with people of a similar mindset to develop long-term solutions to what has become a recurring problem. Being able to identify and deal with a range of cyber threats, of varying levels of risk intensity, means that a cyber security management approach needs to be adopted that is pro-active and benefits the organization and the organizations it does business with. By recognizing that a cyber security manager fulfils a vital and high-profile role within an organization, it should be ensured that emphasis is placed on making the organization more resilient in terms of its business operations and connectivity, and is less vulnerable to attack via a supply chain partner.

The management perspective articulated throughout the book should assist students from various disciplines, researchers and reflective practitioners, to develop their intellectual curiosity in terms of developing approaches to counteract cyber threats and to develop a broad range of solutions that enable senior managers to put in place cyber security systems that are robust enough to make the organization less vulnerable to attack and also better able to defend the organization in real time. The reader will, by the time they have read the book, be more confident in terms of devising and implementing cyber security solutions as they will have a theoretical understanding of how the topics covered are integrated. A number of benefits will become evident. For example, the reader will become more aware of the issues to be addressed and better able to relate to day-to-day cyber security challenges, probe cyber security experts when necessary for advice regarding solving recurring problems and work with managers administering IT projects and subcontractors that provide a range of outsourced services.

The book, which is reinforced by real world examples and cases, will help the reader to identify, from their perspective, what the key cyber security risks are and how a cyber security manager should prioritize them and deal with them. Cyber security has a worldwide reach and law enforcement officers are aware that those carrying out cyber attacks are able to operate from hidden locations and focus their efforts on exploiting known vulnerabilities. Those behind a cyber attack are known to be well informed and well organized, and draw on a range of resources to assist them in their efforts. For example, as the banking industry becomes better able to defend itself against known cyber attacks, the emphasis on stealing money from accounts becomes less obvious and organized criminals move their focus of attention to industries that are less protective in their outlook. Because the focus of attack changes, people are caught off guard as new vulnerabilities are exploited.

Over the years, staff within organizations have been targeted by criminals and have on occasion divulged confidential data and information that has given individuals not connected with the organization access to their computer/database, which has resulted in a data breach or money being transferred to an overseas bank account or a ransom being paid to allow staff to regain access to the organization's files and computer networks. Often, the disruption associated with a successful cyber attack is just as costly as the losses incurred from the immediate financial loss as a disruption in service provision can result in reputational damage and a decrease in the customer base. As well as the immediate loss due to money being stolen from an account, a fine may be imposed on the organization by a regulatory authority if it coincides with a data breach. Also, there are likely to be additional costs as experts are brought in to help deal with the problem and make the organization's computer system(s) and networks more robust. From this, it can be deduced that the cyber security manager needs to draw on current management theory to help to shape new theoretical insights into what is an evolving body of multi-disciplinary knowledge.

Should a ransomware attack occur, it is likely that senior management in the targeted organization will pay a fee to the attacker so that staff can regain control of the organization's computer system(s) and networks; however, ethical considerations need to be addressed. Some governments are adamant that no ransom should be paid and some governments take a less confrontational approach and accept that a ransom can be paid. It is this type of dichotomy that is focusing the minds of those involved in cyber security; hence, it is necessary to view problem solving from the perspective of identifying appropriate management theory that can be used to develop a coherent approach to solving recurring problems. The underlying message is, therefore, that cyber attacks evolve through time, and the cyber security manager needs to understand the motivations of those carrying out the attacks, and how they operate and work with middlemen in order to deceive people and take advantage of them. Those orchestrating a cyber attack are likely to operate through various illicit channels and are apt at disguising who they are and who they represent. This focuses attention on human and psychological factors and legal and management factors.

What the cyber security manager needs to take cognizance of is that organized criminal syndicates operate from countries that are known to have lax legal frameworks in place or in some cases are protected by the government in power. This highlights the complexity of the problem because staff in an organization that has suffered a cyber attack will need to engage with law enforcement personnel and hope that the attacker is brought to justice and held accountable for their actions. Evidence suggests, however, that law enforcement officers have limited jurisdiction overseas and may not be able to approach their counterparts in some countries for a number of reasons, corruption being one of them. It is possible that a cyber security investigation will span several months or even years, and result in additional costs and dilute the management process as attention is focused on a non-competitive business action instead of the actions of competitors and maintaining and growing the company's market share. Bearing in mind that cyber criminals are becoming more selective and sophisticated in the way they study a designated target (either an individual or an organization or a government department), and are ambitious in terms of how much it costs to implement an attack compared with the possible financial returns and publicity gained, forces the cyber security manager to think through how a risk mitigation strategy should be deployed.

Through the examples, the reader will become familiar with understanding why the cyber security manager needs to adopt a *strategic* approach to cyber security management. Because a cyber attack occurs in real time and can be multi-faceted, it is likely that a successful attack will have a substantial impact on the organization that results in an escalation and cascading effect. *Strategic Cyber Security Management* will, it can be argued, provide a basis upon which the reader will be able to develop insights into the phenomenon of cyber security and what it entails and at the same time develop an ethical stance that will prove beneficial from both a self-awareness and reflective perspective and a managing complexity perspective. By being grounded in the role that the cyber security manager adopts, the reader will be able to identify with government policy in relation to the prevention of cyber attacks and encourage others to adopt a pro-active approach to cyber security management that ensures that cyber security management systems, procedures and policies are established, and reinforced through a security culture with cyber security at its heart.

1.4 Promoting a Collectivist and Stakeholder Approach to Cyber Security

Reflecting on the above, it can be deduced that *Strategic Cyber Security Management* is written in order to provide a basis for students and reflective managers to understand and interpret how a collectivist approach to cyber security and the management of it helps the cyber security manager to counteract cyber threats by adopting a pro-active, stakeholder approach to cyber security. At the same time, the reader will place cyber security firmly in an international context. Because cyber attacks vary in form and are carried out by multiple actors, the cyber security manager will need to develop an all-round appreciation of how cyber attackers think, and why they are motivated to carry out an attack in the way they do. The nature of the subject matter does, for example, link criminology with international relations, and this provides both intellectual curiosity and a challenge at the same time.

1.5 The Topics Covered

The reader will note that the main topics covered in the book are an introduction to strategic cyber security management; strategic cyber security management and the stakeholder approach; bridging the government, industry and society divide; strategic cyber security management and strategic intelligence; threat identification and risk assessment; governance and compliance decision making; business continuity management; resilience policy and planning; integrated security and a risk management communication strategy; organizational learning, managing change and security culture; cyber security management and a cyber security awareness programme.

1.6 The Aims of the Book

A number of aims can be identified:

- to provide insights into how to counteract cyber crime;
- to place in context organizational risks and vulnerabilities;
- to provide insights into risk management;
- to explain how cyber security is linked with intelligence theory;
- to place cyber security within organizational policy;
- to explain the role that cyber security awareness plays; and
- to place the role of the cyber security manager in the context of management theory.

Bearing in mind the aims above, the reader will (i) increase their awareness of the kind of cyber attack that is launched on an organization; (ii) develop an understanding of why the cyber security manager needs to be aware of how to defend the organization against various cyber attacks; (iii) develop an appreciation of how to draw on management theory and relevant concepts to better understand the motivation of those that carry out cyber attacks; (iv) apply cyber security management concepts/models/frameworks in order to solve cyber security-related problems and (v) formulate their own view as to how a cyber security manager can develop a collectivist approach to cyber security so that the emphasis is on stakeholder participation.

It can also be suggested that *Strategic Cyber Security Management* has a number of strengths. The reader will be guided to (1) establish how and why certain cyber threats manifest; (2) carry out a threat analysis and place cyber threats in order of severity; (3) formulate appropriate cyber security countermeasures; (4) establish an organization-specific intelligence framework; (5) devise a risk management approach; (6) develop an organization-specific security culture; (7) devise for implementation a cyber security awareness programme and (8) integrate cyber security within an organization's security system.

In addition, the reader will broaden their knowledge base in terms of linking cyber security awareness with intelligence gathering; and deepen their understanding as to why risk assessment and cyber security need to be viewed as a shared responsibility involving co-operation with staff from various business functions (e.g. marketing and IT) and external organizations (e.g. the legal profession and law enforcement). Both students and reflective practitioners will be guided through the process of understanding why it is necessary to adopt a pro-active approach to cyber security and fully understand the complexities involved (e.g. managing across functions and cultures).

1.7 The Objectives of the Book

The reader will identify with the following objectives:

- establish how and why certain cyber threats manifest;
- formulate a cyber security threat analysis;
- formulate appropriate cyber security countermeasures;
- establish an organization-specific intelligence framework;
- develop an organizational specific security culture;
- devise and implement a cyber security awareness programme;

- integrate cyber security within the organization's security system;
- establish how security awareness can be improved through intelligence gathering;
- establish how risk assessment enriches the cyber security management process;
- establish how cyber security is viewed as a shared responsibility involving the co-operation of various business functions and external organizations (e.g. law enforcement);
- develop a pro-active approach to cyber security management and
- develop an appreciation of the complexities involved in devising and implementing a cyber security management policy.

1.8 Learning Outcomes of the Book

As regards the main subject specific learning outcomes, a social science approach and appreciation of cyber security management are advocated. This is achieved through linking various bodies of knowledge gained from security studies, intelligence studies and management studies (including risk assessment), with the ability to develop and test various conceptual models/frameworks. The cases and the questions posed will enable the reader to reflect on current practice and challenge existing ideas and theoretical assumptions. The reader will both understand and challenge the assumptions upon which current cyber security knowledge is based and will develop the confidence to apply concepts and frameworks, and develop new approaches through the development and testing of their own conceptual models/frameworks.

The book has been written in such a way as to provide intellectual fulfilment and this is achieved through the reader developing the ability to evaluate risk-based situations and undertake a threat assessment and possible impact analysis. The mini cases and extended case examples allow for critical reasoning through the analysis of complex subject matter as the discussion component focuses on "what if" type scenarios and encourages the reader to engage in problem solving by establishing cause and effect. Most importantly, the case material will allow the reader to intellectualize through synthesizing complex outcomes (e.g. cyber security problems are defined and then placed in an organizational, political and societal context).

The main learning outcomes are therefore:

- to provide the reader with sufficient knowledge of cyber security management so they can challenge and implement cyber security solutions that are organization- and industry-specific, and which prove influential in terms of managing across organizations;
- to allow the reader to view cyber security from different perspectives: strategic, tactical and operational. The advantage being that the reader will identify cyber security issues and challenges and place them in a management context;
- to provide the reader with confidence to make assumptions as to how and why people act as they do and place an organization at risk;
- to enable the reader to apply the cyber security knowledge gained to solve current and recurring cyber security management problems;
- to allow the reader to adopt a pro-active cyber security threat intelligence management perspective so that a logical and systematic approach is used to solving current and future cyber security problems through a collectivist decision-making process that ensures that cyber security is viewed as a shared responsibility;

- to assist the reader find unique ways to identify and implement cyber security management solutions, which are sustainable and/or based on evidence that results in appropriate practice and knowledge building; and
- to allow the reader to place cyber security management at the heart of security, and help develop a security culture within an organization and in the process contribute to theory building, as security and intelligence are interlinked.

1.9 Conclusion

By placing cyber security at the heart of security and integrating it into a strategic intelligence framework, it should be possible for the cyber security manager to play a visible role in terms of helping the organization become more resilient. Through the process of integrating security with strategic intelligence, individual managers, and the cyber security manager in particular, will be better able to be engaged in risk management, and more able to develop a holistic view of security and place cyber security within a collectivist decision-making context. This should ensure that the cyber security decision-making process embraces a number of management practices that help make the organization and its partners resilient and better able to develop and implement effective countermeasures that result in the partnership arrangement being sustainable.

2 Strategic Cyber Security Management and the Stakeholder Approach

2.1 Introduction

Government representatives, managers and people in society realize that the threat from cyber attack is increasing and criminals are becoming more sophisticated in their approach to deceive people for financial gains. At risk are individuals and all types of organization, whether they are operating in the public sector or the private sector, and charities in particular have been targeted in recent years. It is with this in mind that an argument can be made for members of society to be made more aware of the threats posed by cyber criminals and to be involved more fully in cyber crime prevention. Hence, a stakeholder approach to the problem can be advocated that views cyber security as a shared, collectivist responsibility. The advantage of a collectivist approach is that it will provide a central focus that mobilizes the expertise of cyber security staff, under the guidance of a cyber security manager, so that the resources of government and industry can be harnessed, and results in people joining together to counteract the various types of cyber attack that are launched. As the actions of cyber criminals are thwarted, successful cyber security initiatives need to be highlighted that provide insights into how a cyber security policy and strategy framework can be enhanced, through the actions of a wide public. To make the case for this, reference is made to stakeholder theory and a collectivist view is presented that has practical, day-to-day and policy implications. In order to convince people that a collectivist approach to the problem is required, various real world examples of cyber attacks are made reference to.

This chapter starts by focusing on the learning objectives (Section 2.2) and progresses by placing cyber security in context (Section 2.3) and continues by outlining the need for a collectivist approach to cyber security (Section 2.4). Next, insights into organizational interdependencies and security (Section 2.5) are provided and this is followed by information relating to establishing trust-based relationships (Section 2.6). A learning summary is provided (Section 2.7) and this is followed by a conclusion (Section 2.8). Thereafter is a mini case (Section 2.9) and an extended case (Section 2.10), a set of references (Section 2.11), further reading (Section 2.12) and a bank of questions (Section 2.13).

2.2 Learning Objectives

The reader will be able to:

- establish why the stakeholder approach to cyber security is necessary;
- explain and place in context the collectivist approach to cyber security; and

DOI: 10.4324/9781003244295-2

- establish why the cyber security manager needs to know about organizational interdependencies and trust-based partnerships.

2.3 Placing Cyber Security in Context

Madnick (2017: 23) states that "between 50% and 80% of all cyberattacks are aided or abetted by insiders, usually unintentionally – typically through some kind of 'phishing' expedition". The depth of the problem has been made known by the World Economic Forum (Vina, 2016: 2), which purports that the annual global cost of cyber crime is estimated to be US$445 billion. What this highlights is that senior management, and the cyber security manager in particular, needs to better understand the consequences associated with emerging types of human behaviour and how a computer system and/ or network can be breached. However, people in society do not necessarily have sufficient knowledge of how cyber attacks are devised and implemented, and do not fully understand what security involves (Collins and Mansell, 2005) or how certain risks can be reduced. Often, those using computers at home (e.g. remote working) are not aware of the risks involved and have to educate themselves as to what security precautions should be used (Anderson and Agarwal, 2010). Indeed, the cyber attacks launched on government departments, private and public sector organizations, and members of the public need to be better understood if cyber crime is to be curtailed and the perpetrators of deceptive (illegal) acts are to be prevented from defrauding individuals and institutions in the way that they do.

Davis (2007: 181) has highlighted the concern regarding human deception and suggests that social engineering is used by certain individuals to manipulate or use psychological tricks to gain the confidence of a person so that they share private information with them or are in fact unaware of the value of the information they have and which they fail to safeguard. This suggests that the cyber security manager is required to become better acquainted with other fields of learning such as psychology, because of the growing influence of the Internet and what is known as cyberpsychology (Barak and Suler, 2008). Within the broad context of cyberpsychology, managers need to familiarize themselves with new forms of behaviour and the different forms of deception that exist. They also need to look more generally at what is known as trustworthy software and the provision of trusted services, and establish if the computer software used is vulnerable and represents a threat to the organization. Such an approach is useful when establishing the role that trust (Shu-Chen et al., 2006) and risk (Park et al., 2005) play in online buying activity, and requires that employees are vigilant and perform the tasks expected of them according to the procedures outlined. They also need various forms of authentication when required. In addition, by being better aware of how individuals deal with cyber threats, it is possible to deepen our understanding of the reasons behind their actions. This can be supported through protection motivation theory (Anderson and Agarwal, 2010). Protection motivation theory requires that the cyber security manager has a good understanding of how a fear appeal influences attitudinal change for the better and to fully understand this, an in-depth knowledge is required of (i) the components of a fear appeal (e.g. magnitude of noxiousness, probability of occurrence and efficacy of recommended response); (ii) the cognitive mediating processes (e.g. appraised severity, expectancy of exposure and belief in efficacy of coping response, which result in protection motivation) and (iii) attitude change (e.g. intent to adopt recommended response) (Rogers, 1975: 99).

Interaction (via the Internet and social media) involves varying forms of intensity; hence, human interaction can be defined as directly or indirectly influential, and involves individuals situated in a number of stakeholder networks. The fact that some interactions involve contact between an individual and a person unknown to them means that trust is paramount, especially once data and information start to be shared/exchanged. Unfortunately, invisibility provides a cyber attacker with an opportunity to take advantage of a person/situation and the only way to successfully deal with a cyber attack is in real time, which is not always possible because the attack may occur outside of work hours or in conjunction with other forms of cyber attack.

A cyber attack is, however, seldom an isolated act and a number of attacks are normally carried out simultaneously against a number of individuals/targets, and in some cases are termed persistent. Product innovations are often open to attack from counterfeiters who establish websites in order to market fake branded products. The websites and marketing operations, including packaging, are convincing and unsuspecting consumers are duped into buying the good. Criminals know that they have a limited window of operation because in time, disgruntled customers report matters to various consumer protection bodies, trading standards and law enforcement personnel that result in the website being closed down and the perpetrators taken to court. For example, regarding e-cigarettes (vapes), it was noted that health experts and law enforcement personnel were involved in campaigning to stop young adults making online purchases of e-cigarettes that contained harmful substances (Ungoed-Thomas and Griffiths, 2019). Criminals have been known to use social media platforms to extensively promote fake e-liquids that are purchased by vapers (Das and Horton, 2019). This brings to the fore the interconnection between technology and its use and human behaviour and life style. It is clear, therefore, that illicit market place developments have ramifications for health sector workers and law enforcement personnel. Looking ahead, it is possible to suggest that as people in society embrace more fully social media and social media platforms, cyber security will need to be viewed as a shared responsibility because of the number of potential vulnerabilities that exist in the nodes of the interlinking networks, and the fact that cyber criminals are able to identify opportunities and devise inventive forms of attack, and launch an attack quickly and with limited cost. For example, in 2016, Deliveroo (Fortson, 2017: 5) discovered that customers were receiving phantom orders for food delivery services that were initiated by hackers who had obtained the log-in details in relation to breaches in other systems. To place hacks like this into perspective, it is estimated that in excess of 6 million stolen credentials are leaked every day (e.g. either free or sold in the form of lists) (Fortson, 2017: 5) and this is putting pressure on individuals, companies and banks in particular.

Research that has been undertaken into Internet abuse suggests that addictive behaviour may be partly responsible for the actions of abusers (Morahan-Martin, 2008). In addition, it has been suggested that individuals that possess a deceptive behaviour personality may have developed it through time (Reddy, 2008). Hence, it may be difficult to put in place safeguards to counteract fully the actions of people determined to engage in deceptive behaviour. When looking at the issue of fake websites, it can be noted that there are a large number of types of scam aimed at defrauding people (Langenderfer and Shrimp, 2001) and the Internet provides a platform from which those intent on defrauding targeted individuals can do so from many miles away or from locations that remain hidden. Interestingly, it has been suggested that better educated people are less concerned about the risks associated with using the Internet (Dutton and Shepherd, 2005) due to the fact that they are more informed about the security systems that are in place. Taking into account that trust should be looked at in association with emotion and risk perception (Jackson et al., 2005), those involved in developing online shopping facilities need to think more deeply about the role of trust and how trust-baseds relationships with customers can be built and maintained through time (Lee and Lee, 2010). Bearing in mind the connectivity of organizations, it is clear that the cyber security manager can play a pro-active role in working with training staff and those involved in internal marketing, and produce cyber security awareness training programmes that contribute fully to the organization's cyber security policy and strategy. Partner organizations can also be incorporated into an overarching cyber security policy and strategy framework.

The increasing sophistication of cyber attacks and the existence of the encrypted darknet are motivators for a change in management perception in terms of dealing with cyber orchestrated threats. A successful cyber attack is likely to cause much disruption and lost productivity. The UK Government (2016) has acknowledged that it is not possible for a single government to provide a nation's cyber security on its own. The following quotation from Osborne (2015: 7) highlights the extent of the problem:

> A few years ago mounting a sophisticated cyber attack meant having all the skills that each stage of the attack required, from gathering access to the network to designing the payload that was to go into it. But in the past few years, an on-line market-place has developed, which means all the elements of an attack can now be bought and assembled from the computer of anyone with the money to pay for it. All this is reflected in the cyber breaches that we see reported with increasing frequency and increasing severity.

Bearing the above in mind, the following question surfaces: How can the cyber security manager engage better with stakeholders in order to ensure that the organization's strategic intelligence cyber security framework benefits the wider community? There are two key aspects that senior management need to be aware of when finding an answer to the question. First, staff within the organization need to be able to develop and put in place a strategic intelligence cyber security framework that is able to counteract cyber attacks through having a cyber threat forecasting capability; and second, the cyber security manager needs to be able to integrate cyber security within the organization's security strategy and ensure that it embraces risk communication. Embracing risk communication is crucial because vulnerabilities and impacts need to be reported and acted upon in real time.

It is clear from the above that the cyber security manager is involved in high-level strategic decisions and ensures that cyber security is placed within the organization's security policy, so that a cyber security stakeholder framework materializes. The objective of the cyber security stakeholder framework is ultimately to protect society through various pro-active cyber security counter-measures. If, however, the cyber security counter-measures are to be viewed as sustainable, it is necessary for the cyber security manager to work with industry and government representatives so that a focused approach to the management of cyber security occurs at four different levels: (i) the freedom and protection of the individual; (ii) the freedom and protection of the community; (iii) the employee and the protection of the employee; and (iv) the organization and the protection of the organization. This is the essence of the collectivist approach to cyber security which is based on an employee-organization-community interactive process.

At this juncture, it seems logical to pose the question: How can society be more fully engaged in risk prevention in order to reduce the damage caused by cyber attacks that vary in intensity and sophistication? In a democracy such as the UK, people can lobby government and demand that more resources are put into fighting cyber crime and cyber terrorism. However, it should be noted that acts of cyber crime and cyber terrorism are carried out by different actors with different objectives. Furthermore, protagonists are not always identifiable and reside in different parts of the world. Therefore, it seems logical that the management of cyber security is placed within a collectivist approach that involves cooperation between relevant stakeholders, with the organization taking the lead role and being pivotal in terms of cyber security implementation. The logic underpinning this view is that organizations are increasingly undertaking business online and through connectivity are well positioned to respond to cyber attacks and develop appropriate measures to counteract such actions. The knowledge gained can be made available to a wider community, composed of employees and buyers that purchase goods and services online. The various counter-measures devised can be adopted across all industry sectors and should result in relevant threat intelligence being shared and utilized fully. For example, the Financial Conduct Authority imposed a fine of £16.4 million on Tesco Personal Finance plc (Tesco Bank) for "failing to exercise due skill, care and diligence in protecting its personal current account holders" in relation to a cyber attack on the bank in November 2016, which resulted in £2.26 million being stolen over a 48-hour period (https://www.fca.org.uk/news/press-releases/fca-fines-tesco-bank-failures-2016-cyber-attack). Another cyber attack was launched on Tesco in October 2021, and as a consequence, shoppers were unable to place orders via the company's website and app, and Tesco was required to use a virtual waiting room to manage the level of demand (Hotten, 2021).

The logic underpinning the collectivist approach to cyber security is that members of society should be better informed about cyber attacks and how to deal with and thus prevent cyber attacks from causing the damage they do. By placing the organization at the centre of cyber security provision, the cyber security manager can put in place a number of cyber security awareness initiatives and training programmes that equip employees to develop a cyber security mindset. This will help them to avail themselves of the knowledge they need to better understand how to counteract the actions of those carrying out such attacks. The knowledge gained can be utilized both in the workplace and outside of work, and shared with other members of society through community resilience schemes. The way this can be done is through the development of a cyber security stakeholder framework, which incorporates neighbourhood watch groups connected via WhatsApp, for example.

By applying stakeholder theory, the collectivist approach to cyber security is to view the problem through the lens of an organization that considers cyber security to be an extension of its corporate social responsibility programme. Inspiration for this line of argument is drawn from Crane (2018) who draws on the stakeholder literature to provide a model of stakeholder connectedness and trust. The deployment of stakeholder theory can be viewed as beneficial as it provides insights into why and how views evolve that reflect the need to embrace different stakeholder groups. This helps people to better understand how collectivist action can prevent or limit the damage caused by a cyber attack(s). In addition, the insights provided by Kobeissi and Damanpour (2009), who argue that an organization's social responsibility programme encompasses mutuality in the sense that by carrying out certain organizational activities, both the organization and local communities benefit from the relationships that are put in place, can be considered influential in terms of employee-organization-community engagement.

2.4 The Need for a Collectivist Approach to Cyber Security

Oosthoek and Doerr (2021: 300) are of the view that "Cyber threats have become a permanent threat to society" and refer to Yahoo, which in 2017, "announced that three billion user account details were exposed in a hacking operation dating back to 2013". In order to convince members of society that a collectivist approach to cyber security is needed, a case has to be made that explains that the growing reliance on computer networks has put individuals at risk. The intensity and sophistication of cyber attacks have called into question our view of what security involves. Security provision is multi-faceted and complex. It is worth highlighting, therefore, that critical information technology (IT) security challenges cannot be addressed solely by technology (Arach-chilage et al., 2016). This is because staff fall victim to a variety of online attacks as they do not follow online safety procedures, either knowingly or unknowingly. Hence, the cyber security manager needs to ensure that an appropriate security awareness programme is developed (Shillair et al., 2015: 1999; Trim and Lee, 2019; Alharbi and Tassaddiq, 2021) that ensures that the security standards in place are adhered to and that managers in other business functions do not become complacent in terms of staff adhering to the organization's compliance and cyber security policy. For example, BYOD, which stands for Bring Your Own Device, received much attention a number of years ago when security staff discussed the problems associated with people taking their own computer/device (laptop) into the workplace for the purpose of work and then, taking the device home again and using it for their own personal use and/or allowing their children to download computer games on it and play a game without realizing that they had downloaded a computer virus, which then spread malware and deleted or stole/copied organizational files that were stored on the device and spread the computer virus into the existing organizational computer system and destroyed files or stole data from them. It was a substantial period of time before the vulnerabilities associated with BYOD were discovered. A number of BYOD vulnerabilities were identified, including (Trim et al., 2012) personal data loss, loss of privacy, malicious URLs that disclose sensitive information and intercept passwords. However, knowing about vulnerabilities has not stopped people from using a laptop or a hand-held device for alternative purposes and the risk of infection remains high where inadequate security systems or procedures are in place. For example, business personnel attend conferences in parts of the world where there are known to be lax security systems in place and often, a decision is made to bin the device or have the information wiped from it after the individual has returned to the company.

It can be noted that a cyber attack may be to disrupt an organization as opposed to defraud it. This means that when the cyber security manager carries out a risk assessment, they need to prioritize the risks identified. The work of Esteves et al. (2017) is useful in this respect because in order to understand how and why a cyber attack is carried out against an organization, it is necessary for management to establish what type(s) of attack the organization is vulnerable to and how a cyber security awareness programme (Trim and Lee, 2019) can be put in place to limit the possibility of an attack getting through the organization's defences. The UK's Department for Digital, Culture, Media & Sports (2019) has produced a number of insights into cyber security breaches in the UK and it is important that the cyber security manager makes these known to staff throughout the organization. This government department's website contains specific information relating to how managers can engage with staff to create cyber security awareness and reinforce awareness through specific training programmes. It is useful to acknowledge that: "Cyber security focuses on protecting computer systems from unauthorised access or being otherwise damaged or made inaccessible" (https:www.itgovernance.co.uk/what-is-cybersecurity). Furthermore, Jabee and Alam (2016: 36) define cyber security as "the security of data on cloud from theft, damage or unauthorized access", which is based on their own primary data analysis that showed that 25% of the respondents in a social network users survey (n = 170) had experienced a privacy breach and identity theft, but it also has to be acknowledged that a lot of incidents go unnoticed or unreported.

A growing body of evidence suggests that senior managers need to think in terms of three types of potential cyber attack (Maisey, 2014: 5–6): (i) an opportunistic attack involving, for example, an automated "script kiddie"; (ii) a medium-level attack carried out by an organized crime group, the objective of which is to steal and make use of customer data/information; and (iii) a sophisticated attack that is carried out by a nation–state intelligence service, which is planned, coordinated and persistent. However, not all the attacks on an organization are carried out by outsiders. In order to derive meaning from this, the cyber security manager needs to recategorize these forms of attacks as (i) low risk; (ii) medium risk and (iii) high risk. For example, a low risk attack capability is a fairly unsophisticated attack that is limited in scope and which is not able to penetrate an organization's computer system and network(s), unless a particular vulnerability (insider assisted) is exploited. A medium risk attack capability can be defined as a sophisticated attack that has the capability to penetrate an organization's computer system and network(s) and disrupt or remove data. Finally, a high risk attack capability can be defined as a highly sophisticated, persistent and penetrative attack that enters an organization's computer system and network(s), and removes data without management knowing that the organization's defences have been breached.

As regards expanding business online, the cyber security manager needs to ensure that they keep the trust and confidence of customers (both end users/consumers and those buying for resale). However, it is important to remember that cyberspace users do not necessarily have a sufficient understanding of security (Collins and Mansell, 2005) and what security involves. Also, online users are not necessarily in a position to decide whether an organization or service is deemed trustworthy. The fact that a market has developed for stolen credentials (Fortson, 2017: 5) is worrying and reinforces the need for collective action. In fact, cyber attacks are becoming more sophisticated and increased activities on the darknet are causing much concern to senior management and law enforcement personnel. In 2009, a cyber attack on South Korea and the US witnessed online networks being disabled and document files and computer programs being erased (Andreasson, 2012: 61–63). The cyber attack on Target in 2013 resulted in the theft of payment card numbers and personal data and resulted in reputational damage (Upton and Cresse, 2014: 95–96). The data breach at TalkTalk allowed hackers to access various amounts of data relating to email addresses, names, telephone numbers and bank account numbers, for example (Donnellan and Kerbaj, 2015: 1). More recently, the cyber attack on the UK's Northern Lincolnshire and Goole NHS Foundation Trust in October 2016, and the May 2017 WannaCry ransomware cyber attack on the UK's National Health Service (National Audit Office, 2017: 4–5), resulted in much disruption and highlighted the need for government and industry to work together to counteract the actions of cyber criminals. In addition, it was reported that a cyber attack on a US software company, SolarWinds, which occurred in late 2020, had gone undetected for some time. According to the company, a malware called SUPERNOVA had been placed on a server and resulted in a vulnerability (SUNBURST) within the Orion Platform and the supply chain, which manifested in a number of business customers and the US government departments having their networks breached (SolarWinds, 2021). These events highlight a number of points. First, senior managers are being confronted with rapid advances in communications technology that have both positive and negative consequences, and they need up-to-date guidance that is not always available from one source (e.g. the organization's IT manager). Second, as computer technology advances, employees need to be able to identify possible risks, take appropriate action and communicate with internal specialists in real time. This involves a pro-active approach that warrants infrastructural support in terms of immediate IT support. Third, people in the work environment need to undergo behavioural change so that they are better able to use interactive communications technology and foresee future problems. Using a specific communications technology does not bode well if there are security implications, for example. Fourth, senior managers need to adopt a broader view of connectivity and understand how the organization's computer networks are linked into the country's critical infrastructure (Madnick, 2017: 22). This is because a successful attack on a Supervisory Control and Data Acquisition (SCADA) system is likely to result in the network failing, much disruption and lost productivity.

The October 2016 cyber attack on the UK's Northern Lincolnshire and Goole NHS Foundation Trust resulted in 2,800 appointments being cancelled (National Audit Office, 2017: 5). The evidence provided by the UK's National Audit Office (2017: 4) indicated that 81 health trusts in England were affected by the attack and a further 603 primary care (and other NHS organizations) and 595 General Practitioners were also directly affected. As well as carrying out attacks via the Internet or through physical devices (e.g. USB memory sticks), an attacker may eavesdrop on information and manipulate or trick the receiver into making an unauthorized action (Kreutz et al., 2016: 186–187). So to some extent, the problem under analysis also has a disinformation element (e.g. fake news) and disinformation is something that organized criminal groups, terrorist groups and rogue state actors are happy to be associated with because it promotes confusion and disharmony, and allows them to recruit followers that identify with their cause and relish in the prospect of glorying in the publicity associated with their success (e.g. an atrocity/set of disruptive actions).

The international dimension of the problem is clear for all to see. Indeed, the May 2017 WannaCry attack affected 200,000 computers in upwards of 100 countries (National Audit Office, 2017: 4) and highlights the international challenge associated with interactivity and connectivity. The cyber security manager is required to consider three dimensions: the technological dimension; the human element interaction with technology dimension and the government-society dimension. Although there are further overlaps between these dimensions, additional linking becomes complex because of the right to buy and use the technology or the right and freedom to use technology in the way that benefits the individual or the organization.

Recent examples of the human element interaction with technology dimension include high net worth individuals being monitored by criminal gangs, via their social media activities, to establish when they are abroad and using hacked email accounts, criminals target the individual's finances and make fraudulent requests involving changing the target's bank details and transferring funds from their account(s) without the individual knowing about it (Dunkley, 2019: 3). In addition, Eurofins Scientific, which has 800 laboratories in 47 countries, had to pay a ransom to cyber criminals that locked management out of the organization's own computer system (Meddings and Kerbaj, 2019: 3). It can be reported that a recent cyber attack in France affected thousands of computer users and resulted in much disruption (Cornevin, 2019: 9). Most worrying, some social media platforms, including LinkedIn, have been used by overseas spy agencies to recruit individuals for spying purposes and this has been done through the process of befriending (Wong, 2019: 1), which relies on a form of grooming to ensure that the target is willing to then undertake an action due to their sympathetic understanding of the situation or is trapped. This is because they are compromised through their actions into being manipulated into undertaking an act they would not normally undertake (theft or transfer of data, for example). Befriending takes several forms but is known to involve an individual deceiving another individual into thinking that they are somebody that they are not, and through establishing an emotional attachment, they manipulate the individual/target into passing on information that is usually of a sensitive and/or confidential nature. Drawing on various studies into social engineering, Hatfield (2018) identified the different types and approaches to the subject and makes clear that deceptive behaviour follows a number of forms depending upon the approach used. Identity deception has been linked to social media usage (van der Walt et al., 2018) and Jabee and Alam (2016) are of the view that privacy has become an important issue as a result of sharing information vis-à-vis online social networking sites.

Organized criminals are known to use the Internet to target individuals that work in industries that are profitable and target suspects (end users or employees) with ruthless efficiency. Pharmaceutical companies are known to have robust security systems in place to protect against industrial espionage and ensure that company staff adhere to strict government regulations that are in force. However, rogue pharmaceutical companies that are allowed to operate in countries that have lax laws in place target vulnerable customers in overseas markets. For example, in one week, Interpol carried out action into the trade of fake pharmaceuticals in 116 counties that witnessed 123 illicit websites being closed down; however, the trade in counterfeit medicine is estimated to be over US$10 billion per year in Europe alone (Das et al., 2019: 9). This represents an enormous problem for society due to the additional health risks and side effects, and the additional provision needed to rectify the situation. Fake and unproven medicines and bogus medical treatment surfaced from time to time during the COVID-19 pandemic and were sold via various websites. The U.S. Food and Drug Administration (2021) monitors websites and market development and sent warning letters to firms regarding the selling of fraudulent products in relation to COVID-19 as can be ascertained from the following quotation:

> We are actively monitoring for any firms marketing products with fraudulent COVID-19 prevention and treatment claims. The FDA is exercising its authority to protect consumers from firms selling unapproved products and making false or misleading claims, including, by pursuing warning letters, seizures, injunctions or criminal prosecutions against products and firms or individuals that violate the law.

Some organizations are known to be more at risk to hacking than others; however, if management are negligent in terms of a data breach, the consequences can be severe as the following example indicates (Onita, 2018: 49):

> UBER today was slapped with a fine by British and Dutch regulators over a cyber attack affecting millions of users. The Information Commissioner's Office fined the taxis company £385,000, while the Dutch watchdog is asking for …£531,000. The data breach exposed the details of 57 million customers and drivers in 2016. Also, Uber paid the hackers $100,000 to destroy the data they stole before it told those affected about the incident. ICO director of investigations Steve Eckersley said: "This was not only a serious failure of data security on Uber's part, but a complete disregard for the customers and drivers whose personal information was stolen. At the time, no steps were taken to inform anyone affected by the breach, or to offer help and support. That left them vulnerable". Uber said: "We've learned from our mistakes".

2.5 Insights into Organizational Interdependencies and Security

The term interdependencies is often associated with people and organizations in a specific geographical location. However, it is difficult to define what a community is, and possibly it is more appropriate to think in terms of community groups (Bowen et al., 2010: 302). It is also important to acknowledge that cultural norms may affect the way in which an individual(s) interacts or participates within a community (Natcher and Hickey, 2002). Furthermore, a community identity is subject to change as people move into and out of a location/area. By establishing the link between a vulnerability and an attack, the cyber security manager can anticipate what form an attack will take; how it is likely to develop through time; when it is likely to occur and what the cascading effects might be. It is clear, therefore, that senior management need to identify the organization's vulnerabilities in relation to network connectivity and supply chain management. For example, the WannaCry cyber attack in the UK highlighted the fact that the UK government's cyber security strategy is still evolving and an open dialogue with industry is needed in order to ensure that various forms of cyber attack, which range from disruptive to disabling, are dealt with promptly in real time and have limited cascading effects. Equally, if cyber security managers do not ensure that the basic cyber security measures are in place, a successful attack could result in a loss of organizational reputation and the organization being considered the weakest link through which a future attack can be orchestrated. As regards security measures, with regard to a security policy being fully implemented and remaining functional, the cyber security manager needs to ensure that the organization's security culture embraces security awareness. This view is supported by Arachchilage and Love (2014), who point out that security education helps thwart phishing attacks. Cyber security is, therefore, concerned with preserving the availability and integrity of computer networks and critical national infrastructure, and maintaining the confidentiality of the information that is stored within computer networks and systems (European Commission, 2013: 3). Hence, cyber security can be viewed as a multi-faceted problem (Shillair et al., 2015) and again this gives credence to a collectivist approach to cyber security.

Martin and Kracher (2008) have noted that technological advancements and connectivity have made organizations more vulnerable to a number of threats, including online business protests such as email campaigns and hacking attacks. Hacking takes various forms and is characterized by an individual gaining access to a computer system and/or a network without the necessary authorization. A cyber attack can be carried out by someone external to the organization; by an employee (insider); or a combination involving an insider/employee and an external group (criminal group or state-sponsored organization/agency) or a corrupt individual, whose aim may to be to sabotage a database or destroy certain computer files. A vulnerability can be exposed/targeted by other insiders such as staff employed by a contractor that have not been fully vetted or based within a vendor whose objective is to steal data/information and pass it on to a competitor, possibly for a fee. Those involved in hacking into computer networks range from those with a high skill level to a low skill level and are either based in the country where the attack occurs or based overseas. They may also commit or be involved in a timed cyber attack and be travelling between countries so that they can claim that they were not in a specific location at the time of the attack as they were travelling and have an appropriate alibi.

An attacker may be motivated by curiosity or revenge, and may also be intent on causing disruption or making a financial gain (stealing data for resale or holding the company to ransom by taking over the computer system until an agreed sum of money is paid). The cyber security manager, in particular, needs to be cautious vis-à-vis the use of computer networks and the storage of sensitive data because as Flyverbom et al. (2019: 4) suggest, there are "a host of ethical, political, legal, and right-related issues. Examples include states tracking citizens online, governments filtering or turning off the Internet at will, and corporations using personal data for commercial purposes".

The International Organization for Standardization (ISO) is clear that managers need to both identify and be able to deal with risk. Knowing what the organization's risk appetite is focuses attention on senior management putting in place a risk register, which details not only the type of risk identified but also how the risk is to be mitigated. This brings to attention the concept of Enterprise Risk Management (ERM) which requires management to (Bromiley et al., 2015: 265) "address all their risks comprehensively and coherently instead of managing them individually". Although ERM seems a logical approach, it assumes that there is an adequate risk management system in place and that the form of risk analysis undertaken is valid. Not only does increased uncertainty call into question the type of risk analysis tool that is used but also it calls into question if risk management is undertaken on a continual basis. In terms of Internet governance, a number of international standard-setting bodies exist such as the Alliance for Telecommunications Industry Solutions (ATIS) and the European Telecommunications Standards Institute (ETSI) (Flyverbom et al., 2019: 11). The guidelines they have produced have done much to inform the cyber security manager about the quality standards that need to be in place in terms of a company operating across borders and this is recognition that cyber security should be viewed from an international perspective.

Organizational interdependencies present various challenges for the cyber security manager and thought needs to be given to how evolving networks influence business relationships and how government stimulates market forces (Wind and Thomas, 2010). The interdependency of data is an important issue and can be thought of in terms of decisions, outcomes and actions relating to new products, unmet needs being fulfilled and an improvement in the quality of life. However, business to consumer relationships can be adversely affected by actions relating to hacking where intellectual property rights and marketing plans are copied/stolen and as a result the organization's image suffers as a consequence of reputational damage. Morgan and Hunt (1994) remind us that relationships are preserved through commitment and trust, which, in turn, fuels cooperation. Cooperation, it can be argued, is an essential element of an organization's marketing strategy because marketers embrace the value co-creation concept (Vargo and Lusch, 2004) in order to gain a competitive edge in the market.

The following quotation provides additional insights into the problem confronting the cyber security manager: "Digital technology makes it possible for large volumes of information to be stored in easily searchable formats. As a result, more information is readily accessible to today's 'information consumer' working within the digital environment" (Wonders et al., 2012: 250). Finding ways to protect and secure sensitive and confidential data and information has to be done within financial constraints. Furthermore, internal training programmes are useful with respect to making staff aware of the need for safeguards, which are documented in policies (e.g. procedures and systems). The objective being to counteract deviant behaviour that puts an organization at risk. It is important to reflect on the fact that research suggests that in situations of high perceived risk, people will deploy a risk-reducing strategy based on behavioural choices, which lower their vulnerability to what are regarded as potentially negative outcomes (Cho and Lee, 2006: 119).

Pearce (1976) provided comprehensive guidance regarding what an "Intelligence System" represents and emphasized the fact that control, as well as policy and strategy were to be considered key factors with respect to intelligence work. The organizational aspects of intelligence systems have been made known; however, an organization's information system may not include all the aspects associated with an organization's information system (Brockhoff, 1991: 93). Hence, the cyber security manager needs to be involved in the risk management process and think in terms of developing a model for intelligence gathering (Zinkhan and Gelb, 1985). Intelligence gathering can be associated with information sharing and is underpinned by trust-based relationships. This ensures that threat intelligence information is shared with partner organizations and industry members not on a need to know basis, but in an open and continuous manner to ensure that a cyber attack/potential cyber attack is dealt with as soon as possible and does not have a cascading effect on other organizations. For example, the Department for Digital, Culture, Media & Sport (2019: 3) report entitled *Cyber Security Breaches Survey 2019* outlined the fact that the average annual cost of a data breach was higher for a charity compared with a business, although large firms appeared to have the highest average annual cost of a data breach. It can be reported that managers in the charity sector are now implementing additional health checks, audits and risk assessments in order to deal more effectively with cyber risks compared with previously. As the General Data Protection Regulation (GDPR) receives greater prominence in the UK, it is hoped that managers will become more vigilant and pro-active in terms of dealing with cyber vulnerabilities.

2.6 Establishing Trust–Based Partnerships

Governance of the Internet is complicated because a number of national and international stakeholders are involved that operate under different laws governing the sharing of information and include companies, government agencies and civil society (Flyverbom et al., 2019: 10), all of whom have different objectives, priories and responsibilities. As well as thinking in terms of internal trust (brought about and reinforced through leadership and teamwork), the cyber security manager needs to focus on developing and maintaining external trust that is developed with suppliers, joint venture partners and customers (Huff and Kelley, 2005: 97), but also takes reputational damage into consideration.

Accepting that there are different views as to what trust is and how it can be defined, it is important that the cyber security manager develops their own understanding of what trust is. The view of "public trust" advocated by Pirson et al. (2019: 136) emphasizes public trust in business that "encompasses elements of generalized, institutional, reputation-based, and stakeholder trust". The authors suggest that reputational information as well as an individual's experiences of a company shape the attitudes of people towards an organization. Hence, the stakeholder view of trust is relevant, more so because as Pirson et al. (2019: 133) claim, control mechanisms that are in place to regulate a business may fail in an Internet-based environment. The Internet is about connectivity and interactivity and operates in a global context; therefore, it is not always possible for individuals in society to have all the information they need about a situation and how an organization operates, and few know about or have access to an organization's risk register. Consequently, the cyber security manager needs to ensure that there is an adequate risk communication strategy in place to keep stakeholders informed about events. In addition, ensure that the internal control procedures are given the attention they need (e.g. senior managers are held accountable for their actions). Reflecting on this approach, Pirson and Malhotra (2011: 1099) argue that a stakeholder-specific framework of organizational trust provides a reasonable insight into understanding how stakeholder trust is structured within an organization. Lundqvist (2015: 442) takes this a step further by suggesting that the stakeholder approach views risk, more specifically ERM, as including risk governance, which is essentially about encouraging staff to think in terms of risk-awareness and how the risk management system is controlled. This suggests that risk managers need to adopt a strategic risk perspective and include the possible actions of the organization's competitors as well as make reference to product liability and accidents, for example (Bromily et al., 2015: 268). By undertaking a formal threat analysis, the risks identified can be ranked and contingencies can be assigned. The cyber security manager can gain prominence by adopting a pro-active approach to risk assessment and can work closely with the risk manager, writing reports for top management.

Successful partnership engagement involves coordination and governance, and can be thought of as a form of cooperation (Rese, 2006: 74). Hence, managers need to ensure that staff interact well and are aware of what information is to be shared and with whom.

The communication of risk is a component of the risk management system (Oliva, 2016) and can be deemed one of the responsibilities of the organization's chief risk officer (Aebi et al., 2012). A vital role of the chief risk officer is to facilitate interaction and cooperation and develop a collectivist understanding that acts as a bridge between the various business functions (Kisfalvi et al., 2016: 435). It is important to note that organizations involved in a cooperative partnership are expected to carry out the agreed policies in the way specified and must be convinced of the benefits accruing as well as be assured that cooperation will be maintained at all levels within the partnership arrangement (Wucherer, 2006: 91–92). Senior managers need to think in terms of integrated solutions involving cooperation between internal business units and departments, and across the partnership arrangement. This highlights the role of the cyber security manager in terms of ensuring that end users, partners of various kinds, which includes staff based in research institutes and government agencies, are included in the organization's decision-making process (Windahl and Lakemond, 2006: 816–817). This is so because a holistic view of security is adopted and cyber security is integrated into it and placed at the heart of it. The reason why this is important is because "Insider collaboration with organized crime and activist groups is becoming increasingly common" (Upton and Cresse, 2014: 98). As a consequence, the cyber security manager is being forced to cooperate more and more with staff in law enforcement agencies, both at home and abroad, because those carrying out cyber attacks are becoming more able to use deceptive behaviour and deploy different types of attack depending upon the vulnerabilities identified.

Bearing the above in mind, stakeholder theory can be utilized to provide a framework for analysing how multiple relationships are managed. Rowley (1997) has placed this in context by suggesting that when studying multiple relations involving multiple stakeholders, it is important to take into account stakeholder expectations, which are governed by active communication between the parties and which result in shared behavioural expectations. By adopting a pro-active stance to managing relationships with a multiple set of stakeholders (Donaldson and Preston, 1995), an organization can improve its performance through time (Jones, 1995). Harrison et al. (2010) reinforce this view by suggesting that stakeholders can be involved in value co-creation and if this is the case, trust between the parties increases. Hayibor (2017) builds on the work of Harrison et al. (2010) and promotes the line of argument that "fairness and justice in the firm's treatment of its stakeholders are often regarded as influencing stakeholder behaviour". Referring back to the point about value co-creation, Harrison and Bosse (2013) believe that trustworthiness results in additional trustworthiness and as a consequence, the sharing of valuable information results in and encourages the additional sharing of valuable information. The logic of this is that it takes into account the customer co-creation concept (Khanagha et al., 2017), because it allows managers to exchange and share knowledge, and initiate and implement change that is viewed as necessary and inclusive. For example, the same security policy standard and if necessary technological security system(s) can be adopted by organizations throughout a partnership arrangement and this should set a standard of cooperation that ensures the organizations concerned are aware of the vulnerabilities that exist and make organizational defences as robust as possible to repel any form of cyber attack.

The above suggests that the cyber security manager needs to think in terms of linking organizational resilience with corporate governance, and using existing risk assessment models and frameworks or developing new risk assessment models and frameworks, so that an appropriate risk analysis or methodology can be developed and deployed. There are various models and frameworks available to assist the cyber security manager in their task. For example, Trim and Lee (2010) have placed the development of an organization's cyber security strategy within the context of three interlinked circles representing (i) the external environment; (ii) risk assessment which is embedded within the organization's strategic value system and (iii) the integration of security within the organization's functions so that a security culture emerges within the organization. This approach allows senior management to improve and refine the linkage between an organization's cyber security strategy and the ability to attract and maintain cyber security specialists. Trim and Lee (2010: 4) suggest that:

> by integrating security more firmly into the organization's structure, it should be possible to reduce the organization's level of risk and facilitate information sharing. Information sharing should enhance co-operation between partner organizations and add to the defensive capability vis-à-vis establishing effective counter-cyber attack measures.

The approach supports the view of Pearce (1976: 123–125) who explains the need to distinguish between three types of intelligence (strategic, tactical and operational). In addition, it provides a platform for monitoring and forecasting cyber threats as well as it becomes a basis for senior management to put in place an appropriate intelligence system that incorporates information that is used to make strategic decisions (Jagetia and Patel, 1981) and to think in terms of organizing the counter-espionage operation (Pearce, 1971: 23). This cannot, however, be done without guidance from or cooperation with government.

2.7 Learning Summary

Reflecting on the above, the reader is aware that in order to understand what the collectivist approach to cyber security involves, please see Figure 2.1, it is necessary for the cyber security manager to utilize strategic intelligence, establish organizational vulnerabilities, use risk management and engage with internal and external staff. Through the process of identifying an attacker and how they operate, and knowing what is at risk, information can be shared with staff in partner organizations and a stakeholder approach to cyber security can be adopted.

The reader is now able to:

- understand how the cyber security manager is central to the development of an organization's cyber security strategy;
- understand that knowledge of the human factors involved is crucial to counteracting the actions of cyber attackers;
- understand that it is necessary to monitor the actions of those carrying out cyber attacks and to utilize cyber threat intelligence;
- deploy the stakeholder approach and share information about organizational vulnerabilities; and
- evaluate how staff in an organization work with staff in partner organizations and share cyber security information with a wider community.

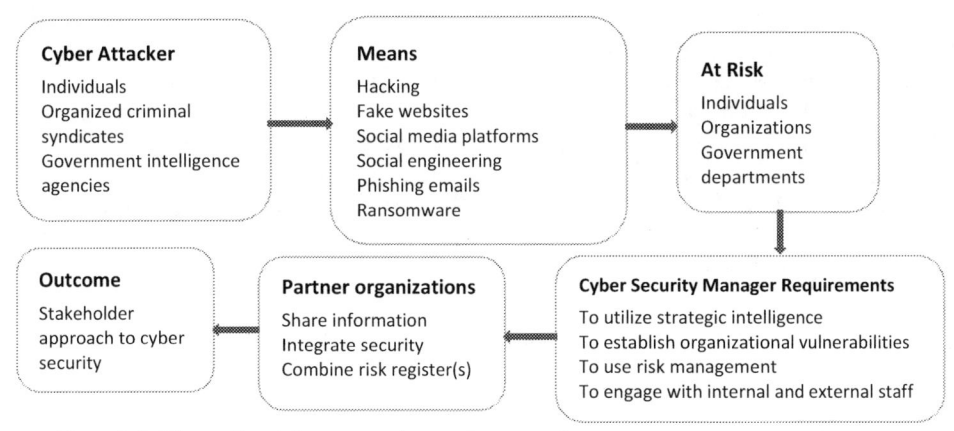

Figure 2.1 The collectivist approach to cyber security.

2.8 Conclusion

Government will, because of both the nature and proliferation of cyber attacks, need to adopt a more transparent role in cyber security, if, i.e., members of society are to become more aware of how to prevent cyber attacks from causing the damage that they do. It is because of this that a collectivist approach to cyber security needs to ensure that there is an appropriate interaction involving employees (individuals living in the community), cyber security managers (employed by various for profit and not-for-profit organizations), law enforcement personnel and members of the community (e.g. hospital administrators). Should this be the case, the management of cyber security will be viewed as a shared responsibility.

2.9 Mini Case: Lost and Not Found

Rob Smith had only been with the company for a couple of weeks when he realized that there was a "who cares" attitude among the staff, which was causing problems for all concerned. Two examples came to mind that he reflected on and had taken action over. The first referred to a Mr. Johnston, who had been with the company for a significant number of years and persisted on knowing everything about everybody and how business was done with partner organizations. Mr. Johnston was not keen on using computers and often wrote down passwords, telephone numbers and business account numbers on a writing pad that was left open on his desk. He was also heard talking about client accounts when travelling on public transport and was known to talk freely on his mobile phone when walking out of the company's security gates. A week after joining the company, Rob Smith was on a train travelling to London and he overheard Mr. Johnson talking on his mobile device, seated behind him. He heard Mr. Johnston say to the person on the telephone:

> Do not worry about that, I am the only one in the carriage and nobody is listening. Now, what did you say about the non-payment... have you talked to the people at Dean's, or did you want me to do it. They know me and they will not give me any nonsense...

Rob Smith was worried that as he sat there, the conversation became more open and more and more information was revealed. When Mr. Johnston had finished the call, he immediately made another call and was heard ordering a gift for his wife. He paid by credit card and was happy to read out the full number and the security code, and then repeat the numbers when asked to do so.

The next day, Rob Smith went to his line manager and reported the incident. His line manager, Andy Jones, looked at Rob and said in a quiet voice: "Well, what do you expect me to do about it? Everybody knows he cannot keep a secret and that is the way he is". After a pause, Rob replied: "I think it would be a good idea if we organized a training course about data and information security, I can run it as I have lots of experience".

"No need", replied Mr. Jones, "You have enough on your plate. Do not worry about small things like that".

The second incident happened about a week later. Rob overheard a conversation between two staff in the marketing department. It seemed that several records in the customer database had been deleted and there was no backup file in existence. Although the services of a cloud provider had been used, the company had not paid the service charge for the past three months and the service had been discontinued. Rob decided to intervene and asked if he could assist in some way. "Not sure you can", said Mrs. Hunter, who was the head of market research, "we will have to wait for Mrs. Billings to return from her holiday, she only left yesterday and will be away for two weeks".

Questions

Question 1: What should Rob Smith do in order to convince people to be more security conscious?

Question 2: How should Rob Smith differentiate cyber security from security?

Question 3: What would Rob Smith need to do to make people take security seriously?

2.10 Extended Case: Technological Change, Society and the Role of Government

Technological change can occur quickly and can result in increased employment and an enhanced life style. However, it can bring about unforeseen challenges that require more than just immediate action by a handful of people. Families, communities and indeed society are often caught up in the process of change and because of this, government officials need to be aware of the challenges and issues faced by people in society.

Moving into the cyber era has not been without problems. People are from time to time reminded of what they need to do in order to stay safe. During the COVID-19 era, face-to-face interaction as we know it was replaced with people distancing themselves from others and communicating online, engaging through Skype, MS Teams and Zoom, for example. At the same time, pressure on the health service (already under pressure due to the demands of an ageing population) meant that people were forced to use apps more to book medical appointments and consultancies. Telephone help lines were available but often the only way to see a doctor was to book an appointment online.

In June 2020, it was reported that when Rory Glover logged onto a GP booking app, he was given access to over 50 recordings of video conferences involving other people, and put out a message via Twitter (Meddings, 2020: 6) telling people about this. The breach was dealt with quickly but questions were raised about how this could have happened and what measures need to be taken to protect people and their confidential data.

Parents working long hours cannot always keep an eye on what their children do on a computer and trust that they are doing their homework or playing an approved computer game. Although some games are free, they may contain certain components (tools and accessories) that require a purchase of some kind, as can be noted from the following quotation in relation to a parent's comments about her daughter playing an online game (Hannah, 2020: 10): "There was hardly any money left. Then I saw all the outgoings -£9.99 at a time, many times a day. At first I thought it was just a couple of hundred pounds..........She spent £400 in a single day". The reason why this happened was because the parent's bank card details had been saved previously on the tablet used and this allowed the transactions to be made once authorized. No doubt, this is not a unique case and other parents have found themselves in a similar situation. The following advice has been provided to parents (Hannah, 2020: 10):

> Turn off in-app purchasing and set up a password in the apps store to manage downloads. Turn on notifications on your devices so that you get a message when payments are made and can take action immediately. Explain to your children how easy it is to accidentally spend real money when playing games. Use gift cards instead of credit cards for any gaming spending.

In 2019, the need to protect the identity of people and their private information received much attention. A number of UK banks made clear to their clients that they should not disclose private information that could be accessed via social networking sites. This was because it became known that cyber criminals were targeting individuals (possibly high net worth individuals) via social media and email as the following example makes clear (Dunkley, 2019: 3): "JP Morgan Private Bank has emailed customers with a cautionary story of a client whose family office was tricked into transferring $250,000 (£205,000) to a fraudulent account. The perpetrator found enough details of the family's holiday to impersonate them and authorize the transfer – with the weak link being a social media profile saying, "headed to Paris with the family! See ya in two weeks!"" Keeping details like this private and not using public wi-fi in airports is essential because "fraudsters use hacked email accounts to intercept expected payment requests and change the bank details to their own account" (Dunkley, 2019: 3).

The ransomware attack on the Brussels-based company, Eurofins Scientific in 2019, caused much concern among the UK government representatives and it was noted that the company, which provides forensic analysis services to the police and security services, went ahead and paid a ransom to those that launched the attack in order that it could regain access to its computers and networks (Meddings and Kerbaj, 2019: 3). This is an interesting case because it highlights the fact that both the intelligence and crime agencies were approached to investigate the situation. It also suggests that a sophisticated cyber attacker does not distinguish between targets and has a technology that can be considered proven and may not be traceable.

Questions

Question 1: Whose responsibility is it to ensure that people are protected from the actions of cyber criminals?

Question 2: What can people do in order not to fall victim to a cyber attack?

Question 3: What data and information can be shared by staff in the private sector and the public sector in order to prevent cyber attacks from causing harm and financial damage?

Case Sources

Dunkley, E. (2019). Private banks warn over Facebook holiday scams. *The Sunday Times* (Business Section), 1st September, p. 3.

Hannah, F. (2020). As I fought the virus, my child spent £2,000. *The Sunday Times* (Money Section), 3rd May, p. 10.

Meddings, S. (2020). Babylon bug sets GP apps shivering. *The Sunday Times* (Business Section), 21st June, p. 6.

Meddings, S., and Kerbaj, R. (2019). Forensics giant pays ransom in cyber attack. *The Sunday Times* (Business & Money Section), 7th July, p. 3.

2.11 References

Aebi, V., Sabato, G., and Schmid, M. (2012). Risk management, corporate governance, and bank performance in a financial crisis. *Journal of Bank Finance*, 36 (12): 3213–3226.

Alharbi, T., and Tassaddiq, A. (2021). Assessment of cybersecurity awareness among students of Majmaah University. *Big Data and Cognitive Computing*, 5 (23): 1–15. https://doi.org/10.3390/bdcc5020023.

Anderson, C.L., and Agarwal, R. (2010). Practicing safe computing: A multimethod empirical examination of home computer user security behavioural intentions. *MIS Quarterly*, 34 (3): 613–643.

Andreasson, K. (2012). *Cybersecurity: Public Sector Threats and Responses*. London: CRC Press.

Appleyard, M.M., and Chesbrough, H.W. (2017). The dynamics of open strategy: From adoption to reversion. *Long Range Planning*, 50: 310–321.

Arachchilage, N.A.G., and Love, S. (2014). Security awareness of computer users: A phishing threat avoidance perspective. *Computers in Human Behavior*, 38: 304–312. http://dx.doi.org/10.1016/j.chb.2014.05.046.

Arachchilage, N.A.G., Love, S., and Beznosov, K. (2016). Phishing threat avoidance behaviour: An empirical investigation. *Computers in Human Behavior*, 60: 185–197. http://dx.doi.org/10.1016/j.chb.2016.02.065.

Barak, A., and Suler, J. (2008). Reflections on the psychology and social science of cyberspace, pp. 1–12. In A. Barak (Ed.), *Psychological Aspects of Cyberspace: Theory, Research, Application*. Cambridge: Cambridge University Press.

Bowen, F., Newenham-Kahindi, A., and Herremans, I. (2010). When suits meets roots: The antecedents and consequences of community engagement strategy. *Journal of Business Ethics*, 95 (2): 297–318. https://doi.org/10.1007/s10551-009-0360-1.

Brockhoff, K. (1991). Competitor technology in German companies. *Industrial Marketing Management*, 20 (2): 91–98.

Bromiley, P., McShane, M., Nair, A., and Rustambekov, E. (2015). Enterprise risk management: Review, critique and research directions. *Long Range Planning*, 48: 265–276.

Cho, J., and Lee, J. (2006). An integrated model of risk and risk-reducing strategies. *Journal of Business Research*, 59 (1): 112–120.

Collins, B.S., and Mansell, R. (2005). Cyber trust and crime prevention, pp. 11–55. In R. Mansell and B.S. Collins (Eds.), *Trust and Crime in Information Societies*. Cheltenham: Edward Elgar.

Cornevin, C. (2019). Une cyberattaque mondiale démantelée. *Le Figaro*, 28th August, p. 9.

Crane, B. (2018). Revisiting who, when, and why stakeholders matter: Trust and stakeholder connections. *Business & Society*, 1–24. https://doi.org/10.1177/0007650318756983.

Das, S., Gregory, A., and Harper, T. (2019). Dangerous fake drugs bought online with Google search. *The Sunday Times*, 1st September, p. 9.

Das, S., and Horton, I. (2019). Dealers on Snapchat openly sell THC juice for £20 a time. *The Sunday Times*, 15th September, p. 19.

Davis, B.J. (2007). Situational prevention and penetration testing: A proactive approach to social engineering in organizations, pp. 175–188. In A.W. Merkidze (Ed.), *Terrorism Issues: Threat Assessment, Consequences and Prevention*. New York: Nova Science Publishers, Inc.

Department for Digital, Culture, Media & Sport (2019). *Cyber Security Breaches Survey 2019*. London: Department for Digital, Culture, Media & Sport.

Donaldson, T., and Preston, L.E. (1995). The stakeholder theory of the corporation: Concepts, evidence, and implications. *Academy of Management Review*, 20 (1): 65–91.

Donnellan, A., and Kerbaj, R. (2015). Carney goes to war against cyber crooks. *The Sunday Times* (Business Section), 1st November, pp. 1, 8.

Dunkley, E. (2019). Private banks warn over Facebook holiday scams. *The Sunday Times* (Business & Money Section), 1st September, p. 3.

Dutton, W.H., and Shepherd, A. (2005). Confidence and risk on the Internet, pp. 207–244. In R. Mansell and B.S. Collins (Eds.), *Trust and Crime in Information Societies*. Cheltenham: Edward Elgar.

Esteves, J., Ramalho, E., and De Haro, G. (2017). To improve cybersecurity, think like a hacker. *Sloan Management Review*, 58 (3): 71–77.

European Commission (2013). *Cyber Security Strategy of the European Union: An Open, Safe and Secure Cyberspace*. High Representative of the European Union for Foreign Affairs and Security Policy. Report JOIN (2013) 1 final (7th February). Brussels: European Commission.

Flyverbom, M., Deibert, R., and Matten, D. (2019). The governance of digital technology, big data, and the Internet: New roles and responsibilities for business. *Business & Society*, 58 (1): 3–9. https://doi.org/10.1177/0007650317727540.

Fortson, D. (2017). 90% of all attempted logins are by cyber-hackers. *The Sunday Times* (Business Section), 2nd April, p. 5.

Harrison, J.S., and Bosse, D.A. (2013). How much is too much? The limits to generous treatment of stakeholders. *Business Horizons*, 56: 313–322.

Harrison, J.S., Bosse, D.A., and Phillips, R.A. (2010). Managing for stakeholders, stakeholder utility functions, and competitive advantage. *Strategic Management Journal*, 31: 58–74.

Hatfield, J.M. (2018). Social engineering in cybersecurity: The evolution of a concept. *Computers & Security*, 73: 102–113. https://doi.org/10.1016/j.cose.2017.10.008.

Hayibor, S. (2017). Is fair treatment enough? Augmenting the fairness-based perspective on stakeholder behaviour. *Journal of Business Ethics*, 140: 43–64.

Huff, L., and Kelley, L. (2005). Is collectivism a liability? The impact of culture on organizational trust and customer orientation: A seven-nation study. *Journal of Business Research*, 58 (5): 96–102.

Jabee, R., and Alam, M.A. (2016). Issues and challenges of cyber security for social networking sites (Facebook). *International Journal of Computer Applications*, 144 (3): 36–40.

Jackson, J., Allum, N., and Gaskell, G. (2005). Perceptions of risk in cyberspace, pp. 245–281. In R. Mansell and B.S. Collins (Eds.), *Trust and Crime in Information Societies*. Cheltenham: Edward Elgar.

Jagetia, L.C., and Patel, D.M. (1981). Developing an end-use intelligence system. *Industrial Marketing Management*, 10 (2): 101–107.

Jones, T.M. (1995). Instrumental stakeholder theory: A synthesis of ethics and economics. *Academy of Management Review*, 20 (2): 404–437.

Khanagha, S., Volberda, H., and Oshri, I. (2017). Customer Co-creation and exploration of emerging technologies: The mediating role of managerial attention and initiatives. *Long Range Planning*, 50: 221–242.

Kisfalvi, V., Sergi, V., and Langley, A. (2016). Managing and mobilizing microdynamics to achieve behavioural integration in top management teams. *Long Range Planning*, 49: 427–446.

Kobeissi, N., and Damanpour, F. (2009). Corporate responsiveness to community stakeholders: Effects of contextual and organizational characteristics. *Business & Society*, 48 (3): 326–359. https://doi.org/10.1177/0007650307305369.

Kreutz, D., Malichevskyy, O., Feitosa, E., Cunha, H., Da Roas Righi, R., and De Macedo, D. (2016). A cyber-resilient architecture for critical security services. *Journal of Network and Computer Applications*, 63: 173–189.

Langenderfer, J., and Shrimp, T.A. (2001). Consumer vulnerability to scams, swindles, and fraud: A new theory on visceral influences on persuasion. *Psychology & Marketing*, 18 (7): 763–783.

Lee, J., and Lee, S-E. (2010). Initial trust with unknown e-tailers in the context of online gift shopping. *Journal of Global Academy of Marketing Science*, 20 (4): 343–352.

Lundqvist, S.A. (2015). Why firms implement risk governance – Stepping beyond traditional risk management to enterprise risk management. *Journal of Accounting and Public Policy*, 34: 441–466.

Madnick, S.E. (2017). What executives get wrong about cybersecurity. Interview with Manglesdorf, M.E. *Sloan Management Review*, 58 (2): 22–24. http://mitsmr.com/2gDSjip.

Maisey, M. (2014). Moving to analysis-led cyber-security. *Network Security*, 2014 (5): 5–12.

Martin, K.D., and Kracher, B. (2008). A conceptual framework for online business protest tactics and criteria for their effectiveness. *Business & Society*, 47 (3): 291–311. https://doi.org/10.1177/0007650307299218.

Meddings, S., and Kerbaj, R. (2019). Forensics giant pays ransom in cyber attack. *The Sunday Times* (Business & Money), 7th July, p. 3.

Morahan-Martin, J. (2008). Internet abuse: Emerging trends and lingering questions, pp. 32–69. In A. Barak (Ed.), *Psychological Aspects of Cyberspace: Theory, Research, Applications*. Cambridge: Cambridge University Press.

Morgan, R.M., and Hunt, S.D. (1994). The commitment-trust theory of relationship marketing. *Journal of Marketing*, 58 (July): 20–38.

Natcher, D.C., and Hickey, C.G. (2002). Putting the community back into community-based resource management: A criteria and indicators approach to sustainability. *Human Organization*, 61 (4): 350–363.

National Audit Office. (2017). *Investigation: WannaCry Cyber Attack and the NHS*. HC 414 Session 2017–2019. London: National Audit Office.

Oliva, F.L. (2016). A maturity model for enterprise risk management. *International Journal of Production Economics*, 173: 66–79.

Onita, L. (2018). Uber fined after millions are hit by a cyber attack. *Evening Standard*, 27th November, p. 49.

Oosthoek, K., and Doerr, C. (2021). Cyber threat intelligence: A product without a process? *International Journal of Intelligence and CounterIntelligence*, 34: 300–315. https://doi.org/10.1080/08850607.2020.1780062.

Osborne, G. Rt. Hon. (2015). Chancellor's speech to GCHQ on cyber security (17 November). https://www.gov.uk/government/speeches/chancellors-speech-to-gchq-on-cyber-security (accessed on 2nd December, 2015).

Park, J., Lennon, S.J., and Stoel, L. (2005). On-line product presentation: Effect on mood, perceived risk, and purchase intention. *Psychology & Marketing*, 22 (9): 695–719.

Pearce, F.T. (1971). INTELLIGENCE: A technology for the 1980's. *Industrial Marketing Management*, 1 (1): 11–26.

Pearce, F.T. (1976). Business intelligence systems: The need, development, and integration. *Industrial Marketing Management*, 5 (2/3): 115–138.

Pirson, M., and Malhotra, D. (2011). Foundations of organizational trust: What matters to different stakeholders? *Organization Science*, 22 (4): 1087–1104. https://www.jstor.org/stable/20868912.

Pirson, M., Martin, K., and Parmar, B. (2019). Public trust in business and its determinants. *Business & Society*, 58 (1): 132–166. https://doi.org/10.1177/0007650316647950.

Reddy, V. (2008). Getting back to the rough ground: Deception and 'social living', pp. 219–244. In N. Emery, N. Clayton, and C. Frith (Eds.), *Social Intelligence: From Brain to Culture*. Oxford: Oxford University Press.

Rese, M. (2006). Successful and sustainable business partnerships: How to select the right partners. *Industrial Marketing Management*, 35 (1): 72–82.

Rogers, R.W. (1975). A protection motivation theory of fear appeals and attitude change. *Journal of Psychology*, 91 (1): 93–114.

Rowley, T.J. (1997). Moving beyond dyadic ties: A network theory of stakeholder influences. *Academy of Management Review*, 22 (4): 887–910.

Shillair, R., Cotten, S.R., Tsai, H-Y., Alhabash, S., LaRose, R., and Rifon, N.J. (2015). Online safety begins with you and me: Convincing Internet users to protect themselves. *Computers in Human Behavior*, 48: 199–207. http://dx.doi.org./10.1016/j.chb.2015.01.046.

Shu-Chen, Y., Wanchiao, H., Sung, K., and Cheng-Kiang, F. (2006). Investigating initial trust toward e-tailers from the Elaboration Likelihood Model perspective. *Psychology & Marketing*, 23 (5): 429–445.

SolarWinds (2021). Solar Winds Security Advisory (29th January). https://www.solarwinds.com/securityadvisory (accessed on 2nd February, 2021).

Trim, P., Hadfield, R., Garlati, C., Smith, M., Austin, J., and Lee, Y-I. (2012). Understanding, explaining and counteracting inappropriate user behaviour: Insights and Recommendations. *IAAC Workshop Paper*. BCS, The Chartered Institute for IT. London: Information Assurance Advisory Council.

Trim, P.R.J., and Lee, Y-I. (2010). A security framework for protecting business, government and society from cyber attacks. *5th IEEE International Conference on System of Systems Conference: Sustainable Systems for the 21st Century*, pp. 1–6. Loughborough: Loughborough University (22nd to 24th June).

Trim, P.R.J., and Lee, Y-I. (2019). The role of B2B marketers in increasing cyber security awareness and influencing behavioural change. *Industrial Marketing Management*, 83: 224–238. https://doi.org/10.1016/j.indmarman.2019.04.003.

UK Government. (2016). National Cyber Security Strategy 2016–2021. London: UK Government.

Ungoed-Thomas, J., and Griffiths, S. (2019). Cannabis vapes laced with Spice put children's lives at risk. *The Sunday Times*, 15th September, p. 19.

Upton, D.M., and Cresse, S. (2014). The danger from within. *Harvard Business Review*, September, pp. 94–101.

U.S. Food and Drug Administration (2021). Fraudulent Coronavirus Disease 2019 (COVID-19) products. https://www.fda.gov/consumers/health-fraud-scams/fraudulent-coronavirus-disease-2019-covid-19-products (accessed on 4th February, 2021).

van der Walt, E., Eloff, J.H.P., and Grobler, J. (2018). Cyber-security: Identity deception detection on social media platforms. *Computers & Security*, 78: 76–89. https://doi.org/10.1016/j.cose.2018.05.015.

Vargo, S., and Lusch, R. (2004). Moving to a new dominant lotic for marketing. *Journal of Marketing*, 68 (November): 1–17.

Vina, G. (2016). Patients in limbo after cyber attack. *Financial Times*, 3rd November, p. 2.

Wind, Y., and Thomas, R.J. (2010). Organizational buying behaviour in an interdependent world. *Journal of Global Academy of Marketing Science*, 20 (2): 110–122.

Windahl, C., and Lakemond, N. (2006). Developing integrated solutions: The importance of relationships within the network. *Industrial Marketing Management*, 35 (7): 806–818.

Wonders, B.J., Solop, F.I., and Wonders, N.A. (2012). Information sampling and linking: *Reality Hunger* and the digital knowledge commons. *Contemporary Social Science*, 7 (3): 247–262.

Wong, E. (2019). China hunts on LinkedIn for potential spy recruits, *The New York Times*, 29th August, p. 1.

Wucherer, K. (2006). Business partnering – A driving force for innovation. *Industrial Marketing Management*, 35 (1): 91–102.

Zinkhan, G.M., and Gelb, B.D. (1985). Competitive intelligence practices of industrial marketers. *Industrial Marketing Management*, 14 (4): 269–275.

Website Addresses

https:www.itgovernance.co.uk/what-is-cybersecurity (accessed on 14th October, 2019).

https://www.fca.org.uk/news/press-releases/fca-fines-tesco-bank-failures-2016-cyber-attack (accessed on 29th October, 2021).

Hotten, R. (2021). Tesco website and app back up after hack attempt. https://www.bbc.co.uk/news/business-59027423 (accessed on 29th October, 2021).

2.12 Further Reading

Esteves, J., Ramalho, E., and De Haro, G. (2017). To improve cybersecurity, think like a hacker. *Sloan Management Review*, 58 (3): 71–77.

Jones, T.M. (1995). Instrumental stakeholder theory: A synthesis of ethics and economics. *Academy of Management Review*, 20 (2): 404–437.

Oosthoek, K., and Doerr, C. (2021). Cyber threat intelligence: A product without a process? *International Journal of Intelligence and CounterIntelligence*, 34: 300–315. https://doi.org/10.1080/08850607.2020.1780062.

2.13 Bank of Questions

Question 1: What role does the cyber security manager play? Provide examples to reinforce your arguments.

Question 2: How can the cyber security manager engage better with stakeholders in order to ensure that the organization's strategic intelligence cyber security framework benefits the wider community?

Question 3: How can cyber security be embedded in the organization's security culture?

Question 4: How can society be more fully engaged in cyber security in order to reduce the damage caused by cyber attacks that vary in intensity and sophistication?

Question 5: Cyber security should not be linked with an organization's corporate social responsibility programme. Critically appraise this view and provide examples to reinforce your arguments.

Question 6: Which factors should the cyber security manager take into account when carrying out a risk assessment?

3   Bridging the Government, Industry and Society Divide

3.1 Introduction

The Internet and social media have an impact as to how people in society interact with each other and what information they share when carrying out their daily activities. Indeed, the Internet is viewed as facilitating relationship building that helps managers to alter business processes and revise the company's business model, improve client information usage and streamline supply chain activities (Lichtenthal and Eliaz, 2003; Makkonen and Vuori, 2014). Through enhanced connectivity, rapid interaction occurs between individuals of a personalized nature and this allows for the acquisition of information, and the consolidation of distribution and storage (Walters, 2008). Future developments in communications technology usage are likely to influence how individuals in society respond to events and how they engage and share information, respond to news, whether genuine or fake, and become influential in terms of writing reviews, for example. Key influencers in organizations and professional bodies and institutions are likely to increase their rapport with government and demand that government departments adopt a pro-active approach to solving cyber security threats as and when they materialize.

This chapter starts by outlining the learning objectives (Section 3.2) and continues with an explanation of what a collectivist-oriented cyber security stakeholder framework involves (Section 3.3). The approach used for establishing a cyber security policy and strategy framework is made clear (Section 3.4) and an analysis of the attacks on a computer system and network (Section 3.4.1), and an analysis of the critical friendship groups (Section 3.4.2) are provided. The relationships between an organization and the known influential cyber security stakeholders are provided (Section 3.5). A learning summary is provided (Section 3.6) and this is followed by a conclusion (Section 3.7); a mini case (Section 3.8); an extended case (Section 3.9); a set of references (Section 3.10) and further reading (Section 3.11). A bank of questions (Section 3.12) is also provided.

3.2 Learning Objectives

The reader will be able to:

- establish how a collectivist cyber security approach fits within a stakeholder framework;
- establish why a cyber security manager needs to think of establishing a cyber security policy within a strategic framework;

DOI: 10.4324/9781003244295-3

- establish why it is necessary and important to analyse attacks on a computer system and network; and
- devise and implement a cyber security management framework.

3.3 A Collectivist-Oriented Cyber Security Stakeholder Framework

Government communication updates are essential during a crisis but are sometimes distrusted or looked upon with scorn as activists provide counterarguments or merely set out to disrupt by providing disinformation. Some critics of government suggest that society is being put at an increased risk because of the fact that an information breach is likely to occur because of how people in society interact with other members of society using electronic devices. Also, cyber security is still underappreciated as it is not that well understood. It is suggested that people take for granted the use of communications technology and assume that they are safe. However, as the sophistication of communications technology increases and people use electronic devices to make payments and book a range of services, some vulnerable people may be exposed to fraud as they have a limited understanding of security per se. The interconnectivity of computer systems and computer networks means that there are multiple providers and stakeholders, all of whom operate in their own way and with their own objectives. This adds to the complexity of the situation because employees share different types of information and data, and use multiple devices, which suggests that they cannot possibly be aware of all the threats that they are exposed to, and even if they were, human weaknesses leave people open to exploitation. For example, an employee may click on a spurious email link that results in them downloading a virus or provide information to somebody making an unsolicited telephone (scam) call that results in the individual targeted giving out personal data or allowing an unknown person to take remote control of their computer that results in them being defrauded or held to ransom in some way.

The UK's Government Communications Headquarters (GCHQ) is an intelligence, cyber and security agency that has responsibility for keeping the UK safe for people to engage in online business. The UK's cyber security mission is led by the National Cyber Security Centre (NCSC), which is a part of GCHQ. The focus of the NCSC is to protect the UK's critical services from cyber attack as well as manage major incidents, and help improve the security of the Internet. The latter involves advice to citizens and organizations vis-à-vis technological improvement. Additional technological support is provided by the Centre for the Protection of National Infrastructure (CPNI), which is accountable to the Director General of MI5 (the UK's security service). Staff at CPNI provide advice regarding how to protect the nation's infrastructure from various acts of terrorism and other threats, and managers and industry specialists can consult with CPNI staff in order to gain insights into increasing organizational security. There is also the opportunity to report an incident to local businessmen via the WARP (Warning, Advice and Reporting Point) programme that focuses on sharing information regarding cyber attacks within a geographical region with staff in various industrial sectors. The WARP programme represents a cost-effective, community approach to identifying and solving cyber security problems in real time, and acts to help identify threats before they manifest into incidents. Staff based at the UK's National Crime Agency (NCA) have a wide brief and focus on critical cyber incidents and are charged with disrupting the activities of criminals. Agency staff work closely with the UK police forces, regional crime units and international law enforcement bodies (e.g. Europol, the FBI and the US Secret Service) as well as organizations in the private sector. The Information Assurance Advisory Council (IAAC) forms a bridge between government and both profit and not-for-profit organizations in terms of advancing Information Assurance (IA). IAAC provides a range of services, including policy recommendations, and through its various activities, promotes a number of cyber security initiates. Indeed, IAAC's Academic Liaison Panel was instrumental in helping to lobby government in terms of the trust-worthy software initiative, which was taken up by the UK government in due course. The Cyber Security Challenge UK is well established and organizes a number of competitions, learning programmes and other events to identify and inspire people from a broad range of backgrounds to pursue a career as a cyber security professional. Get Safe Online is a UK public/private sector partnership supported by the UK government and industry and provides a range of information (advice and reports), relating to online security and safety. Get Safe Online organize an annual event called Get Safe Online week, work with law enforcement personnel in order to improve online safety for all, and have a user-friendly website. The advice provided helps consumers (the general public) and business users to protect themselves, their computers and mobile devices against online threats, including viruses, fraud and identify theft. Advice is also provided as regards how to back up data and information, how to protect people against the cyber threats they may encounter and how to report a crime and who to report a crime to.

Much is being done to combat the actions of fraudsters and the UK's Action Fraud is a national reporting centre for fraud and cyber crime and is accessible to members of the general public that are victims of fraud. The centre is managed by the City of London Police and their staff work alongside staff based at the National Fraud Intelligence Bureau (NFIB). The service is available 24 hours a day and 7 days a week, and offers victims the opportunity to report a fraud and receive help and support. People can also call a telephone helpline and report a telephone scam to British Telecommunications that has an online telephone information scam facility. The following example is extracted from Jill Insley (2021: 13). Question of Money column in the Money Section of The Sunday Times shows how an individual can fall victim to a fraud:

> ...I had a call from …..in New York saying that as I was a shareholder in the packaging company … I was entitled to some shares because a hostile takeover was going on in the USA. ...my entitlement, 5004 shares £2.34 each, and drew up a contract to pay a bond guarantee of £4,119.29, which it said would protect me...I paid the money into an Indonesian account ……I rang my bank,... to make the international payment and asked it if it was normal to pay a bond to a US company and was assured that it was.
>
> I was then put in touch with others ……….. I was told I could pay for a warrant to buy 5,004 more shares costing £11,259, which I did... Then I was told I needed to pay the bank charges to transfer the money and £5,574.78 to the international clearing fund. I asked …. if banks charge such amounts for clearance fees, and ….they did.

> More money was demanded ....I had to sign a form for an anti-money laundering application. ......'.I had to pay $10,000 to the Office of the Comptroller to get my money released, but that I would get $10,000 back strategy away. ...I was being scammed and told the caller so, who hung up.

The above example highlights how easy it is for a person to be duped into parting with sensitive personal information and normally, a victim is approached via a phishing email or a scam telephone call, which appear to be from a genuine source. Cyber criminals are also deploying various phishing techniques via social media sites, including LinkedIn, MySpace, Facebook and Twitter, to trap individuals (Abawajy, 2014). To prevent such occurrences, attention needs to focus on facilitating increased interaction between government, industry and academia, and it is worthwhile to note that the UK government already works closely with industry, in cyber space. For example, the Cyber Security Information Sharing Partnership (CiSP) was established a number of years ago to exchange cyber threat information in real time, so that situational awareness is increased and the potential damage to the UK business from a cyber attack is reduced. Governments around the world, sometimes through formal cooperative agreements, respond in a pro-active manner to various cyber threats in a number of ways. One example that involves international cooperation is the development of Computer Emergency Response Teams (CERTs), the aim of which is to maintain network continuity and promote the use of valid security technology (Choucri et al., 2014: 104). It is also useful at this juncture to make reference to Supervisory Control and Data Acquisition (SCADA) and note that automated systems are essential for maintaining the continuity and control of Critical National Infrastructure (CNI) (e.g. energy, water and transportation) (Cherdantseva et al., 2016: 2). If key components of CNI are attacked and disabled, damage can be inflicted on companies, institutions and society. The fact that the UK government has formed the National Cyber Force (NCF) should protect further UK cyber space by allowing specialized staff to undertake retaliatory attacks on those intent on disrupting national infrastructure and spreading fake news on social media (Kerbaj, 2019: 8). The UK's NCF was established in late 2020 and is composed of staff from the Ministry of Defence, GCHQ and various intelligence agencies, the objective being to undertake offensive and defensive cyber operations to prevent acts of cyber crime and cyber terrorism, as well as counteract the cyber attack methods deployed by hostile states. NCF staff monitor a number of computer and satellite networks and close down digital platforms managed by criminal groups and terrorists (Kerbaj, 2019: 8). It is clear, therefore, that government staff will in the years ahead work more closely with industry-based experts and the wider community, university research departments, to ensure that a more holistic view of cyber security results in increased cyber security awareness and greater cooperation to reduce an organization's vulnerability. In addition, cyber security education and training programmes will receive attention so that a range of cyber security skills and technologies are developed and deployed as necessary.

Countries do, however, adopt a different approach to cyber security and in some countries there are strict laws in place relating to the use of a computer, network or the Internet itself. South Korea, through KISA (Korea Internet & Security Agency), adopts a pro-active approach to protecting Korean citizens from cyber attack and monitors the websites of Korean companies in Korea to ensure that no sensitive data or information is being provided that can be used by an attacker to penetrate a company's defences or launch a focused attack on an individual. KISA houses the Korea National Biometric Test Center and works closely with various companies and research institutes such as the Electronics and Telecommunications Research Institute (ETRI). ETRI has established an international reputation and works with overseas universities in areas such as technology and security. International cooperation in the area of cyber security is considered essential and South Korea and the UK have worked closely together through the formation of the UK Cyber Security Research Network and the Korean Cyber Security Research Network (Trim and Youm, 2014, 2015). In the US, the Cybersecurity and Infrastructure Security Agency (CISA) works closely with the Federal Bureau of Investigation (FBI) and the National Security Agency (NSA) to assess cyber threats and protect CNI from advanced persistent threats (APTs). Senior managers contemplating undertaking business abroad need to avail themselves of a number of factors, including the law relating to the utilization of personal data and information; the rules relating to cooperation regarding public key infrastructure (PKI); the issues and challenges relating to governance, risk and compliance; and certification in relation to computer-based services, including the Cloud.

Taking into account how people are directly or indirectly affected by a cyber attack, it can be suggested that the complexity involved is beyond a single government or a single organization, and this means that the general public are at risk. By acknowledging that a collectivist approach to cyber security is necessary, a stakeholder theory approach to cyber security and the management of it can be viewed as essential. Noting that companies and countries engage in both cooperation and competition (Freeman et al., 2018), the cyber security manager needs to know how to lobby government in order to get the protection needed and at the same time be confident that national security objectives do not override company objectives. As the level of complexity increases through time and new players enter the arena, policy makers need to accept that a negotiated position between parties (government to government) may need to be renegotiated through time, because the circumstances have changed due to a range of factors, including product innovation vulnerabilities, changes in life style and a change in the law, for example. Ethical issues will surface from time to time and will create tension and require solutions. However, Holzer (2008) suggests that those viewed as stakeseekers (e.g. those that assume an external role in the organization's social environment – independent of a government and industry) can play a positive role and be integrated into the cyber security decision making process. Through the process of dialogue, the stakeseekers move from an outside position to an outside-in position and are viewed as an insider/stakeholder. Through the process of lobbying other stakeholders, cyber security awareness (Trim and Lee, 2019) can be made more prominent, and collectivist action can be taken so that cyber security is placed in the context of community responsiveness. Should this be the case, both the organization and the local community will benefit (Kobeissi and Damanpour, 2009) and the stakeholder framework will take shape.

Through the process of achieving organizational goals, senior management can adopt a benevolent approach (Crane, 2018) to non-organizational members and ensure that the corporate social responsibility policy in place meets a number of expectations and cements relations with external interest groups (Freeman, 1984; Kobeissi and Damanpour, 2009). To achieve this, the cyber security manager needs to view stakeholder involvement from a value co-creation (Vargo and Lusch, 2004) network perspective and consider that cyber security is viewed in terms of a shared purpose (Freeman et al., 2018). This suggests that at the heart of the relationship building process is the concept of mutuality and Heugens et al. (2002) support this view by advocating the need for mutual learning. This can be considered important because stakeholders are often involved in exchanging information and may adopt mutually beneficial working practices in order to achieve success/goals/personal objectives. Success does not need to be defined or measured in monetary terms because a relationship ultimately benefits from the collective learning approach (Heugens et al., 2002). Butterfield et al. (2004) purport that collective learning results in situational learning, which gives rise to behavioural learning and ultimately a changed (e.g. for the better) relationship. This is an important consideration because cyber security cannot be viewed as static owing to the fact that cyber criminals are becoming more aggressive and highly sophisticated in launching attacks in various forms from undisclosed locations, and at the same time, there is a possibility that the boundary between acts of cyber crime and cyber terrorism will fade and result in the end objective becoming the same (e.g. disruption through continual action).

A collectivist approach to problem solving is valid and has been given credence by King (2008: 23) who states:

> Collective action consists of coordinated behavior among two or more people that, at least in some minimal way, satisfies individual goals and produces a jointly experienced outcome. Collective action is necessary for stakeholder identity to emerge. Without collective action, constituents would be disconnected individuals lacking a coherent interest in corporate behavior, and managers would fail to perceive these constituents as consequential. By framing their interests vis-à-vis the focal corporation, collective action among potential stakeholders facilitates the emergence of stakeholder awareness, both among the constituents of the organization and in the eyes of managers. This, we should conceive of collective action as an important factor underlying stakeholder influence.

King (2008: 25) adds to our understanding by stating: "For successful collective action, organizers must find some way to motivate individuals to participate". The approach outlined by Moriarty (2014), which suggests that stakeholder theory has two components, distributive (results oriented and the benefits associated with the outcomes in relation to the decisions made) and procedural (the individuals that have had an input into the decision making process), can be considered useful. Crane (2018) takes matters further by suggesting that stakeholders are increasingly interconnected and are part of a system; hence, it is possible to understand how the actions of an individual stakeholder influences other stakeholders in terms of trustworthiness.

A sophisticated cyber attack can, in the case of a small- or medium-sized organization, inflict enough damage to make it vulnerable. The cyber security manager can reduce organizational vulnerability, by adopting the open strategy approach (Whittington et al., 2011; Appleyard and Chesbrough, 2017; Hautz et al., 2017) as it allows managers to think in terms of enhancing strategy formulation through the process approach by engaging with internal and external stakeholders, and at the same time accepting that partner organizations are important sources of knowledge that can be used to aid an organization's strategic problem solving (Olsen et al., 2017). This is relevant because as Freeman et al. (2018) argue, the stakeholder view was developed in order to help strategists organize information that was used in the strategic planning process. Hence, the cyber security manager needs to be mindful of the importance that technology and innovation play in strategy formulation and accept that strategic planners operate in a competitive environment that is undergoing cultural and technological change (Whittington et al., 2011). In addition, the cyber security manager needs to acknowledge that the implementation of an open strategy is dependent upon managers adopting an open approach whereby strategy professionals and others rely on process skills that include coaching, facilitation and communication (Whittington et al., 2011: 541). This, it can be argued, fits well with the mutual learning approach advocated by Heugens et al. (2002).

3.4 Establishing a Cyber Security Policy and Strategy Framework

In order to understand how the cyber security manager can adopt a strategic approach to cyber security management, we draw from a study. For the study, data were collected over a consecutive three-month period in 2016 relating to cyber attacks on a computer system and network, and this was followed up by two critical friendship groups, composed mainly of senior intelligence and security professionals. The fact that the research spanned several fields of enquiry (Mingers, 2001) can be considered a strength because it adds a multidisciplinary dimension to cyber security threat detection and the management of defined cyber threats. A sequential research process (Mingers, 2001; Anderson and Agarwal, 2010) was adopted and the results of each phase of the research process acted as an input for the next phase of the research process. The objective of the research was to provide insights into how the cyber security manager can manage cyber security complexity and devise a cyber security policy and strategy framework.

The findings from the initial phase of the research formed the basis of two conference paper presentations and two subsequent critical friendship group sessions. Two papers relating to organizational and management issues and challenges in relation to cyber security were presented at two closed cyber security conferences at Christ Church College, University of Oxford in June 2018 and June 2019. Each paper presentation was followed by a critical friendship group discussion. The first critical friendship group was composed of 14 intelligence and security specialists and the second critical friendship group was composed of 26 intelligence and security specialists. The probing that occurred during the critical friendship groups allowed a high degree of probing so that those participating brought out and discussed the underlying conditions (Patton, 1990). Notes were taken and the feedback received was written up immediately after each critical friendship group had concluded. This allowed the researchers to think systematically about the themes generated (Strauss and Corbin, 1990). The suggestions offered were in-depth and were supported by real world examples. Indeed, the naturalistic enquiry method (Lincoln and Guba, 1985) provided an opportunity for the researchers to gain insights into real world situations and to make a link between theory and practice. The critical friendship group approach advocated by Golby and Appleby (1995) was used as it allowed the researchers to place their cyber security knowledge within the context of a cyber security framework, which was challenged and rechallenged, and established how cyber security could be viewed and interpreted from a number of stakeholder perspectives.

The first conference paper presentation revolved around top management's role and the second incorporated the development of cyber security knowledge and its use.

Those attending and offering feedback were highly experienced specialists drawn from government, industry and academia, and had all worked on various security projects in different parts of the world. The phenomenological approach adopted (Patton, 1990) allowed the researchers to establish how a collectivist approach could be used to cyber security and how new knowledge could be developed (Whetten, 1989) and placed in the context of a cyber security framework. The critical friendship group participants spoke freely and the interaction with the researcher that presented the papers and received the feedback can be described as conversation-based (Denzin, 1989) as the participants provided both practical and operational knowledge (of the intelligence and security topics covered) (Sinkovics and Penz, 2011). This approach had the added advantage of providing depth by drawing on the experience of those involved (Bennett et al., 1997).

3.4.1 Analysis of the Attacks on a Computer System

The data relating to attacks on a computer system and network over a three-month period are analysed and tabulated and appear in Tables 3.1–3.3. The data were collected from a computer log and a record was made of the different types of attack that had occurred on each day of each month within a 24-hour period. As can be seen from the tables, there is a clear pattern within the data and it is possible to deduce that the majority of the attacks were carried out at set times and in an organized manner. Some attacks can be classified as random and opportunistic, and others can be defined as sophisticated and persistent. It can be noted from the tables that the most commonly occurring attack was a medium-level attack, which is defined as a sustainable attack that has the capability to penetrate an organization's computer system and network(s) and disrupt or remove data. The attacks occurred throughout the day and were at their most intense in the early part of the day (8am to 11am). There were a similar number of attacks per day throughout the three-month period, which suggests that those carrying out the attacks were highly organized and deliberate in their actions.

Table 3.1 Cyber Attacks on a Computer System in January 2016

Type of attack	Number of attacks	Percentage of overall attacks (%)
Low risk attack	7	5
Medium risk attack	119	88
High risk attack	9	7
Total number of attacks for January 2016	135	100
Average number of attacks per day	4.	
Sustained and continuous attack (medium type)	6	4
Thursday 7th January, 2016	0 attacks	
Friday 22nd January, 2016	0 attacks	
Friday 29th January, 2016	0 attacks	
Attacks every five-hour cycle: from 6am to 9pm	53, 41, 35	96
Attacks mostly occur between 8am and 8pm	118	87
Attacks peak between 8am and 10am	31	23

Table 3.2 Cyber Attacks on a Computer System in February 2016

Type of attack	Number of attacks	Percentage of overall attacks (%)
Low risk attack	7	7.5
Medium risk attack	81	85
High risk attack	7	7.5
Total number of attacks for February 2016	95	100
Average number of attacks per day	3.	
Sustained and continuous attack (medium type)	27	28
Saturday 13th February, 2016	0 attacks	
Sunday 14th February, 2016	0 attacks	
Attacks every five-hour cycle: from 7am to 10pm	53, 23, 13	94
Attacks mostly occur between 7am and 8pm	89	94
Attacks peak between 9am and 11am	31	33

Table 3.3 Cyber Attacks on a Computer System in March 2016

Type of attack	Number of attacks	Percentage of overall attacks (%)
Low risk attack	18	15
Medium risk attack	104	85
High risk attack	0	0
Total number of attacks for March 2016	122	100
Average number of attacks per day	4.	
Sustained and continuous attack (medium type)	29	24
Saturday 26th March, 2016	0 attacks	
Attacks every five-hour cycle: from 8am to 11pm	49, 40, 25	93
Attacks mostly occur between 8am and 10pm	109	89
Attacks peak between 9am and 11am	25	21

3.4.2 Analysis of the Critical Friendship Groups

The first critical friendship group session lasted approximately 60 minutes and was managed by the researcher that presented a paper entitled: "How a defined cyber security strategy can help managers counteract cyber threats and make the organization more resilient" (Trim, 2018). The arguments and counterarguments were contextually embedded and contained various spontaneous episodes that fuelled further discussion, highlighting in the process additional examples (Boje, 1991). The topics covered centred around what top management needed to do in terms of ensuring that the organiza-tion's cyber security strategy was robust. After the first conference paper presentation and critical friendship session, a strategic intelligence and cyber security framework was produced (please see Figure 3.1). It can be noted that a commitment to strategic intelligence results in a security policy and strategy that is influenced by the outcome of a threat model and impact analysis. The cyber security framework that manifests is influenced by the organization's security policy.

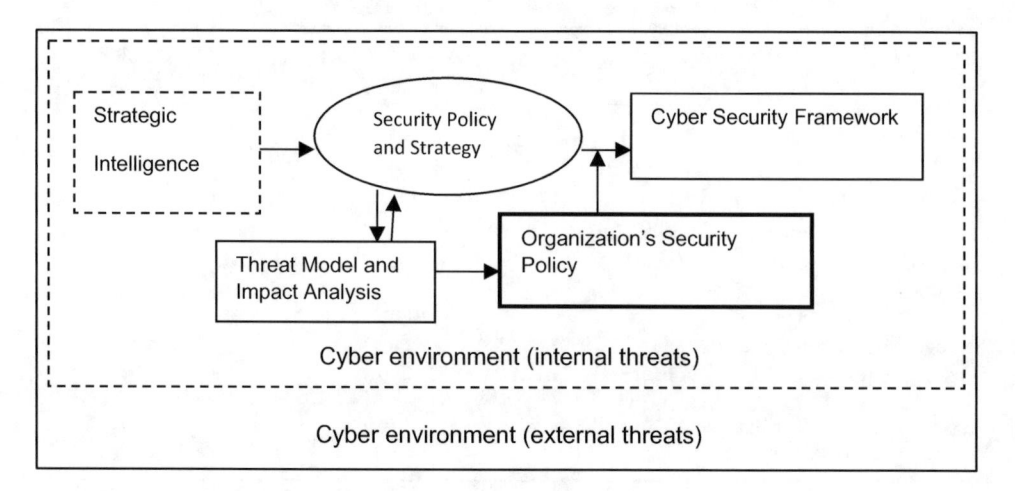

Figure 3.1 Strategic intelligence and cyber security framework.

Following the second conference paper presentation, which was entitled: "Counter-acting cyber threats through organizational learning and training" (Trim, 2019), and critical friendship session, which lasted 50 minutes, Figure 3.1 is amended and a cyber security policy and strategy framework is produced (please see Figure 3.2). By refining the model and building on the discussions stemming from the second critical friendship group, it was possible to place the cyber security framework within the context of an organization's cyber security policy and strategy.

The emphasis of the second critical friendship group session was to establish how cyber security knowledge can be embedded in an organization's cyber security framework. The key point to note about Figure 3.2 is that senior management recognize that it is essential to engage with external stakeholders and bring their knowledge, expertise and interpretation into the threat model and impact analysis component and the cyber security framework. This is because external stakeholders (industry associations, government departments and agencies, and specialist security consultancies, for exam-ple), are sources of up-to-date intelligence and in some cases draw on events overseas, which provide insights into how cyber attacks are evolving and what kinds of impacts certain types of cyber attack have on an organization. The emphasis being to develop a holistic view of cyber security by drawing on the knowledge of the stakeholders, who are deemed to be influential in terms of helping senior management to determine cyber security provision within the partnership arrangement. The second critical friendship group also reshaped the view that an organization's cyber security framework fed into the organization's security policy and strategy as opposed to mainly being an output of it. This is important to recognize because cyber security inputs are considered to influence the type of threat model and impact analysis used, and need to be viewed as transformational as opposed to transactional in nature because the cyber security policy in place is known to change through time, as a result of cyber attacks becoming more sophisticated and new organizational vulnerabilities are identified and rectified.

Figure 3.2 explains how a cyber security policy and strategy framework can be developed that takes into account (i) the level of risk (high, medium and low) associated with a specific cyber attack; and (ii) how various stakeholders can be categorized

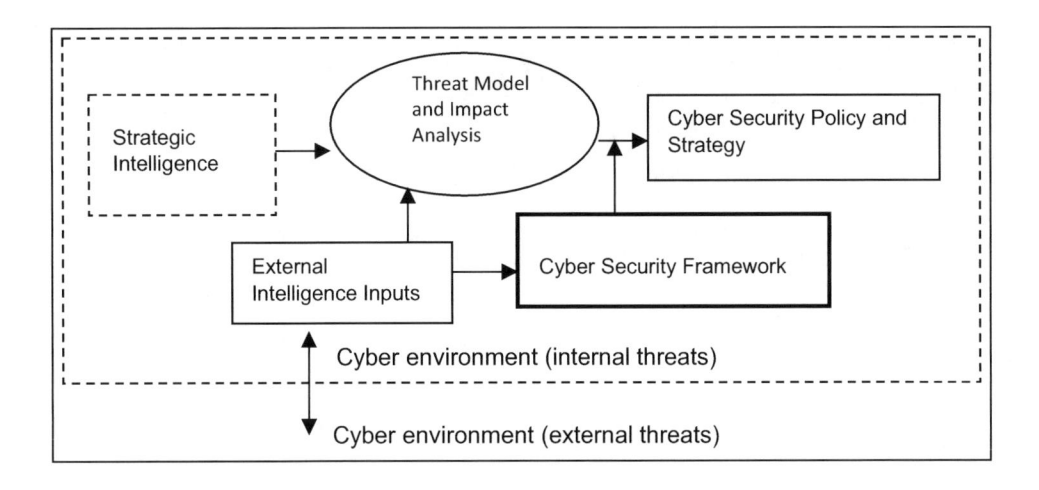

Figure 3.2 A cyber security policy and strategy framework.

according to their influence/impact in terms of counteracting/helping to counteract the type of cyber attack. When using scenario analysis and planning, it is important to remember that managers have at their disposal a technique for dealing with uncertainty and linking actual/possible impact analysis with strategic planning (Ringland, 2006). The cyber security manager needs to view the outcome of such an analysis as being able to explain to people (staff within the organization and staff employed by partner organizations) what cyber security involves and why it is essential to take security seriously. By linking the organization's risk appetite with each influential cyber security stakeholder, it is possible to show how influential each stakeholder is in terms of influencing an organization's cyber security policy and strategy, and their contribution to the community, for example. In addition, by establishing what management need to derive from each of the relationships will determine what type of commitment staff need to make to ensure that an organizational vulnerability can be eradicated.

3.5 The Relationships between an Organization and the Known Influential Cyber Security Stakeholders

In order to place the above into perspective, it is necessary to map the relationships between an organization and the known influential cyber security stakeholders. Figure 3.3 contains a set of relationships between a hypothetical organization and the known influential cyber security stakeholders. It is appreciated that there are both formal and informal relationships between organizational staff and staff in the organizations are listed in the matrix. What can be noted from Figure 3.3 is that as the degree of cyber threat complexity increases and with it the organization's risk appetite, it is likely that national security issues surface and as a result, staff within large and targeted organizations will engage more frequently with staff in government security and intelligence agencies.

By recognizing the complexity of the problem and by understanding that staff do not have the same level of knowledge of cyber security, the cyber security manager can put in place an appropriate staff awareness programme. Staff awareness is reinforced through

Level of influence / Organization's Risk Appetite	Low Level of Influence	Medium Level of Influence	High Level of Influence
Low Risk	WARP Get Safe Online	Independent Cyber Security Consultants NCA Get Safe Online	CERTs
Medium Risk	WARP IAAC Get Safe Online	CPNI NFIB NCA Get Safe Online	CERTs CiSP
High Risk	WARP IAAC Get Safe Online	NCA CiSP	CERTs GCHQ (NCSC) NCF

Figure 3.3 Mapping the relationships between an organization and the known influential cyber security stakeholders.

Legend: WARP (Warning, Advice and Reporting Point); IAAC (Information Assurance Advisory Council); NCA (National Crime Agency); CPNI (Centre for the Protection of National Infrastructure); NFIB (National Fraud Intelligence Bureau); CiSP (Cyber Security Information Sharing Partnership - National Cyber Security Centre); CERTs (Computer Emergency Response Teams); GCHQ (Government Communications Headquarters); NCSC (National Cyber Security Centre); NCF (National Cyber Force)

training and support programmes so that staff at all levels within the organization know about the risks associated with a particular cyber threat and what action they need to take to counteract a specific type of cyber attack. Through the process of sharing information about cyber attacks at various levels (regional, national and international), and engaging continuously with business and the not-for-profit sector, a number of cyber security objectives can be fulfilled that manifest in a wide appreciation of cyber security that is aimed at making society more resilient.

By taking the lead, the cyber security manager in an organization that is at risk from a cyber attack can establish an organization-specific cyber security policy and strategy framework that brings internal stakeholders into contact with external stakeholders, and results in greater public trust of business. Public trust in business does draw on multiple theories of trust (Pirson et al., 2019) but through the process of cyber security enhancement, people in society can be incorporated into an organization's corporate social responsibility programme. Bearing in mind that large companies are known to be at risk to a cyber attack and have the resources to engage more widely with the general public and are better placed to do so than small- and medium-sized organizations, it would seem logical to suggest that they can be at the heart of the collectivist approach to cyber security. Should this be the case, large companies will become beacons (e.g. through sharing cyber security knowledge) and influence behavioural change through the implementation of a strict cyber security behavioural policy and programme. The consequence being that external stakeholders will, through staff using various forms of interaction and electronic word-of-mouth, intensify the relationship they have with organizational staff, and thus promote cyber security awareness more effectively.

The above does, it can be argued, set out the case for a collectivist approach to cyber security and what needs to be understood is that although an organization may have security systems in place (including sensors in its computer networks that indicate if an intrusion is taking place/has taken place) as evidenced in the computer log, it has to be remembered that the actions of individuals and unclear guidance from senior management in terms of BYOD (Bring Your Own Device (to work)), for example, will create additional vulnerabilities that a hardened hacker will probe until access is gained.

The security measures that are put in place need to be viewed as fit for purpose. For example, the cyber security manager can produce guidelines that stop/restrict staff from taking home computer devices and accessories (data sticks) that contain company data and information. All devices that are removed from the organization's premises need to be checked and recorded, and external staff that enter the company's premises need to go through security and receive the appropriate clearance. Hand–held devices can be recorded on a form and left at reception and guarded so that they are safely returned when the person leaves the premises. People can also be checked by electronic means to see if they are carrying a computer device and/or accessories with them when they enter the company's premises. The cyber security manager can keep records relating to the movement of all devices into and out of the organization, and know which laptops are stored in a secure cabinet and kept within the building. Employees that take home a laptop and then misplace it run the risk of having all the data erased, even their own personal data that may be stored on the laptop. Erasing data is done remotely and it is to stop non–authorized access to the data and information stored on the device. By wiping the data and information in this way is known to be a common practice and detailed in company policy.

If senior managers do not ensure that the basic security measures are in place, the organization will remain vulnerable and a successful attack could result in a data breach that leads to the organization losing its reputation. As regards what are deemed appropriate security measures, the cyber security manager needs to take responsibility for cyber security policy and ensure that the cyber security systems and procedures implemented remain functional. The cyber security manager needs to ensure that the firm's security culture embraces security awareness, and staff adopt a collectivist approach to security by drawing on the expertise and knowledge of various stakeholders. What has to be remembered is that an organization's internal and external environments are subject to change as new business models evolve that encompass just–in–time delivery, outsourcing and/or offshoring, and new business relationships with previous competitors such as a strategic alliance. A transparent and open approach to cyber security will help those employed by the organization to relate better to the organization's external environment, develop a better understanding of the cyber threats that exist and at the same time allow them to be more confident in terms of dealing with perceived risks because they have the ability to evaluate a threat more thoroughly (Anderson and Agarwal, 2010). In addition, attention can be given to ensuring that the organization's information security systems are robust enough to withstand an attack (Arachchilage et al., 2016). It has to be remembered, however, that a hacker may not attack a company directly but may seek a route via a vendor or an employee or through a compliance vulnerability (Esteves et al., 2017). Should this happen, organizational vulnerability may increase because of diminishing trust among the channel partners (Håkansson et al., 1977; Davis, 2007; Shillair et al., 2015; Esteves et al., 2017).

An open communication style is known to facilitate information sharing and knowledge transfer within and between organizations (Levinthal and March, 1993) as it takes into account an individual's willingness and motivation to engage in change. Modic and Anderson (2014) acknowledge this and suggest that managers need to understand what the social psychology of persuasion involves and thus understand that security awareness warnings should be non-technical and authoritative in nature. In addition, an appropriate form of security awareness needs to be devised whereby the cyber security manager establishes an individual's knowledge and attitude vis-à-vis their behaviour towards security issues and tailors security awareness programmes to meet the specific needs of individuals. The importance of this has been recognized by Anderson and Agarwal (2010: 638) who purport that management should understand the motivations of employees and what determines psychological ownership, and establish how to influence their security behaviour. Appropriate security messages should be used to reinforce security behaviour and the guidelines in place need to be complete and reinforced though time. However, this cannot be done without management being committed to providing the necessary cyber security resources.

The campaign to provide additional cyber security resources has been running for some time and will continue to gain momentum through initiatives such as those launched by ENISA (European Union Agency for Network and Information Security otherwise known as the European Union Agency for Cybersecurity). Staff at ENISA (2019) are aware of the different stakeholder groups that exist in society and have produced a report relating to Industry 4.0 cyber security, which makes reference to the fact that organizations need additional cyber security knowledge and personnel. NIST (National Institute of Standards and Technology) based in the US does much to promote cyber security and is influential in terms of organizations developing cyber security programmes. Collaboration involving staff from these organizations, government departments, industry and academia will, it can be argued, strengthen cyber security provision.

3.6 Learning Summary

The reader will gauge from Figure 3.4 that inter-organizational cooperation is essential in terms of staff building and maintaining relationships with a range of people and also open communication allows for issues and challenges to be addressed when necessary. The motivation of staff is key and by maintaining the interest and commitment of staff, cyber security awareness will become embedded in the organization's security culture.

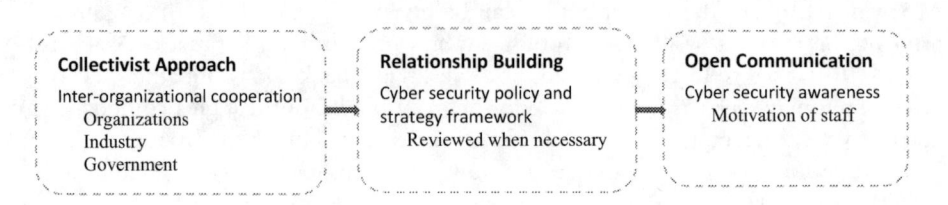

Figure 3.4 A collectivist-oriented cyber security stakeholder framework.

The reader is able to:

- understand the intentions and actions of cyber criminals;
- apply an evidence-based approach to put in place a number of countermeasures that become community focused and owned;
- understand why the cyber security manager needs to develop trust-based relationships that enable internal stakeholders to communicate with external stakeholders through conventional forms of word-of-mouth and current and emerging forms of electronic word-of-mouth;
- make the general public more aware of what has to be done to counteract the various types of cyber threat;
- adopt a responsible approach to how people utilize communications technology in both the workplace and during their leisure time; and
- instigate the process of cooperation and collaboration by embracing stakeholder theory so that there is an appropriate match between technological expertise and psychological understanding, and the realization that the human aspects of security are just as important or more important than technological solutions.

3.7 Conclusion

The cyber security policy and strategy framework outlined in this chapter is derived from the analysis of attacks on a computer system and network, and two critical friendship groups involving highly experienced intelligence personnel, security personnel and academics. The findings suggest that cyber security should be placed in the context of an organization's corporate social responsibility programme and by imbuing a collectivist spirit, stakeholders can be identified and grouped accordingly so that specific trust-based relationships are formed that ensure that everybody in the community remains focused on counteracting the actions of cyber criminals.

There is no doubt that cyber security is a complex subject that will continue to be of high priority in terms of testing management's resolve and will remain on top management's agenda. By recognizing that cyber crime affects all, it should be possible to promote increased engagement so that government to government relations are strengthened, and business takes the lead in terms of devising and implementing a broad set of cyber security initiatives. Accepting that organizations can be at the heart of a cyber security awareness programme bodes well as it allows for uniformity in terms of what is to be done and by whom. By embracing the collectivist spirit, stakeholders can be identified and grouped accordingly and trust-based relationships developed to ensure that everybody remains focused on a central objective, namely, to counteract the actions of cyber criminals.

3.8 Mini Case: Trust and the Community

Mr. Pearson was a well-known organizational consultant and speaker, and had attended a number of international conferences over the years. His most recent engagement was to speak about security and strategy to a group of cyber security managers at an event in London. The group was composed of a wide cross section of people that represented a cross section of industries. What made the planning of the talk awkward was that some were known to have many years of experience and others were known to have very limited industrial experience. It was a mixed group and Mr. Pearson did not want to let people down by appearing too knowledgeable and informative or too predictable and prescriptive.

In order to get his talk started, he wrote down a number of headings, which included leadership, resilience, motivation and unexpected events. He thought long and hard but could not decide which order the concepts should be talked through. Even more surprising, he was unable to think of appropriate examples to reinforce the subject matter and in addition, he could not work out how to link the subtopics. The more he thought about the talk, the more confused he became.

In order to get inspiration, he decided to look through a number of books, reports, academic journal articles and newspaper articles. Still, he drew a blank and then he remembered the work of Kim and Mauborgne (2005), who had approached the concept of strategy in a different way by focusing on a people-oriented approach, suggesting that there were mutually reinforcing elements that made up what was known as the "fair process". Considering the importance associated with cyber security and accepting that the cyber security process had to be managed, it seemed appropriate that he realigns the focus of the talk. Mr. Pearson, who had read the book a number of years ago, familiarized himself with the underpinning theoretical approach of the authors (Kim and Mauborgne, 2005: 175):

> Fair process is our managerial expression of procedural justice theory. As in legal settings, fair process builds execution into strategy by creating people's buy-in up front. When fair process is exercised in the strategy-making process, people trust that a level playing field exits. This inspires them to cooperate voluntarily in executing the resulting strategic decisions.

To win people over is not an easy task he thought to himself. And then he had a brain wave. Picking up on the point relating to commitment, he decided to restructure the talk around the three mutually reinforcing elements identified by Kim and Mauborgne (2005: 175–176), which were engagement; explanation and clarity of expectation. He made a number of notes to help him focus his talk. Engagement refers to involving individuals in the strategic decision making process by asking them to make inputs and at the same time refute the merits of the ideas and assumptions emanating from their colleagues. With regard to explanation, here the emphasis was on getting individuals to understand why final strategic decisions are made. A crucial element of this was to get people to trust in the decisions made and also to place their trust in those that made them. As regards the clarity of expectation, here it is important for staff to acknowledge what the new rules of the game are; after that, the strategy can be finalized. This required that standards were set and responsibilities were clearly defined.

Mr. Pearson now had a way forward. He sketched out the title of the talk: the role of the cyber security manager in strategy formulation. He then listed the topics to be covered: leadership, motivation, strategy and resilience. Leadership was to be defined in terms of dealing with unknown cyber threats; motivation was to be defined in terms of empowerment; strategy was to be given a somewhat broader scope but the "fair process" incorporating engagement, explanation and clarity of expectation was to be pivotal; and resilience was to be reflective in the sense that he would draw on his own experience and highlight the most appropriate examples he was familiar with.

Questions

Question 1: How useful is it to think in terms of defining strategy from the "fair process" perspective involving engagement, explanation and clarity of expectation?

Question 2: What structure(s) should a cyber security manager put in place to deal with unknown cyber threats?

Question 3: How important is it to get staff to engage in cyber security through voluntary behaviour?

Case Source

Kim, W.C., and Mauborgne, R. (2005). *Blue Ocean Strategy: How to Create Uncontested Market Space and Make the Competition Irrelevant.* Boston, MA: Harvard Business School Press.

3.9 Extended Case: Scammers, Internet Providers and Law Enforcement

John Daniels was keen to get the meeting under way. It had been a busy day in the office and John Daniels, who was the head of marketing, was keen to finish the meeting on time as he had another meeting planned, with the company's export manager, which was due to be held in an hour's time.

"Okay, Paul, let us get under way", said John Daniels.

"Yes", replied Paul Maybury, who was the head of domestic retail and had been employed by the company for in excess of ten years.

Paul Maybury continued:

> We have done well during the post COVID-19 period and as we move into a new era, we can look forward to an even sharper rise in online business. In fact, we are 30% up on online orders compared with the previous year, and this month has seen a year on year increase of 44%.

"What problems have emerged from this increase in business?" This was a straightforward question from Simon Gates, the managing director, who was seated opposite his colleagues.

"Well", replied Paul Maybury,

> a number of unexpected concerns have arisen. Let me talk them through and then you can ask me questions at the end......Probably the main concern is that the company's website was hijacked for a short period on Monday last week and since then we have received a number of irate calls from customers that are claiming that they ordered products via our website only to be told that we did not receive their order. As a consequence, there have been some hard hitting comments about the company on various social media networks and a local newspaper reporter has asked to interview me.

Simon Gates frowned and said in a sharp voice: "Nobody told me that the company's website had been hijacked. Can you tell me about it?"

Paul Maybury paused and then said:

> I found out about this from Steven Main in IT and what he said was that our website had been off the air for two hours. In that time, the fraudsters used a very similar or identical website that drove customer traffic to a spurious account. He does not know how many protentional customers placed orders via that website but he thinks it could be a large number because as you are aware the company had just run a sales promotion and we had offers on line.

"This reminds me of an article I have just read", interjected John Daniels.

> It featured browser hacking and spyware. Lately, we have all received numerous telephone scam calls and it is clear that some of our customers may not just have been tricked into believing that they have bought one of our products online, which they have not but also, they may have been subject to a well planned scam. It seems that scammers are pretending to represent Royal Mail and sending out texts in relation to a package for collection. They are told to pay additional postage or the package will be returned to the sender. Of course, there is no package and the scammer can receive payment and get their credit card details and this means they can take more out of their account. Some of our customers were hit by this scam a number of months ago and we had to release a public relations statement and go online and suggest that the company was not involved in it. We lost customers because of it and that month the revenue was down 2%.

"But I did not know this", interrupted Simon Gates. "Nobody told me about this".

"It was during the takeover negotiations and I know some of the people that knew thought it best not to inform senior management as they feared it would disrupt the negotiations, which were at a critical stage", suggested Paul Maybury.

"No excuse", said Simon Gates. "What else have I not been told? John, what else should I have been told?"

John Daniels paused and then said:

> The number of scams are increasing and it looks as if there are two fake websites that have a strong resemblance to our company's website and potential customers are turning to these websites as they are also claiming to have special promotions. What Martha in finance has told me is that some of our existing customers have been approached by a fraudster and have provided their personal details to them without realizing that it was a fake company and a bogus operation. She told me that some scammers are being recruited through playing video games (Hussain, 2021a: 11). The personal data is then traded on to other fraudsters and the people that have released their information then receive telephone calls from a range of "legitimate individuals" that offer one off bargains. Those that fall for it lose their money and other scams are materializing from text messages. It seems there were 39,364 text message frauds in the UK in 2020 and this resulted in innocent people losing £150.3 million according to the newspaper source.
>
> (Hussain, 2021b: 11)

"Yes", said Paul Maybury, he continued:

> there was a data breach involving 500 million Facebook users in 2019 and clearly, according to the same newspaper source, a range of email scams has occurred and over 500,000 fake websites and email addresses as well as fake mobile telephone numbers were known and reported and were acted upon by the authorities.
>
> (Hussain, 2021b: 11)

"This is staggering", replied Simon Gates. "What is our company doing to prevent people from being defrauded?"

"We are doing a lot", Said Paul Maybury.

> We have appointed Johnny Harris to oversee a team led by Helen Wafstaff. They will follow through on customer complaints in relation to cyber issues and problems relating to customers and will work with law enforcement personnel when necessary. Johnny has some experience of cyber crime and Helen was employed in the cyber security industry before she joined the company.

Simon Gates looked rather perplexed and replied: "Why not put Helen in charge of cyber security? Because if I remember, Johnny was involved in overseas trade and not well up on cyber attacks or security for that matter".

"That is a fair point but we have to remember that Johnny had to be redeployed after the mistake he made with that visiting trade delegation", said Paul Maybury.

John Daniels was quick to seize the initiative and said:

> Helen would be a great team player and knows people at the Home Office. She was talking about the EncroChat telephone software system (Smith, 2021) over coffee the other day and seems to have studied the case in much detail. I remember she suggested that the company should set up a group to liaise with law enforcement so that any cyber issues that emerged could be dealt with in real time. The EncroChat phones allowed encrypted messages to be sent to users. What does surface, is that cyber crime is international in context and sometimes it is necessary to deal with law enforcement personnel based overseas. How should we prepare to do this?

Simon Gates paused and then said:

> I think we need to set up a task force to look into all this. I am not convinced the company has sufficient staff to deal with cyber crime and also, we need to ensure that company staff are well able to deal with cyber crime and appear sympathetic to customers. Last year, one of our suppliers was caught using rouge software and that could have impacted on our business had the auditors not found it in time.

"That reminds me", said John Daniels,

> it may be useful to look more closely at how young people are getting involved or being lured into cyber crime. We might be able to help by understanding better why individuals get involved in cyber crime because it seems we need to understand better the incentives involved and who benefits. We could set up a corporate

social responsibility programme and put Johnny Harris in charge, that would make sense. It would mean that Helen could head up cyber security and deal with policy and get a strategy in place.

After the meeting had ended, Simon Gates rushed to his office and started to construct a memorandum for senior management. In the memorandum, he posed a number of questions.

Questions

Question 1: Which factors should senior management take into account when appraising the company's cyber security policy?

Question 2: What are the technological factors that Helen Wafstaff needs to consider when establishing a cyber security policy for the company?

Question 2: What are the human factors that Helen Wafstaff needs to consider when establishing a cyber security policy for the company?

Case Sources

Hussain, A. (2021a). Recruited through video games – The teenage text message scammers. *The Sunday Times* (Money Section), 9th May, p. 11.

Hussain, A. (2021b). There's a fraudster on the line. Why can't phone companies stop him? *The Sunday Times* (Money Section), 2nd May, p. 11.

Smith, D.J. (2021). You've got jail! *The Sunday Times Magazine*, 11th April, pp. 22–25, 27, 29.

3.10 References

Abawajy, J. (2014). User preference of cyber security awareness delivery methods. *Behaviour & Information Technology*, 33 (3): 236–247. http://dx.doi.org/10.1080/0144929X.2012.708787.

Anderson, C.L., and Agarwal, R. (2010). Practicing safe computing: A multimethod empirical examination of home computer user security behavioural intentions. *MIS Quarterly*, 34 (3): 613–643.

Appleyard, M.M., and Chesbrough, H.W. (2017). The dynamics of open strategy: From adoption to reversion. *Long Range Planning*, 50: 310–321.

Arachchilage, N.A.G., Love, S., and Beznosov, K. (2016). Phishing threat avoidance behaviour: An empirical investigation. *Computers in Human Behavior*, 60 (July): 185–197. http://dx.doi.org/10.1016/j.chb.2016.02.065.

Bennett, C., Chapman, A., Cliff, D., Garside, M., Hampton, W., Hardwick, R., Higgins, G., and Linton-Beresford, J. (1997). Hearing ourselves learn: The development of a critical friendship group for professional development. *Educational Action Research*, 5 (3): 383–402. http://dx.doi.org/10.1080/09650799700200035.

Boje, D.M. (1991). The storytelling organization: A study of story performance in an office-supply firm. *Administrative Science Quarterly*, 36 (1): 106–126. https://doi.org/10.2307/2393432.

Butterfield, K.D., Reed, R., and Lemak, D.J. (2004). An inductive model of collaboration from the stakeholder's perspective. *Business & Society*, 43 (2): 162–195. http://dx.doi.org/10.1177/0007650304265956.

Cherdantseva, Y., Burnap, P., Blyth, A., Eden, P., Jones, K., Soulsby, H., and Stoddart, K. (2016). A review of cyber security risk assessment methods for SCADA systems. *Computers & Security*, 56: 1–27.

Choucri, N., Madnick, S., and Ferwerda, J. (2014). Institutions for cyber security: International responses and global imperatives. *Information Technology for Development*, 20 (2): 96–121.

Crane, B. (2018). Revisiting who, when, and why Stakeholders matter: Trust and stakeholder connections. *Business & Society*, 1–24. http://dx.doi.org/10.1177/0007650318756983.

Davis, B.J. (2007). Situational prevention and penetration testing: A proactive approach to social engineering in organizations, pp. 175–188. In A.W. Merkidze (Ed.), *Terrorism Issues: Threat Assessment, Consequences and Prevention*. New York: Nova Science Publishers, Inc.

Denzin, N.K. (1989). *The Research Act: A Theoretical Introduction to Sociological Methods*. Englewood Cliffs, NJ: Prentice Hall.

ENISA (2019). *Industry 4.0 Cybersecurity: Challenges & Recommendations*. Heraklion: ENISA. http://dx.doi.org/10.2824/143986.

Esteves, J., Ramalho, E., and De Haro, G. (2017). To improve cybersecurity, think like a hacker. *Sloan Management Review*, 58 (3): 71–77. http://mitsmr.com/2mXYJdD.

Freeman, R.E. (1984). *Strategic Management: A Stakeholder Approach*. Boston, MA: Pitman.

Freeman, R.E., Phillips, R., and Sisodia, R. (2018). Tensions in stakeholder theory. *Business & Society*, 1–9. http://dx.doi.org/10.1177/007650318773750.

Golby, M., and Appleby, R. (1995). Reflective practice through critical friendship: Some possibilities. *Cambridge Journal of Education*, 25 (2): 149–160. https://doi.org/10.1080/0305764950250203.

Håkansson, H., Johanson, J., and Wootz, B. (1977). Influence tactics in buyer – seller processes. *Industrial Marketing Management*, 5 (6): 319–332. https://doi.org/10.1016/0019-8501(76)90014-6.

Hautz, J., Seidl, D., and Whittington, R. (2017). Open strategy: Dimensions, dilemmas and dynamics. *Long Range Planning*, 50: 298–309.

Heugens, P.P.M.A.R., van den Bosch, F.A.J., and van Riel, C.B.M. (2002). Stakeholder integration: Building mutually enforcing relationships. *Business & Society*, 41 (1): 36–60.

Holzer, B. (2008). Turning stakeseekers into stakeholders. *Business & Society*, 47 (1): 50–67. http://dx.doi.org/110.1177/0007650307306341.

Insley, J. (2021). Letter relating to 'Question of Money'. Barclays' could have done more to stop scam. *The Sunday Times* (Money section), 26th September, p. 13.

Kerbaj, R. (2019). Female spy to net terrorists as head of 'cyber-SAS'. *The Sunday Times*, 8th September.

King, B. (2008). A social movement perspective of stakeholder collective action and influence. *Business & Society*, 47 (1): 21–49. http://dx.doi.org/10.1177/000765030736636.

Kobeissi, N., and Damanpour, F. (2009). Corporate responsiveness to community stakeholders: Effects of contextual and organizational characteristics. *Business & Society*, 48 (3): 326–359. http://dx.doi.org/10.1177/0007650307305369.

Levinthal, D.A., and March, J.G. (1993). The myopia of learning. *Strategic Management Journal*, 14: 95–112.

Lichtenthal, J.D., and Eliaz, S. (2003). Internet integration in business marketing tactics. *Industrial Marketing Management*, 32 (1): 3–13. PII: S0019–8501(01)00198-5.

Lincoln, Y.S., and Guba, E.G. (1985). *Naturalistic Inquiry*. Newbury Park, CA: Sage.

Makkonen, H., and Vuori, V. (2014). The role of information technology in strategic buyer-supplier relationship. *Industrial Marketing Management*, 43 (6): 1053–1062. https://doi.org/10.1016/j.indmarman.2014.05.018.

Mingers, J. (2001). Combining IS research methods: Towards a pluralist methodology. *Information Systems Research; Linthicum*, 12 (3): 240–259.

Modic, D., and Anderson, R. (2014). Reading this may harm your computer: The psychology of malware warnings. *Computers in Human Behavior*, 41: 71–79. http://dx.doi.org/10.1016/j.chb.2014.09.014.

Moriarty, J. (2014). The connection between stakeholder theory and stakeholder democracy: An excavation and defense. *Business & Society*, 53 (6): 820–852. http://dx.doi.org/10.1177/0007650312439296.

Olsen, A.O., Sofka, W., and Grimpe, C. (2017). Solving environmental problems: Knowledge and coordination in collaborative search. *Long Range Planning*, 50: 726–740.

Patton, M.Q. (1990). *Qualitative Evaluation and Research Methods*. Newbury Park, CA: Sage Publications.

Pirson, M., Martin, K., and Parmar, B. (2019). Public trust in business and its determinants. *Business & Society*, 58 (1): 132–166. http://dx.doi.org/10.1177/0007650316647950.

Ringland, G. (2006). *Scenario Planning*. Chichester: John Wiley & Sons.

Shillair, R., Cotten, S.R., Tsai, H-Y., S., Alhabash, S., LaRose, R., and Rifon, N.J. (2015). Online safety begins with you and me: Convincing Internet users to protect themselves. *Computers in Human Behavior*, 48 (July): 199–207. http://dx.doi.org/10.1016/j.chb.2015.01.046.

Sinkovics, R.R., and Penz, E. (2011). Multilingual elite-interviews and software-based analysis: Problems and solutions based on CAQDAS. *International Journal of Marketing Research*, 53: 705–724.

Strauss, A., and Corbin, J. (1990). *Basics of Qualitative Research*. Newbury Park, CA: Sage Publications.

Trim, P.R.J. (2018). How a defined cyber security strategy can help managers counteract cyber threats and make the organization more resilient. *Second Annual Cyber Security Oxford Conference*, Christ Church College, Oxford (5th to 6th June).

Trim, P.R.J. (2019). Counteracting cyber threats through organizational learning and training. *Third Annual Cyber Security Oxford Conference*, Christ Church College, Oxford (3rd to 4th June).

Trim, P.R.J., and Lee, Y-I. (2019). The role of B2B marketers in increasing cyber security awareness and influencing behavioural change. *Industrial Marketing Management*, 83: 224–238. http://dx.doi.org/10.1016/j.indmarman.2019.04.003.

Trim, P.R.J., and Youm, H.Y. (2014) (Editors). *Korea-UK Collaboration in Cyber Security: From Issues and Challenges to Sustainable Partnership*. Republic of Korea: British Embassy Seoul (18th March).

Trim, P.R.J., and Youm, H.Y. (2015) (Editors). *Korea-UK Initiatives in Cyber Security Research: Government, University and Industry Collaboration*. Republic of Korea: British Embassy Seoul (16th March).

Vargo, S., and Lusch, R. (2004). Moving to a new dominant lotic for marketing. *Journal of Marketing*, 68 (November): 1–17.

Walters, P.G.P. (2008). Adding value in global B2B supply chains: Strategic directions and the role of the Internet as a driver of competitive advantage. *Industrial Marketing Management*, 37 (1): 59–68. http://dx.doi.org/10.1016/j.indmarman.2007.06.010.

Whetten, D.A. (1989). What constitutes a theoretical contribution? *Academy of Management Review*, 14 (4): 490–495. https://doi.org/10.5465/amr.1989.4308371.

Whittington, R., Cailluet, L., and Yakis-Douglas, B. (2011). Opening strategy: Evolution of a precarious profession. *British Journal of Management*, 22 (3): 531–544.

Website Addresses

Centre for the Protection of National Infrastructure https://www.cpni.gov.uk/ (accessed on 23rd May, 2019).

Cyber Security Challenge UK https://www.cybersecuritychallenge.org.uk/about (accessed on 23rd May, 2019). See: https://cybersecuritychallenge.org.uk.

Get safe Online https://www.getsafeonline.org/ (accessed on 23rd May, 2019).

Government Communications Headquarters (GCHQ) and the National Cyber Security Centre (NCSC) https://www.gchq.gov.uk/section/mission/cyber-security (accessed on 23rd May, 2019).

Information Assurance Advisory Centre http://www.iaac.org.uk/about/ (accessed on 30th May, 2019).

International Organization for Standardization https://www.iso.org/iso-31000-risk-management .html (assessed on 23rd May 2019).

IT governance https:www.itgovernance.co.uk/what-is-cybersecurity (accessed on 14th October, 2019).

National Cyber Force https://www.army-technology.com/features/national-cyber-force-defending-the-cyber-domain/ (accessed on 4th February, 2021).

National Fraud & Cyber Crime Reporting Centre https://www.actionfraud.police.uk/what-is-action-fraud (accessed on 22nd June, 2019).

National Institute of Standards and Technology, US Department of Commerce https://www.nist.gov/ (accessed on 15th October, 2019).

The Cybersecurity and Infrastructure Security Agency (CISA) https://www.cisa.gov/insights (accessed on 3rd November, 2021).

The European Union Agency for Cybersecurity https://www.enisa.europa.eu/about-enisa (accessed on 15th October, 2019).

The National Cyber Security Centre https://www.ncsc.gov.uk/ (accessed on 30th May, 2019). https://www.ncsc.gov.uk/section/keep-up-to-date/cisp#section_1 (accessed on 30th May, 2019).

The National Cyber Security Centre http://www.warp.gov.uk/background.html (accessed on 23rd May, 2019). See: https://www.ncsc.gov.uk/information/what-warp.

The National Cyber Security Centre https://www.ncsc.gov.uk/information/what-warp (accessed on 15th October, 2019).

3.11 Further Reading

HM Government (2016). *National Cyber Security Strategy.* London: HM Government. https://assets.publishing.service.gov.uk/government/uploads/system/uploads/attachment_data/file/567242/national_cyber_security_strategy_2016.pdf.

Kaminska, M. (2021). Restraint under conditions of uncertainty: Why the United States tolerates cyberattacks. *Journal of Cybersecurity*, 1–15. https://doi.org/10.1093/cybes/tya008.

3.12 Bank of Questions

Question 1: Explain how organizational staff can help government representatives to promote cyber security to a wide community.

Question 2: Which factors should a cyber security manager take into account when establishing a cyber security policy?

Question 3: Which factors should a cyber security manager take into account when establishing a cyber security strategy?

Question 4: A cyber security policy and framework will evolve naturally within an organization and because of this, no additional support is needed from top management. Critically appraise this view and provide reasons for your answer.

Question 5: How important is it for the cyber security manager to ensure that stakeholder relationships are based on trust? Provide examples to reinforce your argument.

Question 6: You are a cyber security consultant and have been asked by the head of human resource management of a company to write a brief outline for an advertisement for a cyber security manager. What would you include in the advertisement for the job?

4 Strategic Cyber Security Management and Strategic Intelligence

4.1 Introduction

Through the process of privatization, a large part of the UK's Critical National Infrastructure (CNI) now rests in the hands of the private sector. This is not the case in a number of countries, which have a more protective government in place and which maintains state ownership of CNI or peruses a more restrictive policy in terms of allowing overseas investment into the country. Whether CNI is privately owned or owned by the state should not detract from the functioning of it, although government is mindful of the fact that malware can be introduced into a network and cause disruption, which then impacts on possibly all industry sectors. Therefore, cyber security, from a government's perspective, needs to be placed in the context of the protection of CNI and Critical Information Infrastructure (CII). In order to understand the issues involved, the cyber security manager needs to have an all-round appreciation of the strategic implications associated with keeping CNI and CII secure.

This chapter addresses a number of issues. First, the learning objectives are cited (Section 4.2) and this is followed by Critical Information Infrastructure Protection (CIIP) (Section 4.3). Next, a strategic Social, Legal, Economic, Political, Technological (SLEPT) analysis is referred to (Section 4.4) and this is followed by Protecting Critical Information Infrastructure against cyber attacks (Section 4.5). After an effective counter threat policy and strategy (Section 4.6), reference is made to the learning organization and organizational learning (Section 4.7) and this is followed by a defined organizational security culture (Section 4.8). Next, attention is given to a learning summary (Section 4.9), a conclusion (Section 4.10), the mini case (Section 4.11) and an extended case (Section 4.12). The references (Section 4.13) are followed by further reading (Section 4.14) and a bank of questions (Section 4.15).

4.2 Learning Objectives

The reader will be able to:

- place cyber security in context;
- establish the need for a collectivist approach to cyber security;
- link cyber security management with the stakeholder approach; and
- establish how organizational interdependencies are developed through trust-based relationships.

DOI: 10.4324/9781003244295-4

4.3 Critical Information Infrastructure Protection

The 11 September 2001 terrorist attack on the US highlights the vulnerability of CNI and CII. According to Cukier (2005: 9 and 27), when the two towers collapsed, a great deal of telecommunications infrastructure in the area was destroyed, and as a consequence 40,000 business and 20,000 residential customers were affected. What needs to be taken into account is that CII is "decentralized, interconnected, interdependent and controlled by multiple actors (mainly private) and incorporating diverse types of technologies" (Cukier, 2005: 14).

Referring to the cyber attacks on Estonia over a two-week period in April/May 2007, Brenner (2009: 10 and 65) raised the stakes in terms of cyber space vulnerability by suggesting that cyberwarfare is subtle and erosive. The aim of the cyber attacks was to cripple the country's infrastructure with the intention of causing both political and economic damages. Botnets have been used to carry out successful attacks on various countries, including the Netherlands and the US, and the window for warning of such an attack is only 30 minutes as sensors based in overseas locations indicate that an attack is being launched. This means that companies and government departments have a very short window in which to prepare a defence and the messages being displayed on a government website or aired via news bulletins allows the perpetrators of the attack to monitor their success, and to plan further action. The vulnerabilities they exploit create an opportunity for like-minded individuals to do something similar or more pronounced. Because CNI and CII are interconnected, what policy makers need to note is that responsibility for safeguarding infrastructure needs to be viewed as a shared responsibility. The interdependence of network systems warrants that stakeholders provide and maintain a level of service that, if disrupted during a successful attack, requires emergency action to restore the situation. Those tackling the individuals/organization responsible for the disruption and damage caused often work across borders and rely on a cooperative and planned emergency response. This is both to rectify the problem and to bring the perpetrators to justice. In the case of the production and consumption of electricity, the UK buys surplus energy from France and also makes energy available to Ireland. So an attack on a French nuclear reactor would have consequences, not only for French householders and businesses, but also possibly for residents and businesses in the southeast of England and Ireland. It is for this reason that policy makers are aware of the cooperation needed to safeguard and maintain the functioning energy supplies and ensure that if an attack manages to disrupt the supply base of a country, it does not cause lasting harm.

Acts of cyber warfare or cyber terrorism are carried out to cause political upheaval and result in a country becoming politically unstable. Bearing the complexities involved, cyber security industry representatives are now of the view that collaboration is required (Zrahia, 2018: 3). Taking into account a cyber attack which can be launched by a person that is intent on inflicting damage and is motivated to succeed because they are personally motivated to do so, a successful attack may not only cause disruption but it will affect people psychologically. Verton (2003: 27) provides a useful real-world example when reporting that in November 2001, a 49-year-old man, using stolen control software, unleased via the Internet, upwards of 1 million litres of raw sewage into a number of public parks and creeks throughout Queensland, Australia, in what was considered a revenge attack. Cyber attacks by disgruntled individuals are of concern to security and intelligence officers, and in-house security officers are trained to help identify possible insiders that know where the organization's vulnerabilities lie and may be motivated to cause damage. The cyber security manager does, therefore, need to adopt a pro-active approach to what is known as the insider threat as can be gauged from the following example. Computer software specialists that work for a company may, having tested a piece of computer software, not have it installed by the company and its suppliers, because they know that it has vulnerabilities. If the software is installed, and an attacker is aware that the software has known vulnerabilities, then it is possible that an attacker would carry out a number of cyber attacks on the company and its suppliers until it was able to penetrate the company's defences. This raises a number of questions regarding the certification that is associated with a company's software products and the company itself. This calls into question what information senior management based within the company would place in the company's risk register and how they would quantify the level of risk identified.

The Centre for the Protection of National Infrastructure (CPNI) in the UK works closely with other UK government agencies and companies to ensure that information security awareness is promoted to all industry sectors. CPNI's staff inform organizations about certain modes of attack and offer advice when necessary. CPNI's website contains information relating to various aspects of cyber security and this is also the case with the Cybersecurity and Infrastructure Agency (CISA) in the US. Staff employed by the CPNI work closely with staff based in various institutions such as the European Network and Information Security Agency (ENISA), KISA (Korea Internet & Security Agency) and the National Institute of Standards and Technology (NIST) in the US, for example. CPNI, ENISA, KISA and NIST provide advice, guidance and documentation to help managers avoid security breaches and are influential in a number of ways. KISA carries out daily checks on Korean company websites to ensure that information of a sensitive nature is not available that can be used for a cyber attack. NIST, through its well-researched publications, provides guidance that can be used by small, medium and large organizations to comply with international security standards. CPNI provides updates and advice regarding certain types of cyber attack and also they work closely with other UK government departments and agencies, and provide training packages that can assist an organization to establish cyber security awareness. ENISA have over the years provided documentation relating to a wide coverage of information technology and information systems issues and challenges, as well as information relating to risk analysis and risk management. Staff in these organizations place emphasis on helping cyber security specialists and nonspecialists to increase cyber security awareness within their organization and ensure that management is compliant in terms of adhering to regulatory procedures and processes.

CPNI, which is known as the engineering arm of MI5, the UK security service, also works closely with GCHQ, the UK Government's Communications Headquarters, which is affiliated to MI6, the UK intelligence service. MI5 and MI6 are both involved in intelligence and security work, but report to different ministers. They also operate under different laws but have a number of common objectives, and work together on specific national security issues. From a stakeholder perspective, it can be argued that staff employed by a security or intelligence agency, some of whom are more visible than others, focus on promoting best practice and also monitor events in order that potential threats can be identified as early as possible, dealt with and contained. MI5 and MI6 officers do, however, operate within strict codes of conduct and are accountable for their actions.

One of the ways in which the UK security service officers safeguard CNI in the UK is to undertake risk assessment reviews of the UK's CNI facilities on an annual basis. The security service officers work closely with staff from relevant government departments and make recommendations as deemed fit. Various overseas law enforcement agencies also work with staff employed by the National Crime Agency (NCA), which has links with all the police forces in the UK. The NCA also works closely with MI5 and this is likely to increase in the future as organized crime syndicates become more involved in cyber crime and cyber-related activities. The objective being to establish ways of working so that law enforcement personnel can deal better with the actions of overseas crime syndicates. What this is resulting in is closer cooperation among staff that are employed in critical industries and staff based at the UK CERT (Computer Emergency Response Team). A country's Computer Emergency Response/Readiness Team has a clearly defined brief. For example, the US CERT

> is charged with providing response support and defense against cyber attacks for the Federal Civil Executive Branch (.gov) and information sharing and collaboration with state and local government, industry and international partners. US-CERT interacts with federal agencies, industry, the research community, state and local governments, and others to disseminate reasoned and actionable cyber security information to the public.
> (http://www.us-cert.gov/aboutus.html: see https://www.cisa.gov/uscert/)

Cyber security specialists employed by government are capable of dealing with and providing advice about the various types of attack launched on a company. They can also draw on the expertise of other specialists and are increasingly being held accountable for their actions. For example, a US government-funded white hat hacker organization that was known to break into government departments and then confront management with the details was asked to stop their hacking activity as it was unlawful. The unit concerned undertook what it considered to be ethical hacking in order to prove to senior management that the security systems in place were inadequate and needed to be updated. This raised the issue of how much funding government organizations should receive and invest in order to improve their security infrastructure, and how the public view such funding, especially during times of economic hardship. The post-COVID-19 period is expected to see an increased amount of spend on security and computer security in particular because during the COVID-19 era, computer hackers became focused on defrauding people that operated from home and also considered some government targets easy prey. What the cyber security manager needs to understand is that regulations change through time and organizational staff need to place more emphasis on the internal audit process so that external auditors are more able to understand how much of a priority cyber security is. As staff engage more in remote working, different pressures arise and additional attention needs to be given to the human aspect, which includes the well-being of staff.

Those concerned with managing CNI need to make clear that staff are just as susceptible to a cyber attack as a company is and they need to take note of the organization's policy relating to compliance. Lovely (2010) states that cyber attacks (including worms, Trojan horses and spybots) on Congress and other government agencies reached 1.8 billion a month that year and the Senate Security Operations Center received 13.9 million attacks each day from both domestic and overseas-based sources. It was noted that spear-phishing attacks via email messages were common. Some of the malicious content was successfully delivered to Senate computers approximately four times each month. Institutions such as INTERPOL and EUROPOL have done much to facilitate information sharing and teamwork involving different European law enforcement officers (Watson, 2005). They have worked hard to combat drug and human traffic smuggling, thwart those committed to undertake acts of terrorism, and also have been involved in various aspects of cyber crime prevention. There are sensitivities, however. It has often been said that a decision made relating to a change in policing in Europe would be leaked to criminal gangs within two hours of a decision being made. It is for this reason that some UK police forces find it difficult to share information with some European and overseas police forces. Because cyber attacks are now being increasingly associated with rogue (military) states, it has to be said that cyber security is no longer clearly demarcated in terms of cyber crime, cyber warfare and cyber terrorism. Organized criminal groups are becoming more ambitious in what they do and are continually seeking new lines of business. At present, telephone scams are reaching record levels in a number of countries and this is resulting in individuals being targeted repeatedly by spurious individuals that claim that they are from a well-known company or government department/agency. The scammer puts time and effort into convincing the person taking the call that they are genuine and have an urgent issue to address, and ask that they log into their bank account or transfer control of their computer to them. Once the bank account details have been provided, the scammer can transfer money from the bank account to their own bank account or a bank account outside the country. In some cases, money is not the target but sensitive data and information is.

Johnson and Williams (2008: 5) suggest that infrastructures create interdependencies and it is these interdependencies that are the weak links (vulnerabilities) in the CII chain. Bearing in mind that infrastructure is a broad-based term, and connectivity is the technological component that has to be managed in a secure way, it can be suggested that a human–centric approach to security will provide the basis for cooperation between stakeholders and result in increased cooperation between the private and public sectors (Jones and Trim, 2009). It is useful to reflect at this point and state that those in the private sector are motivated differently from those in the public sector, even though there is linkage through business associations. Managers in the private sector have access to different resources and align their personal objectives with those of the organization, and heed the fact that the company is owned by shareholders who require a return on their investment. Furthermore, the business models in place in the private sector are evolving through time which means that the priorities of senior managers change and also the underpinning business philosophy is either transaction-oriented or transformational in orientation. This is important to note because the style of management/leadership shapes organizational culture and gives rise to a certain type of security culture.

To facilitate the stakeholder approach to cyber security management, the UK's CPNI has established informal regular meetings involving senior IT staff from industry and CPNI officials, known as "Information Exchanges" (IEs), that cover a range of industry sectors. The objective of these confidential meetings is that members exchange information about current threats and at the same time develop a network of informed contacts that they can draw on in the event of a major cyber attack. Previously, CPNI had provided stakeholders with an opportunity to engage in information sharing via a WARP (Warning, Advice, and Reporting Points) (http://www.warp.gov.uk/warps-explained.

html), which allowed a specific community to share information and solutions, through a website, email, telephone, SMS and face-to-face meeting, with those that could benefit from the IT security advice on offer. Knowledge was also exchanged through a bulletin board and all those that were part of the community (small businesses and local government representatives, service providers and interest groups, for example) could benefit from the information and knowledge available.

As the international environment is increasingly unpredictable, policy makers need to understand that the elimination of risk and the reduction of uncertainty should be viewed as a shared responsibility between government and industry (Trim, 2005a). This means that a community of interest approach assumes that a collectivist approach to security and intelligence work is adopted that results in government-to-government "direct action" and company-to-government "indirect action". Reflecting on this, it can be suggested that a broader-based framework needs to be adopted by senior managers in order that a stakeholder approach is adopted and promoted by senior managers, including the cyber security manager. The Global Intelligence and Security Environmental Sustainability (GISES) model represents a conceptual framework, which has been devised to focus the attention of policy makers and their advisors, on how to disrupt and destroy criminal-terrorist network arrangements (Trim, 2005a, 2005b) through combined action and can be applied to cyber security. The GISES model embraces and utilizes the concept of knowledge management, supports a pro-active approach to leadership and requires those that are within the community to engage in team working and share relevant data and information. The GISES model can be used to integrate the work of intelligence and security professionals with those in the public and private sectors, so that security is viewed as all-embracing and involves business continuity planning. Although the emphasis is on corporate security, it is acknowledged that not-for-profit-organizations are subject to cyber attack and so too are government departments.

The Anti-Terrorist Business-Politico (ATBP) model (Trim and Caravelli, 2007), which is another stakeholder-oriented model, can be used to focus the efforts of those involved in fighting terrorism. It can include inputs from corporate security specialists and be made to have a cyber security focus. The ATBP model, which can be thought of as a generic model, has been designed in mind to focus on inter-government decision-making and the formulation and implementation of action plans to deal with both a particular threat and the consequences and ramifications of an event/incident (Trim, 2009). An additional model, the Environmental and Infrastructural Risk Assessment (EIRA) model, is an output of the ATBP model (Trim and Caravelli, 2007: 149) and focuses attention on counteracting the actions of terrorists. It was conceived to facilitate the coordination of security and intelligence activities and contains inputs from law enforcement personnel.

One of the issues to be addressed by stakeholders is how they equate with vulnerability, bearing in mind that they have different objectives, motivations and interests. It is accepted that risk is linked with probability theory and this means that it can be interpreted in a quantifiable manner. However, it should be noted that although security and intelligence officers make objective risk assessments that support policy decisions, various other stakeholders may view risk differently. Also, risk can be viewed from the perspective of an individual, a group or a community, and it can also be shared but not transferred. This is due to the fact that the outcome of an event is attributable to a cause and/or has repercussions that may be of a physical or psychological nature or both. The resulting impact will affect an individual either directly or indirectly in terms of the organization they work for or the community they belong to. Denney (2005) adds to the complexity by suggesting that the word "Security" has different interpretations. The stakeholder approach to security warrants that the cyber security manager adopts a holistic view of security as this should allow various intra-organizational forms of working to be devised. Because organizations are becoming increasingly interdependent, the cyber security manager needs to take cognizance of the fact that the new business models that are evolving are placing organizational resilience and sustainability in a different context and this requires that senior managers understand that CIIP is to be viewed from a collectivist perspective. The SATELLITE (Strategic Corporate Intelligence and Transformational Marketing) model took this into account as security was designed into the strategic management process (Trim, 2004, Trim et al., 2009). Although the SATELLITE model can be thought of as private sector specific, it can be noted that CII is extensively owned by private sector companies. Hence, the work undertaken by the Corporate Intelligence Staff Support Group, the Strategic Marketing Staff Support Group, the Corporate Security Management Group, the Internet Marketing Group, the Relationship Marketing Advisory Group and the SATELLITE Advisory Group can be considered relevant in terms of the protection of CII. The conceptual model can be used by senior managers to integrate corporate security activities with a broader range of other strategic and operational activities. This is done by defining roles and tasks, and putting in place a structure that enables information to be shared and strategic intelligence to be utilized.

4.4 Strategic SLEPT Analysis

There is a range of cyber security data and information available to the cyber security manager from different sources, including government departments, specialized consultants, banks, university research groups, independent researchers, international institutions, professional associations and security providers. The data and information available cover various cyber vulnerabilities and threats, and guidance is provided as to how organizational staff can put systems in place to make the organization less vulnerable to a cyber attack than it is by staff being able to counteract a specific type of cyber attack. Lee (2009) has indicated that although government departments and agencies have publicized information regarding what future threats are likely to manifest, managers should not be complacent and follow up the information provided and be more proactive in the way that the organization coordinates and manages its response. By being aware of the potential damage associated with a certain type of cyber attack, the cyber security manager can argue the case for investing in cyber security protection and also can be confident in knowing that the recovery plans in place are realistically defined.

In order to have an all-round appreciation of how the organization is prepared to deal with a cyber attack/set of cyber attacks, it is useful if the cyber security manager undertakes a strategic cyber security SLEPT analysis. A strategic cyber security SLEPT analysis will include various risks, such as counterfeiting, for example, because a cyber attack coupled with other forms of attack will increase the intensity of an impact should an organization's defences be penetrated. The cyber security manager and the risk manager will need to prioritize the risks identified and involve internal as well as external stakeholders in the cyber security contingency planning process. The stakeholder approach to cyber security is ideal for coordinating an organization's response to a cyber attack because it allows the cyber security manager to utilize the knowledge of external experts (e.g. government representatives and consultants) and gain the best intelligence so that their actions are current and timely. By ensuring that the organization is secure, government can push forward various digital strategy initiatives and cooperate with various organizations in the process (e.g. scoping, defining, planning, implementing and evaluating).

Although firewalls and other such security measures can be deemed appropriate, the sophistication and frequency of cyber attacks mean that it is likely that some will succeed. Hence, the cyber security manager should work with the risk manager and prioritize the threats and match each threat to a known vulnerability. Improving network security does, therefore, require a collectivist approach and commitment because a range of experts are involved in the cyber security management strategic intelligence process. The stakeholder approach to cyber security will only work if relevant information is exchanged and acted upon, and the cyber security manager has the confidence and trust of those that are engaged in the process. Of course, it can be acknowledged that depending upon others for security can be rather risky and there will be much discussion in-house in terms of what security is to be outsourced if at all. For example, in 2010, Microsoft issued a patch for a 17-year-old vulnerability that had only just been discovered (BBC News website, 2010). Noting that cyber attack software tools are available on the Internet and so too is guidance/expertise as how to use them suggests that cyber crime is well entrenched. Being able to repost a single cyber attack is fine but the ability to counteract a succession of sophisticated cyber attacks is really what the cyber security manager needs to focus on. Bearing this point in mind, the UK companies had fewer security breaches in 2008 compared with 2004, and this may have been associated with a number of factors such as senior managers putting a documented security policy in place, increasing the IT budget spent on security, providing ongoing security awareness training for staff, using strong (multi-factor) authentication and implementing BS 7799/ISO 27001 (PriceWaterhouseCoopers, 2008: 2–3).

A cyber attack trend that is becoming quite pronounced is geopolitically motivated attacks that are carried out by threat actors that are becoming more and more ambitious in terms of espionage activity. PriceWaterhouseCoopers LLP (2021: 4 and 24) have made it known that malware has been used for COVID-19 vaccine development intelligence gathering and that "hacker-for-hire-groups" can be used to carry out an act of espionage. Such groups may complement the work of rogue government agencies or they may operate separately. Most worrying is the fact that ransomware, which is normally undertaken in secret, now takes the form of an attacker (threat actor) exfiltrating data from the target company/individual (victim), next encrypts the victim's files and follows through with setting a deadline for the victim to pay a ransom (PriceWaterhouseCoopers LLP, 2021: 27). Proof is provided that data has been stolen and if a ransom is not paid, the data/some data is placed on a "leak site" which is normally on the dark web (PriceWaterhouseCoopers LLP, 2021: 27). This area of criminal activity now appears to be increasing and evidence of this is that "Ransome-as-a-Service" (RaaS) schemes are appearing, whereby the developer of the malware sells it for a one-off fee (PriceWaterhouseCoopers LLP, 2021: 30).

Another type of cyber crime that is on the increase is cryptojacking, which is when someone gains unauthorized access and use of another person's computer to mine cryptocurrency. Unsuspecting individuals (targets) click on an email phishing link that loads cryptomining code onto their computer and also the malware can be activated from an infected website without an individual knowing (https://www.csoonline.com/article/3253572/what-is-cryptojacking-how-to-prevent-detect-and-recover-from-it.html, 2021).

The cyber security manager needs to be aware of the emergency response procedures that are in place to deal with various types of cyber attack and know how to engage with managers based in partner organizations when necessary. The UK companies have done much in terms of identifying key vulnerabilities and improving their security vis-à-vis backing up critical systems and data, deploying software that scans spyware, filtering incoming email for spam, protecting websites with firewalls, scanning incoming emails for viruses and encrypting wireless network transmissions (PriceWaterhouseCoopers, 2008: 2). This can be considered constructive bearing in mind that organized criminal gangs employ between 300 and 400 people (Smith, 2010: 28), engage in telephone scams and pretend to represent IT companies and fool people into buying "anti-virus" software costing £30, which then releases malware that hacks into computer records. Some gangs resell data and information for profit on the Dark Web/Dark Net and some find a buyer, normally an overseas competitor, that is willing to pay a substantial sum for the stolen data. Sometimes, organized criminal syndicates and hostile government agencies that carry out acts of industrial espionage work in unison and make large amounts of money through bogus "anti-virus" software and ransomware attacks. It has been suggested that the average cost of a worst incident in a year for a small company is between £10,000 and £20,000; and between £90,000 and £170,000 for a large company; and between £1 million and £2 million for a very large company (PriceWaterhouseCoopers, 2008: 2).

Advances in technology are however providing the cyber security manager with a means to counteract the actions of cyber criminals. Bresniker et al. (2019: 46) suggest that artificial intelligence and machine learning can be used to detect a large range of threats and at the same time deal with such threats in seconds. They recommend that: "Global collaboration must be encouraged so that knowledge, strategies and data can be archived and disseminated worldwide and continuously updated to keep up with state of the art in cybersecurity". Bresniker et al. (2019: 49) also explain that automated botnet attacks are likely to increase and this is worrying because managers have plenty of issues on their mind and if a botnet attack results in disruption, and at the same time a number of other threats materialize and impact the company, then it is likely that there will be cascading effects that eventually result in the company being unable to deal with the consequences of the impacts. Again, this is evidence that a stakeholder approach to cyber security is necessary, if, i.e., a consistent and uniform approach to the problem is to be found and the cascading effects are to be reduced.

4.5 Protecting Critical Information Infrastructure against Cyber Attacks

In the UK, the CPNI is responsible for issues relating to CII protection and monitors security issues and challenges, and works with the UK providers and liaises with a range of government agencies inside and outside the UK. There are a number of complexities involved because CIIP can involve state-run defence (e.g. Germany), while others (e.g. the US) have more private sector participation.

The UK strategic framework for CIIP was published by the Cabinet Office in 2010 and outlined nine CII key sectors. The regulatory systems governing each of the sectors are different, but interdependencies exist between the sectors as there is continual interaction involving cooperation between organizations, both public and private, and also interaction involving overseas suppliers and providers. According to Hyslop (2007: 32), "Critical Infrastructure can be damaged, destroyed or disrupted by deliberate acts of terrorism, natural disasters, negligence, accidents or computer hacking, criminal activity, and malicious behaviour". Any disruption to CII is likely to expose unknown vulnerabilities and a vulnerability in terms of CII can be identified in any aspect of connectivity, hosting, security, hardware and software (Hyslop, 2007: 62).

The CPNI is "the Government authority for protective security advice to the national infrastructure relating to national security threats" (Cabinet Office, 2010: 24). CPNI, through website announcements and other initiatives, continually informs and updates members of the public about cyber threats and advice is available from specialists if necessary. A cyber attack may originate from one of a number of sources such as an overseas government agency, an organized criminal syndicate, a terrorist network, activists and disgruntled individuals/employees. New business models involving outsourcing, offshoring and near shoring bring with them unknown risks. CPNI staff are available to offer advice as regards the risks involved but risk management is the priority of staff within the organization and is sanctioned by senior management. As interdependency increases, and equipment, computer systems and networks, and management services are purchased from overseas suppliers, or from domestic suppliers that are under foreign ownership, as a consequence, the issue of political risk becomes more apparent. The asymmetric threats recognized by the security service (e.g. terrorism, weapons of mass destruction, organized crime and espionage) need to be placed in the context of Critical Infrastructure and CII (Hyslop, 2007: 179–180) provision. Political risk is, therefore, dependent on a number of factors, including the commitment to an open market and the concept of perfect competition; pressure on a government from other governments that have a clear ideological perspective and influence; the need to protect "strategic assets" and intellectual property; and the risk of losing a sustainable advantage to another nation state. Cooperation between governments will intensify as private enterprises take more control of CNI and CII. Willis et al. (2009: 342) suggest that:

> Collecting information from the private sector requires coordinating, organizing, and analyzing thousands of disparate information feeds. Local, state, and federal law enforcement face challenges when sharing classified intelligence from the top down and incident reports from the field up. Finally, the public sector faces another set of challenges when considering how to share insight from classified and unclassified intelligence with the private sector.

Senior managers in the private sector will need to think in terms of *processes* as opposed to *facilities* (Willis et al., 2009: 343–344) when formulating strategic, operational and tactical plans, and work with law enforcement officers when required. They will also need to draw more on the knowledge of security professionals for advice with respect to "how security impacts enterprise risk management" (Willis et al., 2009: 344). This is due to the conditions relating extensively to the public sector being different to what they are used to. Hence, they are required to draw on different knowledge as they will receive classified information from government agencies and as a consequence will need to rely on information that "is able to provide an assessment of the credibility of the information." (Willis et al., 2009: 346). While security professionals do acquire and share sensitive and confidential data and information through their own networks, corporate staff in general are reluctant to share information due to four factors (Willis et al., 2009: 346):

i   proprietary information may be leaked to competitors;
ii   if company vulnerabilities become public then customers or investors may defect elsewhere;
iii the company may be liable in some way and
iv   the risk associated with voluntary disclosures which result in regulatory procedures.

In some instances, a company's commercial objectives may militate against the sharing of information with partner organizations, and high-level approval within the organization may be required to share information with intelligence, security and law enforcement officers. Nevertheless, there is no guarantee that when information is passed over that the intelligence and security officers will provide feedback to the company. Normally, an intelligence or security operation requires that the actual source of the threat is identified and tracked, and this means that an instant result is not forthcoming as the operation may span months or even years.

Security clearance takes time and includes a number of hurdles that an individual has to go through. The process should, however, result in useful and relevant data and information being exchanged by public and private sector employees (Willis et al., 2009: 362) that is beneficial to all concerned. The Information Exchanges (IEs) managed by CPNI in the UK are proof of this. By placing CII Protection, which incorporates cooperation and coordination (Pommerening, 2004) within the governance theory body of knowledge as it involves public accountability, it is possible to identify the differences that exist between the similarities and differences between the US and Germany as regards CII Protection. Pommerening (2004: 22) states: "The U.S. clearly has a more elaborate private sector organizational structure responding to cyber threats, while CIIP in Germany is largely attached to state-run civil defense mechanisms". This observation has relevance because it requires more in-depth interpretation of what a stakeholder model needs to include. For example, by incorporating designed-in security (Trim et al., 2009), business continuity planning can be made more robust.

In 2010, the *Strategic Framework and Policy Statement on Improving the Resilience of Critical Infrastructure to Disruption from Natural Hazards*, which proposed "a cross-sector programme to improve the resilience of critical infrastructure and essential services to severe disruption by natural hazards" (Cabinet Office, 2010: 3), was published. The objective being to develop a coordinated approach to improve the resilience of CNI by identifying and assessing risks, and developing a range of options in order to "avoid, transfer, accept, reduce or share those risks" (Cabinet Office, 2010: 6).

CNI has been defined as follows (Cabinet Office, 2010: 9):

Those infrastructure assets (physical or electronic) that are vital to the continued delivery and integrity of the essential services upon which the UK relies, the loss or compromise of which would lead to severe economic or social consequences or loss of life.

The European Union defines Critical Infrastructure in the following way (Cabinet Office, 2010: 9):

> A critical infrastructure (CI) consists of those physical and information technology facilities, networks, services and assets which, if disrupted or destroyed, have a serious impact on the health, safety, security or economic well-being of citizens or the effective functioning of governments.

According to the President's Commission on Critical Infrastructure Protection, 1997, Critical Infrastructures have been defined as "infrastructures which are so vital that their incapacitation or destruction would have a debilitating impact on defense or economic security" (Pommerening, 2004: 1). As indicated in the above, structural change is occurring because of the privatization and investment by the private sector in previously state-owned assets, which has been perceived as beneficial to the state, because it has resulted in an injection of capital that has relieved the public of the responsibility of maintaining what can be described as a cost-intensive service. In some cases, the injection of capital has proved beneficial to the government as it has helped the government to reduce its borrowing requirement and prioritize its spending.

The nine national infrastructure sectors in the UK (Cabinet Office, 2010: 9) are energy, food, water, transportation, communications, emergency services, health care, financial services and government. The key point to note is that as regards regulation, the emergency services sector and part of the transport sector are regulated differently to the water and energy sectors, and because of this, a different approach is needed in order to ensure that these sectors deliver the aims outlined in the programme outlined by the Cabinet Office (2010: 23). In order to highlight the criticality involved, categories from 1 to 5 are used, where 1 represents the loss that would cause a moderate disruption to service delivery and 5 represents a catastrophic impact on the UK (Cabinet Office, 2010: 28).

Bearing this in mind, the appointment of a CIO (Chief Information Officer) within an organization should ensure that information security is an integral part of the strategic management process and this being the case, CIIP will be more complete (Hyslop, 2007: 106). Corporations can ensure that they participate fully in CII Protection by appointing a Chief Information Officer/Chief Security Officer at the boardroom level, which can be considered an aspect of corporate governance (Cukier, 2005: 43). The issues of compliance and governance are integrated and not considered to be separate entities, and require that the cyber security manager focuses attention on relevant industry standards and the work of the regulatory bodies. For example,

> The ability to respond effectively to security events will depend on the ability to monitor and detect security related events and the quality of the response plans in place. This in turn is dependent upon well secured and monitored systems, effective and clear governance and the skills and awareness of personnel.
>
> (CPNI, 2007: 5)

Referring back to work undertaken by the UK Cabinet Office, it can be noted that key areas of focus include areas of investment needed to improve the level of resilience so that the UK's CNI is improved and meets the higher standards proposed for dealing with the UK climate projections and at the same time facilitates the development of CNI sector resilience plans – which allows the work to be placed within a resilience-building framework that takes into account "the differences between sectors and regulatory regimes" (Cabinet Office, 2010: 3). Hence, it is essential to ensure that the "dependencies and inter-dependencies within and between sectors are highlighted and targeted" (Cabinet Office, 2010: 3) and as a consequence, the vulnerability associated with CIIP is reduced.

Verton (2003: 20) points out that infrastructure system providers do not appear to understand the interdependencies among the systems in being and the problem is intensified by the fact that central government, local government and local utilities sometimes write their response plans in isolation. Brenner (2009: 49–50) has indicated that in February 2006, the US Department of Homeland Security's Cyber Storm exercise revealed that organizations that were defending themselves against the attack found it difficult to coordinate their attack response between the public and private sectors and the different public sector agencies. This is a key concern for the cyber security manager because they may need to provide guidance to their peers in times of emergency but also they need to contribute fully to the strategic cyber security strategic management process by providing answers about implementing contingency plans in time of crisis and emergency.

4.6 Effective Counter Threat Policy and Strategy

Suter (2007) suggests that because there are national differences and complexities involving national infrastructures, various CIIP models need to be devised that are country-specific. For example, a CIIP model for one country is not likely to be applicable to other countries due to a range of factors. These factors include the resources available to deal with upgrading and also the differences between the US model and the German model, for example, are due to the difference in state systems and this can be viewed from the stance of the willingness of government to take a lead and either invest in appropriate cyber security defences or work with various stakeholders and ensure that the necessary cyber defence systems are in place (Pommerening, 2004: 1). A key point to be remembered is that, depending upon the country, the ownership of CNI and CII may involve overseas investors that have either partial or full ownership. To place the management of CIIP in context, Suter (2007: 1–4) has developed a generic, Four-Pillar Model of CIIP: (a) prevention and early warning; (b) detection; (c) reaction and (d) crisis management.

A   Prevention and early warning

The aim is to reduce the number of information security breaches and incidents that an organization is confronted with. This is achieved through managers adopting appropriate recommendations and guidelines, and assessing the risk involved and making trade-offs that reduce the organization's level of vulnerability. The emphasis is on adhering to best practice and this is achieved by managers preparing responses in relation to warnings of specific threats. Training is given priority and staff undertake training exercises to prepare them for actual incidents.

B   Detection

Cooperative-based trust-oriented relationships that involve the sharing of intelligence/information allow staff to identify new/emerging threats (technical and/or criminal organizations) and prepare for action.

C   Reaction

Through the process of sharing knowledge with individuals in the sector, it is possible to improve the crisis planning process and improve incident response. Incident response requires that the cause of a disruption(s) is identified and staff know who to contact. Staff can compare emergency CIIP plans and liaise with government representatives.

D   Crisis management

The risks that manifest need to be dealt with in a timely manner and for this to be the case, the CIIP plans in place need to detail the key decision-makers (e.g. organizations and government) so that staff know which organizations are responsible for conducting emergency exercises. The organizations need to know what their responsibilities are and are to be held accountable by government.

Suter (2007: 5–6) has provided guidance as to what a CIIP cooperation model is composed of: (i) a governmental agency (the head of the CIIP unit provides strategic leadership and supervision and is versed in information assurance or Critical Infrastructure protection); (ii) an analysis centre (known as the Situation Center – it has strong links with the intelligence community and the head of the Situation Center should have appropriate legal knowledge and be politically astute, should be able to mentor CII operators and help them raise public awareness) and (iii) a technical centre of expertise (composed of staff members of CERT (Computer Emergency Response Team). It is essential, therefore, that managers are able to work effectively with the CERT team and keep up-to-date in terms of information assurance so that they can deal with early warnings in a rationale manner.

With regard to the sharing of information, there may be legal impositions in place that prevent the full sharing of information. For this reason, the sharing of information needs to be ruled by a commitment to use formal agreements (e.g. non-disclosure agreements) so that the classification levels in place are considered appropriate (Suter, 2007: 14). The OECD (2007) report entitled *Development of Policies for Protection of Critical Information Infrastructures* can be cited in the context of the type and form of information sharing at international level. For example, reference is made to seven countries and the fact that in the countries surveyed, "the national risk management framework is a combination of organisations, processes and government standards leading to actions to manage risk and improve the protection of critical information infrastructure" (OECD, 2007: 14). There are a number of factors that militate against the sharing of information across borders and managers need to be aware of legal restrictions in terms of data protection in relation to cyber crime (OECD, 2007: 26).

CPNI (2007: 6) have advocated the creation of a Process Control Security Response Team (PCSRT) that is

a core element of an organisation's response capability and provides the foundation for effective monitoring, analysis and managing the response to alerts and incidents. The PCSRT must be involved at every step in the process of monitoring a situation, analysing any changes to the cyber threat and initiating appropriate responses.

It is suggested that members of the PCSRT are drawn from (CPNI, 2007: 7) process control; SCADA; automation teams; IT security; IT infrastructure; business management; operations; internal regulators; the legal department; corporate media contact and the corporate security team. This can be viewed as an inclusive approach that ensures the necessary cyber security reporting systems are in place.

4.7 The Learning Organization and Organizational Learning

Learning and the utilization of knowledge are considered essential in terms of a cyber security manager developing appropriate cyber security awareness and finding unique solutions to real-world cyber security problems. Social interaction, characterized by people working "together in a situated activity to construct shared understandings", is deemed relevant as regards the development of an individual's knowledge base (Krajcik and Blumenfeld, 2009: 319) in the case of finding solutions to recurring problems. Cyber security knowledge needs to be fostered by management and supported by intra- and inter-organizational cooperation, but in order to achieve this, senior management needs to be committed to cyber security management strategic intelligence and the cyber security manager needs to be provided with the appropriate authority to get a decision implemented in real time.

Collins (2009: 53) advocates that people can be made to work in pairs to solve problems, and this view is representative of teamwork and the need for senior management to be committed to a learning organization approach that has at its heart, organizational learning. The objective is to raise the cyber security awareness and skill base of employees, and to make them aware that the International Standard for Information Security Management, ISO 27001, can be used to gain guidance (Jones and Trim, 2009: 169) and to harden the organization so that staff are better able to counteract cyber attacks.

In order that organizational staff and staff in partner organizations understand what resilience entails, the cyber security manager needs to draw on the specialisms of their colleagues and exchange ideas and experiences that allow them to identify organizational vulnerabilities and engage in risk management and the mitigation of risk. Bearing in mind that the capability of staff in terms of data and information handling is known to influence the relationship and level of trust between parties (Håkansson et al., 1977), transparency in communication should facilitate inter-functional interaction (Ruekert and Walker, 1987) and result in the flow of inter-organizational knowledge (Easterby-Smith et al., 2008) that manifests in trust-based relationships between staff throughout the partnership arrangement. A key point to note is that:

> knowledge cannot be created without an intensive outside-inside interaction. To create knowledge, the learning that takes place from others and the skills shared with others need to be internalized – that is, reformed, enriched, and translated to fit the company's self-image and identity.
>
> (Nonaka et al., 1996: 844).

Bearing this in mind, the cyber security manager should be well able to influence organizational behavioural change. Hence, by adopting the relationship management approach, the cyber security manager will be able to promote the organization's value system and ensure that a security culture is embraced with cyber security at the centre. Indeed, Arachchilage and Love (2014) are of the view that security education helps thwart phishing attacks and furthermore, cyber security awareness training can be tailored to take into account online activities such as blogging, instant messaging and social networking that employees engage in while at work (Shaw et al., 2009).

4.8 A Defined Organizational Security Culture

A collectivist approach (Trim and Lee, 2006: 151) to counteracting cyber threats has a number of advantages. The cyber security manager can ensure that managers and employees draw on relevant, existing knowledge and are perceived as sensitive to staff in partner organizations in terms of sharing relevant data and information in real time; are seen to be sensitive to events; and are viewed as open-minded, pro-active and supportive of the human-centric approach to security (Jones and Trim, 2009: 166). The security measures in place need to take into account human behaviour and how human behaviour changes through time. As the level of risk increases, cyber security countermeasures need to be put in place and maintained through a leadership model that is underpinned by leadership theory. This is so that the decisions made and implemented are acted upon and managers lead by example. Bass (1990: 21) has paid attention to this and states:

> Superior leadership performance – transformational leadership – occurs when leaders broaden and elevate the interests of their employees, when they generate awareness and acceptance of the purpose and mission of the group, and when they stir their employees to look beyond their own self-interest for the good of the group. Transformational leaders achieve these results in one or more ways. They may be charismatic to their followers and thus inspire them; they may meet the emotional needs of each employee; and/or they may intellectually stimulate employees.

Accepting the view that security involves trust, it can be suggested that a transformational leadership style is useful as it places emphasis on trust between people and the development of trust-based relationships that are aimed at harmonious working conditions and a sustainable business model. A cyber security culture is a subset of a security culture and is reflective of the commitment of staff and the organization's objectives as laid down by senior management. According to Kakabadse (2000), a transformational leader has the quality of being a good listener and the confidence to empower staff so that organizational change is accepted and change occurs in an incremental way. However, a transformational leader needs to manage all tasks adequately, maintain control and embrace ideas that can be acted upon so that the decisions made are implemented when necessary.

The antithesis of the transformational leadership style is the transactional leadership style, which is known to be hierarchical in orientation. Bratton et al. (2005: 216) state that transactional leadership is "rooted in the usual exchange of material rewards for effort", and is the result of a different value system. The transactional leadership style may, it can be argued, be more appropriate during a period of crisis or when change results in a number of unknowns and there is a high level of uncertainty, but it may be appropriate in terms of the organizational value system.

4.8.1 Teamwork and Agency Theory

Reflecting on teamwork, Agency Theory is useful in terms of evaluating how a relationship is formed and developed between two people. There are two distinct schools of thought within Agency Theory: the positive theory of agency (the company is a nexus of contracts) and the theory of principal and agent (focuses on how the principal designs the agent's reward structure) (Douma and Schreuder, 1998: 100). Reward is considered to be beneficial in terms of motivating staff to achieve a set goal(s) and/or set objective(s), and is linked with career progression. The two management approaches may however result in conflict, especially when managers and their subordinates are involved in conflicts arising from dealing with a cyber attack or devising systems to prevent a cyber attack. The management rules and procedures in place, which are enforced by governance and compliance and the need to adhere to external regulatory conditions, ensure that staff operate within a set of defined rules (to prevent a data breach, for example) and are rewarded for taking appropriate action to prevent a cyber attack from damaging the organization. However, Argyris (1999: 56) suggests:

> In real life, most organisations exhibit powerful defensive routines... [which are]... any action or policy intended to prevent the players from experiencing embarrassment or threat, and does so in ways that make it difficult to identify and reduce the causes of the embarrassment or threat. Defensive routines are overprotective and anti-learning...

Taking this into account, it can be suggested that using Agency Theory to define an appropriate reward structure may not always be useful because of the inevitable tension between what Argyris (1999) calls "espoused theories" (that is what we are officially doing, or think we are doing) and "theories in use" (that is what we are actually doing), to which cyber security is particularly vulnerable. When a cyber attack is unleashed on an organization, staff need to respond in a certain way and deal with a number of issues in real time. It may be difficult, therefore, to have in place a reward structure that both prevents unauthorized "security breaches" and rewards sensible use of initiative, especially when staff report to different managers or management groups. This is because although there is an organizational value system in place, the values of the staff employed in different departments within the same organization are different (e.g. cooperative versus non-cooperative), depending upon the sensitivity of the data/information being dealt with and the politics within the organization due to length of service and individual personalities.

4.8.2 Organizational Learning and Cooperation

Lee (2005) suggests that the concept organizational learning is beneficial in terms of senior management developing a unified organizational value system that supports behavioural change and views organizational change as incremental change. In order to achieve transformational change,

> senior managers need to distinguish between leadership and strategic leadership, and adopt a dual leadership approach, in order that junior managers can devise and implement new management models that result in improved decision-making processes. The main advantage of this approach is that it should result in more open communication and an acceptance of what is known as institutionalizing organizational learning, which can facilitate government to government co-operation; government to organization co-operation; and organization to organizational co-operation.
>
> (Lee cited by Trim, 2009: 95)

By senior management providing direction and establishing a unified culture and value system throughout the company, it should be possible to encourage staff to improve their knowledge and skill base through time, to view learning as continuous and cooperate with internal staff and staff based in partner organizations. It can be noted that the level of dependency between partner organizations increases through time as a consequence of managers sharing information (Carlile, 2004) on a frequent basis. Inkpen and Currall (2004: 594–595) suggest that as the level of dependency increases between individuals in partner organizations: "partner willingness to provide access to information is likely to increase, thus providing the foundation for partner learning". If, however, cooperation between individuals is lacking due to insufficient trust or inadequate communication, and the partnership is judged to be failing/not achieving the objectives set, it is likely that the priorities of senior management will need to be reassessed and action taken to realign the priorities of the organizations involved. This may be achieved by staff agreeing to be more transparent in terms of how they operate and where data and information are stored, and more focused on integrating computer networks and continually updating computer systems. By establishing a shared improvement programme, new working practices can be developed and skill and knowledge gaps can be identified that result in tailor-made staff training and development programmes.

4.9 Learning Summary

It is clear from Figure 4.1 that there is a range of support and advice available to the cyber security manager from various organizations and institutions, which can be drawn on when required. Remembering that the objective of an attacker may be to disable and disrupt a nation's CNI and/or CII brings into focus the need for the cyber security

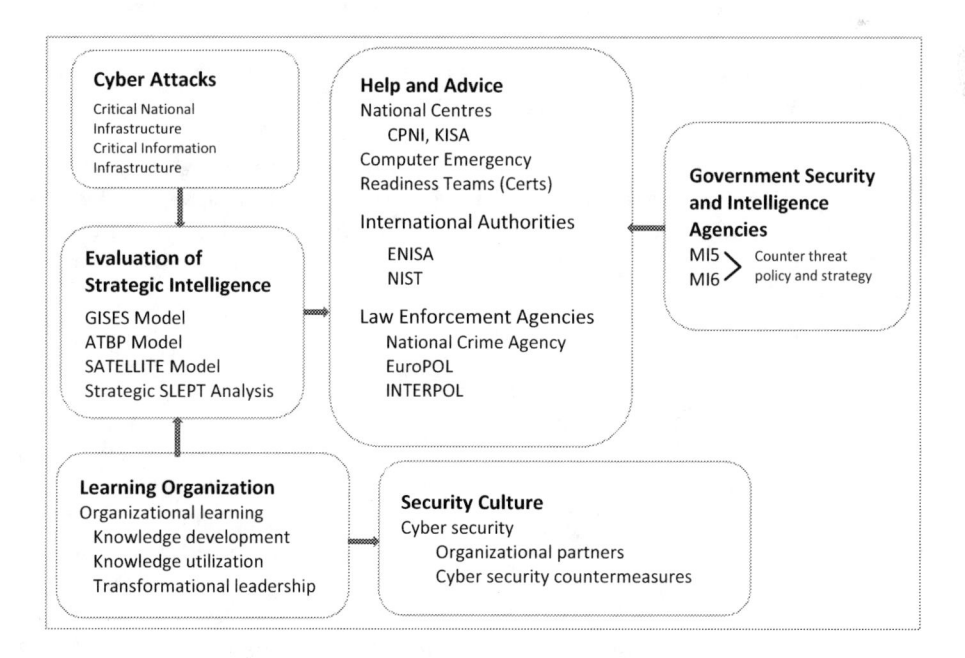

Figure 4.1 Cyber attacks and strategic intelligence.

manager to utilize the knowledge of various cyber security experts and also use models, some of which are conceptual in nature, that can be amended if necessary to meet the needs of the organization. By being committed to developing a learning organization, senior management can develop a cyber security knowledge base throughout the partnership arrangement that embraces a security culture and has cyber security at its centre.

The reader is able to:

- think like a cyber security management specialist;
- identify the complexities associated with cyber security management;
- link cyber security management theory and practice; and
- place cyber security management in a specific business context.

4.10 Conclusion

The cyber security manager is aware that the cyber attacks launched on an organization are changing through time and are in fact becoming more sophisticated and more associated with what are defined as advanced persistent threats (APTs). As a consequence, those carrying out such attacks are known to draw on extensive resources and have both economic and political objectives to fulfil. It is because of this increasing level of complexity that the cyber security manager needs to liaise and work with staff in partner organizations, industry groups and law enforcement personnel, so that Cyber Threat Intelligence (CTI) is shared in real time and a pro-active approach to cyber security results in cyber attacks being reposted.

4.11 Mini Case: Power Outages

Climate change had resulted in a number of freak storms and heavy downpours of rain that had caused flooding on a large scale. The floods had taken down power cables and knocked out a number of electricity substations. To make matters worse, wild fires in Summer had caused water shortages in some parts of the country. Various labour unions were unhappy about pay conditions and were threatening to go on strike and cause more uncertainty and upheaval. Reports had also started to surface suggesting that some haulage companies were unable to meet delivery schedules because of various knock on effects relating to staff shortages and new regulations regarding safety standards. High cost energy supplies were also contributing to the uncertainty and winter was rapidly approaching.

Mrs. Jacobs, the head of an energy company, was only too aware of the problems surfacing as the company had recently lost several contracts to competitors, for reasons unknown to senior management. She had asked the head of strategy, Simon Yates, to compile a report outlining how the company could be positioned in the industry, bearing in mind that there were rumours that several of the competitors were going to Ofgem, the UK's independent energy regulator, to report that they had experienced a number of cyber attacks that were causing concern in relation to the disruption of energy supplies. Several companies had been attacked and it was thought that the attacks were connected with ransomware. The companies involved had all placed messages on their websites indicating that the attacks had not caused serious damage and only some of the computer systems and networks had been put out of action. Although the companies were only temporarily affected, it did seem that their operations had been disrupted. It was reported that internal IT networks were down and the laptops of some of the employees were disabled for a while. In addition, email servers were rendered inoperable and a number of employees could not carry on with their work and had been sent home early. Another reason why staff were sent home was because the restaurant facilities within the company had been closed down. Power supplies had been affected and this had also resulted in no heating in the staff offices. The public relations department of one of the companies affected put out a statement that read: "Fifty years in business and still going strong", as it was known that the company had been planning a celebration for its staff and business partners as it had just completed half a century in business. However, the celebrations had to be postponed because of the cyber attack.

While thinking through his task, Simon Yates considered both organizational and inter-organizational issues, and reflected on what Turner (2006: 115) had written:

> Prediction is made more difficult by the complex and extensive nature of the tasks that must be carried out to fulfill organizational goals of any significance. Many tasks, particularly the more important ones, are loosely formulated, directed to ill-defined or possibly conflicting ends, and lacking unequivocal criteria for deciding when the goals have been attained. This situation is resolved sometimes by creating small areas of certainty which can be handled. At other times the problem is redrawn in a more precise form which ignores features that are difficult to specify or are nonquantifiable.

Questions

Question 1: How serious do the cyber attacks appear to be?

Question 2: How should Mrs. Jacobs and her colleagues rank the problems identified?

Question 3: How useful would it be for all the companies affected to approach Ofgem together?

Case Source

Turner, B.A. (2004). Chapter 8: The organizational and interorganizational development of disasters, pp. 115–135. In D. Smith and D. Elliott (Eds.), *Key Readings in Crisis Management: Systems and Structures for Prevention and Recovery*. London: Routledge.

4.12 Extended Case: Strategic Cyber Intelligence

The increasing complexity of the business environment has resulted in increased government intervention at times, as witnessed in various ransomware attacks and the intervention of law enforcement agencies to help retrieve Bitcoin demands that have been paid. Although senior managers may be hesitant about dealing with law enforcement representatives, evidence suggests that cyber attacks are likely to move from one industry to another, as the attacker finds it more difficult to extort money/ tokens from certain types of business entity. How can senior managers adopt a strategic view of cyber security? This is now a key consideration.

An article by Montgomery and Weinberg (1979: 42) highlighted the need for strategic intelligence systems and various forms of intelligence, including defensive intelligence (assumptions made so that management are not surprised); passive intelligence (benchmark data is provided for objective evaluation) and offensive intelligence (to identify opportunities). By integrating strategic intelligence systems (Montgomery and Weinberg, 1979: 43) into the organization's strategic intelligence cycle, relevant data from the external environment can be collected, analysed and disseminated so that priorities are established and the organization can react to a specific situation. Speed of impact and speed of reaction are judged important and emphasis is placed on gaining intelligence from a range of sources.

It has been suggested that the average time to identify a data breach is 206 days and taking into account it takes 73 days on average to contain a data breach (Oosthoek and Doerr, 2021: 301), senior managers may need to invest more heavily in Cyber Threat Intelligence (CTI). Although companies can receive protection through firewalls and anti-virus software, more needs to be done as this example, drawn from a UK government report (HM Government, 2016: 21), makes clear:

> A cyber attack on western Ukrainian electricity distribution companies Prykarpattya Oblenergo and Kyiv Oblenergo on 23 December 2015 caused a major power outage, with disruption to over 50 substations on the distribution networks. The region reportedly experienced a blackout for several hours and many other customers and areas sustained lesser disruptions to their power supplies, affecting more than 220,000 consumers. Use of the BlackEnergy3 malware has been blamed by some for the attack, after samples were identified on the network. At least six months before the attack, attackers had sent phishing emails to the offices of power utility companies in the Ukraine containing malicious Microsoft Office documents. However, the malware was not likely to have been responsible for opening the circuit breakers which resulted in the outage. It is probable that the malware enabled the attackers to gather credentials that allowed them to gain direct remote control of aspects of the network, which would subsequently enable them to trigger the outage. The Ukraine incident is the first confirmed instance of a disruptive cyber attack on an electricity network. Instances such as this further demonstrate the need for good cyber security practices across all of our Critical National Infrastructure (CNI) to prevent similar incidents occurring in the UK.

A number of issues and challenges emerge from the above. It is clear that industry, government and academia need to cooperate in order to establish how cyber threats can be negated. There are differing views as to how this should be done and how much responsibility government should shoulder in terms of ensuring that cooperation is maintained. Trim (2005) has produced the GISES model that can be used as an outline for furthering partnership arrangements involving intelligence and security agencies, government, law enforcement agencies and interested parties drawn from both the private and public sectors. The objective being to develop and share knowledge that results in a better understanding of how to counteract the actions of those that are focused on harming society or intent on causing disruption.

Questions

Question 1: Explain why managers in a range of organizations should be aware of attacks on a nation's Critical National Infrastructure.

Question 2: Explain what Cyber Threat Intelligence involves and how it can be made industry-specific.

Question 3: Evaluate the arguments put forward in the above and suggest how managers can utilize strategic cyber intelligence.

Case Sources

HM Government. (2016). *National Cyber Security Strategy 2016–2021.* London: HM Government.

Montgomery, D.B., and Weinberg, C.B. (1979). Toward strategic intelligence systems. *Journal of Marketing*, 43 (Fall): 41–52.

Ossthoek, K., and Doerr, C. (2021). Cyber Threat Intelligence: A product without a process? *International Journal of Intelligence and CounterIntelligence*, 34: 300–315. http://dx.doi.org/10.108 0/08850607.2020.1780062.

Trim, P.R.J. (2005). The GISES model for counteracting organized crime and international terrorism. *International Journal of Intelligence and CounterIntelligence*, 18(3): 451–472. http://dx. doi.org/10.1080/08850600590945425.

4.13 References

Arachchilage, N.A.G., and Love, S. (2014). Security awareness of computer users: A phishing threat avoidance perspective. *Computers in Human Behavior*, 38 (September): 304–312. http:// dx.doi.org/10.1016/j.chb.2014.05.046.

Argyris, C. (1999). *On Organisational Learning.* Malden, MA: Blackwell.

Bass, B.M. (1990). From transactional to transformational leadership: Learning to share the vision. *Organizational Dynamics*, 18 (Winter): 19–31.

BBC News website. (2010). Microsoft to patch 17-year-old computer bug. http://news.bbc. co.uk/1/hi/8499859.stm (accessed on 5th February, 2010).

Bratton, J., Grint, K., and Nelson, D.L. (2005). *Organizational Leadership.* Mason, OH: South-Western/Thomson.

Brenner, S.W. (2009). *Cyberthreats: The Emerging Fault Lines of the Nation State.* Oxford: Oxford University Press.

Bresniker, K., Gavrilovska, A., Holt, J., Milojicic, D., and Tran, T. (2019). Grand challenge: Applying artificial intelligence and machine learning to cybersecurity. *Computer*, (December): 45–52.

Cabinet Office. (2010). *Strategic Framework and Policy Statement on Improving the Resilience of Critical Infrastructure to Disruption from Natural Hazards* (March Natural Hazards Team, Civil Contingencies Secretariat). London: Cabinet Office.

Carlile, P.R. (2004). Transferring, translating, and transforming: An integrative framework for managing knowledge across boundaries. *Organization Science*, 15 (5): 555–568.

Collins, A. (2009). Cognitive apprenticeship, pp. 47–60. In R.K. Sawyer (Ed.), *The Cambridge Handbook of the Learning Sciences.* Cambridge: Cambridge University Press.

CPNI. (2007). *Good Practice Guide: Process Control and SCADA Security: Guide 3. Establish Response Capabilities.* London: Centre for the Protection of National Infrastructure (CPNI). http://www. cpni.gov.uk/Docs/Guide_3_Establish_Response_Capabilities.pdf (accessed on 31st December, 2009). See: https://scadahacker.com/library/Documents/Best_Practices/CPNI%20-%20 GPG%20-%2000%20Process%20Control%20and%20SCADA%20Security.pdf.

Cukier, K. (2005). *Critical Information Infrastructure Protection: Ensuring (and Insuring?): A Report by The Rueschlikon Conferences*. Rueschlikon: Switzerland (September).

Denney, D. (2005). *Risk and Society*. London: Sage Publications.

Douma, S., and Schreuder, H. (1998). *Economic Approaches to Organizations*. Hemel Hempstead, Herfordshire: Prentice Hall Europe.

Easterby-Smith, M., Lyles, M.A., and Tsang, E.W.K. (2008). Inter-organizational knowledge transfer: Current themes and future prospects. *Journal of Management Studies*, 45 (4): 677–690.

Håkansson, H., Johanson, J., and Wootz, B. (1977). Influence tactics in buyer – Seller processes. *Industrial Marketing Management*, 5 (6): 319–332. https://doi.org/10.1016/0019-8501(76)90014-6.

Hyslop, M. (2007). *Critical Information Infrastructures: Resilience and Protection*. New York: Springer.

Inkpen, A., and Currall, S. (2004). The coevolution of trust, control and learning in joint ventures. *Organization Science*, 15 (5): 586–599.

Johnson, C.W., and Williams, R. (2008). Computation support for identifying safety and security related dependencies between national critical infrastructures. http://www.dcs.gla.ac.uk/~johnson/papers/IET_2008/National_Critical_InfrastructureFinal.pdf (accessed on 5th February, 2010). See: http://citeseerx.ist.psu.edu/viewdoc/download;jsessionid=45726FF3C4EA6A0B-7C2B0A4983ED2A7E?doi=10.1.1.139.4581&rep=rep1&type=pdf.

Jones, N., and Trim, P.R.J. (2009). Establishing a security culture: Pointers for senior management, pp. 165–179. In P.R.J. Trim and J. Caravelli (Eds.), *Strategizing Resilience and Reducing Vulnerability*. New York: Nova Science Publishers, Inc.

Kakabadse, A. (2000). From individual to team to cadre: Tracking leadership for the third millennium. *Strategic Change*, 9 (1) (January–February): 5–16.

Krajcik, J.S., and Blumenfeld, P.C. (2009). Project based learning, pp. 317–333. In R.K. Sawyer (Ed.), *The Cambridge Handbook of the Learning Sciences*. Cambridge: Cambridge University Press.

Lee, E. (2009). *Homeland Security and Private Sector Business: Corporations' Role in Critical Infrastructure Protection*. Boca Raton, FL: CRC Press/Taylor & Francis Group.

Lee, Y-I. (2005). A strategic model for facilitating inter-organizational and intra-organizational development. *The Second CAMIS Security Management Conference entitled Managing Complexity and Developing Partnership Initiatives*, Birkbeck College, University of London (23rd September).

Lovely, E. (2010). Cyberattacks explode in Congress. http://www.politico.com/news/stories/0310/33987.html (accessed on 17th March, 2010).

Nonaka, I., Takeuchi, H., and Umemoto, K. (1996). A theory of organizational knowledge creation. *Unlearning and Learning for Technological Innovation* (Special Issue), 11 (7/8): 833–845. https://doi.org/10.1504/IJTM.1996.025472.

OECD. (2007). *Development of Policies for Protection of Critical Information Infrastructures*. Ministerial Background Report DSTI/ ICCP/REG(2007) 20/FINAL: Paris: OECD. http://www.oecd.org/dataoecd/25/10/40761118.pdf (accessed on 31st May, 2011).

Pommerening, C. (2004). A comparison of critical information infrastructure protection in the United States and Germany: An institutional perspective. Paper presented at the *Annual Meeting of the American Political Science Association*, Chicago, IL, 2nd September 2004, pp. 1–30. http://www.allacademic.com/meta/p60905_index.html (accessed on 10th November, 2009).

PriceWaterhouseCoopers. (2008). *2008 Information Security Breaches Survey: Technical Report*. London: Department for Business, Enterprise & Regulatory Reform.

PriceWaterhouseCoopers LLP. (2021). *Cyber Threats 2020: A Year in Retrospect*. pwc-cyber-threats-2020-a-year-in-retrospect.pdf (accessed on 4th November, 2012).

Ruekert, R.W., and Walker, O.C. (1987). Marketing's interaction with other functional units: A conceptual framework and empirical evidence. *Journal of Marketing*, 51 (1): 1–19. http://dx.doi.org/10.2307/1251140.

Shaw, R.S., Chen, C.C., Harris, A.L., and Huang, H-J. (2009). The impact of information richness on information security awareness training effectiveness. *Computer & Education*, 52 (1): 92–100. http://dx.doi.org/10.1016/j.compedu.2008.06.011.

Smith, H. (2010). Crooks steal IDs in online 'security' con. *METRO*, 15th November, p. 28.

Suter, M. (2007). *A Generic National Framework for Critical Information Infrastructure Protection (CIIP)*. Zurich, Switzerland: Center for Security Studies (August).

Trim, P.R.J. (2004). The strategic corporate intelligence and transformational marketing (SATELLITE) model. *Marketing Intelligence and Planning*, 22 (2): 240–256.

Trim, P.R.J. (2005a). The global intelligence and security environmental sustainability model: Counteracting organized crime and international terrorism. *The Second CAMIS Security Management Conference: Managing Complexity and Developing Partnership Initiatives*, Birkbeck College, University of London, 23rd September 2010.

Trim, P.R.J. (2005b). The GISES model for counteracting organized crime and international terrorism. *International Journal of Intelligence and CounterIntelligence*, 18 (3): 451–472.

Trim, P.R.J. (2009). Collaborative security: Pointers for government representatives and corporate security personnel, pp. 91–101. In P.R.J. Trim and J. Caravelli (Eds.), *Strategizing Resilience and Reducing Vulnerability*. New York: Nova Science Publishers, Inc.

Trim, P.R.J., and Caravelli, J. (2007). Counteracting and preventing terrorist actions: A generic model to facilitate inter-government cooperation, pp. 135–152. In A.W. Merkidze (Ed.), *Terrorism Issues: Threat Assessment, Consequences and Prevention*. New York: Nova Science Publishers, Inc.

Trim, P.R.J., and Lee, Y-I. (2006). Vertically integrated organisational marketing systems: A partnership approach for retailing organisations. *Journal of Business and Industrial Marketing*, 21 (3): 151–163.

Turner, B.A. (2006). The organizational and interorganizational development of disasters, pp. 115–135. In D. Smith and D. Elliott (eds.). *Key Readings in Crisis Management: Systems and Structures for Prevention and Recovery*. London: Routledge.

Verton, D. (2003). *Black Ice: The Invisible Threat of Cyber-Terrorism*. Emeryville, CA: McGraw-Ill/Osborne.

Watson, N. (2005). Europol: Form, function and implications. *The Second CAMIS security Management Conference: Managing Complexity and Developing Partnership Initiatives*, Birkbeck College, University of London (23rd September 2005).

Willis, H.H., Lester, G., and Treverton, G.F. (2009). Information sharing for infrastructure risk management: Barriers and solutions. *Intelligence and National Security*, 24 (3): 339–365.

Zrahia, A. (2018). Threat intelligence sharing between cybersecurity vendors: Network, dyadic, and agent views. *Journal of Cybersecurity*, 1–16. http://dx.doi.org/10.1093/cybsec/tyy008.

Website Addresses

http://www.us-cert.gov/aboutus.html (accessed on 23rd November, 2010). See: https://www.cisa.gov/uscert/.

http://www.warp.gov.uk/warps-explained.html (accessed on 23rd November, 2010). See: https://www.ncsc.gov.uk/information/what-warp.

https://www.pwc.co.uk/cyber-security/pdf/pwc-cyber-threats-2020-a-year-in-retrospect.pdf (accessed on 4th November, 2021).

https://www.csoonline.com/article/3253572/what-is-cryptojacking-how-to-prevent-detect-and-recover-from-it.html (accessed on 29th October, 2021).

4.14 Further Reading

Chaudhry, P.E. (2017). The looming shadow of illicit trade on the Internet. *Business Horizons*, 60: 77–89.

PriceWaterhouseCoopers LLP. (2021). *Cyber Threats 2020: A Year in Retrospect*. pwc-cyber-threats-2020-a-year-in-retrospect.pdf (accessed on 4th November, 2012).

Trim, P.R.J., Jones, N., and Brear, K. (2009). Building organisational resilience through a designed-in security management approach. *Journal of Business Continuity & Emergency Planning*, 3 (4): 345–355.

4.15 Bank of Questions

Question 1: Which factors does the cyber security manager need to be aware of as regards the protection of Critical National Infrastructure (CNI)?

Question 2: Which factors does the cyber security manager need to be aware of as regards the protection of Critical Information Infrastructure (CII)?

Question 3: What role does the cyber security manager play in producing a SLEPT (Social, Legal, Economic, Political, Technological) analysis?

Question 4: How will a collectivist approach to cyber security help senior management to devise an effective counter threat policy and strategy?

Question 5: Who in the organization should be involved in developing a learning organization culture?

Question 6: How can the commitment to organizational learning be maintained?

5 Threat Identification and Risk Assessment

5.1 Introduction

The Budapest Convention on cyber crime came into force in 2001 as policy makers were: "Convinced of the need to pursue, as a matter of priority, a common criminal policy aimed at the protection of society against cybercrime, inter alia, by adopting appropriate legislation and fostering international co-operation" (Council of Europe, 2001: 1). The UK government ratified the Budapest Convention on cyber crime and invested in a number of initiatives to reduce the threats associated with cyberspace and considered cooperation involving private sector companies and the government to be crucial in thwarting the actions of cyber criminals. It was suggested that attention be given to (Cabinet Office, 2011: 28):

- "exchanging actionable information on cyber threats and strengthening our response to incidents
- analysing new trends and identifying new and emerging threats and opportunities
- working to strengthen and link up our collective cyber security capabilities".

The theft of intellectual property (IP) and information breaches in general are of concern to the cyber security manager as they have repercussions in terms of adverse publicity and manifest in a lost competitive advantage due to the information being exploited by a competitor. The following quotation refers to a significant information breach (Cabinet Office, 2011: 16):

> In the spring of 2011, Sony announced that criminals had successfully targeted the PlayStation network, compromising the personal details of up to 100 million customers and resulting in the network shutting down for several weeks. The costs to Sony are expected to total $171 million.

A former Director of the UK's Government Communications Headquarters (GCHQ), Ian Lobban, stated in 2010 (Atlantic Council, 2021): "There are over 20,000 malicious emails on government networks each month, 1,000 of which are deliberately targeting them". This is evidence of the type of problem encountered by those responsible for protecting an organization's data and information, and requires both a commitment from top management and investment in people and technology to ensure that data and information breaches are limited, and the exfiltration of data and information does not occur.

DOI: 10.4324/9781003244295-5

This chapter starts with defining the learning objectives (Section 5.2) and then makes reference to the different types of cyber attack (Section 5.3). Threat analysis and strategic risk assessment frameworks (Section 5.4) are followed by risk assessment policy and its strategic context (Section 5.5), and Cyber Security SWOT and SLEPT analysis (Section 5.6). Cyber security threats (Section 5.7) are followed by enterprise risk management (ERM) (Section 5.8), which is followed by building trust-based relationships (Section 5.9). A learning summary (Section 5.10) is provided and is followed by a conclusion (Section 5.11). Thereafter is a mini case (Section 5.12) and an extended case (Section 5.13). The references (Section 5.14) are followed by further reading (Section 5.15), and a bank of questions (Section 5.16).

5.2 Learning Objectives

The reader will:

- establish what threat identification involves;
- establish how risk assessment and risk analysis are linked.
- place risk management within a business–global context; and
- establish what an effective counter threat policy and strategy involves.

5.3 Different Types of Cyber Attack

Drawing on the UK Cybercrime Report 2008, Cornish et al. (2009: 3) indicate that 830,000 businesses in the UK in 2007–2008 experienced an online/computer-related security incident and in the order of 84,700, personal identity fraud cases took place online. Extremist groups are known to use the Internet and so too are organized criminal gangs that engage in money laundering. Referring again to the UK Cybercrime Report 2008, Cornish et al. (2009: 7) have reported that in 2007, there were 255,800 online cases of financial fraud and that the losses associated with this activity were £535 million.

The fact that there are thousands of bot-infected computers in existence is of concern and also, Cornish et al. (2009: 8) make reference to the British North American Committee Cyber Attack Report which has indicated that "the cost to business globally of malware and viruses was between US$169bn and US$204bn, and in 2005 the cost of spam transmissions alone was US$17bn in the US, US$2.5bn in the UK, and US$1.6bn in Canada".

According to a survey undertaken by the Federal Bureau of Investigation (FBI) in 2005, the annual loss relating to computer crime to the US organizations was put at US$67.2 billion (United States Government Accountability Office, 2007: 2). In 2006, US$49.3 billion was lost and associated with identity theft and US$1 billion was associated with phishing (United States Government Accountability Office, 2007: 2). One issue that needs more attention is the fact that cyber crime laws vary from country to country (United States Government Accountability Office, 2007: 14) and in some countries it is not illegal to launch a cyber intrusion on another country.

Computer abuse by employees has been increasing over the years. For example, a survey undertaken by the Computer Security Institute found that 64% of the organizations that responded to the survey had encountered a loss of US$378 million in 2001 because of this activity and well over half of the computer abuse was carried out, not by external hackers, but by company employees (Lee and Lee, 2002: 57). Although attempts have been made to increase protection via more appropriate enforcement, security policies and security systems, as well as security awareness programmes, it is clear that human factors and in particular how individuals build relationships with each other are very important (Lee and Lee, 2002). Research has indicated that in order to better understand the motives of those engaging in computer abuse, it is necessary to look at the problem from what causes computer abuse. For example, individuals that have formed strong social bonds with their peers may not engage in such activity owing to the fact that they feel some degree of responsibility to the group, whereas an individual that does not bond with his/her work-based colleagues and mixes socially with those that may be considered to be anti-social in nature may well be inclined to engage in computer abuse (Lee and Lee, 2002: 59).

As regards IP crime, there are two types: counterfeiting and piracy. According to York (IPO, 2009: 6):

> Counterfeiting involves the illegal copying of trade marks on products such as clothing and pharmaceuticals. Piracy involves the illegal copying of content such as music, film, sports events, literary works, broadcasts, computer games and software for commercial gain. Copyright infringement also includes illegal copying and downloading of digital content.

Referring to the Rogers Review, York (IPO, 2009: 9) suggests that criminal gain from IP was estimated at £1.3 billion in 2006 with £900 million going direct to organized criminal groups; however, some considered these figures to be underestimates. The following reinforces the scale of the problem (IPO, 2009: 9): according to the British Software Alliance and International Data Corporation, about 26% of software installed in the UK in 2007 was from non-legal sources; in monetary terms, the UK clothing and footwear industry suffered enormously (the figure is put at £3.5 billion a year). Also, according to the World Health Organization (WHO), about 1% of medicines in the developed world are counterfeit compared with up to one-third in some developing countries (globally the figure is put at 10%). What is worrying to say the least is that the WHO estimates up to 50% of medicines that are sourced from websites that do not make their physical address known are indeed counterfeit. Internet fraud is also on the increase. For example, in the US, Internet fraud was up 33% in 2008 compared with 2007, and the losses associated with this type of crime were in the region of US$265 million (IPO, 2009: 9). The Fifth Annual Global Study of Software Piracy (produced by the Business Software Alliance and the International Data Corporation in May 2008) revealed that the amount of illegal/unlicenced software on personal computers in the European Union was enormous and cost the industry £6 billion (IPO, 2009: 64).

Cyber criminals are becoming more sophisticated and more persistent. It is necessary, therefore, for the cyber security manager to better understand how to deal with the types of attack they unleash and the networks that they belong to and share information and knowledge with. Blyth (2011: 1) has indicated that as regards the challenges associated with advanced persistent threat (APT) agents, the cyber security manager needs to define two key terms in order that they develop an appropriate understanding of the situation:

> *Computer Network Attack* (**CNA**): Includes actions taken via computer networks to disrupt, deny, degrade, or destroy the information within computers and computer networks and/or the computers/networks themselves.

Computer Network Exploitation (**CNE**): Includes enabling actions and intelligence collection via computer networks that exploit data gathered from target or enemy information systems or networks.

Blyth (2011: 1, 2) outlines a risk model and provides background information about sophisticated cyber attacks (e.g. Ghostnet, Operation Aurora and Stuxnet) and explains that:

> computer network attacks have occurred and this illustrates how computer network attacks (CNA) have moved into the area of information acquisition and intelligence gathering via the application of zero-day exploits. This indicates that the nature and capabilities of threats and threat agents continues to evolve, and pose increasing challenges to senior management......To explore and understand the issues referred to above we need to put in place a series of definitions and concepts. The term advanced persistent threat (APT) is used to refer to an individual or group of individuals that are well motivated, well resourced and well trained in the art of computer network attack and computer network enumeration. Typical threat agents that fall into this group are: Foreign Intelligence Services (FIS) and Organized Criminal Syndicates. The term advanced evasion technique (AET) is used to refer to the CAN/CNE techniques that have been engineered to avoid detection and attribution. Analysis of the above allows us to explore the changing face of CAN/CNE. For example, recent attacks have focused on deploying advanced evasion techniques such as zero-day exploits to gain, and maintain, a persistent, presence on the target system so as to exfiltrate information for political and economic ends. In particular attack outcomes include:

- The theft of an individual's online identity.
- The targeted theft and resale of intellectual property.
- The use of the Internet to engage in fraud and extortion.
- The use of the Internet for political influence.

> These security incidents highlight the fact that cyber criminals and foreign state intelligence services are seeking to maintain a level of persistence on a victim's machine and are prepared to use sophisticated techniques to achieve that goal. These techniques include:

1 Targeted social engineering attacks that seek to manipulate existing social/trust relationships to facilitate exploitation of a targeted system.
2 The development and use of zero-day exploits and other advanced evasion techniques (AETs) in order to manipulate existing social/trust relationships.

Ralph (2011) suggests that situational awareness can be used by managers throughout the organization's supply chain to provide adequate risk assessment and has suggested that staff at Lockheed Martin have developed an APT cyber kill chain that is composed of eight steps, which can occur over months: Reconnaissance; Weaponization; Delivery; Exploitation; Installation; Command and Control; Actions; and Clean Up. As well as organizations being vulnerable to cyber attack, it can be argued that countries are also vulnerable in terms of politically or economically motivated cyber attack. Symantec (2010: 7) reported that Brazil has been subjected to increases in all categories of malicious code activity and one attack resulted in a massive power grid blackout, and another cyber attack resulted in a ransom request related to the exposure of valuable data from a government source with various consequences. Another country that has experienced malicious activities is India, which experienced an increase in malicious code, spam zombies and phishing hosts from 2008 to 2009 (Symantec, 2010: 8). This is evidence that those carrying out cyber attacks are prepared to try a range of attacks in order to gain access to the targeted company, individual or government department.

As regards what is known as a "significant" cyber attack on a country (e.g. government agency, a defence company or high-technology company, or an economic crime costing US$1 million and above), the US is top with 156 cyber attacks between 2006 and 2020, followed by the UK with 47; India with 23; Germany with 21; and South Korea with 18 (https://specopssoft.com/blog/countries-experiencing-significant-cyber-attacks/). According to Specops Software, there are three main techniques used to carry out a significant cyber attack. They are Denial of Service (DoS) attack; SQL Injection attack and a man-in-the-middle (MitM) attack (https://specopssoft.com/blog/countries-experiencing-significant-cyber-attacks/). Specops define the terms accordingly: a DoS attack results in a machine or network being made unavailable to its users; an SQL Injection attack is a malicious SQL code that is inserted into a database in order to access sensitive information; and an MitM attack occurs when communication between two parties is intercepted through various means, including an email, social media or through web browsing. There are several purposes associated with an MitM attack (e.g. eavesdropping on communication, hijacking passwords, spying or modifying traffic between parties). Phishing attacks are a common practice and "cyber criminals send emails that appear to be from trusted entities, but are in fact a fraudulent attempt to gain authentication details from victims such as login credentials, payment information, and personal address" (https://specopssoft.com/blog/countries-experiencing-significant-cyber-attacks/).

One of the areas that cyber security specialists need to pay attention to is what information individual employees make available about themselves via their own personal networks. An example of people being vulnerable or through their actions making an organization vulnerable to attack is made clear in the following example. The Hydraq Trojan (referred to as Aurora) infected the computer systems of a number of large companies (Symantec, 2010: 8) through the attackers exploiting information about companies and individuals found on social networking sites that resulted in an unknown vulnerability in computer technology being compromised. The following quotation makes clear the threat faced by the cyber security manager within companies (Symantec, 2010: 8):

> Once the Trojan is installed, it lets attackers perform various actions on the compromised computer, including giving them full remote access. Typically, once they have established access within the enterprise, attackers will use the foothold that they have established to attempt to connect to other computers and servers and compromise them as well. They can do this by stealing credentials on the local computer or capturing data by installing a keystroke logger.
>
> Usually, when this type of attack is performed against individuals or by less sophisticated attackers, the attack is used to gather all the information immediately available and move on to the next target. However, APT attacks are designed to remain undetected in order to gather information over prolonged periods.

Symantec (2010: 9–11) indicated in 2009 that hacking attacks accounted for 60% of the identities exposed and that malicious code that was planted on the network gathered sensitive information and resulted in the theft of 130 million credit card numbers. Those carrying out the cyber attacks were able to cause a data breach and thus remotely acquire data and this is evidence of web-based attacks replacing mass-mailing worm attacks. Also, social engineering methods such as spam messages are used to gather intelligence for an attacker, and once operationalized the user is lured to a website and unknowing to them, the browser and plug-in vulnerabilities are exploited. Once malicious code is installed in the user's computer, they are at the mercy of those perpetuating the attack and may place others at risk by advising them to do the same without being aware of the consequences. Online banking activity has made it attractive for cyber attackers to purchase crimeware kits such as Zeus and customize malicious code that has been designed to obtain data and information illegally.

The cyber security manager needs to pay attention to a number of points (Symantec, 2010: 19–34): malicious activity by country (especially the US, China, Brazil, Germany and India); web-based attacks (compromised legitimate sites and especially crafted malicious sites that have been set up with the intention to target web users, e.g. PDF activity aimed at distributing malicious PDF content); countries of origin for web-based attacks (e.g. once a legitimate website has been compromised by an attacker, a user that visits the website can be attacked in one of two ways – a drive-by download that installs malicious code or the redirection of the user to a website that is hosting malicious code); data breaches that could lead to identity theft, by sector (educational institutions hold large amounts of sensitive data relating to staff and students and thus are a target; and so too are financial institutions and government departments); data breaches that could lead to identity theft, by cause (e.g. missing disks, insecure policy and hacking activity); bot-infected computers (bots are installed computer programs that allow an attacker to control the computer via remote means and launch an attack such as DoS, spam and phishing attacks); distribute spyware, adware and malicious code (and harvest information of a confidential nature); and threat activity – protection and mitigation (this requires that senior managers monitor network-connected computers in order to detect a malicious activity and deploy firewalls and antivirus software).

Symantec (2010: 33–34) recommend the removal of infected computers; companies need to deploy up-to-date antivirus software and install necessary security patches; notify their ISPs of what they consider to be a malicious activity; request that staff only open attachments from trusted or known sources; protect personal data via the Internet; implement a data loss protection solution; restrict access to sensitive information; comply with information storage and transmission standards; ensure that computers containing sensitive information are held in secure locations; ensure that sensitive information is accessed by authorized individuals only and avoid having data on mobile devices that can be misplaced or stolen. Symantec (2010: 46–83) also make clear that managers/administrators should monitor vulnerability mailing lists as well as security websites in order to keep up with new vulnerabilities affecting the organization's assets; monitor trends associated with malicious code and in particular analyse malicious code types (e.g. Trojan, Worm, Virus, and backdoor); monitor phishing, underground economy servers, and spam trends; monitor the countries hosting phishing URLs (e.g. the US, South Korea, Spain, Poland, Romania and Russia) and the most targeted sectors (e.g. financial, ISP, retail and insurance). Furthermore, managers/administrators will also need to monitor the market for automated phishing toolkits; the countries of spam origin (the US, Brazil,

India, South Korea, Poland, China, Turkey, Russia and Vietnam) and how botnets are distributing spam, malicious code and phishing scams (Symantec, 2010: 71–83). As regards the removal of infected computers, it is known that some business personnel that have travelled abroad and attended a business function abroad discard their laptop on returning home, understanding that while they were away attending meetings and using their laptop, it was most likely infected with a virus. In order not to risk transferring the virus to other files or computer systems, they discard/destroy the device.

The mindset and the speed at which cyber criminals carry out their attacks can be deduced from the following quotation (McAfee, 2011: 17):

> Only two hours after the Japanese earthquake and tsunami struck we spotted the first potential scam donation site. During the few next hours we collected more than 500 malicious domains or URLs with the terms *Japan, tsunami,* or *earthquake* in their titles. Most were created in association with spam campaigns, false news sites to distribute malware, and especially fake charity actions. This behavior will never go away.

5.4 Threat Analysis and Strategic Risk Assessment Frameworks

Information security standards form the basis of security management and measurement activities (Martin, 2008) and can be used by the cyber security manager to better understand risk. ENISA (2010: 15) define risk as follows: Risk = f(Asset, Vulnerability, Threat). However, the cyber security manager needs to develop an in-depth appreciation of risk and devise and implement a proactive threat identification process. The SATELLITE model (Trim, 2004) can be used to provide focused market intelligence and adopted and used to establish a Corporate Security Management function that views security as a core activity (Trim, 2005b) with cyber security being a key component. Various stakeholders in the supply chain and marketing channel, for example, can be identified and grouped into four main categories (Chambers and Thompson, 2004: 8 and 16–18): (i) discoverers, (ii) vendors, (iii) users and (iv) coordinators. (i) Discoverers (individuals or organizations) find vulnerabilities and subgroups include a range of people – researchers, staff in security companies, users, government employees and coordinators. (ii) Vendors develop/maintain information system products/services that are judged to be vulnerable and subgroups include information security teams, product security teams, incident response teams, researchers, and a range of specialists, including communications coordinators, legal officers and operators. (iii) Users are defined as those that use a vendor's product, which may be affected by a vulnerability and include governments and the owners and operators of critical infrastructure, and service providers. (iv) Coordinators, this group is composed of those that manage a single vendor's response/multiple vendors' response vis-à-vis a vulnerability. By establishing a stakeholder framework and assigning certain duties to key individuals, and establishing a communication process to facilitate liaison among the stakeholder groups, it should be possible to gain and share all types of cyber threat intelligence in real time. For example, the Infosec team is charged with maintaining or improving information system security; the product security team address problems associated with a vendor's product; an incident response team can be established that is a subgroup of the Infosec team; an incident handler, an individual appointed to manage an IRT response to a vulnerability; operators are those in charge of day-to-day activities associated with maintaining and improving information system resources; communication coordinators are organizational staff in charge of media issues; researchers are a range of individuals who undertake technical research to produce countermeasures; legal officers are those individuals who identify, monitor and address legal issues in relation to vulnerabilities (e.g. product liability, contractual obligations and regulatory requirements) and law enforcement individuals or groups that deal in legal and wider issues relating to national security (Chambers and Thompson, 2004: 20–21).

The potential problem associated with terrorist attacks on communication networks (ENISA, 2008) brings into focus the interdependencies between nations, organizations and infrastructures. Various models and approaches can be used by the cyber security manager to better understand the interdependencies involved and how the complexities can be managed. The cyber security manager has a pivotal role to play and can draw on appropriate frameworks, models and concepts to engage better with cyber security personnel. The GISES (Global Intelligence and Security Environmental Sustainability) model (Trim, 2005a), which can be used to identify organization-policy maker links and relationships, can be used to establish how direct and indirect interactions among those involved in cyber security and those that are drawn in to offer advice and guidance (e.g. legal experts) both obtain and share information among the stakeholder group(s), thus supporting the collectivist view of cyber security. The model is conceptual in nature and facilitates partnership development between industry and government, and organizations in the public and private sectors. The GISES model includes a number of Inputs (intelligence, security and law enforcement objectives); Issues (controllable and uncontrollable factors); Policy (law enforcement and national security risk and uncertainty assessment); Influences (overseas government, international institutions and international agencies) and Outputs (intelligence and security upgraded). The model highlights the importance of learning and the development of intelligence and security knowledge vis-à-vis the sharing of information between parties and makes clear that staff need to undergo training so that they can establish intra- and inter-organizational support in terms of risk reduction.

The ERM approach has been covered by Fox and Epstein (2010: 3) and their work places risk within the organization's "unique strategy, tolerance, culture and governance". This can be viewed as a useful starting point in order to understand and appreciate the issues and challenges that are associated with the interpretation of risk. The cyber security manager can use the ERM approach to apply environmental and intelligence scanning systems to identify risks and match the cyber threats associated with the known risks with internal organizational vulnerabilities, and develop and implement an Enterprise Risk Management Cyber Strategy (ERMCS) that ensures that prioritized risks are documented and evaluated, and contingency plans are drawn up relating to possible outcomes. Scenario planning and futuristic research methodologies can be used by the cyber security manager to identify the antecedent conditions necessary to develop cyber security tools and systems, which can be adopted and deployed by staff in a partnership arrangement (e.g. suppliers and joint venture partners). Taking into account that organizational learning underpins organizational cultural change, cyber security countermeasures can be implemented to ensure that the cyber security risks (and other related security risks) are prioritized and acted upon before they impact the organization. Through the process of the continual monitoring for threats, a formal and systematic approach to environmental scanning (both internal to the organization (e.g. the protection of data stored in in-house databases) and external to the organization (e.g. data held in cloud computing facilities)) can be implemented to ensure that an effective cyber security monitoring system is in place. To ensure that the cyber security monitoring system is robust and current risks are detected, acted upon and future risks are logged, interpreted and communicated to partner organizations, it is essential that a number of controls are in place. The cyber security manager can be aided in their tasks by following and implementing appropriate industry standards. There are a number of advantages associated with this, such as the controls in place will be effective and efficient, both in design and in operation; further information is obtained and this improves the risk assessment process; analysing and learning from events, changes, trends, successes and failures allows lessons to be learned; changes in the internal and the external contexts are detected – risk criteria, the actual risk, and revision of risk treatments and priorities; and the identification of emerging risks is automatic (ISO/FDIS, 2009: 20).

Another approach that can be used to identify future risks is the utilization of the Sequence-of-Events Model (Trim and Lee, 2014: 33–36), which was designed specifically to help managers identify and categorize cyber threats. Thus, the cyber security manager can use the model to counteract a range of cyber threats and devise a resilience-oriented cyber security strategy that incorporates a sustainable counter-intelligence cyber security policy and strategy, the objective of which is to place the management of risk in a business-industry framework. The Sequence-of-Events Model outlines the main cyber characteristics and factors to be borne in mind by top managers, policy makers and their advisors, and security experts and can be considered adaptive.

The Sequence-of-Events Model is a conceptual model that should help the cyber security manager to evaluate the various cyber security threats in existence and identify and prioritize countermeasures to ensure that a problem understanding is attained in relation to acts of cyber crime, cyber warfare and cyber terrorism. It can be incorporated within an Integrated Security Mechanism and a Generic Cyber Security Management Model (GCSMM) (Trim and Lee, 2010, 2011). Furthermore, the GCSMM (Trim and Lee, 2014: 201–202) links the organization's internal and external environments, education and training component and is supportive in terms of the cyber security manager developing a cyber security policy that is embedded within a defined cyber security strategy. The Modified and Extended GCSMM (Trim and Lee, 2014: 202) also incorporates a software tool that monitors a sensor activity in the organization's computer networks so that appropriate managers are informed that an attack on the organization is taking place.

Various approaches to cyber security modelling have been adopted through time with the objective of helping senior managers to better understand the threat landscape and develop in-depth knowledge of the management of computer systems and networks. Cyber security can be interpreted differently by staff, however; hence, it is important to remember that (Le and Hoang, 2016: 1):

> Cyber security can be considered systems, tools, processes, practices, concepts and strategies to prevent and protect the cyber space from unauthorized interaction by agents with elements of the space to maintain and preserve the confidentiality, integrity, availability, and other properties of the space and its protected resources.

The Capability Maturity Model by Humphrey (Le and Hoang, 2016) has proved useful to those involved in software development because it has made them aware that the quality of software is a continual process and that software is developed to enhance the organization's capability. Because the software conforms to the requirements laid down in international standards, the user can be assured that the software will perform in the way expected (Le and Hoang, 2016).

Cotae et al. (2020) utilize game theory and the decision-making process, and have produced a cyber security optimal decision-making model or cybergame model that is focused on perceived damage and the cost in association with potential defensive action. The model includes the benefit to mission and also ensures that risk and uncertainty are taken into consideration. The cyber security manager can use the model to identify possible cyber attacks and establish how they will/might impact the organization and this has the benefit of allowing staff to devise and implement defensive strategies. Wang et al. (2020: 15) designed the Factor Analysis of Information Risk (FAIR) model, which can be used to analyse interactions involving attackers and defenders. To use this model, the cyber security manager is required to have adequate knowledge of security controls and risk mitigation, and have an appreciation of security portfolio and insurance.

Abou el Kalam (2021) supports the view that an inclusive approach to security, known as OM-AM holistic security, can help as regards protecting Supervisory Control and Data Acquisition (SCADA) systems (e.g. in relation to critical national infrastructure). A four-stage OM-AM (objective, model, architecture and mechanism) approach is used that benefits the model builder as it includes an abstract level and a concrete level within it (Abou el Kalam, 2021: 7). An important point to note is that the above models will not only help the cyber security manager to deal more effectively with cyber threats, but have the added advantage of making clear that cyber security education needs to include cyber ethics and also educators need to think in terms of developing ethical cyber theories (Petrie-Wyman et al., 2021).

The Global Cyber Security (GCS) model (Trim and Lee, 2021) places cyber security at the heart of business operations and allows the cyber security manager to have a comprehensive understanding of what cyber security involves. The conceptual model incorporates the role that cyber security specialists play, and can place cyber security in an intra- and inter-organizational risk reduction context. By using the model to establish a comprehensive cyber attack defence system, the cyber security manager can define the organization's cyber security objectives and make sure that they are realistic in terms of liaising with and requiring help from government representatives. This requires that the cyber security manager establishes what the controllable and uncontrollable factors are, draws on in-house intelligence and reports relating to cyber attacks from various external sources (e.g. government, private consultancies and university research teams), and identifies, appraises and prioritizes cyber security risks. It should be noted that it is important to evaluate and update cyber security policy through time, which can be done in consultation with internal staff and external cyber security specialists. A cyber security steering group can have an input into the organization's cyber security objectives and draw on the advice of domestic security specialists. An externally appointed group of cyber security advisors provides information and intelligence that can be used by the cyber security manager to set organizational security objectives. In addition, a range of cyber security specialists are admitted to the cyber attacks monitoring system committee, which is chaired by the Chief Information Officer (CIO) and a cyber attacks monitoring system committee reviews cyber security training and educational programmes. It may be useful for an organization to fund research into cyber security artificial intelligence (AI) as AI is being used in cyber security and is likely to play an increased role in cyber security threat identification in the years ahead.

The reason why such models, concepts and frameworks can be considered useful is because corporate security staff need to communicate widely and seek the views of non-security professionals in order that "security is achieved through the everyday actions of employees right across the company" (Briggs and Edwards, 2006: 13). For this, staff need to be trained in issues relating to security and understand the reason why security is important. Training can be used to reduce theft and acts of grievance (Briggs and Edwards, 2006: 44) and should prepare staff better to spot and deal with actual and/or potential cyber attacks from organized criminal syndicates and terrorist groups. Cornish et al. (2009: 3) indicated that 830,000 businesses in the UK during the period 2007–2008 experienced an online/computer-related security incident and 84,700 personal identity fraud cases took place online, which is evidence of the enormity of the problem.

5.5 Risk Assessment Policy and Its Strategic Context

Mont and Brown (2011: 1) suggest that:

> Security decision-makers need to assess the risks their companies are exposed to (due to current and foreseeable threat environments) and how current security policies effectively address them; the priorities of various stakeholders and business objectives need to be taken into account; they need to understand the implications; at the operational level, of mandating or changing specific policies; they need to decide which investments (e.g., automation, education, better monitoring/compliance, etc.) are necessary and most suitable in order to support these policies.

There are different methods of risk assessment. Some involve mathematical formulas and others are qualitative in orientation and sometimes involve the use of score cards. The degree of risk an organization is subjected to or the level of risk appetite is influential in terms of what type of business model is in place and what type of exposure the organization has. A number of factors need to be taken into consideration, including (1) the size and complexity of the organization; (2) management's attitude to change and innovation; (3) a consideration of the non-human factors and human factors (both internal and external); (4) an appreciation of the fact that those that might launch an attack on the organization have the resources to do so and (5) an overall appreciation of the complexity of the IT resources. The latter includes the internal and external uses of the Internet, the access that the organization's partners (outsourced service providers) have with respect to them accessing the organization's IT networks and resources, the extent with which employees engage in home working and remote working and other considerations such as legal and regulatory requirements and possible breaches, the consequences of an organization not being able to access business critical information from the organization's information systems, changes made to business critical information vis-à-vis an organization's information systems without the knowledge of staff or authorization, and the likely impact on the organization should, for example, the confidentiality of the business critical information on the organization's systems be compromised (ENISA, 2007–2008: 4–8). In addition, the cyber security manager needs to take into account the significance of the organization's information systems with respect to it achieving its business objectives and what the impact on various stake-holders might be should a disaster occur with the organization's information systems (ENISA, 2007–2008: 8).

Sheffi (2005: 20) indicates that "A firm's 'vulnerability' to a disruptive event can be viewed as a combination of the *likelihood* of disruption and its potential severity". Bearing this in mind, the cyber security manager needs to ask the "what if" question. If something can go wrong, the likelihood is that it will go wrong and there will be an impact on the organization. There will of course be consequences associated with such an impact (Sheffi, 2005). It is for this reason that the cyber security manager needs to know what organizational vulnerabilities there are and what contingency plans are in place. McGill and Ayyub (2007: 39) have enhanced our understanding by providing a useful definition of what vulnerability is:

"*Overall vulnerability* is a multidimensional property of a system that describes the degree to which it is susceptible to realizing a specified degree of loss following the occurrence of an initiating threat event".

Strategic risk analysis incorporates an evidence-based analysis. French (2007: 16) suggests that strategic threat assessment "must communicate distinct threat levels for multiple scenarios and it must allow managers to understand what evidence was considered and how it affects the results". By deploying an event tree analysis and threat severity analysis, both of which are based on detailed data and information, it is possible to construct complex scenarios (French, 2007: 16).

The US Department of Homeland Security definition of risk is well accepted (HSSAI, 2010: 3): "the potential for an unwanted outcome resulting from an incident, event, or occurrence as determined by its likelihood and the associated consequences". Hence, the cyber security manager needs to adopt a holistic view of risk and use business continuity as a process to establish impact criticality and what needs to be done in terms of strategic recovery. So the terms risk, criticality, value of the asset (impact on the asset), risk profile (e.g. risk related to individual assets), critical business requirements and business continuity are all linked and should be portrayed in a conceptual risk model that is understood by all those that use it.

The cyber security manager can adapt the ERM model to their particular organization and develop a matrix model, which becomes a generic model of risk. The grounded theory approach (Strauss and Corbin, 1998) can be used to develop and build an ERM model that takes into account risk at various levels (tactical, operational and strategic) and links with a customer relationship strategy. Senior management will, however, need to define the organization's risk strategy and ensure that Enterprise Resource Planning identifies various supporting services that may or may not be viewed as essential and at risk. Interoperability needs to be considered and viewed from the various perspectives of the organizations that make up the partnership arrangement. As well as Enterprise Resource Planning being considered with a holistic view of risk management, it also has a strategic emphasis as it focuses attention on supply chain activity involving cloud computing and how different cloud computing models may require a different or a broader view of what risk is.

According to BSI (2010: 17–18), risk assessment is "the overall process of risk iden-tification, risk analysis and risk evaluation". At the risk identification stage, the cyber security manager needs to identify and list the sources of risk, and make reference to their causes and potential consequences. Scenario analysis can be used to make the consequences of an impact better known and various experts can be consulted to provide insights into an impact and its consequences (BSI, 2010: 17). As regards risk analysis, the cyber security manager can develop an understanding and an appreciation of the risk, the causes and sources of risk, and the consequences and the interdependence of the various risks and their sources. Understanding the level of risk involved, how the level of risk can be communicated and the likely impacts should the risk materialize are important considerations and modelling can be used to explain the intricacies involved (BSI, 2010: 18). Soo Hoo (2000: 3) has provided a useful insight into risk and states that risk assessment "is the process for identifying, characterizing, and understanding risk; that is, studying, analyzing, and describing the set of outcomes and likelihoods for a given endeavour". Soo Hoo (2000: 3) goes on to state that:

> Risk management is a policy process wherein alternative strategies for dealing with risk are weighed and decisions about acceptable risks are made. The strategies consist of policy options that have varying effects on risk, including the reduction, removal, or reallocation of risk.

With respect to risk evaluation, the cyber security manager needs to know how the outcomes associated with risk analysis support the decision-making process and they need to establish which of the risks identified need treatment, and what the priorities are for treatment implementation (BSI, 2010: 18).

In order to place risk management within context, an appropriate definition of resilience is required, for example (HSSAI, 2010: 9):

> the ability of a system to attain the objectives of resisting, absorbing, and recovering from the impact of an adverse event, before, during, and after its occurrence. It is also a dynamic process that seeks to learn from incidents to strengthen capabilities of the system in meeting future challenges. The goals are to maintain continuity of function, degrading gracefully, and recover system functionality to a pre-designated level, as rapidly as desired and feasible.

Resilience principles need to be mapped against resilience objectives (Kahan et al., 2009) as this will indicate the operational capability of the organization as appropriate recovery systems and procedures are implemented in times of a crisis. HSSAI (2010: 6–7) have highlighted four resilience domains: infrastructure, organizations, communities and ecosystems. By interpreting resilience in this way, Critical Information Infrastructure is viewed as a set of interlinked systems and networks, all associated supply chains, all business-related and non-business-related activities, and the links between a community and the physical environment are known and are protected. The wider environment includes where workers live and how they interact with each other when not at work, and also, how corporate social responsibility programmes integrate with local community activities.

Taylor et al. (2002: 3) talk in terms of the survivability of computer systems and the ability of a computer system to be able to recover from an attack and outline the probability risk assessment approach in three stages: (i) risk identification; (ii) risk quantification and (iii) risk evaluation and acceptance. With respect to risk identification, the cyber security manager needs to be aware of what can go wrong and when it might go wrong. As regards risk quantification, the cyber security manager needs to relate probability to causal relationships and model known impacts. With regard to risk evaluation and acceptance challenges, the cyber security manager needs to establish what can be done and outline the options available. The emphasis is to create policy options and make trade-offs vis-à-vis risks and the cost/benefit of risk mitigation.

With respect to a survival strategy, Aaker and McLoughlin (2010: 93) have indicated that strategists need to think broadly and establish (i) what a strategic uncertainty is related to (trends or events impacting a business), the importance of the business and the number of businesses likely to be affected; and (ii) the immediacy of a strategic uncertainty and what it is related to (the probability that something will occur), the timeframe involved and the reaction time necessary to develop and implement an appropriate strategy.

Emergencies will occur from time to time and the US Homeland Security Studies and Analysis Institute (HSSAI, 2010: 15–16) suggest that situational awareness (composed of people, organizations and technology) during an emergency can maintain communications and develop a common operating picture that allows leaders to make appropriate and timely decisions vis-à-vis priorities and objectives, which is a key activity that needs concerted attention. Furthermore, the organizational culture in place needs to stimulate people to be Resourceful (the capability to improvise and innovate after or during an adverse event); and also, the organization itself needs to exhibit a Learning Capacity (the capability to learn from events and the lessons learned are used to improve future performance during adverse conditions).

Kendrick (2010: 14–17) focuses on three types of principal risks associated with Internet technologies: (i) technology risk; (ii) legal and compliance risk and (iii) operational risk. Technology risk is not just associated with computer viruses and encryption, however, and the cyber security manager needs to note that in-house computer security awareness programmes and staff development programmes relating to enterprise security and intelligence issues can be considered beneficial with regard to developing a security culture within the organization, as it can highlight and reinforce the risk management process, as a shared responsibility. As regards legal and compliance risk, the practicalities associated with complying with the various statutory and regulatory provisions that are in place to govern Internet technologies need to be thought through because the legal issues involved are not as obvious or indeed interpretable as the cyber security manager may expect. With respect to operational risk, there is no doubt that managers within organizations devote resources to devising and implementing workable systems and procedures so that employees behave in the way expected in the work environment. Training employees how to handle and safeguard data should be viewed as an ongoing process because a data breach can occur in a number of ways, some of which are less obvious than others. A CIO can be appointed who

> is responsible for the organization's information system planning, budgeting, investment, performance, and acquisition. As such, the CIO provides advice and assistance to senior organizational personnel in acquiring the most efficient and effective information system to minimize supply chain risks within the organization's enterprise architecture.
>
> (Swanson et al., 2010: 8)

The soft systems methodological approach (Checkland and Scholes, 2007) can be used as a methodological process for bringing together various stakeholders to produce a strategic security framework encompassing risk assessment. As well as warning people in society about the dangers associated with giving out passwords and sharing data with people they do not know (mostly through social networks), a community resilience model can be devised that provides a security mindset and makes people aware of the threats and vulnerabilities that are in existence.

Integrating security with intelligence is key and needs to be viewed as such. A multi-disciplinary approach is needed in order to counteract the threats posed by those carrying out cyber attacks and to ensure that the issue of organizational resilience is addressed by the cyber security manager in consultation with the organization's risk manager. The GISES model (Trim, 2005a) can be used to develop a security-intelligence interface and also the SATELLITE (Strategic Corporate Intelligence and Transformational Marketing) model (Trim, 2004) can be deployed to link more firmly the various environmental issues with business intelligence planning. The multi-disciplinary approach to security embedded in these models should enable both the cyber security manager and the risk manager to link security with intelligence, and to provide a focus of momentum that results in a security culture being established within the partnership arrangement. According to Trim and Lee (2010: 4):

> It can also be stated that by integrating security more firmly into the organization's structure, it should be possible to reduce the organization's level of risk and facilitate information sharing. Information sharing should enhance co-operation between partner organizations and add to the defensive capability vis-à-vis establishing effective counter-cyber attack measures.

Samani (2011) suggests that managers need to view information risk management from a multitude of perspectives and need to know how risk is assessed and what metrics are needed to establish the actual level of organizational vulnerability. Prioritizing threats helps to place matters in perspective. Quillinan (2010: 32) suggests that cloud will "revolutionise traditional outsourcing models" and outsourcing needs to be viewed more strategically because a company may be developing a long-term relationship with what may become a major competitor or a supplier that is vulnerable to take over. If an outsourcing arrangement is terminated for whatever reason, the previous outsource company may hold a certain amount of sensitive data relating to the company. It can be suggested that precautions need to be taken from the outset such as the pre-screening and pre-selection stages, which involves senior managers evaluating the risk posed by an outsourcer if confidential data is to be used or exchanged. Issues of compliance and knowing where data is, and the risks associated with losing it (Quillinan, 2010: 33) are key considerations in terms of interoperability, which reflects the way in which user behaviour creates security issues within partner arrangements with virtualization specialists (Adams, 2010: 49). Information assurance and breaches in security that result in leaks of data require that the cyber security manager thinks through what they are safeguarding and who they are accountable to, and if a leak does occur, a damage limitation policy may fail to stop financial losses and/or the identities of individuals being stolen.

Remote working has been given increased attention over the years and Rosch (2010: 35) reported that:

> Barclays plans to cut its energy consumption further too, by replacing standard desktops with thin client terminals connected virtually to a remotely located server. BGRB is also virtualising a lot of its servers, 550 in its Gloucester data centre alone, allowing it to make further significant energy savings.

Attack scenarios can be used in risk assessment to highlight which system components will be affected should an attack be launched on a computer system and this is a constructive way of looking for vulnerabilities in the system (Taylor et al., 2002). Managers in small- and medium-sized companies rely on a scenario analysis to establish how a computer security system is likely to be compromised. However, although scenarios are considered appropriate for highlighting the vulnerabilities of an organization should a certain attack manifest and can be used in order to stimulate brainstorming activities relating to computer security, they have limited scope (Soo Hoo, 2000: 11).

When analysing vulnerabilities in the supply chain, managers need to pay attention to issues such as the obsolescence of systems and in particular, how parts, subsystems and technologies that make up a system become outdated or discontinued (Swanson et al., 2010: 15). It has to be remembered that the supply chain includes all aspects of the product life cycle from design, development and acquisition of custom or what is known as commercial off-the-shelf (COTS) products, as well as system integration and system operation, and ultimately disposal as well as people and processes, and services and products (Swanson et al., 2010: 3). Hence, senior management need to understand that: "Supply chain attacks may involve manipulating computing, system hardware, software, or services at any point during the life cycle" (Swanson et al., 2010: 1).

A business model may change as a consequence of a new shareholder joining and the business model may be extended to incorporate suppliers (which need to be ISO 27000 compliant) and this would provide ISO 27000 end to end coverage. Not all the suppliers may be incorporated as such and the cyber security manager needs to decide which controls are relevant and if a supplier is to be included and audited according to being certified, the criteria for certification must be explicit.

Although there are various interpretations of risk and there are different risk models, the cyber security manager needs to prioritize risks, and identify current and future threats in the short, medium and long terms, and deploy ERM to provide a situational analysis so that senior and junior managers throughout the partnership arrangement understand the threats identified in the internal and external environments. A PESTEL (Political, Economic, Social, Technological, Environmental and Legal) analysis can be used to identify threats, and business continuity management can be used to integrate the sub-areas/topics. By placing risk assessment at the centre of the strategy process, it should be possible to connect with all the other areas of business activity. By focusing on cyber space, it should be possible to place IT security risk management at the centre of a risk assessment policy and this will, if this is the case, integrate the organization's risk management model with the external environment (e.g. supporting infrastructure). What has to be acknowledged is that the cyber security manager needs to be aware that: "risk management in alliances is a complex endeavour that is related to specific types of trust and control" (Das and Teng, 2001: 277). For this reason, it is important to review again the relationship between the different phases of risk management and for top management to sanction a communication risk management strategy that can be used to integrate more clearly a risk assessment policy in the context of a partnership arrangement.

5.6 Cyber Security SWOT and SLEPT Analysis

By adopting an integrated management approach, the cyber security manager can use the outputs of a Cyber Security SLEPT (Social, Legal, Economic, Political, Technological) analysis and the outputs of a Cyber Security SWOT (Strengths, Weaknesses, Opportunities and Threats) analysis to devise cyber countermeasures. A Cyber Security SLEPT analysis can be considered an integral component of corporate intelligence activity as it utilizes environmental scanning that is aimed at (Trim and Lee, 2010: 1–2):

i   identifying the emerging trends in criminal and terrorist behaviour;
ii identifying potential systems failure;
iii identifying legal vulnerability;
iv establishing the effect on society in economic terms should a major cyber attack/series of attacks occur;
v   establishing the main vulnerability and threat drivers confronting senior management; and
vi results in a vulnerability Sequence-of-Events Model.

By harnessing the knowledge of staff based in external organizations (companies, private consultancies, government agencies, international institutions, universities, trade associations, embassies and chambers of commerce and industry, for example), the cyber security manager can synthesize the results of a Cyber Security SLEPT analysis into a Sequence-of-Events Model. The Sequence-of-Events Model can be used by senior managers (IT, finance, marketing, corporate law, security and corporate intelligence, for example) to highlight current and future cyber security threats and to provide guidance for prioritizing each risk identified. As regards what may be referred to as legal factors, the cyber security manager can make staff aware of the influence (direct and indirect) that industry standards have on how the organization functions and how current and future regulations place constraints on an organization's resources. Protecting and sharing IP rights will receive attention through time and as regards economic factors, managers need to pay careful attention to how organizational costs can be kept to a minimum bearing in mind increases in commodity prices and components.

A Cyber Security SWOT (Strengths, Weaknesses, Opportunities and Threats) analysis (Trim and Lee, 2010: 2–3) forms an integral part of corporate intelligence activity and underpins:

i   an organizational strategic governance framework;
ii a business continuity management contingency planning framework;
iii a communication risk management strategy; and
iv a GCSMM and strategic management framework.

When assessing organizational strengths, the cyber security manager needs to authorize an audit to be undertaken that requires that a corporate security function is established and a governance framework is put in place/implemented. Attention will also be given to how a resilience and business continuity policy are formulated and implemented, and how a risk communication policy is communicated that treats as inputs the risks listed in the organization's risk register. As regards identifying and eradicating organizational weaknesses, the cyber security manager needs to identify corporate security gaps and deficiencies, and detail how they are to be eradicated.

The cyber security manager needs to be vigilant in terms of the opportunities that exist and this means identifying the best practice outlined in industry standards; evaluating various cyber law initiatives; identifying evolving market opportunities at home and abroad; and cooperating with government agencies and international organizations. With respect to threats, staff need to constantly monitor the external environment and identify the actions of organized criminal syndicates; gauge the way in which state-sponsored actors carry out industrial espionage and sabotage; identify the actions associated with terrorist networks and money laundering activities; understand how and why activists and small criminals engage in disruptive behaviour; and provide support and assistance to government agencies at home and abroad that implement initiatives aimed at eradicating cyber crime.

To understand fully how current affairs relate to cyber security and management issues, the cyber security manager needs to review the literature (including industry reports) relating to relevant bodies of knowledge and to draw on existing models and frameworks that have a security and intelligence focus/dimension. By amending and utilizing an existing model/framework, it is easier to develop an appropriate model/framework in the sense that it can be made company- and industry-specific. In order that managers throughout the organization participate fully in the model building/framework building process, it is necessary for a holistic view of security to be adopted and for a management logic to be incorporated that ensures that the corporate security framework/model that materializes is robust. Trim (2005b: 496) has stated that:

> Senior management cannot sit back and wait for security systems to evolve naturally, the necessary commitment and stimulation needs to be put in place so that a security culture is created that incorporates an intelligence dimension. The organization's intelligence function needs to have a specific organizational–environment focus. Hence it needs to be organizational specific, industry specific, technology specific and country specific. This being the case, corporate intelligence and security will automatically be linked to governmental transnational intelligence. Transnational intelligence deals with the many but integrated threats that emerge to debilitate a system. Once a system is debilitated, it is both defenceless and vulnerable.

5.7 Cyber Security Threats

What is evident from the above is that the cyber security manager will, in order to put an effective corporate security framework in place, need to embrace the concept of organizational learning so that the level of security awareness is raised. This is because a wide range of diverse cyber threats and related cyber threats confronting senior managers and government representatives have been identified. See Figure 5.1, which contains a diverse range of cyber threats (Trim and Lee, 2014: 20–24).

Cloud computing is perceived by some as a necessary and obvious way forward. However, certain points need to be considered. For example, three different models have been identified (Global Knowledge, 2010: 1–2):

i   Infrastructure-as-a-Service (IaaS), which is where the company owns the software and purchases "virtual power to execute as needed". An example is Amazon Web Services.

ii   Platform-as-a-Service (PaaS), here the provider is responsible for the platform for the service and in particular the system development life cycle, application programme interfaces, website portals and gateway software. GoogleApps is an example.

iii Software-as-a-Service (SaaS), a complete service is offered via a front end or web portal. Salesforce.com provides this type of service.

counterfeiting and brand piracy; insider crime; fraud orchestrated by organized criminal syndicates; cyber attacks from hackers and crackers and government front companies; a lack of skilled cyber security professionals; malware (malicious code) to get into the system; the increasing number of fake software products; companies do not have adequate cyber security policies and security plans in place; the management of cloud computing; poor/ineffective patching; the increasing targeting of social networking activities and resulting identify theft and fraud; product testing and evaluation, and validation against national and international standards; the mitigation of risk and the link with contingency planning and disaster recovery planning; cyber security policy and linkage with the security policy of partner organizations in the supply chain and marketing channel organizations; adequate staff development and educational programmes vis-à-vis skill enhancement and the development of staff; transparency of operations; the security of Supervisory Control and Data Acquisition (SCADA) Systems; technological developments which could result in an untested product or technology being made available; communication between organizations, institutions, private sector companies and government departments; an organizational security culture that places, embeds information security/assurance policy within the risk management strategy; terrorist networks; countries that may become centres for organized criminal syndicates or terrorist groups; industrial espionage; continued threat of attacks against infrastructure (CNI and CII) and tourist attractions; continued expansion of organized crime (money laundering, fraud, kidnapping and extortion), and corruption of government representatives; computer abuse by employees; the actions of rogue governments; identity fraud; increased use of spyware; an untested business model; wireless control systems; increased need to develop timely nuclear counterintelligence policy and responses and to place these within a strategic intelligence context; the growth in the idea of cyber sex; (Yesterday Television Channel, 2010); the growing trend in hoaxing relating to computer viruses; growing vigilante movement to expose Internet bullies to their employers; spurious emails from supposed relatives or those supposedly representing family members; money laundering and drug trafficking; and the illegal and legal actions of organized criminal syndicates.

Figure 5.1 Diverse range of cyber threats.

A number of issues and concerns have been raised about cloud computing which bring to the fore the subject of security controls. It is important to note that (NIST, 2010: 1):

> Security controls are the management, operational, and technical safeguards or countermeasures prescribed for an information system to protect the confidentiality, integrity (including non-repudiation and authenticity), and availability of the system and its information. Once employed within an information system, security controls are assessed to provide the information necessary to determine their overall effectiveness; that is, the extent to which the controls are implemented correctly, operating as intended, and producing the desired outcome with respect to meeting the security requirements for the system. Understanding the overall effectiveness of the security

controls implemented in the information system and its environment of operation is essential in determining the risk to the organization's operations and assets, to individuals, to other organizations, and to the Nation resulting from the use of the system.

Understanding the risk associated with operational activities is key and requires that the cyber security manager places risk assessment within a logical context and in addition places risk mitigation within a security management framework and process. As regards cloud computing services, several questions can be posed regarding whether an organization should engage partially or fully in cloud computing activities and services. The National Institute of Standards and Technology (NIST, 2010: 4) indicates that cryptographic modules and information technology products can be tested, evaluated and validated and these include "operating systems, database systems, firewalls, intrusion detection devices, Web browsers, Web applications, smart cards, biometrics devices, personal identity verification devices, network devices, and hardware platforms using national and international standards".

In the US, the Process Control Security Requirements Forum (PCSRF) was established by the National Institute of Standards and Technology (Stouffer, 2005: 2) "to increase the security of industrial process control systems through the definition and application of a common set of information security requirements for these systems. This will reduce the likelihood of successful cyber-attack on the nation's critical infrastructures". Owing to the fact that cyber security needs to be placed within an international as opposed to a national context, it is not surprising to learn that (Stouffer, 2005: 2):

> Members of the PCSRF represent the critical infrastructures and related process industries, including oil and gas, water, electric power, chemicals, pharmaceuticals, metals and mining, and pulp and paper. There are currently over 650 members, from 32 countries in the PCSRF representing government, academic, and private sectors.

Stouffer (2005: 4–6) has provided some valuable insights into SCADA:

> Supervisory Control and Data Acquisition (SCADA) systems integrate data acquisition systems with data transmission systems and Human-Machine Interface (HMI) software in order to provide a centralized monitor and control system for numerous process inputs and outputs. SCADA systems are designed to collect information, transfer it back to a central computer, and display the information to the operator(s) graphically or textually, thereby allowing the operator to monitor and/or control an entire system from a central location in real time. Based on the sophistication and setup of the individual system, control of any individual system, operation, or task can be automatic, or it can be initiated by operator commands.
>
> SCADA systems are often used for electronic tagging of control and data points. Tags can include control inhibit, alarm and scan inhibit, as well as caution and informational messages as allowed in a utility's operational procedures.....................
> SCADA systems are used to control dispersed assets where centralized data acquisition is as important as control and are used in the distribution operations of water supply systems, oil/gas pipelines, electrical systems and rail systems. ....A large, complex, and geographically dispersed infrastructure system can be operated by a small number of people in a Control Center.......Most current SCADA field devices are highly insecure because encryption, authentication, and other security

measures were not designed in to the devices. An adversary could potentially exploit these insecurities by inserting false commands and responses, modifying legitimate communication, or altering field device behaviour.

Common vulnerabilities in SCADA field devices include (but are not limited to):

* TCP/IP addressability
* Weak or non-existent authentication
* Remote configuration capabilities and modem access
* Open FTP, Telnet, SNMP and HTML ports that allow for remote configuration
* Configuration modes that are protected by passwords sent in clear text
* Unencrypted communications with SCADA MTU
* Lack of configuration backups
* Embedded web servers
* Default OS security configurations
* Uncollected or unexamined system logs.

Power outage, followed by terrorism, bird flu and extreme weather conditions are considered the main threat to businesses and are now placed within the context of risk management processes (EIU, 2006). A combined event, a natural disaster which coincides with a major terrorist attack and reinforced by a hacker/criminal activity, is part of the scenario planning of business continuity experts. But it has to be said that senior managers in the US view the risk of terrorism and its consequences as different to those of European and Asian managers, and there is recognition that disaster recovery plans are important and need to be implemented (EIU, 2006).

The "system of systems" view, explained by Stouffer (2005: 7), is relevant as experts often refer to the US critical infrastructure in this way because

> of the interdependencies that exist between its various industrial sectors. Critical infrastructures are highly interconnected and mutually dependent in complex ways, both physically and through a host of information and communications technologies. What happens to one infrastructure can directly and indirectly affect other infrastructures through cascading and escalating failures.

Agrafiotis et al. (2018: 2) indicate that once management has identified the main risks, they need to select the controls to address the risks identified. Stouffer (2005: 9–10) is right to recommend that management think in terms of management, operational and technical security controls (countermeasures) in order that they mitigate the risk associated with the vulnerabilities identified, and has this to say about the controls:

> Management controls are the security controls (countermeasures) for an industrial control system that focus on the management of risk and the management of the industrial control system. The main management controls focus around the following areas:
>
> * Risk Assessment
> * Developing and implementing a security programme
> * System and services acquisition
> * Security assessments

Operational controls are the security controls (countermeasures) for an industrial control system that are primarily implemented and executed by personnel as opposed to the system. The main operational controls focus around the following areas:

- Personnel security
- Patch and configuration management
- Checklists
- Maintenance
- Network segmentation
- Incident response and disaster recovery
- Physical protection
- Media protection
- Awareness and training

Technical controls are the security controls (countermeasures) for an industrial control system that are primarily implemented and executed by the industrial control system through mechanisms contained in the hardware, software or firmware components of the system. The main technical controls focus around the following areas:

- User identification, authentication and authorization
- Data identification and authorization
- Device identification, authentication and authorization
- Logging and audit
- Secure communications
- Access control
- Intrusion detection and prevention
- Virus, worm and malicious code detection.

5.8 Enterprise Risk Management (ERM)

Bearing in mind that risk can be interpreted from an organizational perspective as many functions of the organization are vulnerable to attack and the cyber security manager needs to monitor and report cyber attacks, a collectivist risk management strategy can be developed that is underpinned by the ERM concept. Fox and Epstein (2010: 3) outline how ERM can be used to establish what an organization can tolerate in the way of risk, and how risk can be related to the business goals and objectives, and place risk within the organization's "unique strategy, tolerance, culture and governance" and build on the work of The Risk and Insurance Management Society, Inc. They advocate an approach whereby senior managers apply an environmental and intelligence scanning system to identify risks and match the threat of risks with internal organizational vulnerabilities, and develop and implement Enterprise Risk Management Cyber Security (ERMCS) that ensures that prioritized risks are documented, evaluated and contingency plans are drawn up relating to possible outcomes. Hence, scenario planning and futures research are useful as they provide insights and add depth to our understanding of what vulnerabilities exist and what needs to be done to eradicate organizational weaknesses. Those organizations that are involved in producing security tools and systems, and/or involved in working on cyber security projects, need to ensure that they are certified and meet compliance standards, because they too are at risk from sophisticated attacks.

As the reader will note from above, the subject of risk covers a wide and sometimes multifaceted area of study and it is known that "the adoption of consistent processes within a comprehensive framework can help to ensure that risk is managed effectively, efficiently and coherently across an organization" (ISO/FDIS, 2009: v). It is clear that the management of risk encourages a proactive management approach to increase the likelihood that the organization will achieve its objectives; improve the identification of opportunities and threats, financial reporting, governance, stakeholder confidence and trust, controls, operational effectiveness and efficiency, loss prevention and incident management, organizational learning and organizational resilience. The proactive risk management approach will make managers comply with relevant legal and regulatory requirements. By doing so, management will establish a reliable basis for decision making and planning, will effectively allocate and use resources for risk treatment; enhance health and safety performance and enhance environmental protection (ISO/FDIS, 2009: v–vi). Taking this into account makes it clear that: "Risk management is part of the responsibilities of management and an integral part of all organizational processes, including strategic planning and all project and change management processes" (ISO/FDIS, 2009: 7).

The cyber security manager can ensure that monitoring is undertaken on a continual basis and that a formal and systematic approach to environmental scanning (both internal to the organization and external to the organization) is undertaken and is viewed as ongoing. A monitoring system will ensure that (ISO/FDIS, 2009: 20) the controls in place are effective and efficient, both in design and in operation; further information is obtained and this improves the risk assessment process; analysing and learning from events, changes, trends, successes and failures allow lessons to be learned; changes in the internal and the external contexts are detected – risk criteria, the actual risk and revision of risk treatments and priorities; and the identification of emerging risks is automatic.

5.9 Building Trust-Based Relationships

In order that the effectiveness of cyber attacks on an organization is reduced, the cyber security manager needs to be aware of how staff are monitored and how their behaviour can change so that they become more cyber conscious. Research suggests that in situations of high perceived risk, people will deploy a risk-reducing strategy based on behavioural choices, which lower their vulnerability to what are regarded as potentially negative outcomes (Cho and Lee, 2006: 119). Stating and reinforcing the threats and penalties relating to computer crime may be worthwhile but this has to be done throughout the partnership arrangement using seminars, workshops and public awareness campaigns.

Building and maintaining trust-based relationships with external partners is key to maintaining long-term sustainable working relationships. However, as well as thinking in terms of internal trust (brought about and reinforced through leadership and teamwork), the cyber security manager needs to focus on developing and maintaining external trust that is trust developed with suppliers, joint venture partners and customers (Huff and Kelley, 2005: 97). Drawing on their research findings, Suh and Kwon (2006: 198–199) state:

> It is safe to say that the success of supply chain rests on the degree of trust that the supply chain partners believe is in the partnership. Many supply chain tools presuppose that each partner behaves in a manner consistent with expectation based on trust. For example, collaborative planning, forecasting and replenishment

(CPFR), a main driver for structural change in the supply chain optimization process requires information sharing, and such information sharing demands trust among and between supply chain partners. Any lack of trust creates an informational balance between partners, which in turn produces unintended inequitable distribution of optimization results (profits) among the partners.

Successful partnership does, therefore, need to be viewed as involving coordination and governance, and can be thought of as a form of cooperation (Rese, 2006: 74). Those organizations involved in a cooperative partnership need to carry out the agreed policies in the way specified and must be convinced of the benefits accruing and also they need to be convinced of the need for cooperation at all levels within the partnership arrangement (Wucherer, 2006: 91–92). The cyber security manager can contribute to the process by advocating integrated solutions (e.g. cooperation between internal business units and departments), but in order for this to be achieved, it is essential that this view is extended to include end customers and partners of various kinds, including research institutes and government agencies (Windahl and Lakemond, 2006: 816–817).

The management of interrelationships is a complex process as it involves applications development platforms, database management systems, systems software and network infrastructure (Someswar et al., 2002: 149). Someswar et al. (2002: 150) have indicated that when thinking about security access control, it is important to first think in terms of both physical access to a building and access to the computer system, which is underpinned by the concept of privacy (only those individuals listed as accessing information in a system should be allowed to do so); integrity ensures that only those individuals allowed to make changes to or amend records are permitted to do so; authentication is key as it ensures "that the origin of an electronic message is correctly identified"; non-repudiation refers to the fact that the person that sends a message cannot deny sending it and also the receiver is not able to deny receiving the message. The term availability refers to the fact that the systems are in place and are available when needed; and DoS manifests in a corrupted hard disk or consumption of entire memory of the system as a result of the site being bombarded by large amounts of data. By taking into account the main components of an e-commerce system (e-commerce development platforms, database management systems, operating systems and infrastructure) (Someswar et al., 2002: 154) and how the various components and tools are linked, it is possible to outline the relationship between technologies and tools.

Alpaslan et al. (2009: 41) suggest that "managerial tasks also include identifying potential/actual corporate stakeholders to a crisis and their concerns and interests, and involving these stakeholders in crisis preparation and response". When addressing the topic of "how to align security with the business", Briggs and Edwards (2006: 13) discovered that corporate security staff need to communicate widely and seek the views of non-security professionals in order that "security is achieved through the everyday actions of employees right across the company". They cite a number of relevant points, including a high turnover of staff that results in security-related problems and the need for training that is aimed at reducing the level of theft and absenteeism and acts of grievance (Briggs and Edwards, 2006: 44). Briggs and Edwards (2006: 49–52) also make reference to the fact that companies have included in their business model offshoring and make reference to the fact that India, which has been a centre for offshoring activity, has been subject to a large number of terrorist attacks over the years and senior managers need to be aware of this, especially if they are working for organizations in sensitive industries. These are, it can be argued, important considerations that the cyber security manager and senior management need to take into account when forming relations with other business partners.

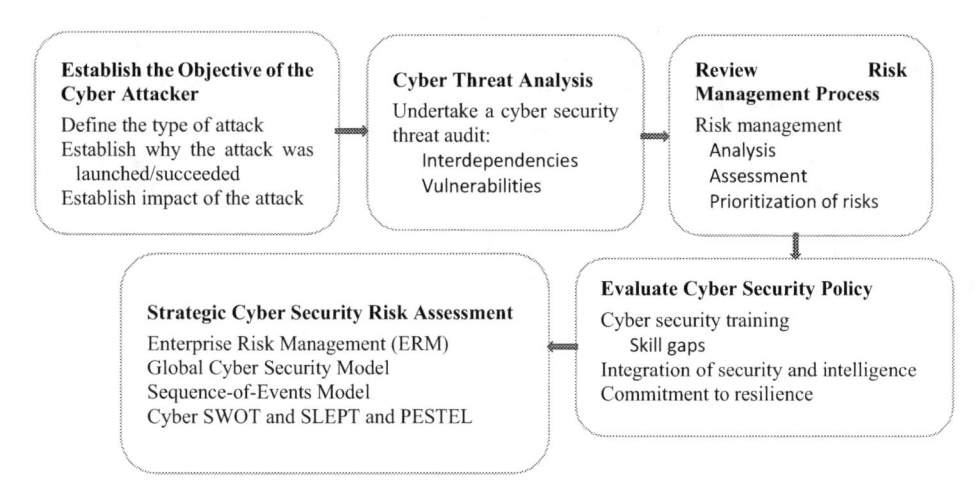

Figure 5.2 Strategic cyber security risk assessment.

5.10 Learning Summary

From Figure 5.2, it can be deduced that strategic cyber security risk assessment is complex and requires that the cyber security manager undertakes a number of tasks, some of which are with colleagues such as the risk manager. By defining matters clearly and by undertaking regular cyber security threat audits, the risk management process will be formalized and so too will cyber security training. A number of models are available to the cyber security manager and can be used to undertake a strategic cyber security risk assessment, which should ensure that plans are put in place to make the organization as resilient as possible.

The reader is able to:

- identify and catalogue organizational vulnerabilities;
- identify and catalogue various cyber threats;
- apply various cyber security management approaches and models; and
- devise and implement cyber security risk management solutions.

5.11 Conclusion

Evidence suggests that organizations will continue to be subjected to various forms of cyber attack and that organized criminal syndicates will find ways to develop more sophisticated forms of attack. Bearing in mind the political aspects involved, the cyber security manager needs to undertake a formal risk assessment and work closely with the risk manager in order to ensure that the cyber security models available are utilized in terms of developing cyber security countermeasures. By adopting an international perspective to cyber security, the cyber security manager can implement a risk management policy in association with staff based in partner organizations and can draw on the expertise of external cyber security experts when necessary.

5.12 Mini Case: Fake News and How to Deal with It

There was much excitement among the company's staff, all of whom had gathered in the canteen to hear the latest news relating to the latest product launch. Jane Mansfield, the company's managing director, had taken the stand and was about to release a statement. Members of the local press had been invited to attend as it was hoped that the additional news coverage would help promote the success of the brand and result in additional business.

Suddenly, Tom Arthur, the company's Marketing Director, rushed forward and asked Mrs. Mansfield to join him on the side of the podium. "What is it Tom?" She asked. "I am just about to start my speech. Can it wait?"

"Please wait", said Mr. Arthur, "I have some disturbing information and need to talk with you about it".

He gained his composure and then explained why he had asked her to wait, step aside and listen to him. Apparently, news was circulating via social media suggesting that the company, which had developed a new form of battery for electric vehicles, had fabricated the results of the experiments and that the battery, which was said to represent a breakthrough in technology, was not as efficient as it was claimed to be. The report on social media, which was from an unknown source, also suggested that the battery had been developed by an overseas supplier that was associated with human right violations. The violations related to the poor and unsafe working conditions of employees, and the use of banned chemical materials.

While Mr. Arthur was talking with Mrs. Mansfield, he received a call on his mobile phone informing him that another social networking site was running a different but equally harmful story about the battery, suggesting that a number of companies that had pre-ordered the product had cancelled their orders due to consumer activism. The online reviews, from a range of sources, including a non-existent research company, an overseas industry association and a number of individuals, were all false and had been made up and posted online.

"This is becoming serious", said Mrs. Mansfield. She continued: "We need to cancel this presentation and get public relations in quickly".

The presentation was cancelled and those present were told that they would be informed about the battery in due course. They were also told that fake news was spreading about the product and management had to take action fast in order to sort the problem out. Time was of the essence because by the time Mrs. Mansfield and Mr. Arthur arrived at the main board room, yet another story was circulating about the company and misinformation was being emailed to staff throughout the company. What appeared to be happening was that a focused attack was being made on the company and the problem was escalating. What became apparent was that staff were not experienced at dealing with such an attack and what senior management feared was staff responding to the attack by releasing information that might cause further harm. For example, a disgruntled employee that had been sacked from the company for stealing components was known to be disputing the charge and had said that he would release harmful information about the company if he was not reinstated. A number of people within the company had been close to the person concerned and had spread a rumour suggesting that the person had been "set-up".

Fake online news can prove difficult to deal with as it involves a number of people and organizations, and can be fuelled by emotional outbursts and individuals pushing a political cause. What baffled Mrs. Mansfield and Mr. Arthur was that the company had, over the past three months, administered a promotion campaign featuring the work of the company and its commitment to a green and safe environment. Indeed, the company produced other green and safe products and had won an industry award for its innovatory practices.

It was clear, because of how the problem was unfolding, that the fake news campaign was being driven by a well-organized and ruthless campaigner, who was out to do damage to the company. Management feared that this was in fact the first wave of the attack and another was planned. Possibly, the second wave would involve key individuals within the company, being targeted and cyber bullying would become evident.

Questions

Question 1: How should senior management deal with the fake news story?

Question 2: What should have been done to prevent or counteract the fake news story?

Question 3: What do senior management need to do in order to convince the company's stakeholders that the stories are not true?

Further Reading

Albright, J. (2017). Welcome to the era of fake news. *Media and Communication*, 5 (2): 87–89. https://doi.org/10.17645/mac.v5i2.977.

Klein, D.O., and Wueller, J.R. (2017). Fake news: A legal perspective. *Journal of Internet Law*, 20 (10): 5–13.

5.13 Extended Case: The Role of the Chief Information Officer (CIO)

It has been suggested that marketers and IT specialists have little in common and inhabit different castles. This appears to be an outdated view because the current view maintains that the CIO is responsible for formulating and implementing a company's digital strategy, which is aimed at improving the customer's experience and keeping them loyal in terms of purchasing the company's products and service. A CIO does therefore perform a substantial task bearing in mind that new business models are being developed that provide workforce flexibility (the opportunity to hot desk, share roles and work from home (remote working)) and connectivity, which provides consumers with the opportunity to surf the web, locate and compare similar products, and enjoy the thrill of virtual shopping. It can be suggested that a CIO is normally found within a large company and has the necessary resources to draw on. Small companies tend to have management thinly spread with one director undertaking two separate functions, and are subject to cash flow issues during periods of economic downturn.

The focus of this case is to highlight the issues confronting a small, family owned, thriving fashion company based in the South East of England. The main shareholder, Mr. Ashcroft, was only too aware of what remote working involved as he had had to close down the company during the COVID-19 pandemic in order to adhere to government lockdown procedures. Reopening the company proved straightforward because of the locally based and committed workforce, and the strong bond the company had with its high net worth customer base. Luxury clothing was in demand and recently, Mr. Ashcroft and his colleagues had diversified into casual sportswear as it was suggested that this market was to expand significantly over the next three years. However, although sales were booming, much was on the mind of the senior management team. For example, Josephine Appleton, head of sales and marketing, was concerned that the company's website was outdated and contained too much personal information about the senior management team. The profiles were comprehensive and covered: where people were born, which schools they attended, the university where they studied, and details about their social interests and where they took their holidays. It was clear that anybody reading the details on the web page could build up a picture of the pattern of behaviour of the individuals cited and establish their lifestyle. Mr. Ashcroft had considered it important to provide such details as transparency was deemed to be equated with trust and an open and honest business relationship. Gone were the days when it was important to hard sell to the trade and customers, including those that purchased for resale; the emphasis now was stability and consolidation through personal relationships. It was this philosophy that underpinned the approach to customer service and the need to have a customer relationship management system in place.

Another area of concern was the rush to incorporate artificial intelligence (AI) as a tool for analysing customer data, profiling customer trends and matching purchase decisions to individual behaviour and the lifestyle of a group of people. Mrs. Appleton considered that the company was rushing to take advantage of technology but did not have the skills in house to utilize the intelligence gained. On a number of occasions, it was clear that those involved in buying and marketing were too ambitious and did not think of safeguarding client data or indeed the data of suppliers in the way expected. The marketing databases operated were activated by simple passwords and those operating them were known to use their name and date of birth as opposed to a complex password containing various characters. Often, staff wrote down a password on a piece of paper and left the paper either on their desk or pinned to a board in front of their desk, or wrote down the password in a writing pad, which was then placed in an unlocked draw. Using Post It Notes was not allowed because they tended to peel away and were often found on the floor. In some instances, they got stuck to the sole of somebody's shoe, and could end up in the car park or somewhere else. Paul Nice, who was head of IT and Human Resource Management, had suggested that security should be improved because a week ago, it had been noticed that one of the company's laptop computers had disappeared from a small back room office. Nobody had seen anything and the company's security camera (CCTV) did not record anything because it had not been working for the past three months.

An apathetic view and approach to security was known to prevail but recent events had drawn attention to the issue of ransomware. For example, Mrs. Appleton had suggested to Mr. Ashcroft that the company might fall victim to a ransomware attack because small companies were viewed as an easy target. Mr. Ashcroft suggested that she should not worry because the company was insured. However, Mrs. Appleton did not know if the company had cyber insurance cover and suggested that the company should hire an external security consultant to undertake a security audit. Mrs. Appleton had on occasion mentioned to Mr. Ashcroft and his business partner, Julia Hart, that the company should employ a CIO to oversee the use of AI and place AI utilization within the company's digital strategy. This had drawn a blank expression from both Mr. Ashcroft and Mrs. Hart, because they were more interested in expanding unit sales than thinking in terms of an integrated business platform. Staff had over a number of months been exposed to email phishing attacks but because it was a small company, such irritations were dealt with through personal contact and word of mouth. What was clear, however, was that as the company expanded and employed more people, it was only a matter of time before a cyber attacker identified a vulnerability and gained access to the company's database or accounts.

In order to convince both Mr. Ashcroft and Mrs. Hart that the company should appoint a CIO, Josephine Appleton produced a two-page report that she entitled: The role and responsibilities of the Chief Information Officer, Past, Present and Future. She considered that it would be eye catching and brief enough to hold their interest. At the same time, it was up-to-date and detailed. The report was divided into various sections and covered a number of points taken from an article entitled: "Five priorities for CIOs" (Pickup, 2021: 12). The points covered regulatory compliance and security; how to modernize IT infrastructure and systems; visibility of critical data; engaging with the workforce and making the most of cloud computing. Mrs. Appleton had gone to length to add depth and interpretation, by incorporating insights into the report drawn from the work of Bresniker et al. (2019). Indeed, the central focus of the work had revolved around how AI can be used to detect cyber attacks on the organization and how a CIO would map out a digital strategy for the company. The main thread being that security and cyber security, in particular, were everybody's responsibility, and senior management were responsible for providing guidance and direction.

Having written the report, Mrs. Appleton reflected and then decided to redraft it. She was worried that it would be viewed as a work of science fiction as opposed to something that could be influential in terms of a policy document. The redrafted report made clear that AI coupled with machine learning could be used to monitor specific types of cyber attack and also could help managers identify a real threat from a possible threat. Currently, the company deployed AI for marketing purposes but it was not connected with security or alerting staff that an intruder was trying to gain access to the company's database. While redrafting the report, Mrs. Appleton took into account that some employees were based at home and only came into the office once a week. In addition, some staff took home a company-owned laptop and sometimes used it for gaming and buying products online. Also, some staff were reluctant to use technology to communicate with fellow staff and because staff were thinly spread, it was clear that staff did not communicate well in real time. Emerging from the report was the need for a CIO to be appointed that had the necessary skill set and knowledge base, to influence change and also had an ability to perceive the future and establish an appropriate organizational culture that ensured staff cooperated and utilized technology in the way expected.

Questions

Question 1: What is the role of a Chief Information Officer (CIO)?

Question 2: How influential is organizational culture in terms of employees adapting to change?

Question 3: What do staff within the company need to do in order to make the company more resilient?

Case Sources

Bresniker, K., Gavrilovska, A., Holt, J., Milojicic, D., and Tran, T. (2019). Grand challenge: Applying artificial intelligence and machine learning to cybersecurity. *Computer*, (December): 45–52.

Pickup, O. (2021). Five priorities for CIOs. The future CIO: Raconteur. *The Sunday Times*, 28th March, p. 12.

5.14 References

Aaker, D.A., and McLoughlin, D. (2010). *Strategic Market Management*. Chichester: John Wiley & Sons Limited.

Abou el Kalam, A. (2021). Securing SCADA and critical industrial systems: From needs to security mechanisms. *International Journal of Critical Infrastructure Protection*, 32: 1–16. https://doi.org/10.1016/j.ijcip.2020.100394.

Adams, D. (2010). Virtual reality. *Financial Sector Technology*, 16 (4): 48–50.

Agrafiotis, I., Nurse, J.R.C., Goldsmith, M., Creese, S., and Upton, D. (2018). A taxonomy of cyber-harms: Defining the impacts of cyber-attacks and understanding how they propagate. *Journal of Cybersecurity*, 1–15. https://doi.org/10.1093/cybsec/tyy006.

Alpaslan, C.M., Green, S.E., and Mitroff, I.I. (2009). Corporate governance in the context of crises: Towards a stakeholder theory of crisis management. *Journal of Contingencies and Crisis Management*, 17 (1): 40–49.

Blyth, A. (2011). The changing face of IA risk management. *Information Advisory Assurance Council (IAAC) Consumerisation of IT: Risk and Advanced Persistent Threat Agent Research Workshop*. Positioning Paper. London: BCS, The Chartered Institute for IT (6th December), pp. 1–3.

Briggs, R., and Edwards, C. (2006). *The Business of Resilience: Corporate Security for the 21st Century*. London: Demos.

BSI. (2010). *Risk Management – Principles and Guidelines*. BS ISO 31000: 2009. London: British Standards Institute.

Cabinet Office. (2011). *The UK Cyber Security Strategy: Protecting and Promoting the UK in a Digital World*. London: Cabinet office (November).

Chambers, J.T., and Thompson, J.W. (2004). *Vulnerability Disclosure Framework: Final Report and Recommendations by the Council*. Cybersecurity & Infrastructure Security Agency: National Infrastructure Advisory Council (NIAC).

Checkland, P., and Scholes, J. (2007). *Soft Systems Methodology in Action*. Chichester: John Wiley & Sons.

Cho, J., and Lee, J. (2006). An integrated model of risk and risk-reducing strategies. *Journal of Business Research*, 59: 112–120.

Cornish, P., Hughes, R., and Livingstone, D. (2009). *Cyberspace and the National Security of the United Kingdom: Threats and Responses*, Chatham House Report. London: Royal Institute of International Affairs.

Cotae, P., Kang, M., and Velazquez, A. (2020). A cybersecurity model for decision-making problems under uncertainty using game theory. *13th International Conference on Communications (COMM)*. Bucharest: IEEE (18th to 20th June), pp. 15–22. https://doi.org/10.1109/COMM48946.2020.9141991.

Das, T.K., and Teng, B-S. (2001). Trust, control, and risk in strategic alliances: An integrated framework. *Organization Studies*, 22 (2): 251–283.

EIU. (2006). *Catastrophe Risk Management: Preparing for Potential Storms Ahead*. London: The Economist Intelligence Unit (EIU).

ENISA. (2007–2008). *Determining Your Organization's Information Risk Assessment and Management Requirements and Selecting Appropriate Methodologies*. Ad Hoc Working Group on Risk Assessment/ Risk Management. Crete: European Network and Information Security Agency (September).

ENISA. (2008). *Report on 4th ENISA CERT Workshop*. Athens: European Network and Information Security Agency (ENISA) (June).

ENISA. (2010). *Mapping Security Services to Authentication Levels: Reflection on STORK QAA Levels*. Heraklion, Greece: European Network and Information Security Agency.

Fox, C.A., and Epstein, M.S. (2010). *Why Is Enterprise Risk Management Important for Preparedness?* White Paper. New York: Risk Insurance Management Society, Inc.

French, G.S. (2007). Intelligence analysis for strategic risk assessments, pp. 12–24. In L. Jackson (Ed,), *Critical Infrastructure Protection: Elements of Risk*. Washington, DC, and Arlington, Virginia: School of Law, George Mason University.

Global Knowledge. (2010). Top 10 security concerns for cloud computing, pp. 1–2. https:// infosecisland.com/blogview/5300-Top-10-Security-Concerns-for-Cloud-Computing.html (accessed on 27th July, 2010). See: https://www.globalknowledge.com/us-en/resources/ resource-library/recorded-webinar/10-security-concerns-for-cloud-computing/#gref.

HSSAI. (2010). *Risk and Resilience: Exploring the Relationship*. Arlington, VI: Homeland Security Studies and Analysis Institute, Department of Homeland Security, Science and Technology Directorate (22nd November).

Huff, L., and Kelley, L. (2005). Is collectivism a liability? The impact of culture on organizational trust and customer orientation: A seven-nation study. *Journal of Business Research*, 58: 96–102.

IPO. (2009). *Crime Group: 2008–2009 IP Crime Report*. Newport: Intellectual Property Office (IPO).

ISO/FDIS (2009). *International Standard: Risk Management – Principles and Guidelines*. Reference Number ISO/FDIS 31000: 2009 (E). Geneva: ISO.

Kahan, J.H., Allen, A.C., and George, J.K. (2009). An operational framework for resilience. *Journal of Homeland Security and Emergency Management*, 6 (1): 1–48.

Kendrick, R. (2010). *Cyber Risks for Business Professionals*. Ely: IT Governance Publishing.

Le, N.T., and Hoang, D.B. (2016). Can maturity models support cyber security? *35th International Performance Computing and Communications Conference (IPCCC)*, pp. 1–7. Las Vegas, NV: IEEE (9th to 11th December). https://doi.org/10.1109/PCCC.2016.7820663.

Lee, J., and Lee, Y. (2002). A holistic model of computer abuse within organizations. *Information Management & Computer Security*, 10 (2): 57–63.

Martin, R.A. (2008). Making security measurable and manageable. Software Assurance Measurement Working Group. Department of Homeland Security/The MITRE Corporation. +http://buildsecurityin.us-cert.gov/swa/ecosystem.html (accessed on 1st December, 2011).

McAfee. (2011). *McAfee Threats Report: First Quarter 2011*. Santa Clara, CA: McAfee Labs.

McGill, W.L., and Ayyub, B.M. (2007). The meaning of vulnerability in the context of critical infrastructure protection, pp. 25–48. In L. Jackson (Ed,), *Critical Infrastructure Protection: Elements of Risk*. Washington, DC and Arlington, Virginia: School of Law, George Mason University.

Mont, M.C., and Brown, R. (2011). *Risk Assessment and Decision Support for Security Policies and Related Enterprise Operational Processes*. HPL-2011–12. Bristol: HP Laboratories, pp. 1–10. http:// www.hpl.hp.com/techreports/2011/HPL-2011-12.html (accessed on 14th September, 2011).

NIST. (2010). *Guide for Assessing the Security Controls in Federal Information Systems and Organizations: Building Effective Security Assessment Plans - Information Security Special Publication 800–53A Revision 1*. Gaithersburg, MD: National Institute of Standards and Technology, US Department of Commerce (June).

Petrie-Wyman, J., Rodi, A., and McConnell, R. (2021). Why should I behave? Addressing unethical cyber behavior through education. *Developments in Business Simulation and Experiential Learning*, 48: 162–179.

Quillinan, J. (2010). Austerity rules. *Financial Sector Technology*, 16 (4): 32–33.

Ralph, S. (2011). Situational awareness and advanced persistent threat agents. *Information Advisory Assurance Council (IAAC) Consumerisation of IT: Risk and Advanced Persistent Threat Agent Research Workshop*. Positioning Paper. London: BCS, The Chartered Institute for IT (6th December).

Rese, M. (2006). Successful and sustainable business partnerships: How to select the right partners. *Industrial Marketing Management*, 35: 72–82.

Rosch, V. (2010). Living the dream. *Financial Sector Technology*, 16 (4): 34–36.

Samani, R. (2011). Is it possible to control security in any cloud service? *Second International Secure Systems Development Conference: Designing in Security*. London: Hilton London Olympia Hotel (18th to 19th May).

Sheffi, Y. (2005). *The Resilient Enterprise: Overcoming Vulnerability for Competitive Advantage*. Cambridge: The MIT Press.

Someswar, K., Ramanujan, S., and Sridhar, N. (2002). A framework for analyzing e-commerce security. *Information Management & Computer Security*, 10 (4): 149–158.

Soo Hoo, K.J. (2000). *How Much Is Enough? A Risk Management Approach to Computer Security*. Stanford, CA: Consortium for Research on Information Security and Policy Working Paper, Stanford University (June). http://iis-db.stanford.edu/pubs/11900/soohoo.pdf (accessed on 14th September, 2011). See: https://fsi-live.s3.us-west-1.amazonaws.com/s3fs-public/soohoo.pdf.

Stouffer, K. (2005). NIST industrial control system security activities, pp. 1–12. *Proceedings of the ISA Expo*, Chicago, IL (25th to 27th October).

Strauss, A., and Corbin, J. (1998). *Basics of Qualitative Research: Techniques and Procedures for Developing Grounded Theory*. London: Sage.

Suh, T., and Kwon, I-W.G. (2006). Matter over mind: When specific asset investment affects calculative trust in supply chain partnership. *Industrial Marketing Management*, 35: 191–201.

Swanson, M., Bartol, N., and Moorthy, R. (2010). *Piloting Supply Chain Risk Management: Practices for Federal Information Systems*. Draft NISTIR 7622. U.S. Department of Commerce, Gaithersburg, MD: NIST (National Institute of Standards and Technology) (June).

Symantec. (2010). *Symantec Global Internet Security Threat Report: Trends for 2009. Volume XV*. Mountain View, CA: Symantec Corporation (April).

Taylor, C., Krings, A., and Alves-Foss, J. (2002). Risk analysis and probabilistic survivability assessment (RAPSA): An assessment approach for power substation hardening. Moscow, ID: University of Idaho, pp. 1–10. http://www2.csuidaho.edu/-krings/publications/SACT-2002-T (accessed on 14th September, 2011). See: https://www.academia.edu/4528115/Risk_Analysis_and_Probabilistic_Survivability_Assessment_RAPSA_An_Assessment_Approach_for_Power_Substation_Hardening1.

Trim, P.R.J. (2004). The strategic corporate intelligence and transformational marketing model. *Marketing Intelligence and Planning*, 22 (2): 240–256.

Trim, P.R.J. (2005a). The GISES model for counteracting organized crime and international terrorism. *International Journal of Intelligence and CounterIntelligence*, 18 (3): 451–472.

Trim, P.R.J. (2005b). Managing computer security issues: Preventing and limiting future threats and disasters. *Disaster Prevention and Management*, 14 (4): 493–505.

Trim, P.R.J., and Lee, Y-I. (2010). A security framework for protecting business, government and society from cyber attacks, pp. 1–6. *5th IEEE International Conference on System of Systems (SoSE): Sustainable Systems for the 21st Century*, Loughborough University (22nd to 24th June).

Trim, P.R.J., and Lee, Y-I. (2011). Cyber social science and information assurance: A generic cyber security management model (GCSMM). Poster paper presentation: *The IAAC Symposium: Information Assurance: Meeting Challenges of Changing Times*. London: College of Physicians (7th September).

Trim, P.R.J., and Lee, Y-I. (2014). *Cyber Security Management: A Governance, Risk and Compliance Framework.* Farnham: Gower Publishing.

Trim, P.R.J., and Lee, Y-I. (2021). The Global Cyber Security Model: Counteracting cyber attacks through a resilient partnership arrangement. *Big Data and Cognitive Computing*, 5(3): 1–17, 32. https://doi.org/10.3390/bdcc5030032.

United States Government Accountability Office (2007). *Cybercrime: Public and Private Entities Face Challenges in Addressing Cyber Threats.* GAO-07–705. Washington, DC: GAO.

Wang, J., Neil, M., and Fenton, N.A. (2020). Bayesian network approach for cybersecurity risk assessment implementing and extending the FAIR model. *Computers & Society*, 89: 1–20. https://doi.org/10.1016/j.cose.2019.101659.

Windahl, C., and Lakemond, N. (2006). Developing integrated solutions: The importance of relationships within the network. *Industrial Marketing Management*, 35: 806–818.

Wucherer, K. (2006). Business partnering – A driving force for innovation. *Industrial Marketing Management*, 35: 91–102.

Television Programme

Yesterday Television Channel (2010). Pornography – A Secret History of Civilisation, 9th August, 11pm to 12pm.

Website Addresses

Atlantic Council (2021). British Intell Chief: "Cyberspace is contested every day, every hour, every minute, every second". https://www.atlanticcouncil.org/blogs/natosource/british-intell-chief-cyberspace-is-contested-every-day-every-hour-every-minute-very-second/ (accessed on 4th October, 2021).

Council of Europe (2001). *Convention on Cybercrime, European Treaty Series No. 185.* Budapest, 23.XI.2001. https://rm.coe.int/1680081561 (accessed on 1st October, 2021).

Specops Software (2021). The countries experiencing the most 'significant' cyber-attacks. https://specopssoft.com/blog/countries-experiencing-significant-cyber-attacks/ (accessed on 1st October, 2021).

5.15 Further Reading

Booz, Allen and Hamilton. (2009). *Cyber In-Security: Strengthening the Federal Cybersecurity Workforce.* Washington, DC: Booz, Allen and Hamilton.

Romanosky, S. (2016). Examining the costs and causes of cyber incidents. *Journal of Cybersecurity*, 2 (2): 121–135.

Someswar, K., Ramanujan, S., and Sridhar, N. (2002). A framework for analyzing e-commerce security. *Information Management & Computer Security*, 10 (4): 149–158.

Trim, P.R.J., and Lee, Y-I. (2021). The Global Cyber Security Model: Counteracting cyber attacks through a resilient partnership arrangement. *Big Data and Cognitive Computing*, 5(3): 1–17, 32. https://doi.org/10.3390/bdcc5030032.

Turner, B.A. (2006). The organization and interorganizational development of disasters, pp. 115–135. In D. Smith and D. Elliott (Eds.), *Key Readings in Crisis Management: Systems and Structures for Prevention and Recovery.* London: Routledge.

5.16 Bank of Questions

Question 1: Identify five types of cyber threat and rank each threat in order of importance.

Question 2: Explain what a cyber threat analysis is composed of.

Question 3: Which factors should a cyber security manager include in a strategic risk assessment framework?

Question 4: The enterprise risk management approach is over complicated and cannot be used in practice. Critically appraise this view and provide examples to reinforce your arguments.

Question 5: Explain how a risk assessment policy can be integrated into the management decision-making process.

Question 6: Design a cyber security management model and explain how it will be implemented.

6 Governance and Compliance Decision Making

6.1 Introduction

An effective organizational strategic governance framework needs to incorporate a set of procedures, plans and systems, which allow the cyber security manager to identify where a cyber attack was launched from, initiate an appropriate response and liaise with appropriate in-house and external personnel, to make sure that the attack is publicized as much as possible. Because cyber attacks are launched from various parts of the world and can impact an organization at any time, it is essential that a cyber attack is registered so that various government bodies and agencies can be informed of the trend that is occurring. Through the process of sharing cyber threat intelligence, the cyber security manager and senior management can establish appropriate management, organizational and structural responses and ensure that if a cyber attack impacts the organization, the damage is contained.

The fact that cyber attacks are becoming more sophisticated places emphasis on the cyber security manager recording full details in the organization's memory so that the cyber attack countermeasures that are in place throughout the partnership arrangement can be managed proactively and scrutinized by outside experts/auditors. This again focuses attention on the fact that in order to have appropriate countermeasures in place, staff need to be both aware of the various types of cyber attack launched on an organization and have the appropriate knowledge and skill base (Baker, 2010) to actively repost the attack. The cyber security knowledge and skills needed to repost an attack can be defined in terms of knowledge relating to system forensics; network forensics; deep pocket installations; Windows; UNIX; PDA defence configurations; log analysis; script development; exploitation and penetration testing; service coding; reverse engineering and counterintelligence (Paller, 2010).

The chapter is constructed in the following way. First, attention is given to the learning objectives (Section 6.2) and this is followed by placing corporate governance in context (Section 6.3). The human dimension is given attention (Section 6.4) and so too is information security governance (Section 6.5). Learning from the past (Section 6.6) is followed by a learning summary (Section 6.7), and a conclusion (Section 6.8). A mini case is provided (Section 6.9), which is followed by an extended case (Section 6.10), a set of references (Section 6.11), further reading (Section 6.12) and a bank of questions (Section 6.13).

DOI: 10.4324/9781003244295-6

6.2 Learning Objectives

The reader will:

- establish why governance is placed in a specific business context; and
- establish the importance and need for compliance.

6.3 Placing Corporate Governance in Context

According to Kendrick (2010: 20–21), corporate governance represents "a business strategy based upon transparent decision making; the establishment of lines of account-ability and responsibility; securing shareholder and stakeholder value; and the adoption of sound risk management strategies, including information security". Kendrick (2010: 21–22) continues by saying that "IT governance is a subset of corporate governance" and suggests that a risk manager can be appointed to head a Risk Management Team. The risk manager has a specific role to play and can work with the cyber security manager, who is also accountable for governance and compliance in relation to cyber security, and who reports to senior management.

Fahy et al. (2005: 2) suggest that "Enterprise Governance is based on the principle that good governance alone cannot make an organisation successful". In other words, the cyber security manager should integrate security more firmly into the strategic management process of the organization and ensure that the governance process is taken into consideration. The Generic Cyber Security Management Model (GCSMM) (Trim and Lee, 2010: 5) can prove useful as it explains the importance of the link and coop-eration between commerce and industry, government and academia, thus allowing the development of resilient management systems and processes.

In order to ensure that governance and compliance are thought of in unison, it is important for the cyber security manager to link organizational resilience with corporate governance. A starting point for this is to place the development of an organization's cyber security strategy within the context of three interlinked circles representing (Trim and Lee, 2010: 5) (i) the external environment; (ii) risk assess-ment which is embedded within the organization's strategic value system and (iii) the integration of security within the organization's functions and an emerging security culture within the organization. This should achieve the objective of linking the organization's cyber security strategy with the organization's ability to develop its cyber security capability through time. By integrating security with intelligence, and other functional areas, it is possible to embrace more effectively the GISES (Global Intelligence and Security Environmental Sustainability) model (Trim, 2005) and to link the GISES model with the SATELLITE (Strategic Corporate Intelligence and Transformational Marketing) model (Trim, 2004). The intelligence-oriented and multi-disciplinary security approach embedded in these models should enable the risk manager, in consultation with the cyber security manager, and various colleagues such as the assistant risk manager, to link corporate security with strategic corporate intelligence, and to provide the necessary stimulation for the development of a secu-rity culture within the partnership arrangement. Trim and Lee (2010: 4) suggest that:

> by integrating security more firmly into the organization's structure, it should be possible to reduce the organization's level of risk and facilitate information sharing.

Information sharing should enhance co-operation between partner organizations and add to the defensive capability vis-à-vis establishing effective counter-cyber attack measures.

As regards new and emerging business models, senior management need to establish formal organizational structures and policies that improve the process of governance, and although networks may be considered reasonably secure, the main vulnerability is in the application layer and Stuxnet is a good example of what has been termed a cyber weapon, because it infiltrated networks and became a worm (Barnell, 2011). Such attacks can prove devastating and the disruption caused can last a long period of time. Bearing in mind that top management are concerned with how the organization performs, the cyber security manager can use the Enterprise Governance model as it incorporates three relevant dimensions: (1) performance; (2) conformance and (3) corporate responsibility (Fahy et al., 2005: 2–10). The model can be adopted to measure how efficient the organization is. For example, performance is measured in terms of how well an organization does in terms of systems, people and processes, in creating value for shareholders. As regards conformance, of key interest here is corporate accountability and how well management do in terms of regulatory codes, corporate legislation and accounting standards. Corporate governance addresses five main areas: risk management and internal controls; corporate culture; stewardship and accountability; board operations and composition; and monitoring and evaluation of activities. As regards corporate responsibility, it is clear that six main areas are addressed: managing/reducing environmental, societal and cultural impact; protecting intangible assets such as reputation; promoting best practice vis-à-vis corporate ethics and governance; engaging in risk management; establishing traceability in supply chain management and procurement; and enhancing employee motivation and productivity (Fahy et al., 2005: 7–8).

According to Sharman and Copnell (Fahy et al., 2005), those involved in corporate governance need to take into account the effectiveness of management structures, the role that the directors play, the accuracy of corporate reporting and understanding the effectiveness of risk management systems. This leads to the view that corporate governance "is the systems and processes put in place to direct and control an organisation in order to increase performance and achieve sustainable shareholder value" (Fahy et al., 2005: 161). The key elements to note are strategy, stewardship, corporate culture, corporate reporting, IT systems and board operation; and because of this compliance can be defined as "a measurement of responsibility to the stakeholder, the environment and the community. Business leaders must be prepared to demonstrate and explain their social contribution on training, employment, income generation, wealth creation, innovation, and supply chain development" (Fahy et al., 2005: 231).

There are also a number of different and emerging business models in place, which exhibit different characteristics. According to Quillinan (2010: 32), cloud computing will "revolutionise traditional outsourcing models"; therefore, the cyber security manager needs to ensure that the cyber security awareness programmes in place provide continual cyber security awareness so that staff in partner organizations adhere to the regulatory controls in place and the partner organizations are compliant. This means that attention has to be given to the security controls that are in place. Security controls that are deployed in an information system provide valuable information with regard to protecting organizational assets, and senior management need to "place risk mitigation within a security management framework and process" (NIST, 2010: 1). The cryptographic modules and information technology products to be tested, evaluated and validated include (NIST, 2010: 4) "operating systems, database systems, firewalls, intrusion detection devices, Web browsers, Web applications, smart cards, biometrics devices, personal identity verification devices, network devices, and hardware platforms using national and international standards".

In order to have an all-round appreciation of what cyber security involves, the cyber security manager can use scenario planning and business continuity planning, to facilitate thinking and develop different perspectives in relation to disaster planning and recovery. In addition, the "system of systems" approach outlined by Stouffer (2005: 7) is gaining acceptance as a means of understanding the complexities associated with how the interdependencies between industrial sectors need to be viewed, for example: "Critical infrastructures are highly interconnected and mutually dependent in complex ways, both physically and through a host of information and communications technologies. What happens to one infrastructure can directly and indirectly affect other infrastructures through cascading and escalating failures".

Stouffer (2005) indicates that management need to think in terms of operational and technical security controls (countermeasures) as this is a means of mitigating the risk associated with vulnerabilities identified. As regards devising a risk management strategy, senior managers need to (NIST, 2009: 13–14):

1 categorize information systems, and then select the security controls;
2 implement the security controls;
3 assess the security controls;
4 authorize the information systems; and
5 monitor the security controls, and then categorize information systems, all of which is encapsulated within a risk management framework.

The person in-charge of internal security is known as the Head of Security and the person in-charge of external security is the Director of Corporate Intelligence. The Head of Security reports to the Director of Corporate Intelligence and has their own department or liaises with external organizations that can provide specialist data and information, when hired to do so. This is supportive of the view put forward by Fox and Epstein (2010: 3) who advocate the Enterprise Risk Management (ERM) concept, which is viewed as context-specific and can be used by the cyber security manager to develop the organization's risk management policy and an understanding of what the organization can tolerate in the way of risk, and how risk can be related to the organization's goals and objectives. The ERM model indicates how important environmental and intelligence scanning is and can be used to establish a formalized scanning operation that identifies internal organizational vulnerabilities. It can also help the cyber security manager and the risk manager to prioritize and quantify risks that are identified through scenario planning. The main objective of which is to produce a number of appropriate cyber security contingency plans, which can be implemented when circumstances demand.

Taking these points into account and understanding that it is not possible to transfer risk, the cyber security manager needs to think in terms of making the nodes in the organization's supply chain (e.g. suppliers) more resilient than they are. To achieve this, it is necessary to think in terms of what constitutes a successful and sustainable partnership arrangement. This is because a supplier that does not implement a cyber security strategy is likely to be open to attack and once breached could make the other organizations in its network vulnerable to further attack. Therefore, the conceptual sustainable partnership development (SPD) model, which has at its core, Monitoring and Evaluation, is useful as it can help the cyber security manager to adopt a strategic intelligence focus (Trim and Lee, 2008). In order for the cyber security manager to become a strategic thinker, it is necessary to adopt and work with an appropriate strategic marketing intelligence framework as this will provide an opportunity to identify information needs and gaps, and share information that facilitates the development and utilization of knowledge (Trim and Lee, 2007: 61). In order that the cyber security manager and influential peers, such as the risk manager, have a positive input into the strategic intelligence process, strategic thinking must be both formalized and holistic, and there must be strong working relationships with staff in all the business functions. For example, staff based in the corporate legal department and in the information systems and technology department are involved in intelligence and security work, and contribute to the counterintelligence decision-making process. Furthermore, staff employed by various external organizations (e.g. trade associations, chambers of commerce and industry, government departments and law enforcement agencies) as well as external experts are all sources of intelligence and can be viewed as stakeholders.

The cyber security manager needs to keep up-to-date in terms of operational security issues and situational awareness vis-à-vis placing strategic intelligence within a cyber security context. By understanding how the main components of an e-commerce system (e-commerce development platforms, database management systems, operating systems and infrastructure) are structured and linked, staff can assist the cyber security manager in terms of deepening their understanding of the relationship between technology(ies) and tools (Someswar et al., 2002: 154–156).

By linking organizational resilience with corporate governance, the cyber security manager can better appreciate how performance, conformance and corporate responsibility (Fahy et al., 2005) are integrated with the people, processes and systems approach. However, in order to achieve the security objectives set, it is necessary for the cyber security manager to re-evaluate the organization's security priorities and to place cyber security in the context of a partnership arrangement, in terms of all the partner organizations being compliant and adhering to strict codes of governance. This means placing governance and compliance within a partner organization's resilience policy and placing resilience in a stakeholder or community context. Should this be the case, each organization's risk communication strategy will be linked with and implemented in terms of the main partner organization's risk communication strategy. But this can only be achieved, however, if the cyber security manager has undertaken an adequate threats analysis and is backed up by senior management as regards investing resources to make the organization as robust as possible.

6.4 The Human Dimension

In an interconnected world, international cooperation involving sharing information relating to cyber issues is crucial because: "Without such cooperation, our collective ability to detect, deter, and minimize the effects of cyber-based attacks would be greatly diminished" (The White House, 2003: 8). This suggests that when looking at the issue of cyber security from a stakeholder perspective, the cyber security manager needs to place much emphasis on the human factor and work closely with the training manager to make sure that staff undertake an appropriate cyber security training programme that is designed to equip staff with an all-round cyber security defence capability so that the organization can achieve sustainability. It is because of this that senior management need to think more deeply about compliance and the fact that "Compliance is now a measurement of responsibility to the stakeholder, the environment and the community" (Fahy et al., 2005: 231).

What top management need to understand is that as an organization becomes more connected, it will become more "net-centric". The Defense Science Board (2009: ix) has provided an insight into what becoming "net-centric" involves:

> This entails networking many different sources of sensor and informational data with multiple processing nodes and geographically distributed users to achieve unprecedented levels of situational awareness, data distribution, and operational coordination. Net-centric operations bring both an increase in capability as well as increased dependence on the viability of the network. Thus, new vulnerabilities are created.

The Centre for the Protection of National Infrastructure (CPNI) have done much to improve governance; for example, the HoMER (Holistic Management of Employee Risk) approach offers guidance and advice to senior management regarding how the risk associated with employees can be reduced. For example (CPNI, 2012a):

> HoMER is an interactive guidance document designed to help organisations manage these risks. The guidance provides examples of good practice principles, policies and procedures, backed up by case studies. The guidance will help organisations build effective countermeasures, and respond to and recover from incidents when they occur. HoMER is aimed at board members and other owners of people risk and shows users the steps that can be taken to change their organisation's approach to personnel security. Through creating a positive culture supported by strong corporate governance and a fair, compliant and transparent legal framework, an organisation can successfully prevent, protect and manage employee risk.

CPNI (2012b) advises:

> Risk of damage from the actions of employees or contractors working on your behalf. Most incidents stem from errors or omissions but there is also a threat of malicious activity including, in extreme cases, actions by criminals, terrorists or foreign powers.........HoMER provides guidance or organizational governance, security culture, and controls to help you mitigate people risk. The key elements of HoMER are:
>
> • Take a risk-based approach
> • Manage people risk holistically
> • Develop the security culture needed by the business
> • Appoint a senior single owner of people risk
> • Act in an ethical, legal and transparent manner.

The cyber security manager will be involved in the formation of human relations policy and can champion the need for strategic intelligence. The strategic intelligence process will, because of the complexities involved, need to be overseen by a steering committee that advises and regulates the work of those undertaking intelligence-gathering activities (Trim, 2001a: 351). Furthermore, the age-old argument that national intelligence is the prerogative of the state (Shpiro, 1998: 545–546) is justified but because organizations, and commercial companies in particular, are being increasingly subjected to cyber attacks orchestrated by government agencies intent on acts of industrial espionage, it can be argued that the concept of corporate intelligence needs to be reviewed so that the cyber security manager considers it to be

> the acquisition of knowledge using human, electronic and other means, and the interpretation of knowledge relating to the environments, both internal and external, in which the organization operates. It provides selected staff within the organization with up-to-date and accurate information, which allows strategists to develop and implement policy so that the organization maintains and/or gains a competitive advantage in the marketplace. It also provides a mechanism for implementing counter-intelligence measures to safeguard corporate data and secrets
>
> (Trim, 2001b: 54–55)

6.5 Information Security Governance

Shurson (2020: 167) is of the view that there is a need to protect peoples' data but at the same time law enforcement authorities need to access data because it represents evidence. West (2010: 2) has suggested that: "Countries need to harmonize their laws on cloud computing so as to reduce current inconsistencies in regard to privacy, data storage, security processes, and personnel training". For example, West (2010: 3) has noted that there are times when "courts often support greater privacy rights with local rather than remote file storage......Potential security problems need to be addressed, but sometimes this involves increasing the level of real or imagined privacy threats... the lack of uniformity in standards across nations". This is also of concern and it means that the cyber security manager is required to pay attention to issues relating to privacy, security, storage and accessibility, for example.

The cyber security manager needs to take cognizance of what is going on in specific countries that the organization is doing business in or wishes to enter. For example, some governments have taken direct action to disconnect the digital networks in their country. Since 1995, 99 countries have been involved in 606 unique incidents that actually resulted in disconnected Internet exchange points or if they did not go that far instead, they blocked significant amounts of traffic from entering the country's networks (Howard et al., 2011: 1). The reasons for such action varied from political actions to social actions but were classified in terms of safeguarding the public. Howard et al. (2011: 7) state:

> The lasting impact of a temporary disconnection in Internet service may actually be a strengthening of weak ties between global and local civil society networks. When civil society disappears from the grid, it is noticed. What lasts are the ties between a nation's civic groups, and between international non-governmental organizations and like-minded, in-country organizations. Certainly not all of these virtual communities are about elections, but their existence is a political phenomenon -particularly in countries where state and social elites have worked

hard to police offline communities. Thus, even the bulletin boards and chat rooms dedicated to shopping for brand name watches are sites that practice free speech and where the defense of free speech can become a topic of conversation. The Internet allows opposition movements that are based outside of a country to reach in and become part of the system of political communication within even the strictest authoritarian regimes. Today, banning political parties could simply mean that formal political opposition is now organized online, from outside the country. It could also mean that civil society leaders turn to other organizational forms permitted by the network technologies. When states disconnect particular social media services, student and civil society leaders develop creative workarounds and relearn traditional (offline) mobilization tactics. This almost always means that target sites, such as YouTube, Facebook, and Twitter, are accessible through other means.

The findings of *Global Risks*, a report produced by the World Economic Forum (2012), and which drew on the expertise of 469 experts and industry leaders, suggest that if there was a cyber disruption that caused cascading failures of critical infrastructures and networks, then a critical systems failure could occur that undermined global governance. Conner and Coviello (2003) suggest that cyber security needs to be a prerogative of people at the apex of the organization and corporate governance includes information security governance. Acknowledging that organizations are diverse, it is suggested that management need to think of developing an approach to information security governance that is considered appropriate for the organization. This is a valid argument because Kim and Mauborgne (2005: 18) suggest that managers need to be aware of the difference between conventional thinking as defined by a Red Ocean Strategy (compete in existing market space, beat the competition, exploit existing demand, make the value–cost trade–off and align the whole system of a firm's activities with its strategic choice of differentiation or low cost) and a holistic view that incorporates the Blue Ocean Strategy perspective (create uncontested market space, make the competition irrelevant, create and capture new demand, break the value–cost trade–off and align the whole system of a firm's activities in pursuit of differentiation and low cost).

Conner and Coviello (2003: 20) have mapped out the responsibilities and functional roles associated with information security governance. It is clear from their analysis that the chief executive officer has the responsibility for corporate security and is held accountable by the board. The organization's security policy, procedures and training are under the control of the chief security officer, the chief information officer and the chief risk officer, for example. It is their duty to respond to known security breaches and audits (e.g. in relation to compliance). Mid-level managers are responsible for sanctioning the audits that take place and communicate policies and manage training programmes. Managers are held responsible for reporting on matters of security and reporting vulnerabilities and breaches, and this is organization-specific. It can be argued that organizational learning is fundamental in terms of developing a corporate governance mentality within an organization but the appropriate management structure, processes and systems need to be in place for this to produce the desired results.

Bearing these points in mind, once a security culture has been established, appropriate behaviour can be maintained through a security awareness programme that is reinforced through an appropriate cyber security policy. Advice has been provided

Devise an inventory of devices that are connected to the organization's network to ensure that only authorized personnel are using the equipment and networks; list all authorized software and monitor for unauthorized software; prevent attackers from exploiting the organization's services and settings vis-a-vis access through networks and browsers; run automated vulnerability scanning tools to check for system vulnerabilities and fix problems identified within 48 hours; deploy automated anti-virus and anti-spyware software to monitor and protect workstations and all types of devices; deploy web application firewalls; allow wireless devices to connect to the network provided that they conform to authorised configurations; remove all traces of an attack by automatically backing up all the information; devise a security skills assessment programme and map training against the skills needed; match the configurations against standards for each type of network device; only allow legitimate users to have remote access to devices and networks; enforce the use of robust passwords that conform to Federal Desktop Core Configuration (FDCC) standards; put in place multilayered boundary defence (eg., firewalls, proxies demilitarised zone (DMZ) perimeter networks); use detailed logs to both identify and uncover an attack; do not allow an attacker to gain access to highly sensitive data (eg., put in place a multilevel data classification scheme and ensure that only authenticated users are given access to nonpublic data and files); ensure that attackers do not impersonate legitimate users; disable business accounts that are not associated with a business process and owner, and encrypt and files associated with such accounts; prevent the unauthorised transfer of sensitive data through the organization's networks that is drived from attacks and physical theft; develop and implement an incident response plan that delineates roles and responsibilities; use a secure network engineering process in order to prevent security controls from being circumvented; and carry-out regular penetration tests so that vulnerabilities can be identified and rectified.

Figure 6.1 Limiting the possibility of a data/information breach.

regarding this. Please see Figure 6.1, limiting the possibility of a data/information breach (CPNI/SANS, 2012).

6.6 Learning from the Past

The insider threat is of concern to the cyber security manager and the work of Randazzo et al. (2004: 1–2) entitled "Insider Threat Study: Illicit Cyber Activity in the Banking and Finance Sector" can be considered informative as regards the variety of insider acts that occur, including employees altering credit reports, changing data in trading systems and implementing a "logic bomb" that deletes files. Randazzo et al. (2004: 4) state:

> The overall goal of the collaborative effort is to develop information and tools that can help private industry, government, and law enforcement identify cyber security issues that can impact physical or operational security and to assess potential threats to, and vulnerabilities in, data and critical systems.

When studying what an insider may have done and the damage caused, it is useful to think in terms of (Randazzo et al., 2004: 4):

1   components of the incident
2   detection of the incident and identification of the insider
3   pre-incident planning and communication
4   nature of harm to the organization
5   law enforcement and organizational response
6   characteristics of the insider and the organization
7   insider background and history
8   insider technical expertise and interests.

Randazzo et al. (2004: 10–20) revealed that as regards 81% of the incidents, the insiders knew what they were going to do as they had planned it in advance of committing the act. It was also found that a high percentage of detection was by individuals not involved in security (61%) and just over one-third of the incidents were reported by customers. It was also noted that a high percentage of the insider attacks originated at the office during normal working hours and went undetected by co-workers. Conrades (2004: 9) has called for more education and awareness regarding the Internet and its use, and has championed the need for education in order that a common level of security understanding is achieved among software developers and in particular that security education is made more accessible. A number of initiatives can be implemented to guard against the actions of insiders. These include sensors in networks that monitor computer usage and security alerts in the form of messages that are sent to individual managers.

Governance and compliance will receive more attention in the years ahead due to the fact that the cyber security manager is required to know about the law and how to keep people's data secure. For example, the UK Data Protection Act 2018 requires an organization to store people's data in a certain way and to safeguard it through encryption (https://www.gov.uk/data-protection). An organization is required to employ a Data Protection Officer (DPO) that can be contacted by an individual in terms of data that the organization holds about them. Data should only be kept for a certain period of time and a data breach is likely to result in a fine (imposed by the Information Commissioner's Office) and result in adverse publicity for the organization. An organization is expected to have a Data Protection Plan in place and GDPR (General Data Protection Regulation) applies to EU countries and provides individuals with more control over their data and the safeguarding of it.

6.7 Learning Summary

Strategic cyber intelligence and security governance as outlined in Figure 6.2 makes clear the fact that security controls need to be in place if, i.e., the organization is to be compliant. The management structures devised are required to provide a basis for a security culture to be established, which is underpinned by a commitment to organizational learning. By having appropriate governance, trust will be established with stakeholders and this will ensure that the commitment to resilience is maintained. Again, risk management is viewed as playing a key role and so too is risk communication, which helps to maintain trust-based relationships with stakeholders.

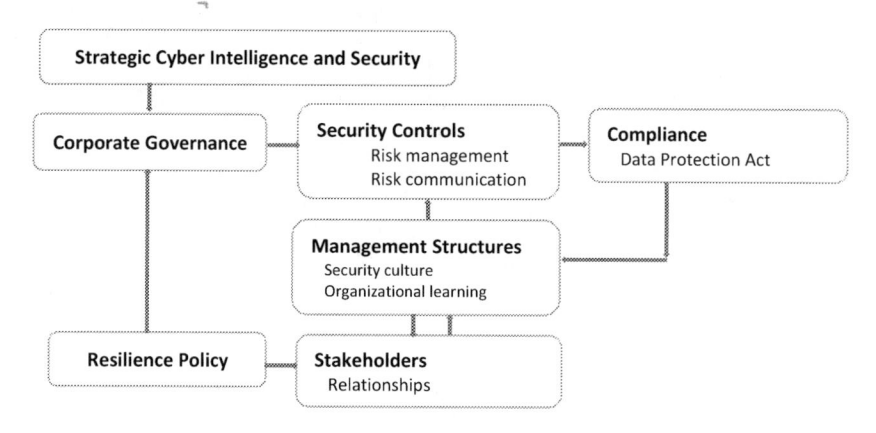

Figure 6.2 Strategic cyber intelligence and security governance.

The reader is able to:

- develop a cyber security governance policy and strategy;
- develop a cyber security compliance policy and strategy;
- implement a cyber security governance policy and strategy; and
- implement a cyber security compliance policy and strategy;

6.8 Conclusion

The cyber security manager is ideally placed to play a pivotal role in terms of developing and implementing a governance and compliance framework throughout the partnership arrangement. What needs to be remembered is that governance and compliance are continual processes and require the constant monitoring of data and information, with attention being given to how it is managed, stored and utilized. In order to safeguard data, the laws in place need to be adhered to and regular audits undertaken to make sure that the systems in place are up to the required security standard. Should staff lack relevant knowledge and skills in terms of how data is acquired and kept safe, then they will need to attend bespoke training sessions so that they can upgrade their skill base and comply with the regulations in place.

6.9 Mini Case: Cyber Security Governance

For some time now, there had been a debate within the company regarding what an appropriate cyber security governance policy would be composed of. It was accepted that governance in general was about systems and mechanisms that ensured that staff within the company acted within the rules laid down by top management when making decisions and liaising with stakeholders. Jason Monday, the head of corporate affairs, had been asked by the managing director of the company, Jack Faraday, to extend the company's governance mission statement and policy, by incorporating cyber security and making the policy as integrative as possible.

Jason Monday considered it useful to read the paper by Rossouw de Bruin and S.H. von Soloms (2016), which he had come across recently. The authors highlighted the fact that there was a link between cyber security and information security and suggested that ISO 27032: 2020 was highly relevant and that "Cybersecurity appropriately lives within Information Security and the security principles are the same – only the way in which they are implemented differs" (de Bruin and von Solms, 2016: 3). Building on their earlier work (de Bruin and von Solms, 2015), which featured a cyber security governance maturity model that was used to assess an organization's cyber security in terms of capability, contingency, capacity building, conformance and threat, the proposed model was extended to include seven aspects, with the additional components being legal aspects and ethics (de Bruin and von Solms, 2016: 5–6). This extended view suggests that there is a direct connection between capacity building and ethics, and that the human resource management department was central to this as viewed from the perspectives of improving the skill sets of individual staff and creating cyber security awareness. The legal aspects that emerged could be passed on to the legal department and this would result in management putting the necessary cyber security legal requirements in place.

Mr. Monday considered that the advice provided by the authors was to be welcomed as it appeared that a collectivist approach to cyber security was being championed. The fact that auditing and reporting were covered suggested that responsibilities had been assigned and people would be held accountable for their actions. Just what was needed he thought.

Questions

Question 1: Who in the organization should be involved in establishing a cyber security governance policy?

Question 2: What are the main benefits of implementing a cyber security governance policy?

Question 3: How will a cyber security governance policy be updated through time?

Case Sources

de Bruin, R., and von Solms, S.H. (2015). Modelling Cyber security governance maturity. 2015 IEEE international Symposium on Technology and Society (ISTAS). IEEE: Dubin, Ireland (11th to 12th November), pp. 1–8. https://doi.org/10.1109.ISTAS.2015.7439415.
de Bruin, R., and von Solms, S.H. (2016). Cyber security governance: How can we measure it? 2016 IST-Africa Week Conference. IEEE: Durban, South Africa (11th to 13th May), pp. 1–9. https://doi.org/10.1109/ISTAFRICA.2016.7530578.

6.10 Extended Case: Ensuring that Staff Are Compliant

Facilitating technology such as the Internet is providing a basis from which companies can increase their global reach but at the same time it is putting managers under pressure because the new business models evolving require additional management skills and knowledge. Evidence of this can be seen in the fact that as computer hackers become more knowledgeable and share their knowledge and successes with fellow hackers online, they become adept at planning, implementing and refocusing an attack on a target company. Hacking software, handbooks and individuals offering their services for a fee are available to assist and provide support to those carrying out sophisticated cyber attacks, often interpreted as Advanced Persistent Threats (APTs). The fact that some organized criminal groups have a research and development unit, have access to computer and legal services, and can move and set up operations in various parts of the world in a short period of time, means that some hackers/groups of hackers are going to become even more innovative in the years ahead as companies and law enforcement officers play catch up, and try and solve recurring problems by working together.

As well as establishing a security culture that places emphasis on risk management and staff being able to carry out risk assessments and deploy effective risk analysis, senior management need to ensure that the cyber security structures and systems in place are maintained through time. This is because a cyber attack on an organization, if successful, may not be detected until some months later or may not be detected at all. Those carrying out an attack may either penetrate a computer system and remove data or copy the data only. As regards the latter, the emphasis is to be undetected so that it is possible to revisit the organization at a later date. If an organization has suffered a breach and does not know or knows but does not report it, then what are the potential consequences for partner organizations and customers? At present, senior managers are aware that it is almost impossible to stop a certain type of attack getting through so they are concentrating attention on preventing the intruder from taking away the data.

The General Data Protection Regulation (GDPR) is comprehensive in terms of detailing an organization's responsibility in terms of collecting, securing and using the personal data of individuals. Bearing in mind people need to provide consent about handing over their data and also can ask for their data to be updated or erased suggests that the onus as regards data protection is firmly in the hands of the organization that utilizes it. Because of this, companies that maintain extensive databases (e.g. personal data relating to customers and their purchases) are required to conform to strict legal guidelines so that the data does not fall into the wrong hands or is used in a harmful way and as a result an individual suffers some kind of discomfort. Emphasis is now placed on an organization that holds personal data to undertake Data Protection Impact Assessments and guidance has been given about this (Information Commissioner's Office, 2018: 146):

> A Data Protection Impact Assessment (DPIA) is a process to help you identify and minimise the data protection risks of a project. You must do a DPIA for processing that is likely to result in a high risk to individuals. This includes some specified types of processing. You can use our screening checklists to help you decide when to do a DPIA. It is also good practice to do a DPIA for any other major project which requires the processing of personal data. Your DPIA must: describe the nature, scope, context and purposes of the processing; assess necessity, proportionality and compliance measures; identify and assess risks to individuals; and identify any additional measures to mitigate those risks. To assess the level of risk, you must consider both the likelihood and the severity of any impact on individuals. High risk could result from either a high probability of some harm, or a lower possibility of serious harm. You should consult your data protection officer (if you have one) and, where appropriate, individuals and relevant experts. Any processors may also need to assist you. If you identify a high risk that you cannot mitigate, you must

consult the ICO before starting the processing. The ICO will give written advice within eight weeks, or 14 weeks in complex cases. If appropriate, we may issue a formal warning not to process the data, or ban the processing altogether.

The Information Assurance Advisory Council (IAAC) has done much over the years to promote cyber security awareness among a wide public and various research initiatives and papers produced by IAAC and various researchers associated with IAAC have reinforced the approach. One of the issues addressed is changing work patterns and the consequences of utilizing new forms of technology and technological device (Trim et al., 2012). It is known that various companies were keen to reduce cost and have allowed their staff to benefit from BYOD (Bring Your Own Device) (e.g. laptop) to work and also utilize the same device at home. Taking into account the number of personal devices that are lost or gone missing, and also the fact that the data on some of these devices is not protected; it does of course raise issues about the protection of data and the consequences associated with the loss of the data. Some individuals that find a lost device may try and sell it or sell the data that they uncover if the files are not password protected or encrypted. As well as laptops that go missing, it can be suggested that Kindles, various types of phone and USB sticks are also lost. What becomes clear, therefore, is that the risk of data loss is not associated with the actions only of outside hackers, but an internal member of staff, who does not adhere to the security guidelines laid down, is also the source of data loss. Having said this, it should be noted that individuals can and do try to ensure that they stay within the guidelines provided by the company they work for but may make an error of judgement or may misplace a device or a document containing sensitive information.

Some companies do not allow laptop devices to be taken off the premises and require that they are locked in a secure cabinet when not in use. Additionally, they require that people from outside the company go through a strict security procedure when they enter the company's premises, and this means that they are asked to declare if they have a laptop or a data stick or other device that can record and send messages. Visitors are required to complete forms and hand in such devices and collect them when they leave. In a high security environment, an outsider may even be asked to show personal identification such as a passport and have their photograph taken and stored in the organization's computer security system, for example.

Security management software can be installed on a device and this allows the company to track where an individual is and where they go. This may be useful if, for example, staff are disgruntled and data and information have been known to be leaked to a competitor. This can happen if a staff member is applying for a job with another company or has already accepted an offer of employment with the company concerned. As well as tracking an individual and monitoring where they go, it is possible to wipe the files on a device through remote action and also operate a remote lock so that the data on the device cannot be accessed. Another point to be made is that staff should be advised not to pick up a laptop or data stick or other device that does not belong to them. It has been known for infected data sticks to be planted so that curious people decide to utilize them and this is also true of laptops. Malware is contained in the files and once the device is activated and linked to another device, the malware becomes active and transfers data from the connected device to an intended source. Viruses can also be activated that enter the files of a company and then destroy the data.

Criminal gangs have been known to follow employees or network at trade fairs or conferences in order to target individuals and steal their laptop. There are several ways this is done and strict policies are in place that disallow certain types of behaviour and the interaction of staff with unknown individuals. One of the dilemmas faced by people using their own personal device is that if they lose it, they will lose a lot of their own personal data and information, as well as company-specific data. If a lost device is to be wiped, then all the data on the device will be erased. This is a sensitive issue as people like to have photographs of their family members stored on their personal device. More sophisticated hackers are prepared to target an individual and find ways to acquire information via various means such as teleconferences, for example.

Questions

Question 1: How can senior managers ensure that staff within an organization are compliant in terms of safeguarding customer data?

Question 2: What can managers do in order to ensure that remote working is secure?

Question 3: With reference to the above, if you were asked to produce a charter outlining appropriate behaviour, what would you outline in the charter?

Case Sources

https://assets.publishing.service.gov.uk/government/uploads/system/uploads/attachment_data/file/711097/guide-to-the-general-data-protection-regulation-gdpr-1-0.pdf (accessed on 12th June, 2021).

Information Commissioner's Office (2018). *Guide to the General Data Protection Regulation (GDPR)*. Information Commissioner's Office (ICO).

Trim, P., Hadfield, R., Garlati, C., Smith, M., Austin, J., and Lee, Y-I. (2012). Understanding, explaining and counteracting inappropriate user behaviour: Insights and recommendations. *IAAC Consumerisation of IT Workshop Research Report*. London: Information Assurance Advisory Council.

6.11 References

Baker, J. (2010). Talk at the Cyber Security Challenge UK, University College London (26th July).

Barnell, D. (2011). Stuxnet – Rethink security, right across the supply chain. *Second International Secure Systems Development Conference: Designing in Security*, London: Hilton London Olympia Hotel (18th to 19th May).

Conner, F.W., and Coviello, A.W. (2003). *Information Security Governance: A Call to Action*. Washington, DC: National Cyber Security Summit Task Force (December).

Conrades, G.H. (2004). *Hardening the Internet: Final Report and Recommendations by the Council*. Washington, DC: National Infrastructure Advisory Council.

CPNI. (2012a). *Holistic Management of Employee Risk (HoMER)*. CPNI website: http://www.cpni.gov.uk/highlights/homer-news/ (accessed 1st October, 2012).

CPNI. (2012b). *Holistic Management of Employee Risk (HoMER): New Guidance to Help Organisations to Reduce the Risk from their Employees*. London: Centre for the Protection of the Protection of National Infrastructure.

CPNI/SANS (2012). *20 Critical Security Controls for Effective Cyber Defence* (Referred to as version 3.1). London: Centre for the Protection of National Infrastructure and SANS. www.cpni.gov. uk/advice/cyber/critical-controls/, www.sans.org/critical-security-controls/.

Fahy, M., Roche, J., and Weiner, A. (2005). *Beyond Governance: Creating Corporate Value Through Performance, Conformance and Responsibility.* Chichester: John Wiley & Sons, Ltd.

Fox, C.A., and Epstein, M.S. (2010). *Why Is Enterprise Risk Management Important for Preparedness?* White Paper. New York: Risk Insurance Management Society, Inc.

Howard, P.N., Agarwal, S.D., and Hussain, M.M. (2011). The dictators' digital dilemma: When do states disconnect their digital networks? *Issues in Technology Innovation Number 13.* Washington, DC: The Center for Technology Innovation at Brookings, The Brookings Institution (October).

Kendrick, R. (2010). *Cyber Risks for Business Professionals.* Ely: IT Governance Publishing.

Kim, C.W., and Mauborgne, R. (2005). *Blue Ocean Strategy.* Boston, MA: Harvard Business School Press.

NIST. (2009). *Recommended Security Controls for Federal Information Systems and Organizations – NIST Information Security Special Publication 800–53 Revision 3.* Gaithersburg, MD: National Institute of Standards and Technology, US Department of Commerce (August).

NIST. (2010). *Guide for Assessing the Security Controls in Federal Information Systems and Organizations: Building Effective Security Assessment Plans – Information Security Special Publication 800–53A Revision 1.* Gaithersburg, MD: National Institute of Standards and Technology, US Department of Commerce (June).

Paller, A. (2010). Talk at the Cyber Security Challenge UK, University College London (26th July).

Quillinan, J. (2010). Austerity rules. *Financial Sector Technology,* 16 (4): 32–33.

Randazzo, M.R., Keeney, M., Kowalski, E., Cappelli, D., and Moore, A. (2004). *Insider Threat Study: Illicit Cyber Activity in the Banking and Finance Sector.* US Secret Service National Threat Assessment Center and CERT Coordination Center, Software Engineering institute, Carnegie Mellon University (August).

Shpiro, S. (1998). Parliamentary and administrative reforms in the control of intelligence services in the European Union. *The Columbian Journal of European Law,* 4: 545–578.

Shurson, J. (2020). Data protection and law enforcement access to digital evidence: Resolving the reciprocal conflicts between EU and US law. *International Journal of Law and Information Technology,* 28: 167–184. https://doi.org/10.1093/ijlit/eaaa011.

Someswar, K., Ramanujan, S., and Sridhar, N. (2002). A framework for analyzing e-commerce security. *Information Management & Computer Security,* 10 (4): 149–158.

Stouffer, K. (2005). NIST industrial control system security activities, pp. 1–12. *Proceedings of the ISA Expo,* Chicago, IL (25th to 27th October).

The Defense Science Board. (2009). *Capability Surprise: Volume 1: Main Report.* Washington, DC: The Defense Science Board.

The White House. (2003). *The National Strategy to Secure Cyberspace.* Washington, DC: The White House.

Trim, P.R.J. (2001a). A framework for establishing and implementing corporate intelligence. *Strategic Change,* 10 (6): 349–357.

Trim, P.R.J. (2001b). Public-private partnerships in the defence industry and the extended corporate intelligence and national security model. *Strategic Change,* 10 (1) (January–February): 49–58.

Trim, P.R.J. (2004). The strategic corporate intelligence and transformational marketing (SATELLITE) model. *Marketing Intelligence and Planning,* 22 (2): 240–256.

Trim, P.R.J. (2005). The GISES model for counteracting organized crime and international terrorism. *International Journal of Intelligence and CounterIntelligence,* 18 (3): 451–472.

Trim, P., Hadfield, R., Garlati, C., Smith, M., Austin, J., and Lee, Y-I. (2012). Understanding, explaining and counteracting inappropriate user behaviour: Insights and recommendations. *IAAC Consumerisation of IT Workshop Research Report.* London: Information Assurance Advisory Council.

Trim, P.R.J., and Lee, Y-I. (2007). A strategic marketing intelligence framework reinforced by corporate intelligence, pp. 55–68. In X. Xu (Ed.), *Managing Strategic Intelligence: Techniques and Technologies*. Hersey, PA: Information Science Reference.

Trim, P.R.J., and Lee, Y-I. (2008). A strategic approach to sustainable partnership development. *European Business Review*, 20 (3): 222–239.

Trim, P.R.J., and Lee, Y-I. (2010). A security framework for protecting business, government and society from cyber attacks, pp. 1–6. *5th IEEE International Conference on System of Systems (SoSE): Sustainable Systems for the 21st Century*, Loughborough University (22nd to 24th June).

Trim, P.R.J., and Lee, Y-I. (2014). *Cyber Security Management: A Governance, Risk and Compliance Framework*. Farnham: Gower Publishing.

West, D.M. (2010). Steps to improve cloud computing in the public sector. *Issues in Technology Innovation, Number 1*. Washington, DC: The Center for Technology Innovation at Brookings, The Brookings Institution (July).

World Economic Forum. (2012). *Global Risks 2012*. Geneva: World Economic Forum.

Website Address

UK Data Protection Act 2018. https://www.gov.uk/data-protection (accessed on 9th November, 2021).

6.12 Further Reading

Hooper, V., and McKissack, J. (2016). The emerging role of the CISO. *Business Horizons*, 59: 585–591.

MoD. (2010). *Global Strategic Trends – Out to 2040*. London: Ministry of Defence.

6.13 Bank of Questions

Question 1: Outline what an organizational strategic governance framework is composed of and who in the organization contributes to it.

Question 2: How can security be integrated into an organization's structure?

Question 3: Why is it important for cyber security to be at the heart of security?

Question 4: Governance is a complex process and the prerogative of top management only. Critically apprise this view and provide examples to reinforce your arguments.

Question 5: By ensuring that the members of a partnership arrangement are compliant, it can be deduced that all the organizations will be resilient. Evaluate this view and provide counter arguments where necessary.

Question 6: Explain how the cyber security manager can establish a set of arguments reinforcing the fact that staff within the organization need to understand what governance and compliance involve.

7 Business Continuity Management

7.1 Introduction

Business continuity management is often viewed as something that managers need to do without having a clear overview of what is involved and who within the organization is assigned to do it. This means that business continuity management is viewed as important but often designated as an administrative role as opposed to an operational role due to the fact that most of the impacts that befall an organization are of a superficial nature. Both the business continuity management process and the business continuity manager are, however, receiving increased attention as a successful cyber attack will result in an impact that affects the functioning of an organization and might result in reputational damage. Therefore, in order that the business continuity management planning framework in place is considered appropriate vis-à-vis the type and severity of a cyber attack, the cyber security manager needs to ensure that senior management are aware of a number of factors, including organizational and structural issues in relation to business model vulnerability; resource availability implications relating to the sharing of data and information; operation-specific factors across the partnership arrangement; and legal and ethical considerations relating to the countries in which the partnership arrangement does business. The appropriate business continuity management planning framework in place requires that the cyber security manager cooperates with managers based in industry partners and various external stakeholders, all of whom subscribe to the concept of business continuity management planning. To be effective, the necessary contingency plans need to be in place and the contingency planning process needs to ensure that business recovery is at the heart of the process. To facilitate this approach, a security culture needs to be established that is underpinned by managers possessing a low probability but high impact occurrence mentality.

This chapter is constructed in the following way. First, attention is given to the learning objectives (Section 7.2) and this is followed by business continuity management (Section 7.3). Next, attention is given to dependency modelling (Section 7.4) and IT (Information Technology), risk management and business continuity (Section 7.5). Intelligence, strategic purchasing and supply chain management (Section 7.6) are followed by a business continuity management planning framework (Section 7.7), which is then followed by education and training (Section 7.8). Next, following the learning summary (Section 7.9) appears a conclusion (Section 7.10), a mini case (Section 7.11), an extended case (Section 7.12), the references (Section 7.13) and further reading (Section 7.14). A bank of questions is also provided (Section 7.15).

DOI: 10.4324/9781003244295-7

7.2 Learning Objectives

The reader will:

*   establish what business continuity management involves; and
*   establish why an organization needs to have an appropriate business continuity management framework.

7.3 Business Continuity Management

Senior management will, in the years ahead, need to think more carefully about business continuity management planning and put in place necessary frameworks. The frameworks need to be robust and able to withstand various impacts and tested at regular intervals using specifically tailored crisis simulation workshops and computerized simulation models. This is so that staff are prepared for all eventualities and adopt a proactive approach to business continuity management, which draws on the organizational learning approach. The training programmes devised need to be reflective of reality (Thierry et al., 2006). The cyber security manager is ideally placed to participate in the business continuity planning (BCP) process because of the knowledge they possess and the fact that they can draw on relevant experience or have access to those that have experience of how to deal with certain types of impact (e.g. cyber attacks). Scenario planning exercises prove beneficial in the sense that they allow the cyber security manager to work with specialist trainers and devise realistic contingency plans that contain measurable objectives. By participating fully in the business continuity management strategic process, the cyber security manager can help senior management to devise a crisis management model that is viewed as stakeholder-oriented and is designed to have continual inputs (e.g. revised plans) from staff throughout the partnership arrangement (e.g. business continuity managers, risk managers, assistant risk managers, cyber security managers and training managers).

Smith (2006: 155) suggests that there are three main areas of focus that managers need to be concerned with: crisis management, operational crisis and crisis of legitimation. With regard to recovery, Upton (2007: 84–85) analysed various emergency exercises and responses, and suggests that emergency response exercises and simulations include a number of benefits such as familiarizing staff with emergency response plans; highlighting errors/shortcomings in plans/operational procedures; enabling staff to make contact with and get to know people that are involved in incidents/incident responses; and confidence building that allows responders (those that deal with a crisis) to participate more fully and to be more effective. What the cyber security manager needs to draw from this is that the crisis and emergency management component of business continuality planning requires highly specialized knowledge and possibly the need for external consultants to be engaged on certain projects from time to time.

In order that a business continuity plan is viewed as "fit for purpose", the cyber security manager will need to work with their peers and formalize the business continuity management planning process. In addition, the cyber security manager will be required to provide adequate leadership (e.g. explain which cyber security vulnerabilities are to be addressed) and provide the required level of hierarchical organizational support. This means that the cyber security manager will need to take part ownership of the business continuity management strategy and adopt a forward-looking perspective, which addresses a number of "what if" scenarios. The argument being put forward is that the cyber security manager needs to work with training and staff development personnel in order to help devise training and staff development programmes that equip staff to deal with a crisis, which may or may not be the result of a cyber attack. Scenario planning and training exercises are known to help managers in various business functions to equip their staff with the necessary knowledge and skills. This is so that the business continuity management planning process can be implemented and managed through time. Working alongside the emergency support services and government agencies will foster relations between the organization and external experts, and result in relevant documentation being devised that is incorporated into the business management continuity strategic process and the business continuity management planning process and framework.

In order to maintain the commitment and continued cooperation of the stakeholders, it is important for the cyber security manager to coordinate communication between individuals, organizations and committees, and ensure that the working relations are harmonious. Should amendments to the framework be required, possibly as a result of changes in the law or a change in the business model configuration due to a new partner joining the business combination, the proposed changes need to be thought through, discussed and approved by all the parties concerned. The significance of this has been pointed out by Simmons (2009: 132, 136): "Business continuity management deals with keeping an organisation functioning after a period of downtime", which suggests that there will be, from time to time, incidents that are beyond the control of senior management (e.g. power outage, floods that put out of service a supplier(s) or disrupt supplies across industry sectors, and faulty components that manifest in a product being recalled from the market). The cyber security manager will, because of their knowledge relating to cyber attacks on computer systems and networks, be well placed to engage with a range of stakeholders and provide advice relating to issues such as setting crisis management priorities and the prevention of cascading effects, the implementation of business continuity plans that involve the cooperation of the emergency services, and disaster recovery, which may involve bringing in specialist experts to track and trace how the problem originated and who were involved in its escalation. The cyber security manager, because of their knowledge and strategic role within the organization, will understand the need to prevent cascading effects and this means that business continuity management has to be viewed from the perspective of resilience. Resilience involves the organization and its partners, and requires senior management to link an impact such as a cyber attack, with recovery and the continuity of business operations. Recovery is, therefore, to be viewed as an outcome of BCP, and the cyber security manager has a key role to play in making an organization resilient. For example, if an organization's databases are penetrated by a hacker, the objective is to stop that attacker manipulating the data or taking out the data. This is so that the organization can continue to perform at the same level of efficiency before the attack was carried out. Simmons (2009: 144) recognizes this and suggests that managers need a holistic view of resilience and need to link resilience with risk management:

> The pillars on which risk management needs to be structured and utilised within a resilient organisation include:

1 Moving business continuity from just impact assessment to plotting likelihood and mitigation of all mutating and evolving risks.

2 The mechanism to combine crisis and risk management, information and corporate security – not just through the prism of either business continuity, risk or security, but together in absolute harmony with enterprise risk management, corporate social responsibility and environmental and ethical polices, thus maturing an holistic view of risk management. This then fully supports corporate governance too.

3 A process predicated on corporate uncertainty vis-à-vis reputation management, rather than maintenance of an ideal status quo.

4 A coherent and holistic business strategy that combines accountability, customer confidence and competitive advantage.

5 A mechanism to advance the reality of corporate uncertainty – where it is not possible to know what events will alter the competitive operating landscape for better or worse and the need to combine, not just compliment a range of existing but discrete activities.

7.4 Dependency Modelling

In order to produce an effective business continuity plan, the cyber security manager needs to be aware of what risk management involves. Hyslop (2009: 157) provides a useful explanation of what risk management is:

> Understanding risk involves understanding why we depend on things we cannot control, through an understanding of Dependency Relationships. The formal part of the organization can be thought of as being under constant attack by the uncontrollable part. Risk Management is about designing the former to be maximally resilient to the latter. While we cannot control the root causes, the uncontrollables, nevertheless the effects are more under our control through management of the dependency relationships within the organization. Interdependency relationships are unique to the particular organization, and only by coming to terms with the actual relationships in that organization can anything really valuable be done to understand, manage and reduce risks.

Hyslop (2009: 157) also states that:

> Dependency Modelling was developed to capture these interdependencies in a highly visual model so that the consequence of failures could be uncovered in the safe, virtual environment of the computer. Having created the model it is relatively easy to:

- Infer the risk to the organization implied by the model.
- Illustrate the risk graphically in easy-to-understand terms.
- Find which scenarios are the most dangerous to the organization.
- Find variations of the organizational structure which carry less risk.
- Evaluate the effectiveness of any countermeasures.
- Determine which factors are important and which can be ignored.
- Support management proposals with evidence.
- Avoid spending money on measures which are likely to be ineffective.
- Find ways of reducing risk without necessarily spending money.

Doz and Kosonen (2008: 17) highlight the need for managers to think in terms of how rapid change and growing systemic interdependencies will affect the process of managing complex organizations. This can be interpreted as the cyber security manager having a strategic view of the organization and bearing in mind that a cyber attack can be launched from anywhere in the world, at any time and through various routes, the cyber security manager needs to work with senior management to ensure that the organization has a risk mitigation plan in place that allows staff to implement procedures to deal with any form of cyber attack. By placing risk mitigation within a security management framework (NIST, 2010), it should be possible for the cyber security manager to take into account the linkage between IT and risk management. By doing this, the vulnerabilities of a computer system, the network(s) through which it operates and outsource providers (e.g. those providing cloud services) will all be documented in the business continuity plan.

7.5 IT (Information Technology), Risk Management and Business Continuity

The Community Cyber Security Maturity Model (White and Huson, 2009: 308) can help managers to control and improve IT-related processes as it can be used by IT staff to assist with software development, project management and risk management. In addition, such models can focus attention on securing a community's computer systems and networks and this should help the cyber security manager to build an effective security environment with cyber security being at the centre. Maturity models have a number of advantages in the sense that they can help a community to establish its level of preparedness, establish what steps need to be taken in order to achieve the required level of preparedness and also establish how to measure the community's level of preparedness. As noted by White and Huson (2009: 308), the word "community" can be interpreted in several ways but a useful approach is to think of a "community" in a geographical context (metropolitan area, city, town or village).

Fox and Epstein (2010: 3) make a useful contribution to explaining what a security environment is by suggesting that staff can engage in environmental and intelligence scanning, which will ensure that senior management view risk from a multi-dimensional perspective and at the same time place emphasis on managing risk in a proactive manner by championing the need for organizational resilience. ENISA (2006: 7) offer advice to managers in terms of using a rating system for IT security risk management: from "high" to "low" in importance and to determine whether something has a high dependency (the disruption of information systems results in severe hindering of the dependent process) or a low dependency (the disruption of information systems results in minor hindering of the dependent process). The cyber security manager can think this through and decide whether to use this kind of approach, which can be defined as qualitative or adopt a more formal, quantitative-type approach (e.g. 1 = minimum risk and 5 = very high risk). ENISA (2006: 9) suggest that:

> An IT security risk is composed of an asset, a threat and vulnerability: if one of these items is irrelevant, then there is no risk to encounter. Aggregation of all single IT security risk results in the total IT risk. A key step in the risk management process is risk assessment; this involved evaluating each IT risk as well as total risk, and then giving them priorities.

The following simplified definitions can assist managers to better understand what is at stake (ENISA, 2006: 9): an asset is anything that has value to an organization; a threat can be viewed as an action/event which has the potential to cause harm; and a vulnerability is a weakness in an asset that can be exploited in terms of one or more threats. Bearing this in mind, it can be suggested that an IT security risk is "a potential event that a threat will exploit vulnerability in an asset and thereby cause harm to the organization and its business" (ENISA, 2006: 10). In order to put this into perspective, it is necessary for the cyber security manager, when formulating an IT security risk management policy in cooperation with the IT manager and the risk manager, to think in terms of controls and the risk management and analysis process. For example, as regards controls, the cyber security manager needs to have a sound understanding of (i) logical controls (protection of data, network assets and access to applications, for example); (ii) physical controls (including alarm systems, fire sensors, physical access control and surveillance, for example); (iii) organizational controls (usage rules, administration procedures, process descriptions and definition of roles, for example); (iv) personnel controls (such as sanctions, confidentiality clauses in contracts, and training and awareness, for example) and (v) security controls, all of which link the situation to the type of control, for example, awareness training for certain managers would be associated with control of personnel type (ENISA, 2006: 12). With respect to the management of risk, the cyber security manager needs to have a clear understanding of (i) risk management, whereby managers need to think in terms of risk assessment, which is about establishing which risks will be treated (the risks that apply to a business will be identified and then evaluated); (ii) risk treatment, the objective of which is to select and implement security controls in order to reduce risks (the different effects include mitigation, transfer, avoidance and retention of risks); (iii) risk acceptance, here the concern is that when a risk has been treated, there may well be residual risks and management need to come to terms with how the risks have been treated; and (iv) risk communication, which is concerned with informing decision makers and involved stakeholders about potential risks and the various controls.

The cyber security manager needs to advise staff throughout the partnership arrangement and also staff based in customer organizations, to keep their applications up-to-date and this means that a patch strategy needs to be in place (ENISA, 2009: 10). As regards information assurance, the cyber security manager needs to make sure that there are clear guidelines for hiring IT personnel and that these are adhered to; and that there is also a security education programme in place. As regards subcontracting and outsourcing, the cyber security manager can engage in a regular audit of subcontractors and make sure third party service levels are of the right quality and are maintained, and that remote access policy is defined and that backup policies and procedures are available and can be scrutinized (ENISA, 2009: 12–13). This reinforces the proactive approach to security and is also linked with maintaining harmonious working relations so that data and information sharing occurs relating to actual and potential cyber attacks and also new knowledge is developed and shared among partner members that allows all types of cyber attack to be reposted.

As regards service level agreements, the cyber security manager can ensure that the policy in place covers the minimum amount of time systems are available; that a documented method exists outlining the details associated with the impact of a disruption; that the recovery point objective and the recovery time objectives are linked with the criticality of the service; advice as to how information security activities are addressed in the restoration process provided; in the event of a disruption, the lines of communication are made known to end customers; the roles and responsibilities of the teams involved with dealing with a disruption are made known; the provider also categorizes the priority for recovery and has defined the relative (low, medium or high) priority (in the case of the end user or customer) to be restored; the dependencies relevant to the restoration process (including suppliers and outsource partners) are outlined; and should a primary site be made unavailable, it is made known what the minimum separation time is for the secondary site to be operational (ENISA, 2009: 20).

With regard to incident management and response, ENISA (2009: 20–21) provide guidance with respect to an organization minimizing the probability of an occurrence or reducing the negative impact of an information security incident. The following areas are highlighted (ENISA 2009: 20–21): a formal process for detecting, identifying, analysing and responding to incidents and establishing how effective the response is; a focus on how the detection capabilities are structured; how the severity levels and escalation procedures are defined; reference is made to how incidents are documented and evidence is collected; reference is made to the controls that are in place to prevent or minimize malicious activities by insiders; reference to a forensic image of the virtual machine offered to the customer and which incident reports are made public; how often are the disaster recovery and business continuity plans tested by the provider is made known; the frequency and occurrence of customer service satisfaction levels, help desk tests, penetration testing, vulnerability testing and rectifying vulnerabilities are all covered.

According to ENISA (2008: 8):

> Business Continuity is the term applied to the series of management processes and integrated plans that maintain the continuity of the critical processes of an organisation, should a disruptive event take place which impacts the ability of the organisation to continue to provide its key services. ICT systems and electronic data are crucial components of the processes and their protection and timely return is of paramount importance.

Reflecting on the above, it is clear that business continuity is perceived as a method of risk treatment to mitigate continuity risks in a proactive manner (agreements and systems are in place to deal with a possible disruption) and a reactive manner (business continuity plans); and a disaster recovery plan details the procedures for restoring IT components, telephony and information after a disruptive event has occurred (ENISA, 2008: 12–13). At this point, it is useful to revisit the concept of corporate governance because doing so helps to emphasize the fact that the cyber security manager, in order to implement business continuity plans effectively, needs to have firmly established trust-based relationships with their counterparts both within the organization and with staff in partner organizations, so that any action that the plans implemented are fully supported. Furthermore, the relationships in place need to be endorsed by senior management and supportive of organizational policy. For example, ENISA (2008: 17) stipulate that:

> Corporate Governance is concerned with improving the performance of companies for the benefit of shareholders, stakeholders and economic growth. It focuses on the conduct of, and relationships among, the Board of Directors, Managers and Shareholders. It generally refers to the processes by which organisations are directed, controlled and held to account. It encompasses authority, accountability, stewardship, leadership, direction and control exercised within the organisation.
>
> [HB 254–2005]

What can be deduced from this is that business continuity management is focused on managing risks so that in the event of an occurrence the organization is able to continue functioning to a "pre-determined minimum level" (ENISA, 2008: 18). Should an impact materialize, it can be suggested that (ENISA, 2008: 19):

> Disaster Recovery Planning is concerned with the actual technical recovery of the IT components and details the procedures to be used to restore the IT components following a failure. As the plan is devised by ICT without the knowledge and understanding of business units as to their IT requirements, it is an orderly but non-prioritised recovery process. …Information Technology Service Continuity Management (ITSCM) ensures that information technology technical and services facilities (including computer systems, networks, applications, telecommunications, technical support and service desk …) can be recovered within required and agreed business timescales.

There is a distinct difference between risk management and business continuity as noted by ENISA (2008: 17) and this is important because the cyber security manager needs to know how the tools and techniques are used to solve unique and recurring problems. For example, risk management focuses on risk analysis, impact and probability, all types of events that are known to affect an organization, with a focus on preventing or reducing incidents vis-à-vis the core business, and various forms of intensity (ENISA, 2008: 17). As regards business continuity management, the cyber security manager needs to be familiar with business impact analysis, the availability of the impact, the events that cause major business disruption, the way in which the organization's core processes will be threatened, with a focus being on incident management and recovery, and being aware of the way an event occurs.

Information Technology Service Continuity Management (ITSCM) is an integral component of BCP and can be placed firmly in the context of emergency planning. A thorough business impact analysis is a highly important element of BCP and needs to (ENISA, 2008: 22) (i) assess risks and impacts; (ii) analyse results; (iii) prioritize recovery and define critical resource requirements. Two other aspects need to be given attention: the delivery of the business continuity process and the way in which the business continuity management programme can be sustained. ENISA (2008: 22) has provided guidance and it is clear that the delivery of the business continuity process needs to incorporate an incident response plan, an incident management plan, a business recovery plan, a recovery support plan, a communications and media plan, an IT service continuity plan and a business resumption plan. As regards sustaining the business continuity management programme, the cyber security manager and his colleagues in senior management need to ensure that staff are adequately trained; the business continuity process is maintained and reviewed; and awareness is developed and maintained.

The cyber security manager can in fact sit on the business continuity steering committee, which is appointed by top management in order to make sure that the organization's business continuity plans are reviewed on a regular basis, tested and updated when necessary (ENISA, 2008: 29). As well as having a business continuity steering committee in place, it is necessary to have a business continuity management team led by the business continuity manager; an incident management team (composed of the senior management team), which will incorporate business continuity steering committee members and which is referred to as the Gold team (e.g. stakeholder management, strategic decision making and media interviews); an incident management team referred to as the Silver team (management of the incident using the incident management plan, tactical decision making, communication briefings and escalation of issues) and a business unit management team known as the Bronze team (management of recovery using business recovery plans, communication with staff, escalation of issues) (ENISA, 2008: 28–31). Such an organizational structure should allow the risk manager to maintain the organization's risk register. Staff in partner organizations need to follow the same logic and have the same or similar organizational structure in place.

Senior management need to think in terms of maintaining three risk registers (ENISA, 2008: 56–57): (i) a corporate risk register (the main risks to the organization); (ii) a business continuity risk register (details about incidents that have occurred) and (iii) an IT risk register (the risks associated with IT and information systems). From information provided by ENISA (2008: 93–95) (drawn from HB 292–2006), it is clear that the business continuity management planning process is composed of six main steps: (i) a definition of what business continuity management represents; (ii) a business impact analysis (e.g. risks are assessed, disruptive scenarios are developed and a business impact is conducted); (iii) BCP (e.g. business continuity management strategies are developed and resource requirements are assessed and collated); (iv) the delivery of recovery plans are outlined (this covers the writing of the plan, activation and development, and the development of a communications strategy); (v) testing the business continuity plan (training and awareness, performance and assurance) and (vi) sustaining the business continuity plan (training and awareness, performance and assurance; overall, it is concerned with regular maintenance to ensure the various plans fit together). In order that business continuity management planning is considered strategic and placed within the core activities of the business (business continuity management is considered an integrated business activity and not a stand-alone business function, for example), it is important to highlight the management and structural, organizational design issues.

The cyber security manager can use scenario planning to improve the BCP process, and identify and implement appropriate training and staff development programmes. The ultimate objective of this is to aid the strategic business intelligence planning. By devising appropriate management models and concepts, managers can link the BCP process to crisis/disaster/emergency planning. It can be deduced, therefore, that effective BCP takes into account the interdependencies between organizations and institutions and is influenced by government guidelines. Underpinned by organizational learning, BCP is perceived as useful as regards focusing the cyber security manager's attention on the vulnerabilities associated with critical national infrastructure and critical information infrastructure, and placing BCP within a holistic security environment. This means that the cyber security manager needs to view security from a strategic perspective.

The strategic marketing intelligence framework produced by Trim and Lee (2007: 61) is a useful aid for business continuity management planning and should enable the cyber security manager to embrace the concept of corporate intelligence and place emphasis on "intelligence gathering which leads to better visioning and more exciting scenario development" (Wright, 2005: 4). For example, by making the organization less vulnerable to a cyber attack, the cyber security manager can promote the concept of resilience. Sutcliffe and Vogus (2003: 95) indicate that "Resilience refers to the maintenance of positive adjustment under challenging conditions", and this is important because the cyber security manager needs to take into account what is known as strategic intent, which, according to Hamel and Prahalad (1994), is about developing further the organization's capabilities and securing additional resources.

7.6 Intelligence, Strategic Purchasing and Supply Chain Management

Porter's (1985) value chain concept has relevance to supply chain management because it can be used to evaluate a comprehensive supplier relations programme (Sheth and Sharma, 1997) and this is important in terms of the continuity of supply and increasing the knowledge base within the organization. Managing knowledge-based strategies (Kaplan and Norton, 2001) allows a manager to promote an intelligence culture within the organization (Trim and Lee, 2008b: 733). Eells and Nehemkis (1984: 75) stipulate that intelligence is:

> the product of collection, evaluation, analysis, integration, and interpretation of all available information that may affect the survival and success of the company. Well-interpreted information, provided by a properly designed intelligence function, can be immediately significant in the planning of corporate policy in all of its fields of operations. Stated in both operational and organizational terms, the main purpose of intelligence is to help the chief executive officer fulfil his wide ranging responsibilities.

Tan and Ahmed (1999) acknowledge that intelligence is essential in terms of a manager analysing, distributing accurate information in a timely manner so that planning is improved and control is exercised. Montgomery and Weinberg (1991: 345) state that a strategic intelligence system is about identifying "what information is relevant and actionable" and not just about the production of data. According to Trim and Lee (2008b: 734), competitive intelligence officers are involved in risk assessment and policy formulation that is aimed at reducing an organization's level of vulnerability, and are "also involved in the development of resilience oriented organizational procedures and mechanisms". The cyber security manager needs to be aware that the strategic decision making process is about improving the flow of information from line managers (Ghoshal and Westney, 1991) so that information is turned into intelligence (Kahaner, 1997: 280). Trim and Lee (2008b: 735) have stated that:

> Scenario analysis and planning is used by competitive intelligence officers to develop possible future worlds, and future world typologies can reinforce the intelligence focus and ensure that marketing intelligence officers and competitive intelligence officers adopt a strategic intelligence approach. Marketing intelligence systems should have a practical orientation and be both adaptable and flexible.

Ghoshal (2004: 382) suggests that managers are confronted with various kinds of risks (macro-economic, policy, competitive and resource) and various levels of management expertise and knowledge are needed in order to manage change and at the same time ensure that the risk management process is appropriate. By working closely with the risk manager, the cyber security manager can monitor the information that goes into the organization's risk register and check that individual staff members are adhering to the organization's security value system.

Jones et al. (2005: 383) have linked a human relations culture orientation with a new computing system, and this focuses attention on how a strategic intelligence policy can be devised to take into account cyber security management. By linking human factors with the application of technology, and by adopting a proactive approach to risk assessment, senior managers should be in a position to devise an organizational resilience value system (Lee and Trim, 2006: 738–739) that incorporates inputs from the managers of the various business functions throughout the partnership arrangement. It is for this reason that a cyber security manager needs to ensure that those in the partnership arrangement are able to organize and formalize the intelligence activities and policies within the organization.

Evidence of the need to do this is provided by Sheffi (2005: 13): "The events of 9/11 have brought home for many U.S. executives the dangers of a terror-based disruption, but accidents and random events such as severe weather or earthquakes can also cause significant disruptions". This reiterates the need for top management to put in place a mechanism for identifying a wide range of threats and to establish how vulnerable the organization is to a cyber attack. The cyber security manager can ensure that the findings from a risk assessment feed into the strategic intelligence process and that the counter-intelligence strategy in place is owned by all the organizations in the partnership arrangement. By ensuring that this is the case, the corporate security operation will feed into the organization's strategic intelligence operation (Trim and Lee, 2008b: 737) and the cyber security manager will perform the role of the cyber security intelligence liaison officer.

Senior managers will need to ensure that counter-intelligence activities have a strategic component (Trim, 2001b, 2004) because as a wide range of threats are visible, including counterfeiting and industrial espionage, and it is important that the cyber security manager works closely with the organization's managers, and those involved in corporate intelligence and corporate security, so that the managers in the partnership arrangement deal with cyber attacks in a proactive manner. Trim (2001a: 54–55) defines corporate intelligence as:

> the acquisition of knowledge using, human, electronic and other means, and the interpretation of knowledge relating to the environments, both internal and external, in which the organization operates. It provides selected staff within the organization with up-to-date and accurate information, which allows strategists to develop and implement policy so that the organization maintains and/or gains a competitive advantage in the marketplace. It also provides a mechanism for implementing counter-intelligence measures to safeguard corporate data and secrets.

Top management can formalize matters by appointing a corporate intelligence steering committee to oversee, advise and regulate the work of the intelligence unit and an Executive Intelligence Alliance Policy Strategy Monitoring Group can be established that has the principal aim of monitoring the work of the intelligence unit (Trim, 2001b: 351–352). Having an appreciation of what intelligence and security involve will, it can be argued, manifest in a holistic view of security. The strategic intelligence approach, coupled with the contingency management approach, can provide a basis for understanding how operational security and situational awareness are linked, and can help the cyber security manager to place strategic intelligence within a cyber security context.

Baily et al. (1994: 167) have outlined a seven-step multi-meeting negotiation process (the pre-negotiation stage, the introductory meeting, the preparation for discussion meeting, the discussion meeting, the preparation for agreement meeting, the agreement meeting and the post-negotiation meeting) that can be used as a basis for developing a business continuity plan. The nine-stage BCP process incorporates the multi-meeting phases outlined by Baily et al. (1994: 167) and can be viewed as an extension of their seven step model. It can be suggested that the BCP process is not confined or limited to an annual planning cycle but can be implemented as and when necessary. It is possible for there to be a minimum of two and a maximum of four *discussion meetings* and as a consequence there will be two or four *preparation for agreement meetings* (Trim and Lee, 2014: 68). By adopting a formal process as outlined, all the issues relating to BCP will be discussed and the manuals/documentation used will be accurate. At this point, it can be noted that the organization's business continuity plan(s) need to fit well with local and national government contingency plans, so that the recovery system is implemented in a timely manner (Trim and Lee, 2014: 68).

7.7 A Business Continuity Management Planning Framework

It can be suggested that a business continuity management planning framework is composed of the following components (Trim and Lee, 2014: 70–71):

A proactive leadership approach that (i) facilitates internal marketing (departments, subsidiaries and partner organizations) and relationship building with external organizations and stakeholders (government, trade associations, suppliers and subcontractors for example); and (ii) facilitates communication and advice (public relations and legal for example) vis-à-vis corporate social responsibility.

A staff development and training programme incorporating simulation exercises and scenario planning.

A model of crisis management linked with emergency planning and disaster recovery, which includes customer satisfaction levels.

A model of strategic corporate intelligence that is linked to corporate security and (i) embraces risk assessment and management and (ii) incorporates counter-intelligence.

A maturity model underpinned by information assurance that incorporates stakeholder resilience and ethical policy that is (i) partner focused and (ii) based on trust.

A clearly defined controls and risk management policy and strategy that identifies logical controls, physical controls, organizational controls, personnel controls and security controls (ENISA, 2006: 10). Also included are risk management, risk treatment, risk acceptance and risk communication.

(ENISA, 2006: 12)

An Information Technology (IT) Service Continuity Process that (i) underpins the organization's commitment to corporate governance and (ii) ensures that if there is an event of any kind, the organization can recover and be operational again within an agreed timescale.

(ENISA, 2008: 8–19)

A business continuity management department is in existence that is presided over by a business continuity manager. Business impact analyses are undertaken and feed into strategic situation(al) analysis, and both internal events (brought about by an insider) and external events (brought about by an external computer hacker) are placed in context. Staff produce an incident response plan, an incident management plan, a business recovery plan, a recovery support plan, a communications and media plan, an IT service continuity plan, and a business resumption plan (ENISA, 2008: 22). Most importantly, an incident management team is in being (e.g. Gold, Silver and Bronze Command) (ENISA, 2008: 28–31). Furthermore, a nine stage business continuity planning process is also in being.

A business continuity steering committee is appointed to review, test and update the organization's business continuity plans (ENISA, 2008: 29). The business continuity management policy and strategy is monitored and various functions and processes are audited.

A risk manager is appointed and takes responsibility for maintaining the organization's risk registers (a corporate risk register, a business continuity risk register, and an IT risk register).

(ENISA, 2008: 56–57)

The business continuity management planning process is deemed comprehensive and is composed of six steps: (i) a definition of what business continuity management represents; (ii) a business impact analysis; (iii) business continuity planning; (iv) outlining the delivery of recovery plans; (v) testing the business continuity plan; and (vi) sustaining the business continuity plan.

(ENISA, 2008: 93–95 (drawn from HB 292–2006))

The business continuity management planning framework is contained within a strategic marketing intelligence framework and key aspects are included such as supply chain management.

A comprehensive security management and education and training programme ensures that internal staff and staff employed by external organizations (suppliers and outsource partners and selected organizations in the marketing channel) upgrade their skill base.

By having in place a business continuity management planning framework that outlines how relationships within an organization function and also how relationships with external staff (e.g. partner organizations) are formed and maintained will prove beneficial in terms of helping the cyber security manager to relate better to the various stakeholders.

7.8 Education and Training

Any form of major disruption will have ramifications for both industry and government, affect intra-firm trade (Brooks, 2005: 25) and have knock-on-effects for the community. Hambrick (2007) has done much to focus on the development of theory and its applicability, and it can be noted that scenario planning can be used by managers to develop robust business continuity plans and planning processes. Lindgren and Bandhold (2003), and Ringland (2006) have made reference to the benefits associated with scenario planning and the cyber security manager, working with the training manager, can ensure that this type of training vehicle is fully utilized to promote BCP.

In order for the learning associated with business continuity management planning and contingency planning formulation to be effective, the cyber security manager needs to select appropriate simulation exercises that include a debriefing element at the end of the simulation exercise in order that the lessons learned can be logged and recorded in the organization's memory, and acted upon to improve organizational learning. The written and verbal feedback that is provided by multiple stakeholders at the end of the simulation exercise needs to be comprehensive, accurate and reinforce the organization's learning aims and objectives, and also needs to contain constructive criticism. Weaver (2006: 379) is right to suggest that feedback needs to be produced that assesses individual performance and results in improvements, and those conducting a simulation exercise "can appoint an experienced observer (teacher/trainer) to monitor the actions of each person involved in the simulation" (Trim and Lee, 2008a: 56–57). Furthermore, Trim and Lee (2008a: 57) suggest that when individuals are placed in break-out groups to discuss data and information at various stages of the simulation,

> it should be reasonably straight forward for the observer(s) to monitor both individual and group involvement and attainment, and to establish how key decisions were reached, how plans were implemented, and how reflection resulted in a change in understanding/interactive action that resulted in a different approach/strategic objective.

Reflecting on the role of the cyber security manager and how scenario planning can reinforce BCP, Trim and Lee (2008a: 57) cite the following benefits:

1 develop a holistic view as to what business continuity is in the context of crisis/disaster and emergency management situations;
2 develop a holistic view as to what crisis management involves, from the perspectives of policy and planning;
3 devise new methodological approaches to study crisis/disaster and emergency situations and to model them more effectively;
4 encourage the development of international project teams that can use models, simulations and scenarios;
5 encourage the development of new management theory and insights; and
6 encourage the use of inter-disciplinary/multi-disciplinary approaches that place business continuity within an international security context.

Simulation exercises are deemed useful as regards comparing security procedures with information management security systems, so that a comprehensive organizational security policy is devised and put in place (Irvine and Thompson, 2003: 8–9). Trim and Lee (2008a: 54) state: "Those involved in business continuity training exercises, need to be skilled at assessing technical, interpersonal and leadership skills, as well as assessing both an individual's and a group's teamwork and motivation level". The cyber security manager can find ways to facilitate knowledge sharing and increase skill enhancement at various levels within the organization as Hyslop (2007: 198) notes: "Resilience in Critical Infrastructure and Critical Information Infrastructure Protection has implications at international, national, local, corporate, individual, and political level". It is important to understand that many of the lessons learned from BCP need to be disseminated more widely by those individuals occupying positions of responsibility for dealing with crises and emergencies (Brear, 2007), if, i.e., business continuity knowledge is to be shared and theory developed. For example, Turner (2006: 125) has indicated that organizational exclusivity (the disregard of non-members) can prove problematic because a mentality may exist suggesting that "it was automatically assumed that the organization knew better than outsiders about the hazards of the situations with which it was dealing".

7.9 Learning Summary

Figure 7.1, strategic cyber security business continuity management, shows a comprehensive outline of what business continuity management planning is concerned with and makes clear what the cyber security manager needs to be aware of. In addition, the cyber security manager needs to be involved in the preparation of a set of contingency plans that can be implemented during times of crisis/emergency. Emphasis is placed on establishing IT security risks and also there is an expectation that the organization will be impacted by a successful cyber attack at some stage in its development, hence mention of a disaster recovery plan that is cited within resilience policy. It is with this in mind that the risk management policy is tailored to take into account the interdependencies between organizations and establish how senior management can prioritize dependency relationships.

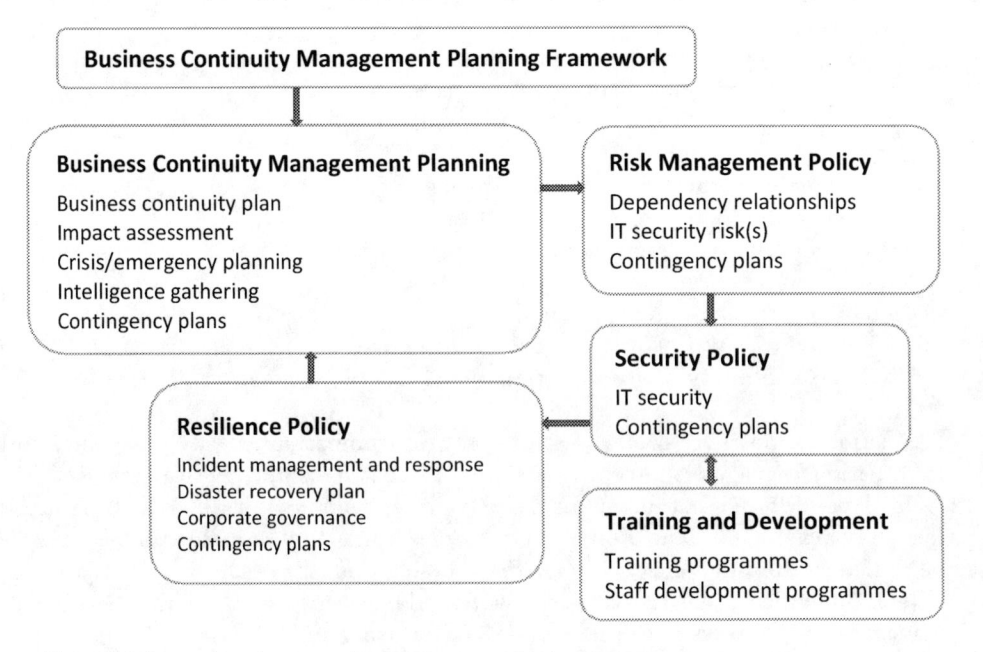

Figure 7.1 Strategic cyber security business continuity management.

The reader will be able to:

- apply the business continuity management approach; and
- devise an appropriate business continuity management framework.

7.10 Conclusion

BCP is a formal process that requires an input from a number of in-house staff and external specialists. The cyber security manager, together with the risk manager, can take the lead and ensure that a business continuity management framework is developed that includes inputs from partner members, but they will need to provide guidance as to what to do if an organization is impacted in any way. This is so that a speedy recovery is achieved. A theoretical approach that embraces dependency modelling can help the cyber security manager define the risks involved that need to be monitored. Such a view will reinforce the fact that more attention needs to be given to education and training in the context of security management and intelligence.

7.11 Mini Case: Blockchain Technology and Business Continuity

Mrs. Greenish, a consultant, entered the board room of the company and greeted all those present. She started her talk by suggesting that the company was rather dysfunctional. Her investigation into the company suggested that some managers were not communicating with their peers. Because of this, a number of internal production targets had been missed and conflict among staff had occurred. She was aware that Mr. Yardley, head of marketing, was very frustrated because a number of deliveries had been missed and he had received some very harsh comments from customers that were buying to resell; a change in mentality was needed.

Mrs. Greenish had been asked to look into how the blockchain concept could be utilized by the company to improve its performance. She drew on the work of Downey et al. (2018: 87) and explained that the blockchain represented distributed database technology that allowed those using it to work with a shared ledger, which is updated every time a transaction occurs. The advantage being that each manager who is provided with the appropriate security (authentication that is verified) is able to see a shared copy of the record of the transaction. The main benefit of the blockchain concept is that it allows for checks to be made on the technical work that has been undertaken and the administrative work that has been completed (Downey et al., 2018: 87). From the talk provided by Mrs. Greenish, it was clear that the company had to improve its operating capability by improving the workflow and getting internal staff to communicate more. In some instances, it was proven that emails that should have been sent were withheld, and some information that should have been provided at a specific time was also withheld. There was generally a lack of communication within the company and it was known that technology and production staff were apathetic towards suppliers, some of whom had not been able to supply components on time. The company's "just-in-time" management system had been nicknamed the "about time" system, because of the delays and the knock-on-effects caused.

Mr. Yardley appeared worried. "I am not sure staff are ready for change", he said. He continued: "They all seem to work in their own world, and some, have lost track of time and what is important to the company".

"Well", responded Mrs. Greenish, "We will see about that".

She explained that the blockchain concept had the added advantage of allowing threat information to be shared among those using a shared ledger and also that it would help managers to keep data and information secure. She referred to an article she had read recently relating to the transfer of data from one country to another and the ramifications involved vis-à-vis GDPR (Karasek-Wojciechowicz, 2021). This resonated with Mr. Yardley, who had recently informed a member of the marketing team that they were wrong to provide an overseas dealer with the names and addresses of some of their customers. This was at a time when the company's marketing database was inaccessible and the dealer was exerting pressure on the company to make its deliveries on time.

Questions

Question 1: How should senior management deal the issues raised by Mrs. Greenish?

Question 2: What can be done to utilize blockchain technology?

Question 3: How can blockchain technology help make the company more resilient?

Case Sources

Downey, L.X. Bauchot, F., and Röling, J. (2018). Blockchain for business value: A contract and work flow management to reduce disputes pilot project. *IEEE Engineering Management Review*, 46 (4): 86–93. https://doi.org/10.1109/EMR.2018.2883328.

Karasek-Wojciechowicz, I. (2021). Reconciliation of anti-money laundering instruments and European data protection requirements in permissionless blockchain spaces. *Journal of Cybersecurity*, 1–28. https://doi.org/10.1093/cybsec/tyab004 (accessed on 11th December, 2021).

Further Reading

Rawat, D.B., Chaudhary, V., and Doku, R. (2021). Blockchain technology: Emerging applications and use cases for secure and trustworthy smart systems. *Journal of Cybersecurity and Privacy*, 1(1): 4–18. https://doi.org/10.3390/jcp1010002.

7.12 Extended Case: Ensuring that People Are Aware of Cyber Security Issues and Challenges

The post-COVID-19 era will focus the attention of the public more on cyber security issues and challenges, not only because cyber attacks are becoming better publicized and more widely talked about, but also because cyber, which is characterized by connectivity and interactivity, is now so dominant in the lives that people lead. Completing forms online, transferring images and photographs, and making comments on Twitter remind parents that they need to understand that their teenage children are growing up in a world dominated by technology and as a consequence, human interaction with technology demands certain skills and discipline. Whether young adults use a smartphone to talk with their friends or complete school-based assignments on their iPad, they are immersed in a world of networks and competing associations.

Business people that were unable to travel during the COVID-19 period due to government-enforced lockdowns are now able, having gained experience of using technology to engage in e-negotiation deals, to understand why it is important to be selective when sharing sensitive documents online and also are aware of how technology can present problems if the supporting infrastructure is inadequate.

Technology should not be taken for granted. For example, Glenny (2020: 22) reminds us of the perils of using online facilities for a public event by recalling an incident that occurred at a Palm Sunday church service when Zoom was used:

> We were all set up and ready to go …..when somebody started shouting……Next, to the horror of the congregation, pornography, photos of dismembered bodies and videos of extreme violence filled the screen. The new sport of "Zoombombing" had come to the home counties…

No doubt incidents such as this cause much concern and result in some people convincing themselves that technology should not be used and also parents need to be better aware of what their children may be viewing online when they are unattended by their parents. Monitoring how children use technology and what they have access to suggests that parents can have a hands-on approach and ensure that their children are safe online. This is because cyber bullying can, if unchecked, present all sorts of problems that can cause harm to specific individuals.

Cyber bullying has been reported over the years but it is still a concern because not all the incidents are reported. Although bullying is known to happen (in school, organizations or at specific events where prejudice is evident), it has to be said that cyber bullying adds another dimension to the problem because of the fact that those who carry out such attacks are not visible to the person receiving the threats and nasty messages, and it is not always possible to stop the insults being transmitted. Kowalski and Limber (2013: S13) suggest that "Cyberbullying involves bullying through the use of electronic venues, such as instant messaging, e-mail, chat rooms, websites, online games, social networking sites, and text messaging".

UNICEF (2021) state:

> Cyberbullying is bullying with the use of digital technologies. It can take place on social media, messaging platforms, gaming platforms and mobile phones. It is repeated behaviour, aimed at scaring, angering or shaming those who are targeted. Examples include:
>
> - spreading lies about or posting embarrassing photos of someone on social media
> - sending hurtful messages or threats via messaging platforms
> - impersonating someone and sending mean messages to others on their behalf.
>
> Face-to-face bullying and cyberbullying can often happen alongside each other. But cyberbullying leaves a digital footprint – a record that can prove useful and provide evidence to help stop the abuse.

If unchecked, bullying can cause harm to an individual and it is for this reason that various organizations have come into being to help those affected by it and their family, to deal with the issues. There are other issues that concern people about how technology is used and who controls it. Glenny (2020: 22) also revealed that a hacking group published stolen patient data from a medical trial company online, which included passport details and other sensitive information. This raises a number of questions relating to the ethical guidelines in place that govern how people secure, protect and utilize other people's data and information and also how staff in an organization are made to comply with regulations so that they stay within the country's Data Protection Act and ensure that the rules governing GDPR are adhered to.

Glenny (2020: 22) outlines seven points that will enable people to become more cyber-secure:

> 1 Always keep your operating system (Mac, Windows and so on) apps and software up to date. 2 Install an anti-virus and anti-malware program. 3 Do not use the same password twice. Use a password generator. 4 Do not keep sensitive data on devices connected to the internet or put it in an email. 5 If there is even a hint of something unusual about an email or message, do not open the attachments or click links. 6 Make sure your children know the risks. If a hacker gets into their computer, they can get into yours via your home wi-fi network. 7 Check the website haveibeenpwned.com to see which accounts linked to your email address have been breached. Change relevant passwords immediately.

Questions

Question 1: Which factors should a cyber security manager take into account when producing a business continuity charter?

Question 2: How relevant is the advice provided by Glenny (2020)?

Question 3: How can the advice provided by Glenny (2020) be taken into consideration when producing a business continuity plan?

Case Sources

Glenny, M. (2020). The virus lit the fuse. Now it's boom time for hackers. *The Sunday Times*, 24th May, p. 22.

Kowalski, R.M., and Limber, S.P. (2013). Psychological, physical, and academic correlates of cyberbullying and traditional bullying. *Journal of Adolescent Health*, 53: S13–S20. http://dx.doi.org/10.1016/j.jadohealth.2012.09.018.

UNICEF. (2021). Cyberbullying: What is it and how to stop it: *10 things teens want to know about cyberbullying*. https://www.unicef.org/end-violence/how-to-stop-cyberbullying (accessed on 10th June, 2021).

7.13 References

Baily, P., Farmer, D., Jessop, D., and Jones, D. (1994). *Purchasing Principles and Management*. London: Pitman Publishing.

Brear, K. (2007). Isomorphic learning in business continuity: A review of processes employed to capture and disseminate the business continuity lessons identified, following the events which occurred in London on the 7th July, 2005, pp. 1–42. *The Third CAMIS Security Management Conference: Strategizing Resilience and Reducing Vulnerability*, Birkbeck College, University of London (5th to 7th September).

Brooks, S.G. (2005). *Producing Security: Multinational Corporations, Globalization, and the Changing Calculus of Conflict.* Princeton, NJ: Princeton University Press.

Downey, L.X., Bauchot, F., and Röling, J. (2018). Blockchain for business value: A contract and work flow management to reduce disputes pilot project. *IEEE Engineering Management Review,* 46 (4): 86–93. https://doi.org/10.1109/EMR.2018.2883328.

Doz, Y., and Kosonen, M. (2008). *Fast Strategy: How Strategic Agility Will Help You to Stay Ahead of the Game.* Harlow: Pearson Education Limited/Wharton School Publishing.

Eells, R. and Nehemkis, P. (1984). *Corporate Intelligence and Espionage: A Blueprint for Executive Decision Making.* New York: Macmillan Publishing Company

ENISA. (2006). *Risk Assessment and Risk Management Methods: Information Packages for Small and Medium Sized Enterprises (SMEs).* Athens, Greece: European Network and Information Security Agency, pp. 1–20 (30th March).

ENISA. (2008). *Business and IT Continuity: Overview and Implementation Principles.* Athens, Greece: European Network and Information Security Agency, pp. 1–179 (February).

ENISA. (2009). *Cloud Computing: Information Assurance Framework.* Athens, Greece: European Network and Information Security Agency, pp. 1–24 (November).

Fox, C.A., and Epstein, M.S. (2010). *Why Is Enterprise Risk Management Important for Preparedness?* White Paper. New York: Risk Insurance Management Society, Inc.

Ghoshal, S. (2004). Global strategy: An organizing framework, pp. 377–394. In S. Segal-Horn (Ed.), *The Strategy Reader.* Oxford: Blackwell Publishing.

Ghoshal, S. and Westney, D.E. (1991). Organizing competitor analysis systems. *Strategic Management Journal,* 12: 17–31.

Hambrick, D.C. (2007). The field of management's devotion to theory: Too much of a good thing? *The Academy of Management Journal,* 50 (6): 1346–1352.

Hamel, G. and Prahalad, C.K. (1994). Strategic intent, pp.3–28. In P. Barnevik and R.M. Kanter (Eds.), *Global Strategies: Insights from the World's Leading Thinkers.* Boston, MA: Harvard Business School Press.

HB 254-(2005). *Governance, Risk Management and Control Assurance Handbook.* Sydney, Australia: Standards Australia/Standards New Zealand.

HB 292-(2006). *A Practitioners Guide to Business Continuity Management.* Sydney, Australia: Standards Australia/Standards New Zealand.

Hyslop, M. (2007). *Critical Information Infrastructures: Resilience and Protection.* New York: Springer.

Hyslop, M. (2009). Towards the hardened organization, pp. 149–163. In P.R.J. Trim and J. Caravelli (Eds.), *Strategizing Resilience and Reducing Vulnerability.* New York: Nova Science Publishers. Inc.,

Irvine, C.E., and Thompson, M. (2003). Teaching objectives of a simulation game for computer security, pp. 1–15. *Proceedings of the Informing Science and Information Technology Joint Conference,* Pori, Finland (24th to 27th June). http://cisr.nps.navy.mil/cyberciege/papers.html (accessed on 22nd January, 2008).

Jones, R.A., Jimmieson, N.L., and Griffiths, A. (2005). The impact of organizational culture and reshaping capabilities on change implementation success: The mediating role of readiness for change. *Journal of Management Studies,* 42 (2): 361–386.

Kahaner, L. (1997). *Competitive Intelligence.* New York: Touchstone.

Kaplan, R.S. and Norton, D.P. (2001). *The Strategy-Focused Organization: How Balanced Scorecard Companies Thrive in the New Business Environment.* Boston, MA: Harvard Business Review.

Lee, Y-I. and Trim, P.R.J. (2006). Retail marketing strategy: The role of marketing intelligence, relationship marketing and trust. *Marketing Intelligence & Planning,* 24 (7): 730–745.

Lindgren, M., and Bandhold, H. (2003). *Scenario Planning: The Link between Future and Strategy.* Basingstoke: Palgrave Macmillan.

Montgomery, D.B., and Weinberg, C.B. (1991). Toward strategic intelligence systems, pp. 341–358. In B.N. Enis and K.K. Cox (Eds.), *Marketing Classics: A Selection of Influential Articles.* Boston, MA: Allyn and Bacon.

NIST. (2010). *Guide for Assessing the Security Controls in Federal Information Systems and Organizations: Building Effective Security Assessment Plans – Information Security Special Publication 800–53A Revision 1.* Gaithersburg, MD: National Institute of Standards and Technology, US Department of Commerce (June).

Porter, M. (1985). *Competitive Advantage: Creating and Sustaining Superior Performance.* New York: The Free Press.

Ringland, G. (2006). *Scenario Planning.* Chichester: John Wiley & Sons.

Sheffi, Y. (2005). *The Resilient Enterprise: Overcoming Vulnerability for Competitive Advantage.* Cambridge: The MIT Press.

Sheth, J.N. and Sharma, A. (1997). Supplier relationships: Emerging issues and challenges. *Industrial Marketing Management*, 26: 91–100.

Simmons, A.C. (2009). A journey towards resilience: Lessons from the British experience, pp. 130–148. In P.R.J. Trim and J. Caravelli (Eds.), *Strategizing Resilience and Reducing Vulnerability.* New York: Nova Science Publishers, Inc.

Smith, D. (2006). Beyond contingency planning: Towards a model of crisis management, pp. 147–158. In D. Smith and D. Elliott (Eds.), *Key Readings in Crisis Management: Systems and Structures for Prevention and Recovery.* London: Routledge.

Sutcliffe, K.M., and Vogus, T.J. (2003). Organizing for resilience, pp. 94–110. In K.S. Cameron, J.E. Dutton and R.E. Quinn (Eds.), *Positive Organizational Scholarship.* San Francisco, CA: Berrett-Koehler Publishers, Inc.,

Tan, T.T.W. and Ahmed, Z.U. (1999). Managing market intelligence: An Asian marketing research perspective. *Marketing Intelligence & Planning*, 17 (6): 298–306.

Thierry, T., Pauchant, C., and Mitroff, I.I. (2006). Crisis prone versus crisis avoiding organizations: Is your company's culture its own worst enemy in creating crises? pp. 136–146. In D. Smith and D. Elliott (Eds.), *Key Readings in Crisis Management: Systems and Structures for Prevention and Recovery.* London: Routledge.

Trim, P.R.J. (2001a). Public-private partnerships in the defence industry and the extended corporate intelligence and national security model. *Strategic Change*, 10 (1): 49–58.

Trim, P.R.J. (2001b). A framework for establishing and implementing corporate intelligence. *Strategic Change*, 10 (6): 349–357.

Trim, P.R.J. (2004). The strategic corporate intelligence and transformational marketing (SATELLITE) model. *Marketing Intelligence & Planning*, 22 (2): 240–256.

Trim, P.R.J., and Lee, Y-I. (2007). A strategic marketing intelligence framework reinforced by corporate intelligence, pp. 55–68. In M. Xu (Ed.), *Managing Strategic Intelligence: Techniques and Technologies.* Hershey, PA: Information Science Reference.

Trim, P.R.J., and Lee, Y-I. (2008a). An explanation of how case study research and simulation can be used to teach negotiation exercises relating to international security, pp. 49–62. In K. Tan, L. Muyldermans and P. Johal (Eds.), *The International Simulation and Gaming Research Yearbook: Teaching and Learning Through Gaming and Simulation*, Volume 17. Edinburgh: SAGSET.

Trim, P.R.J., and Lee, Y-I. (2008b). A strategic marketing intelligence and multi-organizational resilience framework. *European Journal of Marketing*, 42 (7/8): 731–745.

Trim, P.R.J., and Lee, Y-I. (2014). *Cyber Security Management: A Governance, Risk and Compliance Framework.* Farnham: Gower Publishing.

Turner, B.A. (2006). The organizational and interorganizational development of disasters, pp. 115–135. In D. Smith and D. Elliott (Eds.), *Key Readings in Crisis Management: Systems and Structures for Prevention and Recovery.* London: Routledge.

Upton, D. (2007). Official crisis simulations in the UK and elsewhere, pp. 70–88. In P.R.J. Trim and Y-I. Lee (Eds.), *The International Simulation and Gaming Research Yearbook. Volume 15, Effective Learning from Games and Simulations.* Edinburgh: SAGSET.

Weaver, M.R. (2006). Do students value feedback? Student perceptions of tutor' written responses. *Assessment & Evaluation in Higher Education*, 31 (3): 379–394.

White, G.B., and Huson, M.L. (2009). An overview of the community cyber security maturity model, pp. 306–317. In K. J. Knapp (Ed.), *Global Security and Global Information Assurance: Threat Analysis and Response Solutions*. Hershey, PA and New York: Information Science Reference,

Wright, S. (2005). The CI marketing interface. *Journal of Competitive Intelligence and Management*, 3 (2): 3–7.

7.14 Further Reading

Boyes, H. (2015). Cybersecurity and cyber-resilient supply chains. *Technology Innovation Management Review*, (April): 28–34.

Turner, B.A. (2006). The organizational and interorganizational development of disasters, pp. 115–135. In D. Smith and D. Elliott (Eds.), *Key Readings in Crisis Management: Systems and Structures for Prevention and Recovery*. London: Routledge.

Trim, P.R.J., and Lee, Y-I. (2010). A security framework for protecting business, government and society from cyber attacks, pp. 1–6. *5th IEEE International Conference on System of Systems (SoSE): Sustainable Systems for the 21st Century*, Loughborough University (22nd to 24th June).

7.15 Bank of Questions

Question 1: Explain why managers must adopt a formal as opposed to an informal approach to business continuity management and planning.

Question 2: Explain how dependency modelling can be used to aid the risk management process.

Question 3: With reference to specific vulnerabilities in the supply chain, explain how the cyber security manager, the risk manager and the business continuity manager can put in place various contingency plans to deal with a crisis when it occurs.

Question 4: Outline what a disaster recovery plan contains and how it is implemented.

Question 5: What role does the business continuity steering committee play?

Question 6: It has been suggested that strategic intelligence is only concerned with the analysis of known facts. Critically appraise this view and provide examples to reinforce your arguments.

8 Resilience Policy and Planning

8.1 Introduction

Bearing in mind that management can expect a cyber attack to be launched on the organization at any time and some attacks will indeed get through the organization's defences, the cyber security manager should have in place various contingency plans so that either an attack can be reposted in real time or preparation can be made to counteract an attack. Working in close cooperation with the head of corporate security, the cyber security manager will be responsible for ensuring that the corporate security plan in place prioritizes the various types of attack and ensures that the organization is resilient and able to keep functioning. The term *corporate security* does, therefore, need to be placed in a broad context as Trim (2009: 213) suggests:

> …a robust stakeholder security architecture requires that attention is given to intra-government and inter-government working arrangements based on information sharing. It also requires that trust-based relationships between companies that provide disaster relief services and institutions that coordinate disaster relief operations are solidified through time…a more robust global disaster and emergency management policy and strategy [will] emerge and be implemented…[and will] reinforce the fact that a more pro-active approach is needed with respect to dealing with disaster and emergency situations and [furthermore] the international community needs to view disaster and emergency management from the perspective of stakeholder security.

This chapter starts by defining the learning objectives (Section 8.2) and continues with risk and resilience defined (Section 8.3). Next, attention focuses on the need for resilience (Section 8.4), which is followed by resilience policy (Section 8.5). After promoting resilience (Section 8.6), there are resilience domains and features (Section 8.7). Security awareness and organizational learning (Section 8.8) is followed by formulating a resilience policy (Section 8.9), and a learning summary (Section 8.10). A conclusion (Section 8.11) is provided, and this is followed by the mini case (Section 8.12) and an extended case (Section 8.13). The references (Section 8.14) are followed by further reading (Section 8.15), and a bank of questions (Section 8.16).

DOI: 10.4324/9781003244295-8

8.2 Learning Objectives

The reader will:

* establish what a resilience policy is;
* establish why a resilience policy and strategic mapping are necessary; and
* evaluate the role of the cyber security manager in terms of resilience planning.

8.3 Risk and Resilience Defined

Rid and McBurney (2012) are firm in their view as to what a cyber threat represents and have made reference to what a cyber weapon is. Cyber weapons can be grouped according to their potential to cause damage, which can be viewed from a psychological perspective as well as a physical perspective. Looking to the future of cyber weaponry, Rid and McBurney (2012: 10) state: "It would be surprising if an intelligent coded weapon capable of learning had not been developed yet. A learning weapon could observe and evaluate the specifics of an isolated environment autonomously, analyse available courses of action and take action". This is in fact alluring to the fact that artificial intelligence and machine learning are key aspects of cyber security management, which is increasingly having to encompass a geo-political dimension as well as a technological dimension. Bearing this in mind, the cyber security manager needs to answer the following question: how can the organization's leadership model be aligned with the nation's political leadership model in the area of cyber security defence? Longstaff et al. (2010: 7) have provided an insight into this and are right to suggest that leadership can be viewed as a "vital community resource" and used to produce innovation and learning. Longstaff et al. (2010: 9) suggest that: "When a community possesses a high level of all three traits – institutional memory, innovative learning, and connectedness – it, in turn, possesses a high capacity to adapt to changes in the environment". The reason why an organization needs a robust resilience policy in place is because of the "complex consideration of threatening events, interdependencies with other infrastructures, and impact of human behaviour on systems performance" (Steinberg et al., 2011: 28). Furthermore, top management need to ensure that they adapt the security policies of the organization in accordance with threat information received and that they are able to mitigate threats in real time (Anand et al., 2012).

A survey undertaken by the Chartered Institute of Management (CIM, 2011: 13) found that a third of the organizations that participated in the survey had been infected by a virus/malicious software during a 12-month period and 10% of the organizations had lost confidential information. The figures may, however, represent an under-representation because some IT staff may not be aware that the organization's defences have been breached or do not wish to report it; and also, there are cyber security attacks which do not get through an organization's defences.

In order that a resilience policy is accepted by organizational members, it needs to be holistic and embrace security and intelligence. The organizational structures in place need to facilitate the sharing of data and information, but also safeguard sensitive data so that only key senior managers, including the cyber security manager and the risk manager, have full details regarding the organization's counter-intelligence policy. The fact that organized criminal syndicates and state-sponsored organizations are carrying out cyber attacks on organizations and individuals, and are keen to acquire intellectual property rights, places emphasis on the cyber security manager being able to profile all the types of attack the organization and its partner members are likely to be subjected to and have contingency plans in place that will allow the organization to continue trading. The complexity is increased because the issues and challenges relate to threats from current and future competitors; impositions resulting from government regulators; the actions of activists and lobbyists; overseas governments that are undertaking industrial espionage activities; organized crime syndicates; terrorist networks and natural disasters (e.g. floods) that cause damage to and disrupt infrastructure. The cyber security manager is concerned with preventing physical damage to the organization and psychological harm to the employees and the wider community; and it is because of this that the cyber security manager needs to work with a range of security and intelligence staff, some of whom will be external and employed by law enforcement agencies. Increasingly, the cyber security manager is concerned with acts of industrial espionage, which can manifest from organizations and government agencies, in both friendly and hostile nations, and which are predominantly aimed at stealing intellectual property rights in relation to inventions. Both organized criminal syndicates and individual "criminal" entrepreneurs are involved in selling hacker tools on the world wide web; and various documents are also available on the world wide web that can be considered both sensitive and not for general circulation. This is evidence that the cyber security manager needs to be pro-active in terms of identifying and dealing with potential and actual threats, and needs to work closely with staff from human resource management to ensure that staff are both informed about such threats and are able to respond in an appropriate manner when necessary.

The US Homeland Security Studies and Analysis Institute (HSSAI, 2010) explored the link between risk and resilience and explained what risk is and what resilience is. For example, the US Department of Homeland Security definition of risk has been adopted widely (HSSAI, 2010: 3): "The potential for an unwanted outcome resulting from an incident, event, or occurrence as determined by its likelihood and the associated consequences".

The following definition of resilience has been deemed appropriate (HSSAI, 2010: 9):

> Resilience is the ability of a system to attain the objectives of resisting, absorbing, and recovering from the impact of an adverse event, before, during, and after its occurrence. It is also a dynamic process that seeks to learn from incidents to strengthen capabilities of the system in meeting future challenges. The goals are to maintain continuity of function, degrading gracefully, and recover system functionality to a pre-designated level, as rapidly as desired and feasible.

8.4 The Need for Resilience

Kendrick (2010: 11), referring to the PriceWaterhouseCoopers *Information Security Breaches Survey 2010*, indicates that the cost of a breach is between £27,500 and £690,000. Kendrick (2010: 14–17) explains that there are three types of principal risk associated with Internet technologies: (i) technology risk, (ii) legal and compliance risk, and (iii) operational risk. As regards technology risk, the cyber security manager is concerned with computer viruses and their ability to affect the performance of a computer system or network and cause it to fail. Furthermore, the transfer of sensitive and confidential information within an organization and between organizations is an issue, and encryption is often considered to be the answer. Educating staff at all levels within the organization vis-à-vis the use of computers and computer networks is considered important with respect to enhancing and maintaining security. As regards legal and compliance risk, it needs to be noted that top management are required to view this from several perspectives. As well as complying with the various statutory and regulatory provisions in place that result in heavy fines if it is discovered that the company was negligent due to an information breach, for example, there is also the issue of reputational damage in the sense that customers may take their business elsewhere, if they feel that the company is not deploying appropriate safeguards. With respect to operational risk, of key importance here are the systems and procedures in place for governing employee behaviour in relation to the production of goods and services. By participating in the formulation and implementation of security policies and plans, the cyber security manager can influence the way in which an organization invests (e.g. money and manpower) in devising and implementing security solutions, legal compliance and training employees how to handle data. These are important considerations with respect to safeguarding against reputational damage and managing relationships with customers (Kendrick, 2010: 17). Such an approach also helps to place resilience firmly in the context of corporate security.

The board of directors are responsible for corporate governance, which has been defined by Kendrick (2010: 20–21) as "a business strategy based upon transparent decision making; the establishment of lines of accountability and responsibility; securing shareholder and stakeholder value; and the adoption of sound risk management strategies, including information security". Kendrick (2010: 21–22) goes on to state that:

> IT governance is a subset of corporate governance....IT governance is essentially a framework within which IT is designed, deployed and managed in such a way as to ensure that its employment and application remain aligned to the organisation's business objectives.....Project governance may be regarded as a subset of corporate governance...[and].is a set of principles that addresses the development, management and conclusion of projects.

Outsourcing is an area of increased attention and the cyber security manager needs to be at the centre of the decision-making process because the decision to outsource or offshore/near shore is not made on financial criteria alone. Because there are various risks associated with outsourcing such as leakage of data and information, it can be suggested that the risk management process be placed under a risk manager who heads a risk management team (Kendrick, 2010: 25). The risk manager can be held accountable to the board of directors or a senior manager (e.g. head of corporate security) and can liaise with the cyber security manager on a day-to-day basis.

With regard to cloud computing, it can be stated that as regards the consumerization of information technology, the issues of (i) availability, (ii) integrity, (iii) authentication, (iv) confidentiality and (v) non-repudiation (Singh et al., 2009: 294–295) are given increased attention. Organizations are now using various forms of authentication to approve transactions and this is to ensure that ownership, control and the all-round resilience of a system/organization are maintained. The various attacks implemented by cyber attackers are aimed at exploiting the weakest link and they continue to attack computer systems and networks until they gain access and try and extract or sabotage the data.

During the St George's House Annual Lecture 2010, Lord Winston (2011: 7), talking on the theme of "Scientists & Citizens", stated:

> In our digital economy, government can be remarkably careless about the information it stores on our behalf. Unbelievably, the UK government lost the national insurance numbers of 17,000 citizens in 2008. In retrospect, it seems farcical that this digitally stored data was sent by routine post. If that were not enough, the Ministry of Justice lost information affecting more than 45,000 people, in some cases revealing their criminal records and credit histories. Details of 25 million child benefits claimants vanished last year, and the Home Office lost the personal details of 3,000 agricultural workers – including passport numbers when two CDs went missing in an envelope. In five separate cases, the Foreign Office mislaid information affecting about 190,000 people. And the Department for Transport misplaced personal data on six separate occasions, including 3 million records of driving test candidates in May 2007. One might reasonably expect that where national security is involved, officials would encourage particular care – yet the Ministry of Defence lost an unencrypted laptop computer containing 620,000 personal records, including bank account and national insurance numbers and information on 450,000 people named as referees or next of kin by would-be servicemen and women.
>
> These breaches do not necessarily mean that these data will be used by unauthorised persons. But the potential for damage to the individuals concerned is substantial and long-lasting, ranging from financial losses to loss of reputation. Moreover, if when using a personal computer we have our identity stolen we may even be accused of crimes we didn't commit. Other risks undoubtedly include threats to personal safety and the potential for physical or psychological harm. One high profile threat is that posed to children.

Lord Winston (2011: 12) has provided a number of conclusions and recommendations, which include:

> ...every society needs to ensure that the scientific education provided is of the highest quality. Governments need to reflect on a current trend and question whether investing in science education simply because it is valuable to the economy is sound policy. Rather, they should consider investment in science education vital because it is the best way of ensuring that we, our children and grandchildren will live in a safer and healthier society.
>
> In being more science-literate, we might consider that the announcement of a new discovery is almost [always] heralded by exaggerated claims for its immediate value, that many technological advances have a threatening aspect which is not usually recognised at the time of the invention, that most human advances have beneficial applications which are not envisaged when the discovery is first made and that many really important discoveries are arrived at by serendipity...
>
> Communication is a two-way process. Good engagement with the public involves not merely imparting information, but listening to and responding to the ideas, questions, and concerns of the public....We should consider the ethical problems raised by the application of our work...........

Commercial interests so often promoted by governments and universities cannot be disregarded if technology is to be exploited for public good. But scientists need to be aware of the dangers of conflicts of interest. The history of science shows that the pursuit of commercial interests can lead to the loss of public confidence.

The move to remote working is providing both opportunities in the sense that it is allowing employers and employees to have greater flexibility in terms of where employees are based to undertake their duties, but it is also bringing to the fore a number of challenges such as the security of the work environment and the possibility that online business transactions will be intercepted by fraudsters. Also of interest are how counter-intelligence measures can be put in place to stop employees making mistakes and providing access to fraudsters who are intent on carrying out unlawful acts vis-à-vis taking over control of an individual's computer or carrying out industrial espionage through acts of befriending and entrapment. Remote working is considered to have both economic and environmental benefits in the sense that employees working from home can spend more time on work-related issues and less time on travelling and this can increase their productivity. For example, Rosch (2010: 35) reported that Barclays reduced the use of desktops with client terminals that were connected to a remotely located server. Such initiatives can help transform an organization's business model but there may also be challenges that need to be overcome, such as interoperability, for example.

President Obama stated in 2009 that a resilient nation is (HSSAI, 2010: 4) "one in which individuals, communities, and our economy can adapt to changing conditions as well as withstand and rapidly recover from disruption due to emergencies". The UK Foreign Secretary William Hague (2011), speaking on the theme "Security and Freedom in the Cyber Age – Seeking the rules of the road", stated:

> Many government services are now delivered via the internet, as is education in many classrooms. In the UK 70% of younger internet users bank online and two thirds of all adults shop on the internet. This is not a phenomenon confined to any one part of the world. In less than 15 years the number of web users has exploded from 16 million in 1995 to more than 1.7 billion today, more than half of whom are in developing countries. By 2015, it is said that there will be more interconnected devices on the planet than humans.
>
> Along with its numerous benefits, cyberspace has created new means of repression, enabling undemocratic governments to violate the human rights of their citizens.
>
> It has opened up new channels for hostile governments to probe our defences and attempt to steal our confidential information or intellectual property.
>
> It has promoted fears of future 'cyber war'.
>
> It has enabled terrorist networks to plan atrocities, flood internet chat rooms with their ideology and prey on the vulnerable from thousands of miles away.
>
> And it provides rich pickings for criminals. On-line criminals steal the identities of ordinary citizens. They empty bank-accounts, extort money from firms and defraud government departments, and cost the global economy as much as $1 trillion annually...
>
> Cyber-security is on the agendas of some thirty multilateral organisations, from the UN to the OCSE and the G8. NATO's Lisbon Summit in November launched

a new programme to defend NATO's communication systems from cyber attack. But much of this debate is fragmented and lacks focus.

We believe there is a need for a more comprehensive, structured dialogue to begin to build consensus among like-minded countries and to lay the basis for agreement on a set of standards on how countries should act in cyberspace. How this dialogue is organised is up for discussion. But we need to get the ball rolling faster...

So in Britain's view, seven principles should underpin future international norms about the use of cyberspace:

The need for governments to act proportionately in cyberspace and in accordance with national and international law;

The need for everyone to have the ability – in terms of skills, technology, confidence and opportunity – to access cyberspace;

The need for users of cyberspace to show tolerance and respect for diversity of language, culture and ideas;

Ensuring that cyberspace remains open to innovation and the free flow of ideas, information and expression;

The need to respect individual rights of privacy and to provide proper protection to intellectual property;

The need for us all to work collectively to tackle the threat from criminals acting online;

And the promotion of a competitive environment which ensures a fair return on investment in network, services and content.

We are open to the ideas of others and we have already begun to discuss cyber with our allies in Washington, Paris, Berlin, Canberra and elsewhere. We must widen the debate over the coming year. We have a major opportunity to promote the Budapest Convention on Cyber Crime, which the UK will look to do when we chair the Council of Europe from November. Here, as in every debate about how to fashion collective responses to the security challenges of our time, Britain is ready to play its part.

As regards the benefits of cloud computing, Clapperton (2010: 17) has stated:

> In general, though, cloud specialists provide more efficient environments than their customers could achieve in-house, Craig-Wood says, not just through virtualisation improvements, but also through investing in mass automation of data centres, which results in reduced power and hardware requirements. Companies should consider outsourcing to the cloud via two routes, she advises: IaaS (infrastructure as a service), which involves renting servers that reside in the cloud; and SaaS (software as a service), where email hosting and other applications are provided as a cloud-based service.

This raises a number of interesting and linked topics: data storage and the use of a data centre, and the energy savings that can be made, which translate into carbon savings. For example, Bray (2010: 19) states:

> Within the data centre, organisations need to consider two aspects: the IT equipment itself (servers, storage, networking equipment, etc), and the infrastructure that supports it (cooling, ventilation, humidification, power supply etc). As a rule of

thumb, for every pound you spend buying a server you can reckon to spend another pound to manage it and two pounds to power and cool it, so energy considerations should be an important part of the procurement decision.

The process of virtualization is, according to Hamilton (2010: 41), "a technology that allows firms to abstract IT services from an underlying infrastructure" and "in simple terms, offer[s] a trustworthy path to slashing energy costs and reducing data centre space", and needs to be placed in the context of an organization's long-term IT strategy. More generally, Hamilton (2010: 41) has explained this by stating that:

> Boards understand cost, but they also understand that in today's world you need to be more responsive and that means having the ability to release new financial products that meet rapidly changing market demands. To enable these core demands to be met, other key elements in the migration to the cloud will be critical. These include refreshing older applications, some of which can't handle the demands of cloud computing, and equally important, ensuring that, for example, IT operational processes are optimised to reflect the importance of on-demand computing in the private cloud.
>
> What are some practical actions you can take to start achieving these objectives? Assessing the readiness of your IT infrastructure and processes to deliver cloud-based services is a good place to begin. Many firms are also developing financial models and business cases to determine the feasibility of cloud for their operations. Workshops with application and business stakeholders can establish priorities for cloud-enabling applications, align business requirements to IT service levels, and clarify compliance and security requirements.

Speaking on the topic of controlling security in the cloud, at the Second International Secure Systems Development Conference, Raj Samani (2011) made it known that there are five key challenges:

1   Assure the multitude of third party conditions in a scalable manner.
2   Be able to objectively and reliably measure the risk management maturity of third parties.
3   Ensure that all risk management requirements are reflected in contracts (and will be applicable in the future).
4   Perform the due diligence required within current resourcing constraints.
5   Find an approach that leverages existing investment and will be adopted by suppliers.

Samani (2011) is of the view that managers need to devise an approach that allows information risk management to be incorporated objectively into the tender process; and also establish a way in which to compare risk maturity between different suppliers. This suggests that there does need to be full transparency with regard to auditing. By ensuring that the auditing process is thorough and undertaken according to strict criteria, the partnership arrangement will be judged to incorporate mutuality and the stakeholders will be viewed as trustworthy.

A point to note that emerged from the Second International Secure Systems Development Conference was that mobile computing will drive cloud services and as a result security problems will increase. Harper (2011), speaking at the same conference, indicated that in excess of US$288 billion is spent worldwide each year on information security and that 75% of the attacks are on the application layer. It is believed that 10–100 vulnerabilities are evident in core applications and although the case can be made for more penetration testing, penetration testing is not a solution in itself. For example, penetration testing normally occurs at the stage of pre-introduction and it should take place at the start of the software development life cycle (Harper, 2011).

8.5 Resilience Policy

Although networks are considered reasonably secure and the main threat appears to be via the application layer, it has to be remembered that Stuxnet infiltrated networks and became a worm (Barnell, 2011). To avoid this happening, it is recommended that managers take the following into account (Barnell, 2011):

1 Carry out continual monitoring in order to identify suspicious behaviour.
2 Implement an adequate information assurance programme.
3 Use file-level encryption.
4 Check advice offered on the security response websites.
5 Investigate contractors to ensure that they are reputable and that they will share responsibility for risk.
6 Ensure that contractors are not using stolen software (this is how Stuxnet penetrated the network).

With respect to the traditional System Development Life Cycle (SDLC), Virgona (2011: 6) states:

> Disaster recovery is dependent on the SDLC for ensuring disaster recovery planning is integrated throughout the technology development process: the requirements for the system's recovery are defined in the analysis phase, the system is designed to provide service during a disaster within the specified timeframes and testing the recovery capabilities is part of the creation of the project, thus ensuring continued use during a disaster.

Monitoring employees, either directly (CCTV usage and computer logs) or indirectly (through peer reviews), is a controversial subject and is related to trust or a lack of trust (Cialdini et al., 2004: 71). Trust-based relationships are developed through time and it is accepted that "Organisational politics, combined with apathy and distrust, can militate against the formation and development of trust based relationships" (Trim et al., 2009: 350). According to Dawson (1996: 268–269), a number of issues and factors need to be taken into account by managers when analysing an organization:

1 Organizations are interactive systems, with change in one aspect having repercussions for others, sometimes in an unintended or unanticipated way.
2 Organizations are highly complex systems in which there is a great deal of uncertainty.
3 There is no one best way to act in organizations: an appropriate path should be taken through paradox and contradiction in a manner appropriate to the context.

4 Resources are always scarce, and any action is likely to have financial or social costs as well as benefits.
5 Organizations are arenas for the activities of different interest groups which are linked through patterns of conflict, consensus and indifference.
6 People in organizations perceive varying sources of opportunities for, and constraints on, possible action.
7 Activities in, and outcomes from, organizations can be analysed in terms of the level of the individual, group, organization or society; it is very important to identify the levels that are appropriate to the problems, issues or opportunities with which any practitioner or analyst is concerned.

Dupont (2019) is of the view that resilient organizations are able to learn from events and in addition implement improvements that increase their preparedness. Lee (2009) suggests that organizational learning or a commitment to it is an essential aspect of an organization's development because senior managers need to manage inter-organizational as well as intra-organizational relationships. By devising and deploying an adapted leadership style, which becomes more obvious a task when managing internationally and experiencing different cultural groups (Lee, 2009: 192), the cyber security manager can link security training needs with specified cyber security learning objectives. They will need to take into account the psychology of cyberspace (Barak and Suler, 2008) because of people's behaviour in cyber space and how customers engage with information about products and services, and how workers, possibly working remotely, need to be managed and motivated.

8.6 Promoting Resilience

According to the US Homeland Security Studies and Analysis Institute (HSSAI, 2010: 18):

> Promoting resilience can help achieve the fundamental goal of reducing and managing risk, while risk assessments can inform resilience policies....Risk and resilience both involve operationalized planning and allocation of resources. Risk-informed resource allocation seeks to lower risk in cost effective ways. Likewise, resilience ways and means seek to allocate resources that increase resilience in cost effective ways.
>
> Resilience planning can provide a framework for risk reduction that can be applied to risk assessment and management...
>
> ...risk assessments can inform operational planning for system resilience by providing an understanding of the likelihood and consequences of the dangers facing those assets....

Kahan et al. (2009: 29–30) have looked at the relationship between resilience principles and resilience objectives and mapped them as below:

1 Threat and hazard limitation is principally associated with the resistance objective.
2 Robustness is principally associated with the absorption objective.
3 Consequence mitigation is principally associated with the restoration objective.
4 Adaptability, risk-informed planning, risk-informed investment, harmonization of purposes and comprehensiveness of scope are critical considerations for all three resilience objectives.

5 The resistance objective is inherently linked to prevent and protect missions.
6 The absorption objective is inherently linked to protect and respond missions.
7 The restoration objective is inherently linked to respond and recover missions.

Bearing the above in mind, the cyber security manager can promote the concept of resilience throughout the organization and partner organizations in various ways, but will need the continued support of top management. To be effective, however, both the means and key success factors need to be identified (Trim and Lee, 2014: 109). As regards the means, top management should ensure that (i) a Resilience Charter is in place; (ii) transparent communication exists at all levels and (iii) in-house seminars and workshops (e.g. talks, table top exercises and complex scenarios) are used for imparting information and knowledge, and sharing experiences. The key success factors could be (i) an appropriate leadership model is in place; (ii) the risk mitigation policy is appropriate; (iii) there is contingency planning across all functions; (iv) the recovery process is logical and documented; and (v) there is an appropriate allocation of resources or access to resources.

8.7 Resilience Domains and Features

The US Homeland Security Studies and Analysis Institute (HSSAI, 2010: 6–7) has identified four resilience domains: (1) infrastructure: engineered assets, systems, networks, both physical and cyber, including interconnected nodes – telecommunications or power stations, known as systems of systems; (2) organizations: a range of public sector and private sector organizations are included with functional subcomponents and defined objectives, and which have associated supply chains; (3) communities: all aspects of society are included – a city where people live, community groups, businesses, buildings, facilities and social capital, for example; (4) ecosystems: living organisms, the physical environment where people live and the interrelations they have.

The US Homeland Security Studies and Analysis Institute (HSSAI, 2010: 15–16) has identified 11 resilience features: (1) pre-event activity (individuals, organizations, communities and certain systems anticipate challenges and plan and prepare to deal with threats and hazards); (2) situational awareness (people, organizations and technology during an emergency maintain communications and develop a common operating picture that allows those in leadership positions to make appropriate and timely decisions vis-à-vis priorities and objectives); (3) resistance (various countermeasures "to actively redirect, thwart, or attenuate a threat, hazard, or other disruption before or at time of arrival"); (4) cushionability (the ability of a system to absorb a blow and degrade slowly); (5) robustness (when internal or external stress is placed on a system, this reflects the capability of the system to maintain its critical functions); (6) redundancy (alternative options exist and critical assets and resources can be substituted; hence, there is no complete dependence on a subsystem); (7) resourcefulness (the capability to improvise and innovate after or during an adverse event); (8) restoration (this reflects how well a system can perform its functions after an event and also at what level it can perform this functionality); (9) rapidity (the time taken for a system to recover after an event and perform at certain levels); (10) learning capacity (the capability to learn from events and the lessons learned are used to improve future performance during adverse conditions) and (11) affordability (fiscal feasibility and practicality associated with the capabilities designed into systems that ensure that they cope with adversity).

Writing on resilience, McCreight (2009: 4–5) states that:

> Resilience and recovery are very similar, both focusing on the same objectives and outcome. Their shared goal: a survivable and viable community that has withstood disaster and emerges from it wounded, but fully capable of conducting governmental and commercial operations. The main distinction is the emphasis on planning and strategic mitigation, which is embedded in the notion of resilience. It assumes a community committed to every conceivable and robust pre-disaster activity aimed at assuring its survival and continuation. Recovery, by contrast, tends to focus more on the immediate operational, logistical, sociological, and commercial aspects of bringing a damaged community back to life in the aftermath of a disaster. Here the emphasis is on what specific tasks must be performed to restore essential community institutions, neighbourhoods, and related environments. Resilience aims to thwart, diminish, or curtail a disaster's worst effects well in advance of calamity, while recovery attempts to restore to 'nearly normal' as quickly as possible. One is short term, immediate, and temporary. The other is deliberate, strategic, and enduring for the affected community.

Five main dimensions to resilience are evident:

1 personal and familial socio-psychological well-being;
2 organizational and institutional restoration;
3 economic and commercial resumption of services and productivity;
4 restoring infrastructural systems integrity; and
5 operational regularity of public safety and government.

The five dimensions must be assessed independently, and then recombined in a comprehensive manner to resemble a unified strategy. Resilience is, therefore, the result of a deliberative process with built-in assumptions and intentions reflecting a community's firm commitment to its own survival and restoration.

McCreight (2009: 5) defines further the five points cited and states:

> The socio-psychological aspect deals with the public's emotional consciousness, its attachment to (and influence by) the disaster itself, along with the human spirit of grit, determination, and survival. Organizational and institutional restoration deals with social and mediating institutions like schools and influential community groups. Commercial and economic activity is resumed to offer those services and commodities that the disaster nullified. Key infrastructures in power, water, sewer, communications, and related functions are demonstrably back in operation. Finally, government services and public safety must be restored. This raises the fair and urgent question of how a community achieves resilience both as a goal and a yardstick for enhancing its survivability and continuation in facing future disasters.

8.8 Security Awareness and Organizational Learning

There is a link between an individual's behaviour in an organization and their legal responsibility, which is embedded within the organization's culture (Garlati cited in Trim et al., 2012a: 2). Through the process of linking an individual's behaviour with security awareness, it is possible to establish what organizational learning is to achieve.

An immediate topic of attention that the cyber security manager and their peers need to focus on is how to manage organizational cultural change. Because the insider threat is very real, the cyber security manager needs to be vigilant and ensure that the cyber security systems in place are robust enough to prevent cyber criminals circumventing computer security systems and befriending staff with the intention of stealing data/information or carrying out an act of sabotage.

Smith (cited in Trim et al., 2012b: 3) suggests that it is not surprising to learn that acts of fraud and unintentional behavioural patterns (writing down passwords on Post-it Notes, leaving computer files open while employees are not at their work station, and passing out information to unknown individuals via social networks) are common practice that can and does result in a security breach. This highlights the fact that the main security threat to an organization is from people as opposed to technology (Davis, 2007: 185). However, a combination of a lack of IT security and an apathetic attitude among staff can be considered to increase the risk of a data/information breach. It is because of this that security needs to be placed in a wider context, namely, human resource management. This requires that policies are in place to deal with deviant behaviour and at the same time, the organization's value system has to be capable of reinforcing the fact that a resilient organization requires staff to have a security mentality.

Trim et al. (2012b) drew information from an IAAC research workshop that focused on "Understanding, Explaining and Counteracting Inappropriate User Behaviour", which was held in London at BCS, The Chartered Institute for IT on 13 March 2012. The workshop was attended by 31 security experts and addressed six questions:

> What measures can be put in place to prevent individuals engaging in inappropriate behaviour?
>
> How can policy be formulated that takes into account the challenges and threats posed by BYOD (Bring Your Own Device), as IT processes are simply not designed for this?
>
> How can the attitudes of employees be influenced in order to change behaviour so that the necessary security procedures are embraced?
>
> How useful is it to incorporate litigation based case studies in order to teach risk management and ensure that the IT policies in place are workable?
>
> How can management ensure that the behaviour of employees conforms to what is classified as 'secure behaviour'?
>
> If the behaviour of employees is deemed inappropriate, how can management begin the process of influencing staff attitudes towards information assurance and cyber security?

Reflecting on the above questions, the cyber security manager needs to note that it is possible to have a mix of informal and formal procedures in place to curtail inappropriate behaviour; however, the punishments and rewards need to be viewed as fair. Because security priorities may change through time, it is important that resources are put into cyber security awareness programmes and bespoke cyber security training sessions at the same time. Otherwise, there is likely to be a mismatch and staff will not be able to upgrade their skill and knowledge base in order to maintain the organization's level of resilience. Being aware of what type of attack is being launched on the organization and acting in real time to defend the organization is crucial if cyber attacks are to be thwarted. Case studies and case examples are effective learning vehicles and a distinction needs to be made regarding training, which is related to skill enhancement; and education, which is about the transfer and utilization of knowledge. By testing staff on a regular basis, it should be possible to identify the skills and knowledge they have and how they undertake their tasks. For example, if an individual member of staff clicks on an email attachment and they should not have done so, it would seem appropriate for them to undergo a cyber security training programme. If, however, a deeper under-standing of the subject is required, it may be appropriate to use a simulated exercise and link it with a round table discussion.

8.9 Formulating a Resilience Policy

The monitoring of employees is considered controversial because it is associated with a lack of trust (Cialdini et al., 2004). It can be noted that trust-based relationships are developed through time; hence, in order to develop trust, attention needs to be given to how the concept of organizational learning can be embraced and how top management can provide the type of leadership required that allows cyber security to be embedded in inter-organizational and intra-organizational relationships, which embrace different cultural settings (Lee, 2009: 192). Embracing this view, the cyber security manager can ensure that the partnership arrangement (suppliers, manufacturer, wholesalers, retailers and other stakeholders) actively engages in cyber security. A question arises, however. In order to produce a sustainable cyber defence-focused partnership arrangement, what formal structures need to be in place between the parties in order that the information exchanged is viewed as necessary?

Humphrey (2012) suggests that organizations adopt a selective approach to shar-ing information because organized criminals target organizational vulnerabilities. For example, the insider threat is considered a major risk and Hoskins (2012), in a talk entitled "Regulation problems resulting from an EU directive", has suggested that there are two to three breaches each week that are reported to the customer and the relevant authorities. A CPNI Representative (2012) has indicated that data leakage can occur via storage sites, social media sites, printers and photocopiers (as they possess memories), smartphones and tablets, mobile phones, laptops, anything portable that has a storage or write facility, for example. This suggests that the cyber security manager needs to know how information is managed, how it is stored, who has access to it and where it is accessed from. Just as importantly, the cyber security manager needs to be aware of how people dispose of information when it is no longer required. It could be that infor-mation is collected in a secure unit and then destroyed. Questions can be asked about whether this is done on the organization's premises or by a subcontractor. Furthermore, it may be that staff are not allowed to download certain types of information from an organization's own computer network and if they do, a warning is flagged in the com-puter log that is instantly available to the IT manager, the risk manager and the cyber security manager. In addition, computers and other devices that are deemed unusable and are to be discarded need to be wiped of the data and information contained on them and this needs to be done in-house by the IT department. Should a policy be in place to recycle equipment/electronic devices, it is essential that if an external company is involved, all the data and information are removed from the device and a check is carried out to ensure that this is the case. The cyber security manager also needs to be aware of how and where data is stored. If data is stored in the cloud; it needs to be fully protected, available on request and destroyed without any trace of a back-up.

According to Humphrey et al. (2012: 4): "The need exists for more appropriate advice to be given to people concerning practical steps to be taken to prevent data breaches and to implement corrective action if a breach has occurred". It is possible that if a device is lost, company policy demands that the data is automatically wiped. If an employee is in breach of protocols, then it is possible that company policy will dictate that all the files on the computer are erased (Humphrey et al., 2012: 4). In order that the company has a robust security policy in place, employees may be required to sign a document/nondisclosure deal that protects the company itself and other employees working for the company.

Remote working is now receiving a great deal of attention and it is clear that the cost of a breach, both in monetary terms and in psychological terms, needs to be better understood than it is at present. This is an additional factor that the cyber security manager can take responsibility for and working with their peers in marketing can develop new business models that provide insights into online customer experience (Hsu and Tsou, 2011) and online community promotion (Casalo et al., 2010). Those producing innovative products will need to take into account purchase intentions and especially brand association and utility, and social or hedonic utility (Arruda-Filho et al., 2010: 480). Garlati (cited in Trim et al., 2012a: 2) states that employees do not understand the implications of using their personal devices at work and a formal cyber security awareness programme will do much to change this. Insufficient education and training in security awareness is a concern to the cyber security manager and a formal and continually updated cyber security education and training programme can be established that keeps employees informed about the evolving cyber risks and how best to approach the concept of BYOD (Bring Your Own Device) to work.

8.10 Learning Summary

To be effective, strategic cyber security resilience, please see Figure 8.1, needs to include contractor policy because business models are changing and in some instances, work is being subcontracted to overseas providers. In addition, the outsourcing, offshoring and near-shoring approaches have become well established and this has both solved but in some cases resulted in technological as well as human challenges. Developments in cloud computing mean that organizations have an opportunity to use the services

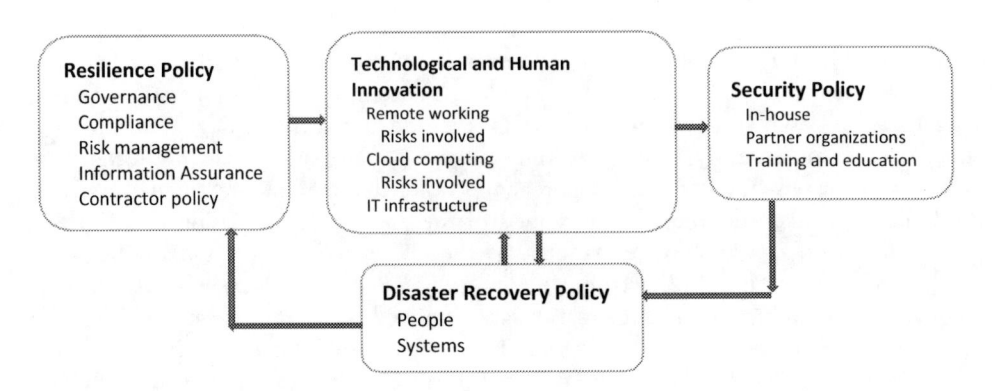

Figure 8.1 Strategic cyber security resilience.

of specialist computer companies and at the same time, however, a number of threats and problems can be identified. What is significant is that an organization's resilience policy is influential in terms of partner organizations' security policy and will require managers from the various organizations in the partnership arrangement to formulate a disaster recovery policy, based on how people operate the systems in place.

The reader will be able to:

- devise a resilience policy;
- implement a resilience policy; and
- develop an integrated strategic resilience management model.

8.11 Conclusion

By having a sound appreciation of information assurance, the cyber security manager will be able to devise robust organizational countermeasures that decrease risk and allow adequate organizational countermeasures to be developed that are co-managed by staff in partner organizations. The cyber security manager can help senior management to devise a Resilience Charter that outlines what all the organizations in the partnership arrangement need to do in order to ensure that the reputation management programme in place is as informative as it should be. The adapted leadership style ensures that management pay adequate attention to risk management, security and intelligence work, and that they adhere to governance and compliance issues, and engage adequately in business continuity management. This is because resilience is about putting in place structures and mechanisms that ensure that if a cyber attack does get through the organization's defences, the damage caused is minimal and the organization is able to continue trading.

8.12 Mini Case: Dealing with Ransomware

John Hargreaves, the Chief Executive Officer (CEO) of a medium-sized company that had its headquarters in London and operated various subsidiaries and partnership arrangements throughout the world, was quietly confident about winning a business contract with a new customer. The company was known to be innovative and a leader in the industry in which it competed, and had over the years both been nominated for and won various industry prizes. Senior management had invested in security over the years and the security systems in place had been updated through time. Owing to recent events, however, senior management had on the agenda, the topic of ransomware, which was known but not understood well by John Hargreaves and his colleagues.

In Spring 2021, John Hargreaves commissioned a cyber security consultant to produce a report outlining what cyber threats the company was likely to face over the next five years and how contingences should be put in place to deal with them. Mr. Hargreaves was rather astonished to discover that the main malware threat to the company was in the way of ransomware. According to the author of the report, who cited the work of Richardson and North (2017: 10), ransomware can be of two types: one type is crypto ransomware that encrypts files and data and the other is locker ransomware, which acts in a way to lock the computer/device so that the user cannot use it. What was clear from the work of Richardson and North (2017: 10) is that even if a company concedes and pays a ransom (usually in the form of Bitcoin), there is no guarantee that the attacker will provide the encryption key and allow management to unlock the computer/device and return to normal. If management find that they have been attacked and they cannot regain control of the computer systems(s) necessary to manage the company, they could be vulnerable to continuing in business as existing clients disengage and take their business elsewhere.

Ransomware attacks are regularly conducted against the UK and US firms, and as a consequence senior managers in the UK and US firms have got to be aware that ransomware attacks are likely to increase in the years ahead. Bearing this in mind, John Hargreaves commissioned another report from the same cyber security consultancy that dealt with how to avoid a ransomware attack. What he wanted to know was which factors would contribute to a ransomware attack and how much such an attack would cost the company should it be necessary to pay the ransom. Of concern was reputational damage and also investing in higher grade computer systems to avoid such a problem from occurring.

The second report drew on the work of RUSI (the Royal United Services Institute) and outlined how an attacker carries out such an attack (Sullivan and Muir, 2021). Reading through the information, Mr. Hargreaves realized just how complex the problem was. The main problem centred around the company losing its operational capability if the computers were disabled and the employees could not operate as normal. However, paying a ransom was not always possible because of the size of the fee or because the government may not condone such an action. If a fee was paid, would it leave the company open to additional ransomware attacks by other organized criminal groups? Mr. Hargreaves decided to ask his management team to compile a report outlining the key aspects relating to ransomware that needed to be answered.

Questions

Question 1: What do staff need to do in order to prevent a ransomware attack on the company?

Question 2: What should staff do in order to stop a ransomware attack on the company becoming public knowledge, should it cause damage in some way?

Question 3: Bearing in mind a ransomware attack can be launched on a company or a partner organization, what should senior management do in order to ensure that if a partner organization is attacked, the problem is dealt with in a positive way through combined action?

Case Sources

Richardson, R., and North, M. (2017). Ransomware: Evolution, mitigation and prevention. *International Management Review*, 13 (1): 10–21.

Sullivan, J., and Muir, J. (2021). *Ransomware: A Perfect Storm*. London: Royal United Services Institute (RUSI).

8.13 Extended Case: Biometrics – A Solution for All

Simon Bates was the head of marketing for a small UK start-up company that had recently won an order from a large company that traded worldwide. Simon Bates and the senior management team were elated with the order and considered that it would provide the company with an opportunity to strengthen existing business ties and expand and consolidate business relations. It would also, through the association with the new customer, allow the company to gain more business. It was a win–win situation and one to be celebrated.

Six weeks later, an issue arose that caused much concern. An email had been received by the accounts department suggesting that a supplier of the large company that the company had just signed the contract with was demanding an up-front payment of US$100,000 for partially completed work that had been sanctioned by the partner company on behalf of Mr. Bates' company. Various senior managers were involved in discussions about the email request, which appeared to be on valid, company-headed notepaper. Several telephone calls had been made by staff from Mr. Bates' office to representatives of the large company but people had not been cooperative. Follow-up emails had been sent to explain the situation and provide evidence that an invoice had been received and that the company involved was threatening legal action.

After a number of days, Mr. Bates and his colleagues were able to prove that the invoice was fake and they alerted various industry bodies and law enforcement representatives so that they were aware that a scam was being operated. This was not the only scam to befall the company however. Two weeks after the scam had been solved and eradicated, an individual arrived at the company's headquarters asking to see Mr. Finch, the head of finance. Mr. Finch was away from the office on holiday and not expected to return for another week. He was away on a cruise in the Mediterranean and difficult to contact.

Instead of meeting Mr. Finch, a meeting was hastily arranged with Mr. Jenkings, the head of accounts. Mr. Jenkings met the individual concerned but was not impressed. The person concerned had no real purpose and he considered that his suspicious behaviour suggested that he was either gaining knowledge about the company and how it operated or was in fact working for a competitor and trying to gain as much intelligence about the company as possible. During the discussions, it appeared that the individual knew about individuals that had LinkedIn accounts and had studied the profiles of various people.

Following Mr. Finch's return to the office, a meeting was held with the senior management team and the topic discussed was identifying and authenticating individuals, their backgrounds and their companies. This was timely because of recent events but also because during the cruise, Mr. Finch had talked with someone that had fallen victim to deceit. Mr. Finch recanted the story he had been told by the person concerned on the cruise ship. Basically, a small company had entered into a business deal with an overseas supplier only to be defrauded of a large sum of money. The background to the story is that the company was approached by an individual claiming to represent a supplier company, which in fact did not exist, and although company representatives visited the country where the illusory company was based, they were wined and dined in a hotel and did not visit the company's site, which turned out to be a vacant plot of land. Company staff had not followed up or carried out due diligence and as a consequence they got involved in a business deal that led the company to lose a great deal of money.

In order not to fall into such a trap, it was decided that the company should invest in a range of technology to improve staff's ability to authenticate people, especially as there was a trend towards e-negotiations and e-procurement. One of the issues discussed was the useful of biometric identification in poor countries (Gelb and Clark, 2013: 3). This was because it may not always be possible to obtain legal documents and other documentation to prove that people are who they say they are. Dealing with people abroad was known to be time-consuming but as the UK had recently emerged from BREXIT, it was considered necessary as the UK companies were known to be looking for business opportunities outside Europe.

According to Gelb and Clark (2013: 9), biometrics is used for two identity-related purposes. The first priority is to identify an individual and establish if that person is real; and second, biometrics is used to authenticate an individual against a record so that the individual can be identified as the actual person. Mr. Finch and his colleagues considered it necessary to invest in biometrics because of this and also biometrics was known to work well as a number of technologies could be utilized such as finger-scan technology, facial-scan technology, iris-scan technology and voice-scan technology (Nanavati et al., 2002).

Questions

Question 1: Which factors should senior management take into account when undertaking a vulnerability study of their company?

Question 2: How can biometrics technology be utilized?

Question 3: Why is it important not to rely on biometric technology alone for authentication purposes?

Case Sources

Gelb, A., and Clark, J. (2013). *Identification for Development: The Biometrics Revolution*. Working Paper 315. Washington, DC: Center for Global Development. https://www.cgdev.org/publication/identification-development-biometrics-revolution-working-paper-315 (accessed on 11th June, 2021).

Nanavati, S., Thieme, M., and Nanavati, R. (2002). *Biometrics: Identify Verification in a Networked World*. Chichester: John Wiley & Sons, Inc.

8.14 References

Arruda-Filho, E.J.M., Cabusas, J.A., and Dholakia, N. (2010). Social behavior and brand devotion among iPhone innovators. *International Journal of Information Management*, 30: 475–480.

Barak, A., and Suler, J. (2008). Reflections on the psychology and social science of cyberspace, pp. 1–12. In A. Barak (Ed.), *Psychological Aspects of Cyberspace: Theory, Research, Applications*. Cambridge: Cambridge University Press.

Barnell, D. (2011). Stuxnet – Rethink security, right across the supply chain. *Second International Secure Systems Development Conference: Designing in Security*, Hilton London Olympia Hotel, London (18th to 19th May).

Bray, P. (2010). Getting down to brass tacks, pp. 18–20. *The True Cost of Your IT: A Guide to Environmentally Friendly Computing*. London: Lyonsdown Media Group.

Casalo, L.V., Flavian, C., and Guinaliu, M. (2010). Relationship quality, community promotion and brand loyalty in virtual communities: Evidence from free software communities. *International Journal of Information Management*, 30: 357–367.

Cialdini, R.B., Petrova, P.K., and Goldstein, N.J. (2004). The hidden costs of organizational dishonesty. *MIT Sloan Management Review,* 45 (3) (Spring): 67–73.

CIM. (2011). *Managing Threats in a Dangerous World*. London: Chartered Institute of Management.

Clapperton, G. (2010). Clouds, not smoke, pp. 16–17. In *The True Cost of Your IT: A Guide to Environmentally Friendly Computing*. London: Lyonsdown Media Group.

CPNI Representative (2012). Potential impact upon critical infrastructures: Data leakage and consumerisation. *IAAC Consumerisation and Information Sharing Workshop*, BCS, The Chartered Institute for IT, London (17th January).

Davis, B.J. (2007). Situational prevention and penetration testing: A proactive approach to social engineering organizations, pp. 175–188. In A.W. Merkidze (Ed.), *Terrorism Issues: Threat Assessment, Consequences and Prevention*. New York: Nova Science Publishers, Inc.

Dawson, S. (1996). *Analysing Organisations*. Basingstoke: Palgrave.

Dupont, B. (2019). The cyber-resilience of financial institutions: Significance and applicability. *Journal of Cybersecurity*, 1–17. https://doi.org/10.1093/cybsec/tyz013.

Hague, W. (2011). Security and Freedom in the Cyber Age – Seeking the Rules of the Road. *Munich Security Conference*, Munich, Germany (4th February). http://www.fco.gov.uk/en/news/latest-news/?view=Speech&id=544853682 (accessed on 1st July).

Hamilton, S. (2010). Private clouds. *Financial Sector Technology*, 16 (4): 41.

Harper, D. (2011). Building security into software. *Second International Secure Systems Development Conference: Designing in Security*, Hilton London Olympia Hotel, London (18th to 19th May).

Hoskins, M. (2012). Regulation problems resulting from an EU directive. *IAAC Consumerisation and Information Sharing Workshop*, BCS, The Chartered Institute for IT, London (17th January).

HSSAI. (2010). *Risk and Resilience: Exploring the Relationship*. Arlington, MA: Department of Homeland Security, Science and Technology Directorate (22nd November).

Hsu, H.Y., and Tsou, H-T. (2011). Understanding customer experiences in online blog environments. *International Journal of Information Management*, 31: 510–523.

Humphrey, M. (2012). The current challenges for information sharing. *IAAC Consumerisation and Information Sharing Workshop*, BCS, The Chartered Institute for IT, London (17th January).

Humphrey, M., Hoskins, M., CPNI Representative and Trim, P. (2012). *Information Assurance Advisory Council Consumerisation of IT Research Workshop Report: Questioning Existing Policy and Setting the Scene to Avoid Predictable Pitfalls: A Call to Action and the Way Forward*. London: Information Assurance Advisory Council (January).

Kahan, J.H., Allen, A.C., and George, J.K. (2009). An operational framework for resilience. *Journal of Homeland Security and Emergency Management*, 6 (1): 1–48.

Kendrick, R. (2010). *Cyber Risks for Business Professionals*. Ely: IT Governance Publishing.

Lee, Y-I. (2009). Strategic transformational management in the context of inter-organizational and intra-organizational partnership development, pp. 181–196. In P.R.J. Trim and J. Caravelli (Eds.), *Strategizing Resilience and Reducing Vulnerability*. New York: Nova Science Publishers, Inc.

Longstaff, P.H., Armstrong, N.J., Perrin, K., Parker, W.M., and Hidek, M.A. (2010). Building resilient communities: A preliminary framework for assessment. *Homeland Security Affairs*, 6 (September): 1–23.

McCreight, R. (2009). Resilience as a goal and standard in emergency management. *Journal of Homeland Security and Emergency Management*, 7 (1): 1–7.

Rid, T., and McBurney, P. (2012). Cyber-weapons. *RUSI Journal*, 157 (1): 6–13.

Rosch, V. (2010). Living the dream. *Financial Sector Technology*, 16 (4): 34–36.

Samani, R. (2011). Is it possible to control security in any cloud service? *Second International Secure Systems Development Conference: Designing in Security*, Hilton London Olympia Hotel, London (18th to 19th May).

Singh, P., Singh, P., Park, I., Lee, J-K., and Rao, H.R. (2009). Information sharing: A study of information attributes and their relative significance during catastrophic events, pp. 283–305. In K.J. Knapp (Ed.), *Cyber Security and Global Information Assurance: Threat Analysis and Response Solution*. Hershey, PA: Information Science Reference.

Steinberg, L.J., Santella, N., and Zoli, C.B. (2011). Baton Rouge post-Katrina: The role of critical infrastructure modelling in promoting resilience. *Homeland Security Affairs*, 7 (February): 1–34.

Trim, P. (2009). Placing disaster management policies and practices within a stakeholder security architecture, pp. 213–227. In P.R.J. Trim and J. Caravelli (Eds.), *Strategizing Resilience and Reducing Vulnerability*. New York: Nova Science Publishers, Inc.

Trim, P., Hadfield, R., Garlati, C., Smith, M., Austin, J., and Lee, Y-I. (2012a). Understanding, explaining and counteracting inappropriate user behaviour. *IAAC Consumerisation of IT Positioning Paper*. London: Information Assurance Advisory Council (March).

Trim, P., Hadfield, R., Garlati, C., Smith, M., Austin, J., and Lee, Y-I. (2012b). Understanding, explaining and counteracting inappropriate user behaviour: Insights and recommendations. *IAAC Consumerisation of IT Workshop Report.* London: Information Assurance Advisory Council.

Trim, P.R.J., Jones, N.A., and Brear, K. (2009). Building organisational resilience through a designed-in security management approach. *Journal of Business Continuity & Emergency Planning*, 3 (4): 345–355.

Trim, P.R.J., and Lee, Y-I. (2014). *Cyber Security Management: A Governance, Risk and Compliance Framework.* Farnham: Gower Publishing.

Virgona, T. (2011). A decade on, what business continuity and information security lessons have been learned? *The Business Continuity Journal*, 4 (3): 1–15.

Winston, L. (2011). Scientists & Citizens. St George's House Annual lecture 2010, pp. 4–11. *St George's House Annual Review, 2009–2010.* Windsor: St George's House, Windsor Castle.

8.15 Further Reading

Anand, V., Sanije, J., and Oruklu, E. (2012). Security policy management process within Six Sigma Framework. *Journal of Information Security*, 3: 49–58.

Wang, Y., Han, J.H., and Beynon-Davies, P. (2019). Understanding blockchain technology for future supply chains: A systematic literature review and research agenda. *Supply Chain Management: An International Journal*, 24 (1): 62–84.

8.16 Bank of Questions

Question 1: How can an organization's leadership model be aligned with the nation's political leadership model in the area of cyber security defence?

Question 2: Explain your understanding of the view that an organization's resilience policy needs to be viewed as holistic and embrace security and intelligence.

Question 3: Provide a definition of resilience and outline why you have chosen this definition as being representative.

Question 4: How can cloud computing be integrated into the organization's resilience policy?

Question 5: How can the concept of resilience be promoted throughout a partnership arrangement?

Question 6: In order to produce a sustainable cyber defence-focused partnership arrangement, what formal structures need to be in place between the parties in order that the information exchanged is viewed as necessary?

9 Integrated Security and a Risk Management Communication Strategy

9.1 Introduction

The fact that a market exists for illicitly collected data and information is a reminder that data and information breaches will occur and that the cyber security manager needs to ensure that data and information are safeguarded as much as possible because data can be transferred quickly via the Internet, and tracking it is often a hopeless cause. Internal marketing plays a key role in the communication process and because of this, the cyber security manager will be involved in the development of an internal marketing programme that involves the preparation of a cyber security awareness programme. The strategic marketing process, which involves a strategic management dimension, can help senior management to establish and maintain a sustainable competitive advantage (Aaker, 1984; Cady, 1984). The relationships that are built between organizational partners will help the cyber security manager to reinforce the collectivist approach to cyber security by staff linking the organization's business continuity planning process with those of partner organizations. This is to ensure that there are no weak links (suppliers or wholesalers or retailers, for example) through which a cyber attack can breach the defences of the partner organizations. The planning and strategy formulation approach advocated by Baker (1996) is very much at the heart of the approach and the cyber security manager can include a communications component that allows the risks identified to be communicated to the various stakeholders, both directly and indirectly, by having them listed in the organization's risk register.

This chapter starts by stating the learning objectives (Section 9.2) and progresses with the integrated security concept (Section 9.3) and the consumerization of IT (Section 9.4). Next, attention is given to culture and communication (Section 9.5), reflecting on the virtues of business continuity management planning (Section 9.6) and risk management communication strategy (Section 9.7). After a learning summary (Section 9.8), there is a conclusion (Section 9.9), and a mini case (Sections 9.10). The extended case (Section 9.11) is followed by a set of references (Section 9.12), further reading (Section 9.13) and a bank of questions (Section 9.14).

9.2 Learning objectives

The reader will be able to:

*   evaluate a risk management communication policy;
*   establish what a risk management communication strategy entails; and
*   establish the role performed by an integrated security mechanism.

DOI: 10.4324/9781003244295-9

9.3 Integrated security concept

The cyber security manager and senior management are aware that a more integrated view of security is required if, i.e., data and information breaches are to be prevented. The cyber security manager, working alongside corporate security staff, the risk manager and corporate legal staff, needs to monitor the actions of those involved in acquiring and making available in the market, illegally acquired data and information. Mahmood and Hookham (2011: 19) highlight the scale of the problem by suggesting that over 150 online criminal "superstores" exist that deal in stolen bank details and that websites are trading debit and credit card numbers with their three-digit security numbers included. Mahmood and Hookham (2011: 19) state:

> The names, addresses, dates of birth, email addresses and telephone numbers of British victims who have had their card details stolen are also easily available... Many of the websites operate for only a few months before they are detected by law enforcement agencies and shut down.

The former UK Prime Minister, David Cameron, informed those attending the London Conference on Cyberspace, which was held on 1 November 2011, that (http://www.number10.gov.uk/news/cyberspace/):

> First, we have come together because we passionately believe in the internet as a force for economic, social and political good. The internet has changed the way we change our world. Go to Cairo or Tripoli and you'll meet people whose lives have been transformed because technology gave them a voice. Go to the poorest parts of Kenya and you'll find people accessing financial services for the first time via their mobile phones, finally getting a foot-hold in the economy.
>
> And the internet has profoundly changed our economies too. Studies show it can create twice as many jobs as it destroys. It's estimated that for every 10 per cent increase in broadband penetration, global GDP will increase by an average of 1.3 per cent. So to grow our economies and get our people back to work, we've got to push harder than ever for wider access – and that's what we're doing in the UK.
>
> Second, we have come together to tackle cyber crime. This costs the UK an esti-mated £27 billion a year. Globally, it's as much as $1 trillion. It costs just 69p – about the price of a song on iTunes – to buy someone's credit card information online. Cyber criminals have their own 'online shopping websites' where they can buy and sell stolen credit card details in just the same way you'd buy a book from Amazon.
>
> And threats come not just from criminal gangs. Every day we are seeing attempts on an industrial scale to steal valuable information from individuals and companies. Britain will shortly set out a new approach for better online security, crime preven-tion and public awareness. But a cross-border problem needs cross-border solutions, which is why the world needs to act together.
>
> Third, we are here because international cyber security is a real and pressing concern. Let us be frank. Every day we see attempts on an industrial scale to steal government secrets – information of interest to nation states, not just commercial organisations.
>
> Highly sophisticated techniques are being employed. This summer a significant attempt on the Foreign Office system was foiled. These are attacks on our national

interest. They are unacceptable. And we will respond to them as robustly as we do any other national security threat.

So Britain has prioritised cyber attacks as a tier one threat – and put £650 million towards improving our cyber defences. And internationally, we're inviting others to join us in a network wide enough and powerful enough to face this threat down.

So our task today and in the future is to strike a balance. We cannot leave cyber space wide open to the criminals and terrorists that threaten our security and prosperity.

But at the same time we cannot go the heavy-handed route. Do that and we'll crush all that's good about the internet – the free flow of information, the climate of creativity that gives life to new ideas and new movements. Governments must not use cyber security as an excuse for censorship, or to deny their people the opportunities that the internet represents.

Although laws are in place to protect individuals from identity theft, identity theft is perceived by criminals as a means to access data and to benefit from it. The data that is targeted ranges from marketing and sales data (e.g. customer lists and contract details) to an individual's personal wealth (e.g. bank account details, share holdings and life policies), and this is why fraudsters either develop in-house computer-related expertise or go into the market and hire in the expertise from external providers, as they are focused on their target and know how to carry out a cost-effective operation.

Cyber security can be increased through planning and international cooperation, and the Joint EU–US Cyber Security Exercise held on 3 November 2011 achieved much in terms of focusing attention on what can be achieved, as can be deduced from the following quotation (http://www.prnewswire.com/news-releases/first-joint-eu-us-cyber-security-exercise-conducted-today-3rd-nov-2011-133138608.html: see https://www.enisa.europa.eu/news/enisa-news/first-joint-eu-us-cyber-security-exercise-conducted-today-3rd-nov.-2011).

In the first scenario, a targeted stealthy cyber-attack (Advanced Persistent Threat – APT) attempts to infiltrate and publish online, secret information from EU Member States' cyber security agencies. The second simulation focuses on the disruption of supervisory control and data acquisition (SCADA) systems in power generation infrastructures.

More than 20 EU Member States are involved in the exercise, 16 of them actively playing, with the European Commission providing high-level direction. Cyber Atlantic 2011 is part of an EU–US commitment to cyber security which was made at the EU–US summit in Lisbon on 20 November 2010. The aims are to '*tackle new threats to the global networks upon which the security and prosperity of our free societies increasingly depend.*'[1] The exercise draws on lessons learned in the first pan-European cyber security 'stress test' exercise, Cyber Europe 2010, which was facilitated last year by ENISA.[2] ENISA's role involves supporting EU Member States in organising cyber security exercises and formulating national contingency plans, with good practice guides and seminars.

---

1 Joint Statement, EU–US Summit, Nov.2010:

    http://www.consilium.europa.eu/uedocs/cms_data/docs/pressdata/EN/foraff/117897.pdf

2 ENISA Cyber Europe 2010 exercise reports: http://www.enisa.europa.eu/act/res/ce2010

    http://www.enisa.europa.eu

9.4 Consumerization of IT

As regards the consumerization of IT and the general topic of information assurance, the cyber security manager needs to revisit the issues of availability, integrity, authentication, confidentiality and non-repudiation (Singh et al., 2009: 294–295). Singh et al. (2009: 283) advocate that as well as safeguarding information, information can be "securely shared, if required, among a set of related groups or organizations that serve a common purpose". This raises the issue of communication and requires that the cyber security manager takes cognizance of what the Intelligence Cycle concept is, and how it can be extended to include the Critical Thinking Process so that "an in-depth end product for sound decision making" (Patton, 2010: 139) is produced. The difference between the Intelligence Cycle process and the Critical Thinking Process has been made clear by Patton (2010: 139): the *Intelligence Cycle* involves (i) planning and direction; (ii) collection; (iii) processing; (iv) analysis and production; and (v) dissemination. The *Critical Thinking Process* involves (i) purpose; (ii) question at issue; (iii) information; (iv) interpretation and inference; (v) concepts; (vi) assumptions; (vii) implications and consequences; and (viii) point of view.

The cyber security manager can use the Critical Thinking Process to identify immediate and future threats, and reflect and revisit issues and challenges identified. During the process, management policies can be integrated, systems and procedures can be developed to harness knowledge (both internal to the organization and external to the organization), and a systematic process can be devised to manage risk and engage in risk mitigation. Patton (2010: 154) suggests that: "The Rings of Defense or Defense in Depth concept is a proven approach to make penetration of an asset much more difficult than without the rings". The main objectives are to deter, detect and neutralize identified threats through kinetic or non-kinetic manoeuvres (Patton, 2010: 155). Knowledge of the Social Net/Network within which interactions between individuals take place is important with respect to comprehending the movement of people and data, and how threats materialize. However, complexity is evident because as Patton (2010: 158) suggests, "several networks exist within systems", and relevant analysis often requires that threats are prioritized. What the cyber security manager needs to remember is that at each stage of the process, the communication process itself needs to be evaluated to ensure that it is as comprehensive as possible. By doing this, it will become evident if a stakeholder is included in the process and is participating in the way expected.

Coveney and Highfield (1995: 7–8) suggest that:

> ... the majority of real-world problems – and therefore most of those in modern industries and societies – do not fit into neat compartments. To solve them, people must be able to communicate across traditional boundaries, to approach issues in a collaborative, integrated way.

Trim and Lee (2010: 4) have recognized the importance of an organization developing a security culture:

> It can also be stated that by integrating security more firmly into the organization's structure, it should be possible to reduce the organization's level of risk and facilitate information sharing. Information sharing should enhance co-operation between

partner organizations and add to the defensive capability vis-à-vis establishing effective counter-cyber attack measures.

Through the process, the interaction between the stakeholders will be intensified and solutions will be found to cyber security-related problems.

9.5 Culture and communication

By placing a risk management communication strategy within the context of strategic marketing, top management will provide an appropriate base from which the cyber security manager can link the contingency plans devised with crisis/emergency procedures that can be implemented during a natural disaster or a man-made cyber attack, for example, so that the appropriate contingency plans can be put into action. However, a disaster could have wide repercussions:

> Localised but significant failure of Internet service in all or part of their territory, possibly occasioned by failure at a major Internet Exchange in turn caused by fire, flood, bomb, failure of electricity supply. Such a failure would disconnect the population as a whole from online government guidance and information and would also inhibit the role of emergency responders.
>
> (Sommer and Brown, 2011: 79)

The cyber security manager needs to be aware of the organization's role within the community because organizational staff may be called upon to help provide back-up services during a crisis/emergency and will need to work with the risk manager in order to coordinate matters. The organization's risk management strategy does need to focus on the entire risk management process and how the communication channels are to be utilized (ENISA, 2011: 3). In addition, attention is required in terms of how the communication policy is embedded within the management of risks. In order that senior management produce a coordinated communication policy and strategy, it is essential that there is an internally oriented risk management communication strategy and an externally oriented risk management communication strategy (Trim and Lee, 2014: 77). In order to be effective, risk management needs to become part of the organization's culture; hence, creating awareness about risk is very important, as ENISA (2011: 3) have indicated:

> External communication and consulting by specialized consultants, as well as exchange of information and cooperation with other organizations, should also be planned and implemented on a regular basis. The exchange of this knowledge and experience can prove extremely helpful for addressing issues related to both the risks and the process to manage these risks, leading thus to a view on risks that is free from subjective estimations. Furthermore, involving external personnel in such activities contributes towards the renewal of available know-how and risk perception.

As regards knowing who to communicate with when there is a crisis, the cyber security manager in consultation with the risk manager can devise a list of risks and prioritize them. By assigning roles to individuals based in partner organizations, it is possible to network the risks in such a way that both direct and indirect stakeholders are assigned duties. For example, possible contacts include local businesses; community groups; competitors; suppliers; government regulators; and various cyber security advisory and support groups. The cyber security manager can reflect on how an organization's value system can be developed and embrace the human factors concept (experience of staff, ambition, commitment, motivation, consciousness) and how risk mitigation (actions to be taken if a disgruntled employee sabotages the computer system or network or plants malware) can be managed. Risk mitigation falls under the control of the risk manager; however, the cyber security manager can be called upon to provide support and devise various types of communication in association with the public relations team. Bearing in mind that organizational learning requires a high absorptive capacity that has two major elements – prior knowledge base and intensity of effort (Kim, 1998: 506), any impact on an organization is likely to result in a transformation in management practice and/or the implementation of a contingency plan; however, this has to be done in a pro-active way and made effective in real time.

Duncan and Weiss (Kim, 1998: 507) state that organizational learning "is the process whereby knowledge is created, is distributed across the organization, is communicated among organization members, has consensual validity, and is integrated into the strategy and management of the organization". The word "communication" is evident and it is clear that top management are required to ensure that communication procedures take into account both internal and external relationships, and how individuals respond to events (e.g. hierarchical controls in place) that influence or consolidate the relationship building process.

By evaluating each cyber threat and establishing both the known and potential consequences associated with an impact and the knock-on-effects, the cyber security manager can monitor the cumulative impact of a series of events that may occur at the same time or result over a long period of time. By putting in place a security policy and a security education policy that incorporates risk assessment, and has cyber security at the centre, the cyber security manager can identify the threats that are most likely to materialize. When they do materialize, they can be dealt with in a collectivist manner and a postmortem evaluation can establish who did what and how effective it was. Evidence will be produced relating to which party or group communicated well and how the less effective forms of communication can be replaced with more effective forms of communication. The analysis undertaken should cover the event/impacts in the short term (up to three months), the medium term (three months to six months) and the long term (in excess of six months). These time periods are not fixed in stone and can vary depending upon what is viewed as a relevant time period. As regards communication with external stakeholders, by prioritizing threats, the cyber security manager will be able to share information with appropriate staff and this will help to establish management hierarchies and organizational structures, and establish who reports to who and how the reporting system in place is maintained and backed up. This is to prevent stone walling and non- or delayed intervention. Trim and Lee (2007: 110) highlight the importance of this by suggesting that during a disaster,

> a number of emergency staff (including firemen and medical staff) work and liaise with a range of scientists and technical people, and staff from the media, the general public and various government departments. Issues such as working

practices, communicating with the general public, and utilizing the assistance of both domestic and overseas based disaster and emergency experts is key.

During a cyber attack, which may cause a power outage, there are likely to be business-to-government and government-to-government interactions and interactions with the wider community. In order to prepare staff for a crisis/emergency/disaster, the cyber security manager can use training simulations to help prepare staff to face the consequences of a cyber attack and communication models can be devised that outline how a range of experts and their organizations can produce more relevant inputs relating to solving a cyber attack and dealing with its consequences. The cyber security manager can develop their understanding of how governments cooperate and facilitate inter-agency interaction, and how simulation exercises are developed that provide training that is underpinned by, in the case of simulation exercises, relevant methodological approaches that link the learning process with forward thinking, and the use of scenario analysis and planning.

With specific reference to an international exercise relating to a cyber attack, the cyber security manager can work with the training manager to establish how individuals interact and communicate information (e.g. procedures) with each other during the crisis/attack stage and how they relate to each other during the aftermath of an episode/attack, in terms of revising and amending management procedures. Cultural differences exist and this means that those involved in an international exercise need an appreciation of the "concepts of the self and others (as assumptions located *within* persons) as well as to a model of interaction *between* people" (Usunier and Lee, 2009: 43). The emphasis on understanding cultural differences is clear and underpins the communication process itself. For example, societies with an *individualistic* value system are likely to be self-sufficient and less dependent in their outlook, while those from a collectivist society are highly influenced by the norms and duties emanating from the in-group (Usunier and Lee, 2009: 43–44). The cyber security manager can draw on this interpretation and develop their own knowledge base so that they better understand how cultural value systems influence the communication process and the communication process can be made more effective in terms of avoiding cultural sensitivity.

The interactionist communication model, which focuses attention on how views are recreated and interpreted with the "self" being an active participant vis-à-vis the creation of meaning (Schiffman et al., 2001: 159), needs to be understood because the psychological factors that are embedded in communication processes are complex. It can be noted that the "self" is an object (a "me") (consciousness) and "subject" ("I") of action. The term *cultural embeddedness* is important and other communicative symbols in the communication process are placed in a cultural context (Schiffman et al., 2001: 160), and this suggests that both verbal and non-verbal forms of communication play a part and influence the communication process. It is for this reason that the cyber security manager needs to view interaction as a continual process that involves indirect as well as direct communication, and informal as well as formal communication.

The Elaboration Likelihood Model of persuasion can be used by the cyber security manager and staff in public relations to ensure that the message of cyber security awareness is received, decoded and related to (Trim and Lee, 2014: 79–78, 2019). Hence, the model can be used to construct a message and also influence the way in which the message is received. What needs to be remembered when formulating a message is that the message content, the arguments and counterarguments put forward, and the supporting arguments all need to be taken into account because individuals receiving a message have their own beliefs which are formed, reformed and evaluated (Schiffman et al., 2001: 179–180).

9.6 Reflecting on the Virtues of Business Continuity Management Planning

By understanding what risk management involves, the cyber security manager can help establish the relationship between the different phases of risk management and devise a risk communication process that senior management adhere to in terms of risk acceptance and what the organization's risk appetite is. In other words, the business continuity management planning process should not be viewed as fixed but fluid and malleable, meaning that it can be updated through time. As regards service level agreements, senior management need to ensure that the overarching policy covers the minimum amount of time systems are available; that a documented method is in being outlining the details associated with the impact of a disruption; that the recovery point objective and the recovery time objectives are linked with the criticality of the service; that advice as to how information security activities are addressed in the restoration process is provided; that in the event of a disruption, the lines of communication are made known to end customers; that the roles and responsibilities of the teams involved with dealing with a disruption are made known; that the provider also categorizes the priority for recovery and has defined the relative (low, medium or high) priority (in the case of the end user/customer) to be restored; that the dependencies relevant to the restoration process (including suppliers and outsource partners) are outlined and should a primary site be made unavailable, it is made known what the minimum separation time is for the secondary site to be operational (ENISA, 2009: 20).

With respect to incident management and response, ENISA (2009: 20–21) provide guidance that the cyber security manager can draw on. For example, it is important for management to provide direction with respect to an organization minimizing the probability of an occurrence or reducing the negative impact of an information security incident. ENISA highlight the following areas: a formal process for detecting, identifying, analysing and responding to incidents and establishing how effective the response is; a focus on how the detection capabilities are structured; how the severity levels and escalation procedures are defined; reference is made to how incidents are documented and evidence is collected; reference is made to the controls that are in place to prevent or minimize malicious activities by insiders; reference to a forensic image of the virtual machine offered to the customer and which incident reports are made public; how often the disaster recovery and business continuity plans are tested by the provider is made known; the frequency and occurrence of customer service satisfaction levels, help desk tests, penetration testing, vulnerability testing and rectifying vulnerabilities are all covered.

A risk management communication strategy must, therefore, be grounded in the business continuity management planning framework and ownership of it must be shared among appropriate staff (e.g. the cyber security manager, the risk manager and public relations staff). If it is judged that training and staff development are key, then the training manager must be admitted to the inner sanctum. This is because if an impact does occur, the recovery process is managed according to set procedures, which are adequately documented, thus helping those who are new to the process to fully comprehend what they need to do, when it needs to be done and who they report to. Those in charge or associated with the recovery process need to be competent and ensure that the business continuity management planning process goes according to plan and the computer systems and networks in place are secure against attack. The cyber security manager plays both an important and visible role in terms of preventing a cyber attack having both a physical and psychological effect on an organization, and if an impact does occur, the consequences are known as they have been researched and the solutions are based on an analysis that senior managers can relate to and understand.

The cyber security manager has a good understanding of what virtualization requires and is aware that management will need to adopt a different view as to what security is and who in the organization takes responsibility for it. The managers that head the various business functions may have a reasonable understanding of what the physical and virtual networks within the organization and partner organization look like, but will they understand how cloud computing will change business-to-business relationships in view of the fact that different forms of working and different accountability and responsibility levels, and greater movement of people between organizations and industries, are likely to stimulate the development of a range of business models, most of which are unknown and some of which may be unsustainable?

Managers do not always understand the type of risks the organization is confronted with and the situation is compounded by the fact that there are different business models for the same industry as well as different business models for different industries. Because managers can adopt either a quantitative or a qualitative approach to risk assessment, it is not always possible to establish which risk approach method is applicable. Austin (2011) has concentrated on how data in the cloud is to safeguard vis-à-vis relationship building involving the service provider and it is clear that managers need to carry out a security analysis of data needs at various levels and address the issue of how the information architecture takes account of various types of risk. As a consequence, top management do need to be aware of a number of factors, which are (listed in priority) data governance; identity management; an overarching security policy (people, process, technology, end point environment); type of possible solution; enterprise solution versus consumer solution; the logic associated with an organization having a kill pill that can be used to solve "the basic problem" and eradicate the problem completely; and the need for monitoring to be constantly applied. These factors affect the perception of trust in relation to cloud computing and how managers work with law enforcement staff when they are required to do so.

9.7 Risk Management Communication Strategy

By now, the importance associated with a risk management communication strategy will be clear. According to Rouse and Rouse (2002: ix–xx), culture can be considered a framework that enables communication to occur and also a framework for interpreting communication, and strategy is viewed as drawing business communications together. Building on the work of Mitchell et al. (1997) relating to relevant stakeholders, Rouse and Rouse (2002: 246–248) extend the concepts of *power* (defined as "the ability of one person or group to influence or force change in another's behaviour"); *legitimacy* (defined as "the behaviour or status of individuals, groups or other organizations that are socially accepted as being proper or appropriate") and *urgency* (which "refers to the idea that stakeholders have variable degrees of urgent claim on some of the value being generated by an organization"). By mapping stakeholders and the interactive process and by placing this within a network configuration, it should be possible for the cyber security manager to identify the attributes and the interests of each stakeholder, and also, ascertain their strengths and weaknesses. This should have a positive impact on creating and delivering communication messages that enable stakeholders to share information when necessary.

9.8 Learning summary

There is no doubt that a risk management communication strategy needs to be developed so that a risk communication strategy can be activated on occasion. As can be gauged from Figure 9.1, the cyber security manager needs to view this from a holistic perspective as the emphasis is on risk management. For example, a shared security culture will allow senior managers within the organization as well as those based in partner organizations, to formulate a unified set of values that give rise to a standardized risk mitigation approach. Cooperation among staff will ensure that the relationships in place can be drawn on for advice and support during times of known cyber attacks. Because the business continuity management planning process is concerned with the functioning of computer systems and networks and takes into account the link with and association with stakeholders, cyber security threats can be analysed in a pro–active manner.

The reader will:

- develop a risk management communication policy;
- develop a risk management communication strategy; and
- devise and implement an integrated security mechanism.

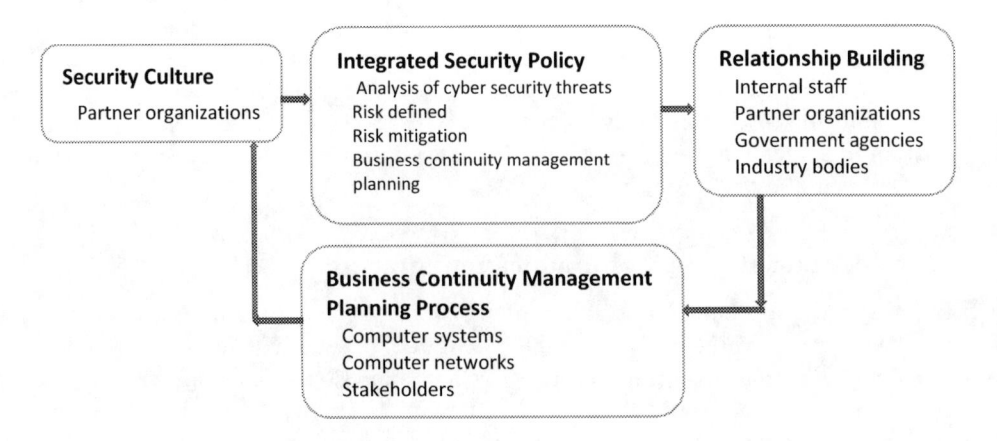

Figure 9.1 Strategic cyber security risk management communication strategy.

9.9 Conclusion

A crisis/disaster/emergency calls into question how people are trained to deal with such an eventuality; how they record the outcome in the organization's memory; how they use the experience to generate new insights into management training and staff development procedures; and how organizational learning produces knowledge. Because effective business continuity planning takes into account the interdependencies between the organization and its stakeholders, and is influenced by government guidelines, the cyber security manager needs to ensure that the risk management communication strategy is grounded in an ethical framework and is considered an integral component of the business continuity management planning process. By integrating the roles and responsibilities of the cyber security manager with those of the risk manager, senior management can develop a strategic corporate intelligence capability that raises the profile of the corporate security function.

Placing security in context is paramount, if, i.e., an organization is to continue to operate effectively. Risk managers in particular are charged with understanding the threats posed by current and evolving complexities in the business environment; however, cyberspace requires that attention is also given to the socio-cultural factors and issues that are shaping the environment in an economic and political context. Opportunities associated with cloud computing, cyber security and information assurance abound. Managers need to stand back and think of how to highlight and reinforce the link between information assurance and cyber security, and promote a security culture that permeates from one sector to another. The logic of this is that both public sector organizations and private sector organizations will be involved in various aspects of harmonizing security practices and policies.

9.10 Mini Case: The Case of the Insider

Mr. Bloomfield, head of security, had just been given a report by an external security company that had been commissioned over the Summer. It made interesting but slightly depressing reading. The main focus of the report was a dissatisfied employee, indeed a long serving employee that had been with the organization for more than 23 years. The individual concerned had been found to manipulate data in the organization's customer database. The problem had come to light when a longstanding customer organization had a contact cancelled for non-delivery of goods. On investigation, it was found that the person under investigation held a high position within the management hierarchy and had access to various internal databases, and was able to manipulate the data in customer accounts. The case proved worrying to Mr. Bloomfield because customer details and accounts were password-protected and he was worried if the details had been passed on to competitors. This was because the data had been changed recently. Further investigation showed that the member of staff, who was about to be suspended, had entered several databases frequently over a two-month period, sometimes two or three times a day.

Another fact that had been unearthed by the security company was that the person concerned had been known to lead an expensive life style and owned a number of cars. He was known to attend horse racing events and had been behaving oddly over a number of months. It was possible that he had lost money on the horses and may be addicted to gambling. Although the quality of the work undertaken by the suspect was still of a high standard, the managing director of the customer organization that had the contract cancelled was furious and was threatening legal action. Mr. Bloomfield was worried that legal action against the company might result in reputational damage and in addition, there might be other issues that surfaced and needed attention.

Reading through the report, Mr. Bloomfield realized that the organization's computer systems and networks were not that well protected and that staff lower down the organizational hierarchy did not have the appropriate security skills and knowledge that were needed to work in a computer-oriented work environment. He was worried that this would all become public knowledge and that he would be held accountable for the organization's failings. One of the recommendation's from the report was that a security audit be undertaken in order to establish the depth of the problem with a view to installing sensors in the organization's computer networks that could flag up an unusual activity or inform certain managers that an individual was accessing a certain database.

The report also highlighted the economic and psychological aspects of cyber crime and it was realized that staff would need to be counselled in relation to the insider's criminal actions and that emphasis needed to be placed on rebuilding trust. This was also the case with staff in the external company that had the contract cancelled.

The report also highlighted the actions of an overseas government agency that had set up a number of front companies abroad, one of which was a fake IT company, and was using the front companies to obtain data and information in various ways. On checking the expense claims of certain employees, it was discovered that several of the organization's staff had held meetings with individuals from several fake companies on the list and that it appeared that the inter-organizational relationships developed were based on some type of social and emotional rapport. The interactions had been going on for well over six months.

Questions

Question 1: How should Mr. Bloomfield rank the problems identified?

Question 2: What security countermeasures should Mr. Bloomfield put in place to deal with the issues raised?

Question 3: How would the appointment of a cyber security manager make the organization more robust?

9.11 Extended Case: The Cyber Security Manager and Risk Communication

The cyber security manager, who fulfils both an operational role and a strategic role, will, in the years ahead, need to pay increased attention to how cyber security issues arise and how the challenges can be managed. For example, the nature of cloud computing and the context within which it is placed is not always understood or appreciated. In addition, internal vulnerability brought about and linked to the insider threat is something that can and does result in reputational damage; however, senior management are not always prepared to admit that a problem exists or has been dealt with. Adding also the fact that managers in the organization's functions have different priorities and are motivated differently means that problems associated with cyber security are multi-faceted and compounded by issues such as untrustworthy software. Bearing in mind also the problems associated with identity and authentication, and identity theft, means that doing business online is known to be risky at times and the cyber security manager is going to be called upon to advocate more strongly the need for more open and continual communication, with internal staff as well as staff based in partner organizations.

To achieve continuity of operations, the cyber security manager needs to ensure that trustworthiness predominates and trustworthy relationships are developed and maintained through time. As regards human resource management, several questions arise regarding how much influence a cyber security manager has over managers in other business functions and calls into question the support needed from corporate security staff who are responsible for implementing security policy and are involved in the preparation of cyber security awareness programmes.

One way in which risk can be communicated is to have in place various defined cyber security operations such as penetration testing methodologies, which are used to identify vulnerabilities and validate the policies and procedures in place. Bavisis (2010: 259) has outlined what a comprehensive penetration test involves: information gathering; vulnerability analysis; external penetration testing; internal network penetration testing; wireless network penetration testing; IDS penetration testing; Firewall penetration testing; router penetration testing; denial of service penetration testing; password cracking penetration testing; social engineering penetration testing; stolen laptop/PDA/cell phone penetration testing; VoIP penetration testing; database penetration testing; physical security penetration testing; application penetration testing; VPN penetration testing.

By making known what penetration testing involves should encourage staff to have a greater interest in cyber security technology and the management of it, and should provide a basis upon which security awareness is communicated much more forcibly. As regards communication and its importance, ENISA (2018: 14) state:

> What is emerging from these studies is the need to improve communication, collaboration and the working relationship between security specialists and other functions in the organisation. There have been a number of examples of creative security engagement techniques (first mentioned by Dunphy et al., 2014) with employees, consumers or citizens. They are encouraged to reflect on security in their environment, the emotions they feel, the constraints they experience, the pressures that they undergo as well as the actions and the tasks that they perform when generating and sharing information. All of this generates insights on what is needed to make security work for a particular group, in the context of their goals and daily activities, and the physical and social environment in which this takes place.

Questions

Question 1: Why is it important for the cyber security manager to ensure that communication is viewed as an essential element of the cyber security management process?

Question 2: How does the risk management process reinforce the cyber security objectives of the organization?

Question 3: How can an integrated security mechanism be maintained through time?

Case Sources

Bavisis, J. (2010). Chapter 9: Penetration Testing, pp. 247–270. In J.R. Vacca (Ed.), *Managing Information Security*. Burlington, MA: Elsevier/Syngress.

Dunphy, P., Vines, J., Coles-Kemp, L. Clarke, R., Vlachokyriakos, V., Wright, P., McCarthy, J., and Olivier, P. (2014). Understanding the Experience-Centeredness of Privacy and Security Technologies, pp. 83–94. In *Proceedings of the 2014 Workshop on New Security Paradigms*. Workshop NSPW 2014 (September). https://doi.org/10.1145/2683467.2683475.

ENISA. (2018). *Cybersecurity Culture Guidelines: Behavioural Aspects of Cybersecurity*. Attiki, Greece. https://doi.org/10.2824/324042.

9.12 References

Aaker, D.A. (1984). *Strategic Market Management*. Chichester: John Wiley & Sons Limited.

Austin, J. (2011). Placing shared services in context: A technology-management perspective. *Second Information Assurance Advisory Council Consumerisation Research Workshop: Common and Shared Services in the Context of Cloud Computing*, BCS, Chartered Institute for IT, London (17th November).

Baker, M. (1996). Marketing strategy, pp. 3333–3347. In M. Warner (Ed.), *International Encyclopaedia of Business and Management*. London: Routledge.

Cady, J.F. (1984). *Strategic Marketing Management: The Course*, Harvard Business School Paper Number 9–584-076. Boston, MA: Harvard Business School Publishing.

Coveney, P., and Highfield, R. (1995). *Frontiers of Complexity: The Search for Order in a Chaotic World*, pp. 7–8. London: Faber and Faber Limited.

ENISA (2009). *Cloud Computing: Information Assurance Framework*. Athens, Greece: European Network and Information Security Agency, pp. 1–24 (November).

ENISA (2011). *Risk Management*. European Network and Information Security Agency, pp. 1–108. http://www.enisa.europa.eu/act/rm/cr/risk-management-inventory/rm-process (accessed on 27th February 2011).

Kim, L. (1998). Crisis construction and organizational learning: Capability building in catching-up at Hyundai Motor. *Organization Science*, 9 (4): 506–521.

Mahmood, M., and Hookham, M. (2011). On sale at £3.70: your stolen credit details. *The Sunday Times*, 6th November, p. 19.

Mitchell, R., Agle, B., and Wood, D. (1997). Toward a theory of stakeholder identification and salience: Defining the principle of who and what really counts. *Academy of Management Review*, 22: 853–886.

Patton, K. (2010). *Sociocultural Intelligence: A New Discipline in Intelligence Studies*. London: The Continuum International Publishing Group.

Rouse, M.J., and Rouse, S. (2002). *Business Communications: A Cultural and Strategic Approach*. London: South-Western, Cengage Learning.

Schiffman, L., Bednall, D., Cowley, E., O'Cass, A., Watson, J., and Kanuk, L. (2001). *Consumer Behaviour*. Frenchs Forest: Pearson Education Australia Pty Limited.

Singh, P., Singh, P., Park, I., Lee, J-K., and Rao, H.R. (2009). Information sharing: A study of information attributes and their relative significance during catastrophic events, pp. 283–305. In K.J. Knapp (Ed.), *Cyber Security and Global Information Assurance*. Hershey, PA: Information Science Reference.

Sommer, P., and Brown, I. (2011). *Reducing Systematic Cybersecurity Risk*. Paris: OECD.

Trim, P.R.J., and Lee, Y-I. (2007). An extended multi-cultural communication model for use in disaster and emergency simulation exercises, pp. 108–118. In P.R.J. Trim and Y-I. Lee (Eds.), *The International Simulation and Gaming Research Yearbook Volume 15, Effective Learning from Games and Simulations.* Edinburgh: SAGSET.

Trim, P.R.J., and Lee, Y-I. (2010). A security framework for protecting business, government and society from cyber attacks, pp. 1–6. *5th IEEE International Conference on System of Systems Conference (SoSE): Sustainable Systems for the 21st Century,* Loughborough University (22nd to 24th June).

Trim, P.R.J., and Lee, Y-I. (2014). *Cyber Security Management: A Governance, Risk and Compliance Framework.* Farnham: Gower Publishing.

Trim, P.R.J., and Lee, Y-I. (2019). The role of B2B marketers in increasing cyber security awareness and influencing behavioural change. *Industrial Marketing Management,* 83: 224–238. https://doi.org/10.1016/j.indmarman.2019.04.003.

Usunier, J-C., and Lee, J.A. (2009). *Marketing across Cultures.* Harlow: Pearson Education Limited.

Website Addresses

http://www.number10.gov.uk/news/cyberspace/ (accessed on 4th November 2011).

http://www.prnewswire.com/news-releases/first-joint-eu-us-cyber-security-exercise-conducted-today-3rd-nov-2011-133138608.html (accessed 4th November 2011). See: see https://www.enisa.europa.eu/news/enisa-news/first-joint-eu-us-cyber-security-exercise-conducted-today-3rd-nov.-2011).

9.13 Further Reading

ENISA. (2018). Cybersecurity Culture Guidelines: Behavioural Aspects of Cybersecurity. Athens, Greece. https://doi.org/10.2824/324042.

Trim, P.R.J., and Lee, Y-I. (2019). Cyber security: Communication and risk management. *Sécurité & Stratégie,* 32 (April/June): 26–31.

9.14 Bank of Questions

Question 1: How useful is the Intelligence Cycle concept in terms of cyber security management?

Question 2: How useful is the Critical Thinking Process in terms of cyber security management?

Question 3: How relevant is the interactionist communication model in terms of getting a message across? Provide examples to reinforce your arguments.

Question 4: Why it is important for the cyber security manager to have a good understanding of the organization's cultural value system?

Question 5: Explain why the risk management communication strategy needs to be grounded in the business continuity management planning framework.

Question 6: How can the cyber security manager ensure that risk management communication is embedded in the organization's security communications strategy?

10 Organizational Learning, Managing Change and Security Culture

10.1 Introduction

The cyber security manager needs to be aware of the different skills that are required as the organization's business model transmutes and staff are required to develop their knowledge and skill base in order to deal with new and emerging cyber threats. By acknowledging the role played by organizational learning, staff can update their skill base through time and develop insights into the threat environment and identify centres of knowledge to be drawn on when necessary.

This chapter starts by looking at the learning objectives (Section 10.2) and continues with training, staff development and strategy implementation (Section 10.3). Next, attention is given to the learning organization concept and organizational learning (Section 10.4), and changing organizational attitudes and mindsets (Section 10.5) is followed by an effective counter threat policy and strategy (Section 10.6). After a strategic cyber security framework (Section 10.7) appears a learning summary (Section 10.8) and a conclusion (Section 10.9). The mini case (Section 10.10) is followed by the extended case (Section 10.11), the references (Section 10.12), further reading (Section 10.13) and a bank of questions (Section 10.14).

10.2 Learning Objectives

The reader will be able to:

- establish what managing change requires;
- establish what the learning organization concept entails; and
- establish why a cyber security culture is necessary.

10.3 Training, Staff Development and Strategy Implementation

The cyber security manager is aware of the complexities associated with managing complex organizations and the need to deal with unforeseen events and impacts, which require input from various individuals, often referred to as first responders. As managing change needs to be planned and coordinated, it can be said that the cyber security manager needs to adopt a pro-active approach to training and work closely with the training manager so that the training courses and programmes available to staff increase the skill base of employees and allow them to become positive agents of

DOI: 10.4324/9781003244295-10

change. Therefore, the organization's cyber security objectives need to be aligned with the organization's strategic security objectives, and be embedded within the organization's strategic intelligence framework. This is so that staff involved in security work are provided with the appropriate guidance and support, and know who their counterparts are in partner organizations.

In order that partner organizations cooperate and the organization's security policy is adhered to, top management need to provide both vision and leadership, and ensure that there is a commitment to security at all levels throughout the organization's hierarchy (Lee, 2009: 181). Deploying the learning organization concept can prove influential in terms of the cyber security manager and the training manager working alongside each other to devise and implement policies and strategies that ensure that the organization remains sustainable. The cyber security manager may use the benchmarking approach when formulating cyber security policies as this will allow the organization to keep up with current practice but benchmarking per se may not always prove useful, especially in a fast-moving and turbulent environment where constant change is evident.

Appelbaum and Gallagher (2000: 49) focus attention on why top management need to have a strategic vision, suggesting that "training is important with respect to staff being able to close the gaps between an organization's current reality and its future transformation". This suggests that the cyber security manager can work with the training manager, and various people, including the IT manager and the risk manager, and devise cyber security training programmes that are aimed at different levels of cyber security awareness. Acknowledging that cyber security staff development programmes fulfil a different purpose to cyber security education programmes, the objective is to enable staff to develop knowledge of an organization's cyber security vulnerabilities and help find a remedy. Through the process of raising the cyber security skill base of staff, it should be possible for management to put in place a structure for dealing with the latest security issues and to coordinate an effective counter cyber threat policy among stakeholders. Furthermore, attitudinal surveys are useful with respect to establishing how satisfied a workforce is, and can be used to detect undercurrents of discontent and possibly areas of vulnerability. Training and staff development programmes can also be used to provide support and reassurance, in times of uncertainty (mergers, economic downturns and new regulatory policy), and can reinforce the organization's value system, through reward programmes linked with attending and passing a cyber security training programme.

During periods of crisis, top management may implement a restructuring programme that does much to innovate and bring about organizational change that is aimed at repositioning the organization in the industry in which it competes. Such an approach may be considered structuralist in nature and an opposing approach, known as the reconstructivist view, put forward by Schumpeter, suggests that innovation "is the product of the ingenuity of entrepreneurs and cannot be reproduced systematically" (Kim and Mauborgne, 2005: 210). It can be argued, therefore, that the cyber security manager can adopt an entrapreneurial approach to cyber security and create a simulated crisis in order to create behavioural change through tailored cyber security training programmes.

As well as the cyber security manager having to deal with external threats, they also need to deal with internal threats. Owing to the fact that it is not possible to predict the behaviour of employees (and temporary employees (those employed by sub-contractors, for example)), it can be suggested that an internally orchestrated (insider) attack can be more damaging than an externally orchestrated attack, because the attacker is already inside the organization and can access various computer systems and networks without raising suspicion. Often, an insider will plan their action months in advance and execute their plan of attack when they feel that the organization is most vulnerable (e.g. when people are on holiday and there is limited staff cover in the office). The sophisticated insider knows how to cover their tracks and may not just think in terms of defrauding the organization. For example, an insider may instigate acts of sabotage when they are threatened with redundancy or when a takeover by a rival organization results in their services being terminated prematurely. Monitoring employee behaviour and changes in an individual's life style are not easy issues for top management to address, as there are a number of ethical considerations and legal issues to contemplate, but they may be indicators that an individual is living above their means and needs to find extra finance to support their life style.

The ability of a person to deceive or continue on a path of deceiving may be to do with their own personality and their closeness to the perceived victim. For example, Reddy (2007) indicates that deceiving may have to do with the type of communication engaged in, and the fact that cyber space provides anonymity and cover for individuals carrying out an attack in cyber space. In addition, cyber criminals take pleasure in relating their successes to other criminals, so they gain esteem from committing unlawful acts and getting away with them. The cyber security manager needs to be aware that cyber attacks are sometimes planned by individuals external to the organization and executed internally, by one person or a group of people. Those that feel dissatisfied with or alienated by employment policy may decide to take revenge on the company – steal data/information and/or delete files or provide passwords that allow somebody to access a computer system. Bearing this in mind, it can be suggested that the emotional state of employees needs to be monitored through time in order to gauge if people are satisfied or likely to be a threat. To guard against inside threats manifesting, top management can reinforce the need for security and ensure that the organization's value system promotes acceptable behaviour relating to the safe keeping and transfer of sensitive data and information, and reward staff for detecting and reporting unusual behaviour that relates to a certain online activity.

10.4 The Learning Organization Concept and Organizational Learning

The concept of organizational learning can be interpreted from several perspectives. Nevertheless, the basic concept places skills, knowledge and the experience of employees within an organizational framework that promotes self-development and improvements in working practices and management systems, policies and procedures, and strategy formulation and implementation (Trim and Upton, 2013: 172). Senge (1999: 14) states that a learning organization is "an organization that is continually expanding its capacity to create its future" and although adaptive learning (known as survival learning) is important, it "must be joined by 'generative learning' that enhances our capacity to create". Organizational learning is, therefore, "a management process, which equips employees with the knowledge and skill they need in order to undertake their duties in a systematic and logical manner, and thus improve the organization's way of doing business" (Trim and Upton, 2013: 172). Realizing this, the cyber security manager can view knowledge creation from two perspectives: knowledge development and knowledge utilization. A third aspect, knowledge implementation, occurs when the knowledge creation process is deemed to be successful and in the case of cyber security is encapsulated within a cyber security framework and strategy. However, a broader view of what organizational learning constitutes is necessary because individuals possess different views as to what it is and how to apply it. The work of Argyris (1996: 8) is informative and can be used to provide the cyber security manager with the appropriate guidance:

Learning is defined as occurring under two conditions. First, learning occurs when an organization achieves what it intended; that is, there is a match between its design for action and the actuality or outcome. Second, learning occurs when a mismatch between intentions and outcomes is identified and it is corrected; that is, a mismatch it turned into a match.

The view of Argyris (1996) is that organizational learning rests with individuals and gives rise to certain behaviour that results in a learning outcome and in order for managers to have an in-depth understanding of what organizational learning involves, they need to be aware of the difference between single-loop and double-loop learning. This is because errors are likely to occur and when they do, the consequences need to be thought through and corrective action taken. In addition, lessons need to be learned and acted upon. Argyris (1996: 8–9) explains this:

Single-loop learning occurs when matches are created, or when mismatches are corrected by changing actions. Double-loop learning occurs when mismatches are corrected by first examining and altering the governing variables and then the actions. Governing variables are the preferred states that individuals strive to "sacrifice" when they are acting. These governing variables are not the underlying beliefs or values people espouse. They are the variables that can be inferred, by observing the action of individuals acting as agents for the organization, to drive and guide their actions. ……learning may not be said to occur if someone (acting for the organization) discovers a new problem or invents a solution to a problem. Learning occurs when the invented solution is actually produced. The distinction is important because it implies that discovering problems and inventing solutions are necessary, but not sufficient conditions, for organizational learning. Organizations exist in order to act and to accomplish their intended consequences.……Single-loop learning is appropriate for the routine, repetitive issue – it helps get the everyday job done. Double-loop learning is more relevant for the complex, non-programmable issues – it assures that there will be another day in the future for the organization.

Morgan et al. (1998: 357) outline the two steps associated with organizational learning: (i) adaptive learning, which embraces existing knowledge in order to improve both the quality and the efficiency of existing operations; and (ii) generative (double-loop) learning, which is the next stage of the adaptive learning process and can be viewed from a cognitive and intellectualizing stance of problem definition and solution. Herbiniak (Morgan et al. 1998: 358–359) consider that the issue of organizational capabilities is important and can be viewed from two perspectives: utilitarian capabilities and psychological capabilities. As regards utilitarian capabilities, the cyber security manager needs to focus on organizational learning in the context of strategic planning (improved managerial skills and coordination between functions); and as regards psychological capabilities, the focus is on cognitive benefits derived from management processes and systems. Organizational learning is, therefore, a means by which the cyber security manager and those charged with cyber security that are based in partner organizations can develop and utilize knowledge, enhance their skill level and most importantly influence the organization's value system so that security permeates through it. The development and utilization of knowledge, and the benefits associated with knowledge transfer, are key aspects that the cyber security manager and the training manager need to be concerned with. Lee et al. (2009: 741) state: "For a learning organization culture to be established, it is essential that senior managers pay attention to how individuals learn and how they develop their skill and knowledge base". Kolb and Kolb (2008) explain that "Learners embrace challenge, persist in the face of obstacles, learn from criticism, and are inspired by and learn from the success of others". But guidance needs to be given because individuals undergoing a training programme have different needs and absorb knowledge in different ways. Understanding what experiential learning involves can help the cyber security manager to relate to "concrete experience" and get those on the training programme to reflect and feel comfortable with their new experience (Kolb and Kolb, 2008: 13).

Argyris (1996: 8) is of the view that behaviour is fundamentally important in terms of learning, and bearing this in mind, the cyber security manager can understand that organizational learning is the beneficiary of and the engine that drives a certain leadership style/model, which, in turn, gives rise to an organization's cultural value system. In order that change is managed well, top management need to be aware of how the business environment is changing and what skills are required, and cyber security awareness programmes need to be developed for various levels of skills. Those undertaking cyber security training include staff directly employed by the organization and employees of partner organizations: suppliers, dealers and distributors, and retailers, for example. Taking this into account, senior managers may "need to make a distinction between transformational leadership and transactional leadership, and take notice of the fact that a dual leadership style can be deployed in a culturally sensitive organizational environment" (Lee, 2009: 181). To be effective, however, the cyber security manager needs to ensure that the cyber security objectives are embedded in the security objectives, and the security objectives are incorporated within the organization's strategic objectives. Bearing in mind that top management are charged with establishing and maintaining a sustainable competitive advantage, the overriding objective of the organization and the partnership arrangement itself is to ensure that it is resilient and able to withstand any form of cyber attack. This means that the process of change has to be managed carefully and needs to be a prerogative of senior management.

Trim and Lee (2007: 335–336) add to this by suggesting that senior managers need to understand:

> that the concept of organizational learning can be used to bring about change and that the change process needs to be managed in an incremental and pro–active manner. One way in which to bring about organizational change is to institutionalize the learning process and to empower people to take responsibility for their personal development. The process of institutionalizing organizational learning is complex; however, an international project group approach can be used to facilitate the transformation process......

With regard to the international project group approach, the cyber security manager can pool cyber security knowledge from organizational members and staff employed by partner organizations, and gain additional intelligence from suppliers, wholesalers and retailers. The way the company is configured and the type of business model that is in place will determine the composition of the international project group members and what their objectives are. The cyber security manager needs to help devise a cyber security plan that is rolled out among all the partner organizations. This means that interoperability and actionability are incorporated and responsibilities are outlined. In addition, attention is required in terms of which leadership model and leadership style are to be deployed as the business model may be evolving or several business models within the partnership arrangement exit and need to be integrated.

The usefulness of the international project group approach is that it allows the cyber security manager to focus on identifying which organizational vulnerabilities are likely to be targeted by those carrying out cyber attacks, and which staff in the partner organizations (security, marketing intelligence, business intelligence, business continuity planners, financial analysis, IT support staff, strategy, organizational support and human resource management specialists) together with external specialists (CPNI, ENISA, the US Department of Homeland Security, academics and industry experts, for example) will be involved in finding a possible solution to the identified problem associated with a technology/technological application or an evolving business model that has a greater number of interdependencies associated with it (Trim and Upton, 2013: 180–181). An increased number of interdependencies may make each organization in the partnership more vulnerable to a cyber attack. For this reason, organizations in the UK need to develop a robust, collectivist cyber security approach and avail themselves of advice offered through the Information Exchanges set up by the UK's Centre for the Protection of National Infrastructure (CPNI).

In the context of an organization operating across borders, international project groups are a means of harnessing the knowledge and expertise of people throughout an organization and more specifically can act as coordinating vehicles for devising ways to implement plans and strategies (Trim and Upton, 2013: 177–178). Trim and Lee (2007: 337) suggest that the main purpose of an international project group is for staff "to work on 'secret' projects that are deemed essential to the future survival of the organization". International project groups are useful with regard to building trust-based working relationships involving staff based in partnership organizations, some of whom may be based abroad, and can act as a catalyst for the development of new ideas, for promoting and managing organizational change through initiatives in interoperability involving IT systems, and can facilitate the development of new management methods and decision-making styles (e.g. achieved through small team relationship building exercises and in-house project-based competitions) (Trim and Upton, 2013: 178). The cyber security manager can contribute to the process of managing organizational change by providing inputs into information management security as well as cyber security. By working with the risk manager and the train-ing manager, workable solutions can be found through embracing organizational learning and being committed to the process of continual improvement. Further-more, by establishing a number of strategic project groups, some of which can be viewed as permanent or semi-permanent (ad hoc and with a limited life), it should be possible to ensure that once a discovery takes place, new training and staff de-velopment programmes are designed and put in place (Trim and Lee, 2007). The advantage of this is that the learning process is enhanced and leads to new cyber security knowledge.

A strategic project group can be established that has involvement from industry, government and academia. The work it undertakes can be reinforced through various initiatives such as the UK-Korea Cyber Security Network (Trim and Youm, 2014, 2015), which has done much to promote cyber security cooperation between the UK and South Korea. Currently, much emphasis is placed on identifying evolving cyber threat trends and specific types of cyber attack; developing appropriate cyber security countermeasures; identifying the risks associated with cloud computing; identifying the problems associated with the implementation of new business models and new ways of doing business (e.g. outsourcing, offshoring and nearshoring); implementing cyber security training programmes to enhance the skill base of employees; incorporating personal security into staff development programmes relating to identify theft and ransomware attacks; how to establish information sharing procedures with law enforcement agencies; how to establish cooperation with organizations in the supply chain to ensure that vulnerabilities are protected; how to embed cyber security within the organization's security value system; how to establish a leadership model that promotes security throughout the partnership arrangement and how to be more responsive to the wider community (e.g. through corporate social responsibility programmes) that helps promote the concept of resilience. As regards establishing a leadership model that promotes risk management and security awareness throughout the partnership arrangement, it is worth noting that top management must take the lead and ensure that risk management and security awareness are incorporated in the organization's value system and that there is a documented and consistent policy in place for dealing with risk management and security in relation to cyber attacks.

Some observers might suggest that the stakeholder view, which according to Johnson and Scholes (1999: 61) represents the political view of strategy development and they suggest that "strategies develop as the outcome of processes of bargaining and negotiation among powerful or external interest groups (or stakeholders)", is more appropriate today than, for example, the Agency Theory approach, which according to Douma and Schreuder (1998: 99) is "in its simplest form …the relationship between two people, a principal and an agent who makes decisions on behalf of the principal". The resource-based view of the firm, which maintains that "a resource can only be the basis of a competitive advantage if that resource has certain properties" (Douma and Schreuder, 1998: 159), can be considered relevant as it focuses top management's attention on resource availability, replication, substitution and the law of competition. What is important is that senior managers develop an organizational configuration (structure and systems) that facilitates the development of cyber security knowledge and the utilization of in-house and external cyber security expertise. A pro-active approach to crisis management and cyber security should help staff to deal with an impact if indeed a cyber attack is successful. Kim (1998) suggests that it is possible to construct a crisis in order to focus the creative energies of staff. Hence, it should be possible for the cyber security manager, working with other senior managers, to create a crisis-oriented approach that is cyber-specific and which can result in a solution or set of solutions being generated that can be implemented in real time in order to make the organization more resilient.

The cyber security manager working with the training manager can ensure that double-loop learning occurs, which results in individuals being given the power and authority to create new learning systems (Argyris, 1996). This should result in knowledge being "continuously derived from and tested out in the experiences of the learner" (Kolb, 1984: 27) so that learning is viewed as a "the process whereby knowledge is created through the transformation of experience" (Kolb, 1984: 38). Kolb (1984: 40–41) explains that "the process of experiential learning can be described as a four-stage cycle involving four adaptive learning modes – concrete experience, reflective observation, abstract conceptualization, and active experimentation".

10.5 Changing Organizational Attitudes and Mindsets

As well as working with the IT manager to have the necessary information security systems in place, the cyber security manager will need to work closely with the training manager. For the staff running development programmes to ensure that staff become aware of how to conduct themselves during their employment and not put the organization at risk, attention will need to be given as to how they can change their behaviour. This is so that they implement the organization's security policy in terms of data handling, data storage, data transfer, data utilization and the destruction of data when necessary. Thus, it can be seen that by developing a security culture and having cyber security at the heart of it, reinforced by cyber security awareness, an appropriate leadership model can be put in place. This will provide a platform from which the cyber security manager and the risk manager can work with various managers throughout the partnership arrangement to categorize the risks identified. Once this is achieved, they will establish how much risk the organization (e.g. the organization's risk appetite) and its partners can be exposed to.

Various models can be used to help staff relate better to the cyber risks identified. The Sequence-of-Events Model (Trim and Lee, 2014: 17–38) can help the cyber security manager to establish the characteristics and factors necessary to identify which threats relate to cyber crime, cyber warfare and cyber terrorism. This is important because cyber threats evolve through time and it is important to help staff identify how a threat is changing and how it will impact the organization. Key stakeholders (suppliers, customer organizations, investors and shareholders) as well as regulators and auditors, for example, will be able to help the cyber security manager establish if the organization's approach to risk management is appropriate. In addition, cyber security experts can be brought into the organization to establish if the organization's risk appetite is defined well. External advice can prove advantageous in terms of an objective view and in-house security seminars and workshops can be devised that help staff understand how to contribute to the organization's strategic security decision-making process.

Caballero (2010: 37) is of the view that management must identify the "weakest element in the security formula that is used to secure systems and networks"; hence, the cyber security manager needs to work with the IT manager and the training manager and devise cyber security awareness activities, including role-based training that raises cyber security awareness throughout the organization. It is known that "what-if" scenario training simulations prove beneficial in terms of this with the focus being on highlighting low-probability, high-impact events that can have a devastating impact on an organization. Caballero (2010: 38) suggests that lectures, case studies, workshops and hands-on practice prove useful in terms of raising the skill level of employees. Aids such as environmental scanning techniques can help the cyber security manager to gain insights into how a threat may evolve and materialize, and can help those charged with implementing cyber security policy to evaluate a range of cyber threats simultaneously. A pro-active approach to resilience is underpinned by an organizational value system that embraces cultural change, and supports open communication and the development of trust-based relationships that give rise to information sharing.

10.6 An Effective Counter Threat Strategy

Bearing in mind the above, it is possible to understand how Critical Information Infrastructure Protection (CIIP) models can be devised (Suter, 2007) and made industry- and country-specific. This can be considered appropriate because a CIIP model for one country may not be applicable to other countries (Pommerening, 2004: 1). By linking organizational learning with cyber security knowledge development, and strategic security, cyber defence systems can be developed that are based on the Four-Pillar Model of CIIP (Suter, 2007: 1–4): (a) prevention and early warning; (b) detection; (c) reaction and (d) crisis management. The collectivist approach to cyber security requires that managers adopt a holistic approach to security and share information with staff based in partnership organizations. Through the process of interaction, the cyber security manager and the risk manager can engage in the monitoring, analysis and detection of cyber threats and liaise with the IT manager when necessary. By devising an appropriate and effective incident response programme, the cyber security manager can implement actions that neutralize threats and record such events so that they remain in the organization's memory. Through the process of working with staff in government agencies, the cyber security manager will help establish unilateral and bilateral government dialogue that manifests in cooperative agreements between nations that results in the harmonization of cyber laws. Both the benefit of this and the need for it become clear as the focus of attention moves more to the actions of rogue states and their unrestricted use of cyber crime and the move to cyber warfare. Therefore, the cyber security manager needs to pay attention to geo-political forces and embrace the work of the intelligence and security agencies.

Aldrich (2012: 56) has indicated that intelligence agencies are moving from "retail surveillance" (warrants or court permissions are needed to observe individuals/small groups) to "wholesale surveillance" (the use of algorithms to search though large data groups/sets in order to identify patterns), otherwise known as robotic spying, facilitated by supercomputers. As governments become familiar with the benefits provided by supercomputers and quantum computing in particular, which uses parallel processing, new opportunities in the area of data security, intelligence and security will emerge as law enforcement personnel will be able to track, trace and bring cyber criminals to justice (Parsons, 2012: 48).

It is useful to make a link between strategic marketing, marketing intelligence, resilience and cyber security, as it helps senior managers to reflect on both the technological and human/behavioural perspectives of security, and have a holistic view of cyber security (Trim and Lee, 2008a, 2010, 2013). In addition, staff in partner organizations need to play their part and understand that the objective of a strategic cyber security defence is to reduce an organization's vulnerability to cyber attack by strengthening its business-to-business, business-to-consumer and business-to-government links, as well as helping the wider community to remain safe. The following example provides evidence of why a holistic view of cyber security is needed. Andreasson (2012: 61–63) reported that a cyber attack on South Korea and the US in 2009 resulted in disabled online networks and hard drives in PCs being hijacked and remotely controlled, and document files and computer programs being erased. An investigation carried out by authorities in Japan found that eight servers in Japan had been used as stepping stones for the cyber attack.

Advocates of the holistic cyber security approach maintain that as well as cyber security training being provided within a partnership arrangement, there needs to be a broader appreciation of the view that scenario and simulation exercises can help to update emergency response skills (Lee et al., 2009). Evidence of this is that in various critical national areas, such as health and safety, an "exercise culture" already exists (e.g. the Control of Major Accident Hazards (COMAH)). Legislation requires that the operators of large, potentially dangerous sites such as oil refineries, and the authorities and agencies in their area, hold regular joint exercises to make sure that not only is the facility safe but if there was an incident (e.g. the fire at Buncefield in 2015), it could be dealt with and the damage contained. Such a culture brings several benefits: response plans are more coordinated, regularly tested and validated; and during the process the responders get to trust each other and this results in the dissemination of new ideas and information (Trim and Upton, 2013: 92).

In the US, the National Infrastructure Simulation and Analysis Center (NISAC, 2009) "conducts modeling, simulation, and analysis of the nation's critical infrastructure" and its analysts "assess critical infrastructure risk, vulnerability, interdependences, and event consequences". NISAC benefits from the sharing of information between the public and private sectors, and the expertise of its staff is used in the areas of risk mitigation and policy planning. In the EU, the DIESIS project (Design of an Interoperable European federated Simulation network for critical InfraStructures) assessed the feasibility and later helped to establish European Infrastructures Simulation and Analysis Centres (EU-ISACs) (https://www.isacs.eu/). Masucci et al. (2009: 1) put forward the case for linking areas of education and training, with CII policy formulation and implementation, and argues for developing a Knowledge Base System (KBS) to "discover new inter-dependencies among critical infrastructure models".

Reflecting on this, it can be argued that an effective incident response programme will help the cyber security manager to implement actions that neutralize threats as and when they materialize. Working closely with government agencies, the cyber security manager can ensure that the government-to-government cooperative agreements in place allow information to be shared as soon as the type of cyber threat is known.

10.7 Strategic Cyber Security Framework

Bearing in mind that solving real-world problems is complex and requires a multi-disciplinary approach (Coveney and Highfield, 1995: 7–8), the cyber security manager, working with the risk manager, can deploy the systems-of-systems approach to bring various stakeholders together and produce a strategic security framework that is the outcome of the organizations in the partnership arrangement. The growing threat from internally orchestrated attacks (Trim, 2008c; Koo, 2011) is focusing the mind of senior management and the cyber security manager needs to monitor the threat environment. According to Aaker and McLoughlin (2010: 93), strategists need to think in terms of (i) what a strategic uncertainty is related to (trends or events impacting a business, the importance of the business and the number of businesses likely to be affected); and (ii) the immediacy of a strategic uncertainty and what it is related to (the probability that something will occur, the time frame involved and the reaction time necessary to develop and implement an appropriate strategy).

This means that senior management need to adopt a more holistic approach to corporate governance because enterprise governance "is based on the principle that good governance alone cannot make an organisation successful" (Fahy et al., 2005: 2). The SATELLITE (Strategic Corporate Intelligence and Transformational Marketing) Model provides guidance as to how security is built into the strategic management process of the organization (Trim, 2004). The SATELLITE Model specifies the type of work to be undertaken and identifies who will undertake the work. For example, various groups of specialists are in existence and include a Corporate Intelligence Staff Support Group; a Strategic Marketing Staff Support Group; a Corporate Security Management Group; an Internet Marketing Group; a Relationship Marketing Advisory Group and a SATELLITE Advisory Group. The SATELLITE Model is used by senior managers to integrate all aspects of corporate intelligence and security work, and incorporates and links with staff based in stakeholder organizations and places emphasis on linking organizational design with data and information security (Trim et al., 2009). The case is made for the Corporate Security Management Group to take responsibility for a strategic approach to security. The cyber security manager can use such models to devise a cyber security programme, which is composed of a cyber security strategy, cyber security policies and plans, cyber security practices, cyber security controls and cyber security supporting controls (Mehan, 2008: 189). As regards the Internet Marketing Group, Kendrick (2010: 10–11) has outlined how Internet technologies have given rise to enhanced email enabling communications; marketing and transactional opportunities via websites; the development of intranets that facilitate the recording and archiving of an organization's intellectual property; the development of extranets that facilitate links with strategic alliance partners and provide access to customers; Internet technologies that enable economies of scale of the production of goods and services; Internet technologies for use in specialist and niche markets; and web technologies that provide an opportunity for further business opportunities.

In order that the cyber security manager can convince senior management that it is necessary to devise realistic defensive strategies based on counter-intelligence, security needs to be viewed as a core activity (Trim, 2005b). This will, should it succeed, result in a pro-active approach to security that manifests in a security culture that imbues organizational security awareness. The security culture is in fact an outcome and a subset of the learning organization culture, which gives rise to security awareness policies and programmes, which are reinforced through internal marketing campaigns. The security awareness programmes produced are adapted and made available to staff in partner organizations, and this results in trust-based relationships being formed that become strategic intelligence-focused partnerships (Trim and Lee, 2008b). The linkage that occurs between commerce and industry, government and academia, means that there is a stakeholder foundation upon which to build organizational resilience.

Reflecting on the international project group concept, Trim and Lee (2007: 337) suggest that the strategic project groups established may not be permanent but should be focused on three areas (Trim and Lee, 2014: 215–218): (i) business continuity, (ii) risk and (iii) IT. The first strategic project group, which is managed by the business continuity manager, is responsible for a number of internal, organizational duties and externally orchestrated duties. The internal duties include working with risk and IT staff to develop cyber security inter-organizational and intra-organizational policies and procedures; information assurance policy and educational and training programmes, which have as inputs foresight planning and scenario analysis. Contributing to risk assessment is vital and staff are very much concerned with issues relating to damage limitation, recovery and the management of reputational damage. The external duties of this strategic group include monitoring behaviour within social networks and working with marketing personnel vis-à-vis integrating a response in the context of integrated, multi-media channels and the deployment of multi-media tools. The second project group, under the risk manager, is concerned with risk assessment, risk analysis and liaising with experts (both at home and abroad), who deal with threat prevention. The third strategic group is under the control of the IT manager, and is very much concerned with all the technical and technological aspects of cyber business and management practices (e.g. BYOD). The GISES (Global Intelligence and Security Environmental Sustainability) Model outlined by Trim (2005a) will assist managers to develop a security-intelligence interface and a hybrid security culture. In addition, the SATELLITE Model (Trim, 2004) can be used to link more firmly environmental issues with business intelligence planning, and will reinforce the organization's hybrid security culture.

10.8 Learning Summary

The organizational learning concept has been given much attention over the years and has proved instrumental in terms of changing the attitudes of employees. As can be noted from Figure 10.1, organizational learning and cyber security policy, it should be possible to harness the benefits of organizational learning by establishing an appropriate cyber security awareness mindset among employees. This can be done through bespoke training and staff development programmes. By putting in place an international project group and a number of strategic project groups, strategic intelligence can be fully utilized. This is necessary because cyber threats, and in particular, Advanced Persistent Threats (APTs), are becoming the norm, and close involvement with the higher education sector is advisable to ensure that research is undertaken to develop effective cyber security software and also the opportunity to hire graduates with software knowledge and skills, at the end of their studies. By developing an effective cyber security counter threat policy and strategy, which is based on strategic intelligence, the cyber security manager can, with other senior managers, ensure that the systems in place are robust. For example, by working with the marketing manager and the IT manager, the organization's marketing databases and website can be made secure. Furthermore, by accepting that the organization is ethically driven, it should be possible for staff to share their knowledge and experience with a wide public through a corporate social responsibility programme. The latter may be tied in with a university and certain projects for the local community.

The reader will be able to:

- devise an appropriate learning organization framework; and
- create a cyber security culture.

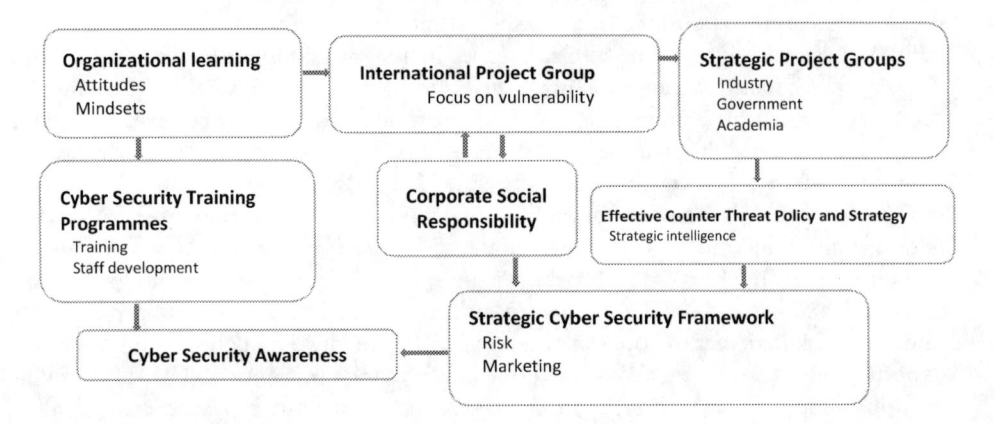

Figure 10.1 Organizational learning and cyber security policy.

10.9 Conclusion

The organization-learning concept allows managers to develop a holistic view of what training is and what it is to achieve. However, in order that organizational learning is viewed as a continual process, top management need to be committed to establishing a learning organization that welcomes the development, utilization and sharing of knowledge. By including senior managers from partner organizations in the organization's learning model, a range of initiatives can be implemented, including the formation of an international project group and more specialized subgroups known as strategic project groups. This being the case, a cyber security culture can be developed that is at the heart of security. The objective is to reinforce security awareness and ultimately influence the organization's value system and the value system of partner organizations.

10.10 Mini Case: Establishing a Cyber Security Culture

Mrs. Rose was the managing director of a distribution consultancy company and had earned a master's degree in innovation management, which had helped her to view innovation from two perspectives: the production of innovatory services and the introduction of an innovatory, work from home human resource management strategy, that saw her elevated to positions of responsibility early in her career. In order to make sure staff stayed committed and were fully participative in the decision-making process, she had commissioned an external management consultancy to undertake a study of how a security culture could be developed that was considered inclusive. The report made interesting reading.

Selecting the three pivotal recommendations, Mrs. Rose asked the head of human resource management, Mrs. Smith and the head of marketing, Mr. Jason, to join her in a brief meeting to discuss how the company could take matters forward. The meeting went well at first and then it seemed to tail away as what had appeared logical and easy to implement recommendations appeared to have issues associated with them.

The first recommendation revolved around inclusivity and the fact that everybody had to undergo regular cyber security training. The consultancy that had produced the report had suggested that half a day be set aside over six weeks so that the material could be covered. It was suggested that Monday was the most appropriate day for the training programmes because staff would be relaxed from their weekend off. Mrs. Smith was supportive of this but Mr. Jason was not. He was firmly convinced that Monday was the busiest day of the week and that his staff normally spent half the day talking with actual and potential clients on the telephone about issues and problems that had surfaced towards the end of the previous week. He reminded those present that business conditions were still uncertain and that the company suffered reduced earnings due to the issues of BREXIT, the COVID-19 era and also the takeover of a client company and the cancelling of a contract.

The second recommendation was also viewed as contentious. The report suggested that the human resource management function should take responsibility for establishing what it called a transparent security culture and that staff that did not abide by the rules should be punished in some way. Various forms of punishment were cited, including reduced pay, suspension and extra security training. Mrs. Smith was keen to embrace the recommendation but Mrs. Rose had her doubts. The company had yet to appoint a training manager and she was not that convinced that those in human resource management should take on the extra responsibility. By making human resource management staff responsible for security was considered not a good idea by Mr. Jason because he felt that they needed somebody that could understand the operational issues the company faced as well as how the issues and challenges that materialized, were dealt with by other companies. Mr. Jason was of the view that Mrs. Smith and her colleagues should be involved in security but they needed somebody that could understand the risks involved and also had a good understanding of legal matters.

The third recommendation drew a number of comments from those present but again they were undecided. The consultancy company suggested that all the company's data and information was moved to the cloud and that even sensitive areas of business operation, such as design work, research and development, and finance and contracts, were moved into the cloud. A number of examples were highlighted to reinforce this view but a number of questions surfaced. Mr. Jason was worried about security within the cloud and also what happened to all the company's data if the cloud provider went into liquidation. Mrs. Rose was aware that a number of points needed more clarification and brought the meeting to a close.

Questions

Question 1: Who should take responsibility for establishing a security culture?

Question 2: What cyber security training programmes should be devised and implemented?

Question 3: What questions should be answered before a decision was made to place data and information in the cloud?

10.11 Extended Case: Opportunities in Retailing – Avoiding the Pitfalls

The COVID-19 pandemic resulted in much change in the retail sector as government-enforced lockdowns forced shoppers to buy non-essential items online and as a result, online shopping soared. The IMRG Capgemini Online Retail Index showed that total online retail sales were well up, standing at over 36% in 2020 compared with the same period for 2019 (Jahshan, 2021). Change in the retail sector has over the years been aided by technology such as artificial intelligence (AI) (e.g. chatbots) (Gregg et al., 2020; Kalaignanam et al., 2021), and this is likely to remain so in the years ahead. As marketers develop a better understanding as regards analysing Big Data, they will be better placed to understand the psyche of consumers and work with strategists and establish an appropriate business model that takes into account future trends in retailing.

Staff employed by retail companies are aware that communication with customers is vital in terms of relationship building and brand awareness. They are also aware of the need to manage supply chain relationships and embrace sustainability, which includes recycling and better care of the environment. Indeed, Villanova et al. (2021: 127) suggest that retailers are keen to sign up customers to the company's mailing list and/or get the customer to follow the company via social media so that they can learn about discounts and new products, for example. As well as balancing practical considerations such as fine tuning the marketing-mix, retail staff also need to take into account how supply chain management decisions result in best practice. For example, senior managers are aware of the pressure on companies to be socially aware and environmentally friendly. Various business models are developing and sustainability can be linked with customer satisfaction (Vadakkepatt et al., 2021) and customer activism.

Retail specialists consider that technology such as AI is beneficial as it can be used to help marketers enrich a customer's shopping journey experience (Luo et al., 2019; Pizzi et al., 2020). This is done by making customers more aware of the products that are available and matching the product's features closely to their needs. Marketers can also benefit from AI by having instant data relating to purchase behaviour and can use the data to devise and implement marketing plans, and retail strategies. Taking into account that suppliers and outsource companies are targets for computer hackers, it can be noted that in order to reduce a company's vulnerability to a cyber attack penetrating the company's defences, it is necessary to think in terms of supply chain resilience. Resilience is a broad-based term but managers need to view it from the perspective of a company being able to "bounce back from a disruption" (Sheffi and Rice, 2005: 41).

New forms of business venture are emerging, however, and as a consequence vulnerabilities will materialize as the business model undergoes transformation through time. Hurr Collective use a rental platform that provides the owners of clothes with the opportunity to rent out their personal items to others for a fee and this appears to appeal to environmentally conscious young shoppers (Anonymous, 2021: 5). Clothes rental and retail sites are expected to gain in popularity as the pressure associated with fast fashion and the ethical concerns relating to the disposal of unsold clothes becomes more pronounced. A company breaking new ground is Nordstrom that operates "See You Tomorrow", which makes available returned and damaged clothes (Vadakkepatt, 2021: 68). The second-hand clothes rental market is expected to challenge traditional retail models and also more retailers are expected to provide recycling bins in store and link returned clothes with a discount scheme. To be successful, a functional information technology system needs to be in place that can track and trace clothes and ensure that ethical guidelines are followed. In addition, the legal considerations also need to be covered.

The 2020–2021 government lockdown resulted in people not going out shopping but turning to online shopping, not only to buy items of clothing but also as a means of entertainment. Hence, retailers are now perfecting avatars to help potential customers have a positive virtual shopping experience, and chatbot facilities are being deployed to help the potential customer find products quickly online. Making sure that the product range is appropriate and that end users as well as those that buy for resale are satisfied with the quality, design, availability and price charged, requires that information technology is utilized and information technology systems are linked (e.g. designer, supplier, retailer, reseller and end user).

Are initiatives in retailing likely to provide adequate financial returns? It has been suggested that by renting out an item of clothing for an eight-day period brings in a fee equivalent to 15% of the retail price of the item (Anonymous, 2021: 5). The costs can be high, however. Rented out clothes have to be cleaned (by the customer or the owner/provider) and in addition, attention needs to be given to how the item is made available to the customer. Is the item sent via the postal system? Or is a click and collect operation in place? If the clothing is damaged, who is responsible, and how does the owner receive compensation (especially if the customer moves address or is in continual transit)?

When hiring out the items of clothing, it seems that specific customer data is required and possibly the end user could use a false name or somebody else's identity when they undertake the transaction. There does appear to be a niche marketing opportunity, however, and evidence of this is provided (Anonymous, 2021: 5):

> Despite the challenges, high street chains are viewing rental as a trend they cannot ignore….John Lewis hires out furniture…. Moss Bros, which has long been in the hire business, last month launched "Moss Bow", a subscription service where customers can rent two garments a month for £65.

What retailers need to take into consideration is the life style of those that are comfortable with renting clothes and also the amount of work that needs to go into ensuring that the clothes meet the expectations of people. The security in place needs to be robust in order to protect client data, ensure that the goods are clean and undamaged and also ensure that there is a regular supply of clothes to meet demand. Because young consumers in particular are keen to share information online, marketers have to be aware that harsh online reviews can manifest in reputational damage and in addition, electronic word-of-mouth can spread rapidly from social network to social network.

Questions

Question 1: Outline the various security problems, both present and future, which are likely to occur in the retailing sector.

Question 2: Why is it important to ensure that retail staff are compliant in their actions?

Question 3: Explain how a comprehensive cyber security system can both protect a retailing business and provide the basis for innovation and growth.

Case Sources

Anonymous. (2021). Millennials turning wardrobes into money machines. *The Sunday Times* (Business & Money Section), 6th June, p. 5.

Gregg, B., Kim, A., and Percy, J. (2020). Leading with purpose: How marketing and sales leaders can shape the next normal. *McKinsey & Company*, April, p. 10.

Jahshan, E. (2021). Online Retail Sales Growth Hit 13-Year High in 2020. *Retail Gazette* (13th January). https://www.retailgazette.co.uk/blog/2021/01/online-retail-sales-growth-hit-13-year-high-in-2020 (accessed on 9th May, 2021).

Kalaignanam, K., Tuli, K.R., Kushwaha, T., Lee, L., and Gal, D. (2021). Marketing agility: The concept, antecedents, and a research agenda. *Journal of Marketing*, 85 (1): 35–58. https://doi.org/10.1177/0022242920952760.

Luo, X., Tong, S., Fang, Z., and Qu, Z. (2019). Frontiers: Machines vs. humans: The impact of artificial intelligence chatbot disclosure on customer purchases. *Marketing Science*, 38 (6): 937–947. https://doi.org/10.1287/mksc.2019.1192

Pizzi, G., Scarpi, D., and Pantano, E. (2020). Artificial intelligence and the new forms of interaction: Who has the control when interacting with a chatbot? *Journal of Business Research*. https://doi.org/10.1016/j.jbusres.2020.11.006.

Sheffi, Y., and Rice, J.B. (2005). Supply chain view of the resilient enterprise. *MIT Sloan Management Review*, 47 (1) (Fall): 41–48.

Vadakkepatt, G.G., Winterich, K.P., Mittal, V., Zinn, W., Beitelspacher, L., Aloysius, J., Ginger, J., and Reilman, J. (2021). Sustainable retailing. *Journal of Retailing*, 97 (1): 62–80. https://doi.org/10.1016/j.jretai.2020.10.008.

Villanova, D., Bodapati, A.V., Puccinelli, N.M., Tsiros, M., Goodstein, R.C., Kushwaha, T., Suri, R., Ho, H., Brandon, R., and Hatfield, C. (2021). Retailer marketing communications in the digital age: Getting the right message to the right shopper at the right time. *Journal of Retailing*, 97 (1): 116–132. https://doi.org/10.1016/j.jretail.2021.02.001.

10.12 References

Aaker, D.A., and McLoughlin, D. (2010). *Strategic Market Management*. Chichester: John Wiley & Sons Limited.

Aldrich, R. (2012). The ultimate spy. *Focus*, (248) (November): 55–59.

Andreasson, K. (2012). *Cybersecurity: Public Sector Threats and Responses*. London: CRC Press.

Appelbaum, R.S., and Gallagher, J. (2000). The competitive advantage of organizational learning. *Journal of Workplace Learning: Employee Counselling Today*, 12 (2): 40–56.

Argyris, C. (1996). *On Organizational Learning*. Oxford: Blackwell Publishers limited.

Caballero, A. (2010). Information security essentials for IT managers: Protecting mission-critical systems, pp. 1–46. In J.A. Vacca (Ed.), *Managing Information Security*. Burlington, MA: Elsevier.

Coveney, P., and Highfield, R. (1995). *Frontiers of Complexity: The Search for Order in Chaotic World*. London: Faber and Faber Limited.

Douma, S., and Schreuder, H. (1998). *Economic Approaches to Organizations*. Hemel Hempstead, Hertfordshire: Prentice Hall Europe.

Fahy, M., Roche, J., and Weiner, A. (2005). *Beyond Governance: Creating Corporate Value through Performance, Conformance and Responsibility*. Chichester: John Wiley & Sons Limited.

Johnson, G., and Scholes, K. (1999). *Exploring Corporate Strategy: Text and Cases*. Hemel Hempstead: Prentice Hall Europe.

Kendrick, R. (2010). *Cyber Risks for Business Professionals*. Ely: IT Governance Publishing.

Kim, L. (1998). Crisis construction and organizational learning: Capability building in catching-up at Hyundai Motor. *Organization Science*, 9 (4): 506–521.

Kim, W.C., and Mauborgne, R. (2005). *Blue Ocean Strategy: How to Create Uncontested Market Space and Make the Competition Irrelevant*. Boston, MA: Harvard Business School Press.

Kolb, A.Y., and Kolb, D.A. (2008). The learning way: Meta-cognitive aspects of experiential learning. *Simulation & Gaming.* https//doi.org/10.1177/10468781083225713 (accessed on 20th October, 2008).

Kolb, D.A. (1984). *Experiential Learning: Experience as the Source of Learning and Development.* Upper Saddle River, NJ: Prentice Hall, Inc.

Koo, M. (2011). An information war? Balancing national security, trade secrets and the rights on the individual. The Strand, London: Australia House (19th May).

Lee, Y-I. (2009). Strategic transformational management in the context of inter-organizational and intra-organizational partnership development, pp. 181–196. In P.R.J. Trim and J. Caravelli (Eds.), *Strategizing Resilience and Reducing Vulnerability.* New York: Nova science Publishers, Inc.

Lee, Y-I., Trim, P.R.J., Upton, J., and Upton, D. (2009). Large emergency-response exercises: Qualitative characteristics—A Survey. *Simulation & Gaming: An International Journal of Theory, Practice and Research,* 40 (6): 726–751.

Masucci, V., Servillo, P., Dipoppa, G., and Tofani, A. (2009). Critical Infrastructures ontology based modeling and simulation. Chapter of a book. http://www.diesis-project.eu/include/Publications/paper.pdf (accessed on 31st December, 2009).

Mehan, J.E. (2008). *Cyber War, Cyber Terror and Cyber Crime: A Guide to the Standards in an Environment of Change and Danger.* Ely: IT Governance Publishing.

Morgan, R.E., Katsikeas, C.S., and Adu, K.A. (1998). Market orientation and organizational learning capabilities. *Journal of Marketing Management,* 14: 353–381.

National Infrastructure Simulation and Analysis Center (NISAC). (2009). http://www.dhs.gov/xabout/structure/gc_1257535800821.shtm#2 (accessed on 31st December, 2009).

Parsons, P. (2012). The quantum revolution is here. *Focus,* (249) (December): 46–51.

Pommerening, C. (2004). A comparison of critical information infrastructure protection in the United States and Germany: An institutional perspective. Paper presented at the *Annual Meeting of the American Political Science Association,* Chicago, IL, 2nd September 2004, pp. 1–30. http://www.allacademic.com/meta/p60905_index.html (accessed on 10th November, 2009).

Reddy, V. (2007). Getting back to the rough ground: Deception and 'social living', pp. 219–244. In N. Emery (Ed.), *Social Intelligence: From Brian to Culture.* Oxford: Oxford University Press.

Senge, P.M. (1999). *The Fifth Discipline: The Art & Practice of the Learning Organization.* London: Random House.

Suter, M. (2007). *A Generic National Framework for Critical Information Infrastructure Protection (CIIP).* Zurich, Switzerland: Center for Security Studies (August).

Trim, P.R.J. (2004). The strategic corporate intelligence and transformational marketing (SATELLITE) model. *Marketing Intelligence and Planning,* 22 (2): 240–256.

Trim, P.R.J. (2005a). The GISES model for counteracting organized crime and international terrorism. *International Journal of Intelligence and CounterIntelligence,* 18 (3): 451–472.

Trim, P.R.J. (2005b). Managing computer security issues: Preventing and limiting future threat and disasters. *Disaster Prevention and Management,* 14 (4): 493–505.

Trim, P.R.J. (2008). Effective communication and persuasion for behaviour change. *Master Class session, The Malicious Exploitation of Information Systems Conference,* University College London (7th November).

Trim, P.R.J., Jones, N.A., and Brear, K. (2009). Building organisational resilience through a designed-in security management approach. *Journal of Business Continuity & Emergency Planning,* 3 (4): 345–355.

Trim, P.R.J., and Lee, Y-I. (2004). Enhancing customer service and organizational learning through qualitative research. *Qualitative Market Research: An International Journal,* 7 (4): 284–292.

Trim, P.R.J., and Lee, Y-I. (2007). Placing organizational learning in the context of strategic management. *Business Strategy Series,* 8 (5): 335–342.

Trim, P.R.J., and Lee, Y-I. (2008a). A strategic marketing intelligence and multi-organizational resilience framework. *European Journal of Marketing,* 42 (7/8): 731–745.

Trim, P.R.J., and Lee, Y-I. (2008b). A strategic approach to sustainable partnership development. *European Business Review*, 20 (3): 222–239.

Trim, P.R.J., and Lee, Y-I. (2010). A security framework for protecting business, government and society from cyber attacks, pp. 1–6. *5th IEEE International Conference on System of Systems Conference (SoSE): Sustainable Systems for the 21st Century*, Loughborough University (22nd to 24th June).

Trim, P.R.J., and Lee, Y-I. (2013). How the strategic marketing approach can underpin cyber security in partnership arrangements involving European and Asian organizations. *2013 CAMIS, KSMS and GAMMA Joint Symposium*, Birkbeck, University of London (4th January).

Trim, P.R.J., and Lee, Y-I. (2014). *Cyber Security Management: A Governance, Risk and Compliance Framework*. Farnham: Gower Publishing.

Trim, P.R.J., and Upton, D. (2013). *Cyber Security Culture: Counteracting Cyber Threats through Organizational Learning and Training*. Farnham: Gower Publishing Limited.

Trim, P.R.J., and Youm, H.Y. (2014) (Editors). *Korea-UK Collaboration in Cyber Security: From Issues and Challenges to Sustainable Partnership*. British Embassy Seoul: Republic of Korea (18th March).

Trim, P.R.J., and Youm, H.Y. (2015) (Editors). *Korea-UK Initiatives in Cyber Security Research: Government, University and Industry Collaboration*. British Embassy Seoul: Republic of Korea (16th March).

Website Address

European Infrastructures Simulation and Analysis Centres (EU-ISACs) https://www.isacs.eu/ (accessed on 7th December, 2021).

10.13 Further Reading

Charan, R. (2001). Conquering a culture of indecision. *Harvard Business Review*, 79 (4): 75–82.

David, D.P., Keupp, M.M., and Mermoud, A. (2020). Knowledge absorption for cyber-security: The role of human beliefs. *Computers in Human Behavior*, 106 (11th January).

Senge, P.M. (1999). *The Fifth Discipline: The Art & Practice of the Learning Organization*. London: Random House.

10.14 Bank of Questions

Question 1: The learning organization concept cannot be applied in all organizations because most management teams are reactive as opposed to pro-active in outlook. Critically appraise this view and provide examples to reinforce your arguments.

Question 2: Explain how organizational learning can help senior managers to identify and deal with organizational vulnerabilities.

Question 3: How useful is the international project group approach?

Question 4: Explain how a strategic project group can be developed and managed through time.

Question 5: Why is it important to have staff members involved in or informed about the organization's counter threat policy and strategy?

Question 6: Explain how the cyber security manager can devise and implement a strategic cyber security framework.

11 Cyber Security Management

11.1 Introduction

In order that the cyber security manager develops an integrated approach to cyber security management, a close working relationship needs to be formed with the training manager and colleagues in the human resource management function. This is so that cyber security solutions can be implemented through bespoke cyber security training and staff development programmes. To be effective, these programmes need to be aligned with current cyber security issues, and also fit within a partner organization's corporate security and resilience policy. Making sure that staff understand and are committed to cyber security management is an ongoing responsibility that needs to be championed by the cyber security manager. When evaluating what corporate security is, managers need to consider that a robust stakeholder security architecture includes intra-government and inter-government working arrangements that are based on and incorporate information sharing. Noting that trust-based relationships facilitate disaster and emergency management policy and strategy across borders, it can be suggested that this constitutes the international stakeholder security view.

This chapter starts with defining the learning objectives (Section 11.2) and then places cyber security in context (Section 11.3). Next, security in a broad context (Section 11.4) is followed by the learning summary (Section 11.5), a conclusion (Section 11.6) and a mini case (Section 11.7). An extended case (Section 11.8) is followed by a set of references (Section 11.9), further reading (Section 11.10) and a bank of questions (Section 11.11).

11.2 Learning Objectives

The reader will be able to:

- establish what cyber security involves;
- establish how cyber attacks can be prevented; and
- establish the context within which security is operationalized.

11.3 Cyber Security in Context

In order to be effective in the role, the cyber security manager is required to have a wide appreciation of the security issues confronting the organization and its partners, and also reflect on and be able to predict how a specific type of cyber threat will manifest. This requires a good understanding of risk and how to establish risk priorities. For example,

DOI: 10.4324/9781003244295-11

Botnet attacks, whereby computers and devices are linked in a coordinated manner and then taken over by the attacker to create a Denial of Service (DoS), are commonly used to disrupt computer operations. Botnets bring into focus the technology and human interface from several perspectives: the attacker, the infrastructure and service provider, the user, government and the expert consultant, for example. As regards technology risk, managers need to be aware of how computer viruses affect the performance of a computer system (Kendrick, 2010: 14–17). The IT manager is responsible for the functioning of computer systems and networks. With respect to the transfer of sensitive and confidential information, encryption is considered important and can be used but it may not be the complete solution. Hence, educating staff in the use of technology is important from the perspective of maintaining an organization's security but managers also need to be sensitive to individual members of staff and their needs because they possess different skill sets. This places emphasis on the cyber security manager being motivated to keep up with technological trends and computer innovations, and how systems work, and know what is involved as regards legal requirements and compliance risk, but also how people feel and how they maintain their level of motivation. By developing an appropriate cyber security knowledge base, the cyber security manager can keep senior management informed about how the organization is going to comply with the various statutory and regulatory provisions governing Internet technology usage. As regards operational risk, the cyber security manager needs to have an in-depth knowledge and appreciation of the systems and procedures in place that govern employee behaviour in relation to the production of goods and services, and how they can embrace organizational polices. This places emphasis on the cyber security manager working closely with the training manager, the risk manager and the IT manager, as information security is about implementing effective security solutions and adhering to legal compliance. This suggests that regular training programmes need to be devised to train employees how to manage data, store data and how they should restrict the use of the data.

Accepting that not all the members of the board of directors of a company are familiar with computer systems and how computer networks operate, and acknowledging that some have in-depth but limited industry experience, the cyber security manager needs to be pro-active in terms of providing corporate governance advice to the board. It should be noted that Kendrick (2010: 21–22) suggests that "IT governance is a subset of corporate governance". Also, bearing in mind that outsourcing may be considered both practical and financially justified, the cyber security manager needs to pay increased attention to the type of risk that arises as the business model is transformed through time and new, unforeseen risks emerge. An unforeseen risk may occur if a deal is agreed with an overseas supplier who is reluctant to integrate their contractors' details into the database of the new parent company. Because of the nature of the work and the sensitivity involving some of the issues covered, the cyber security manager should be admitted to the risk management team, which is under the responsibility of the risk manager (Kendrick, 2010: 25). This is to help formulate risk management policy, which takes into account whether a specific type of risk analysis tool will be used or an alternative approach will be adopted. Ultimately, the risk manager is accountable to the board of directors or a senior manager, and can be viewed as highly influential in terms of working with senior managers throughout the partnership arrangement. This also has the advantage of providing an integrated international stakeholder security view that allows for uniformity of approach among partner organizations. The main priorities being to identify organizational vulnerabilities and put in place contingency plans. As regards emerging issues such as controlling security in the cloud, Samani (2011) states that all risk management requirements are covered in the contracts entered into and an important consideration is how the cyber security manager, the risk manager and the contracts manager develop sufficient knowledge and expertise to make sure that all the eventualities are covered in the contract(s) entered into. Hence, by working closely with the IT manager, it should be possible to link current IT needs with future needs, and view information and communications technology (ICT) as embracing computer systems and networks. As a consequence, the cyber security manager will gain full knowledge of the range of electronic devices that people use to share and utilize information.

Real world examples can be drawn on to highlight why it is essential for the cyber security manager to keep up with events and develop an understanding of how cyber attacks originate and what they involve. Stuxnet, which has been referred to as a cyber weapon (Barnell, 2011), proved to be highly effective in terms of the damage it caused. To guard against such forms of attack on a network, Barnell (2011) suggests that seven points need to be adhered to: (i) continual monitoring; (ii) an adequate information assurance programme needs to be in place; (iii) file level encryption; (iv) the advice provided on security response websites needs to be checked and adhered to; (v) contractors should undergo regular checks to ensure that they are reputable; (vi) the responsibility for risk is shared and (vii) checks are made to ensure that contractors are not using stolen software. Indeed, McAfee (2021) reported that:

> Stuxnet was a multi-part worm that traveled on USB sticks and spread through Microsoft Windows computers. The virus searched each infected PC for signs of Siemens Step 7 software, which industrial computers serving as PLCs use for automating and monitoring electro-mechanical equipment. After finding a PLC computer, the malware attack updated its code over the internet and began sending damage-inducing instructions to the electro-mechanical equipment the PC controlled. At the same time, the virus sent false feedback to the main controller. Anyone monitoring the equipment would have had no indication of a problem until the equipment began to self-destruct.

If an organization suffers from advanced persistent attacks that manifest in advanced persistent threats (APTs), it is likely that the hackers will gain access to the organization's computer systems, in which case the cyber security manager and the IT manager will need to work closely with the risk manager and public relations/marketing manager and implement a disaster recovery programme and a reputational damage limitation programme at the same time. During times of a crisis/emergency, staff work closely together and the multiple relationships in place, both inter-organizational and intra-organizational, help staff to implement plans/policies that allow the organizations in the partnership arrangement to recover and continue trading. The cyber security manager does, therefore, need to pay attention to the formation and maintenance of trust-based relationships (Trim et al., 2009), and accept that each crisis/emergency may need the involvement of a number of external experts. However, as Dawson (1996: 268–269) has indicated, "Organisations are arenas for the activities of different interest groups which are linked through patterns of conflict, consensus and indifference". This calls into question the ability of the cyber security manager to use foresight and utilize the knowledge they have as well as draw on the experience and expertise of additional contacts. The network of contacts will be expanded through time and will bring new individuals into the network based on the personal recommendation of existing network members. The security profession is composed of people from various backgrounds (intelligence, security, the police, the military, law and computer science, for example), and tends to be rather insular. By expanding the envelope of contacts, the cyber security manager can ensure that inter-organizational and intra-organizational relationships are governed and influenced by an adapted leadership style (Lee, 2009: 192) that places cyber security at the heart of security.

11.4 Security in a Broad Context

The UK's Cyber Security Strategy (CSS) aimed to achieve a "resilient and secure cyberspace" by 2015 and incorporated four objectives (Cabinet Office, 2011: 8 and 21):

> Objective 1: The UK to tackle cyber crime and be one of the most secure places in the world to do business in cyberspace.
> Objective 2: The UK to be more resilient to cyber attacks and better able to protect our interests in cyberspace.
> Objective 3: The UK to have helped shape an open, stable and vibrant cyberspace which the UK public can use safely and that supports open societies.
> Objective 4: The UK to have the cross-cutting knowledge, skills and capability it needs to underpin all cyber security objectives.

With reference to CSS objective 4, the UK universities were to focus on increasing the number of appropriately skilled cyber security students at various levels (school, university and post-experience/practitioner levels); cooperate more with government and industry; work with interested parties to produce relevant practical models for business and academia to cooperate fully; work with various stakeholders to develop and distinguish education and training provision in the fields of cyber security and information assurance; and engage more with professional groups and associations (IAAC, 2012a).

At an IAAC (2012b) workshop, which was held jointly with the Cabinet Office in London on 31 January 2012 to discuss the implementation of the UK Government's CSS objective 4, it was suggested that training and education in the field of cyber security needed to be expanded. The reason being that those going into management positions needed to be able to manage risks more effectively due to the changing nature of cyber attacks. In addition, it was noted that there needed to be better integration between companies and universities as regards educational and training provision. More emphasis was needed in terms of increasing the nation's cyber security knowledge base and skill level so that the cyber security knowledge gap could be closed. At the same time, opportunities would be created for young people that wished to embark on a career in cyber security. Through the process of promoting cyber security awareness, individuals would be able to gain the cyber security skills necessary and contribute to the country's cyber defence when they took up employment.

Both the cyber security manager and the risk manager can be considered influential in terms of identifying what type of skills the organization needs to defend itself against various forms of cyber attack. Working with the head of training, a cyber security management programme can be produced that promotes cyber security awareness among a wide group of people that have different expertise, experience and responsibility. In order to avoid the development of knowledge silos and focus on what will make the organization resilient, the cyber security manager can place cyber security at the heart (the inner circle) with security generally (the outer circle) and resilience dissecting the circles. The range of experts (referred to as influencers) that provide intelligence, security knowledge and security expertise are matched with various stakeholders (information security professionals, government representatives, academics, senior managers and various other interested parties), and work together in order to devise a range of courses and programmes of study that can be delivered to different users.

In view of the fact that remote working has gained much acceptance in recent years, the logic underpinning Bring Your Own Device (BYOD) to work has gained momentum and is likely to continue to do so as remote working becomes more entrenched. BYOD relates to an individual user/employee having the right/opportunity to "choose their own working conditions and operating environment" (Simmons, 2012a: 1). Furthermore, BYOD demands that managers consider a number of ownership-related and responsibility-related points (Simmons, 2012a: 1):

> Data storage, including emails, spreadsheets, documents, presentations etc., which will cause problems for 'legal discovery' identifying what has been done on behalf of the organisation. Information classification – in order to be able to identify what is personal information, and how it is to be excluded from storage, transfer, usage etc.; other data types including GPS tracks, photos etc., may also be subject to discovery.
>
> The growing integration of devices and services needs to be understood and scoped. Smartphones and other personal mobile devices may be synchronized with a home PC; users may be utilizing services such as Dropbox etc.; they may also, in the mid term be using their TV for remote access. Their phone may have been plugged in to an in-car display system. All of these situations will make it hard for organisations to know where their information has gone, even if the user is still working for them, and, of course, produces a very large attack surface. There are implications for both the individual and the organisation with regard to managing this future.

Simmons (2012b) is of the view that managers need to identify the potential risks and impacts associated with BYOD because of the explosion of data and the resulting consequences. IT personnel will in the years ahead be under pressure to think of keeping data secure but there is the increased risk associated with the threat posed by employees using their own devices for the purpose of work. For example, either the device is provided by the organization or each member of staff is given a sum of money to purchase a device and utilize it in accordance with strict guidelines. The employer must be held responsible for the device and how it is used, and the safeguards in place ensure that an employee does not breach company policy. However, unforeseen events will occur (e.g. devices are lost or stolen) and it is crucial that the member of staff affected is confident enough to report the matter as soon as possible to the appropriate person within the organization. Because identity theft can be related to a stolen device (e.g. a device stolen to order) or result from personal data/information being placed on a social media networking site, additional attention will need to be given to employees as regards how they can change their behaviour in order not to be targeted in any way. Increasingly, those carrying out a cyber attack will turn to exploit a vulnerability using personal data and evidence of this is when a company executive's stolen personal data/ information is used to unlock company accounts.

By placing data in the public cloud, it has to be recognized that issues will arise that need to be addressed. Hogg (2012) has outlined the growing interest in cyber insurance and suggests that the risk manager needs to pay more attention to what a risk register contains and also the topic of reputational risk needs to be understood. Risk assurance managers are focused on assessing risk exposure, and this requires that the cyber security manager thinks in terms of risk also in relation to the networks and in particular the data stored on networks, especially the physical damage caused during an attack and the financial and emotional harm caused. Working with the risk manager, the following aspects need to be considered: costs (forensic costs in particular), risk mitigation costs, physical costs and a range of issues linked with flexible manufacturing systems. Hogg (2012) is of the view that most of the costs are non-physical and customer lists need to be guarded as they can be considered as intellectual property rights. Physical injury claims would include emotional distress/damage, as well as personal injury and damage. The issue of privacy liability is important and so too are security liability and contractual liability. In particular, extortion, fraud and the bad behaviour of employees can be considered under the umbrella of risk and need to be monitored through time because of the problems associated with reputational damage.

There are a number of topics that can and will be discussed. For example, it is envisaged that from time to time, the cyber security manager, the risk manager and the IT manager will discuss software design issues, and in particular faulty or suspect software; faulty products and product liability; a cloud provider and insurance risk cover; and the fact that an insurance policy is a negotiated contract. However, also of key interest is the knowledge that cloud providers have and how the cyber security manager can avail themselves of the knowledge. Cloud providers need to meet certain standards: incentivization, better rates and better practices, if, i.e., they are to maintain their unique product and service offering. By establishing what the organization's risk appetite is, it should be possible to define the level of insurance cover needed and at the same time make sure that the information in the risk register(s) is valid and the risk management communication strategy is clearly defined. This calls in question the threat modelling approach in use and how senior members of staff such as the chief information officer, the chief technology officer, the cyber security manager, the risk manager, the IT manager and the training manager formulate and implement cyber security policy within the context of the organization's security policy. The risk manager needs to take cognizance of the personal liability of employees, criminal liability and how the management model in place is within a strategic cyber security framework (Trim and Lee, 2014: 128–129).

11.5 Learning Summary

It is clear from the discussion that a cyber security culture, underpinned by a commitment to cyber security and risk awareness, can increase the organization's level of resilience. For this to happen, the cyber security manager needs to be ensured that all members of staff embrace the procedures in place and are compliant. This is made clear in Figure 11.1, which also emphasizes the fact that top management need to establish a cyber security knowledge base that draws on various cyber security expertise. This is because security problems will surface from time to time that require a unique solution. By accepting that cyber security can be viewed widely, it should be possible for senior

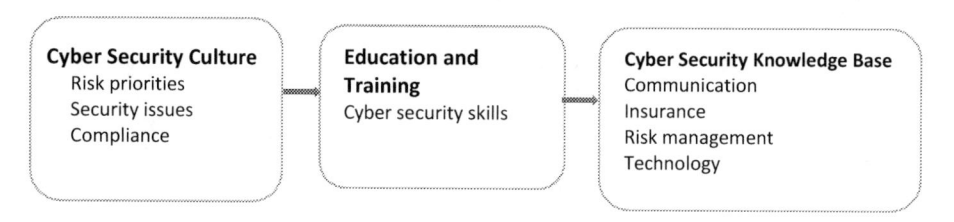

Figure 11.1 Cyber security management process.

management to ensure that staff gain the necessary cyber security skills they need and which are updated through time; and staff develop a cyber security knowledge base that takes cognizance of issues such as cyber insurance, for example. By having a good appreciation of the risks involved and the opportunity costs, a logical approach can be adopted to cyber-related issues and this should facilitate the human-technology interface and strengthen the organization's cyber security knowledge base and those of its partners.

The reader will be able to:

- devise and implement an integrated cyber security management approach; and
- devise a strategic cyber security knowledge base.

11.6 Conclusion

In order to develop an all-round appreciation of what the cyber security management process involves, the cyber security manager must work closely with designated senior managers throughout the partnership arrangement and be an influential member of the senior management team. By working closely with the risk manager, the IT manager and the training manager, the cyber security manager can help to establish a cyber security knowledge base and influence cyber security policy. By doing this, a cyber security culture will be established. Furthermore, the cyber security culture will be strengthened through time as government provides additional clarity and guidance in terms of what they propose to do to develop further the nation's cyber security strategy.

11.7 Mini Case: All Together Now

The company outing was an annual event that was scheduled for a week in July, when the weather was fine and those on the day trip could enjoy a homemade picnic and take in the sea air. The current outing was no exception. The weather was fine, the people were jolly and all was going well until the person in charge, Dan Sheriff, received a call on his mobile phone.

"What is this about", he said to the person at the end of the call. "Oh, I see…No. leave it to me. I will deal with it".

He finished the call and then went over to Mr. Grove, the IT manager, who was finishing his lunch with his wife.

"Can we have a few words", said Mr. Sherrif. "Yes of course", replied Mr. Grove.

They excused themselves and went off to talk through a few points that had surfaced during the telephone conversation that Mr. Sheriff had just had, with an external consultant brought in to assess the organization's cyber security defence capability.

The conversation between Mr. Sheriff and Mr. Grove was friendly and they covered a number of points in a short period of time. The key topics covered were the organization's cloud computing policy, which was considered dated and ineffective. In addition, one of the service companies, that had been contracted in to undertake a project, was known to be using suspect software and also of concern was the fact that a supplier of the organization had been selling some of the company's product designs to a competitor. The designs in question were dated, but it was not clear as to how long this had been going on.

Another point that had been noted was that the company was receiving an increased number of cyber attacks on its computer networks and it was possible that somebody within the company was liaising with an outside criminal syndicate to gain access to the company's accounts.

Mr. Grove looked rather taken aback and said that he would look into these points when he returned to the office on Monday. From the information supplied by the external consultant, it seemed that there was an insider issue and also the person looked as if they were working to steal data and information to order. The pattern uncovered suggested that two departments within the organization were affected and this meant that there were possibly two members of staff colluding and working together.

Questions

Question 1: What other issues may the external consultant have uncovered?

Question 2: How should Mr. Grove prioritize matters?

Question 3: Who should work with Mr. Grove in order to identify the main problems(s)?

11.8 Extended Case: Unexpected Threats

A company involved in smart house design and smart house gadgets was due to hold a management meeting when the head of design received a telephone call from his wife. She was upset and needed to talk with her husband about a family problem. Jerry Anderson took the call in his office and soon became aware that the call was in relation to his son and the theft of his drone, which he had been flying in a local park with a group of friends.

Mark, Mr. Anderson's son, had been given a drone for Christmas and being aware that there were reports in the newspaper about a drone disrupting flights at Gatwick Airport, he and his friends had found a safe place to fly the drone, which was a park nearby to where he lived. The park was far away from residential properties and aircraft, and safe because those involved in flying the drone were aware that they should keep it low in the sky and aimed to keep within a safe distance of people and houses. Mark had been schooled in being responsible and not taking risks, as he had only flown the drone once before in the company of his father.

The local park selected was deemed safe and everybody assumed that it was a secure environment. It was not that well used but children did gather there to play various games on occasion. On the day, Mark was with his older brother Tom, who was responsible for looking after the group and a close friend of the family, Mr. Buckingham, was also in attendance.

Mark stood in the middle of the park (a safe distance from the others) and was able to get the drone off the ground at the third attempt. Once the drone was airborne, it was made to move about in a gentle and controlled manner. Suddenly, Mark looked at his brother in astonishment and said that he was not controlling the drone, and he could not return it to the landing site. The drone went higher and higher into the sky until it disappeared from view. Mr. Buckingham shouted to the group to get their belongings together and once ready, the group moved off in the direction that the drone was known to have headed. They walked out of the park and along the path, leading to the west end of the village. They passed a young man standing by a motor bike looking out towards a field, but nobody else was around and they continued their journey along the path. The drone was not recovered.

Mr. Anderson listened to what he was being told and then said that he had known of a colleague at work, whose son experienced a similar incident and again, although the father and son had gone off together to try and retrieve the drone, they never recovered it. Mrs. Anderson told her husband that Mark had gone onto the worldwide web and looked up hacked drones. She told him how easy it was for somebody to take control of another person's drone by using either a mobile phone or a laptop computer, and thefts of these devices were rather common. Thinking about the incident made Mr. Anderson aware of just how vulnerable people are to a cyber attack, and how those carrying out such an attack are invisible and detached from the emotional hurt they cause.

Bearing in mind what had happened, Mr. Anderson went into the meeting and informed those present that they would start the meeting with a brainstorming session, the objective being to move forward a key point on the agenda so that they could follow through before they engaged with suppliers. The focus of the brainstorming session was to answer the question: how can we ensure that the smart devices in the smart house are secure?

What came out of the brainstorming session was considered highly relevant. For example, Jenny Margate, who was in charge of planning interior design within new build projects, made reference to the fact that people were already connected to a range of services through electronic devices and mentioned that it was not uncommon for millennials, in particular, to have accounts with online retailers that linked the house holder to an automatic ordering system with inter-connected devices. In order to make her points clear, she drew on the insights of Frean (2016: 20):

> The system only works with internet-connected household appliances. Users connect these to their Amazon Prime account using their home wi-fi network and smartphone and select the products they want to order. The device measures usage – for example, how many loads of washing have been run – calculates when new supplies are needed and automatically transmits orders through the user's account.

Mrs. Margate went on to explain that she was being asked to design complete, integrated Internet-connected systems in houses so that a home owner could set the music system to play music as soon as the front door was opened; turn on the kettle automatically so that the water had boiled by the time the person was ready to relax on the sofa and if they wished, they could do their shopping via their television set and plan to have the item purchased, delivered at a specific time over a 24- to 48-hour period.

After she had finished, Mr. Anderson suggested that they should next discuss the security-related issues that people could identify. He started by explaining that if the lights are turned on automatically at a certain time, then anybody watching the property would know when to expect the person returning home. If also, somebody hacked into one of the electronic devices in the house, they would probably be able to switch off all the appliances or gain access to the person's bank account. Reflecting on what his wife had told him over the telephone, he decided to adopt a hardheaded approach to establishing where the vulnerabilities were and suggested that it may not be safe for home owners to have an outside connection that allowed them to plug their electric car into a socket and power up the vehicle overnight. He also suggested that it may be possible for a hacker to gain access to somebody's solar energy power source and steal energy from it. Not only would this be disruptive, but the home owner would be confronted with certain costs they had not expected.

Questions

Question 1: How secure is a smart house from a possible cyber attack?

Question 2: What precautions should a smart house owner take to ensure that they do not fall victim to a cyber attack?

Question 3: What due diligence should be undertaken by a seller of a smart product before they release it on the market?

Case Source

Frean, A. (2016). Household appliances order their own refills, *The Times*, 31st August, p. 20.

11.9 References

Barnell, D. (2011). Stuxnet – Rethink security, right across the supply chain. *Second International Secure Systems Development Conference: Designing in Security*, Hilton London Olympia Hotel, London (18th–19th May).

Cabinet Office. (2011). *The UK Cyber Security Strategy: Protecting and Promoting the UK in a Digital World*. London: Cabinet Office (November).

Dawson, S. (1996). *Analysing Organisations*. Basingstoke: Palgrave.

Hogg, M. (2012). Cyber insurance: What is it about? *Governance and Consumerisation Workshop. Who Should do What?* BCS, The Chartered Institute for Technology, London: Information Assurance Advisory Council (15th February).

IAAC. (2012a). Academic Liaison Panel. BCS, The Chartered Institute for Technology, London (25th January).

IAAC. (2012b). *The UK Government's Cyber Security Strategy Key Issues, Joint IAAC and Cabinet Office Workshop*. BCS, The Chartered Institute for Technology, London (31st January).

Kendrick, R. (2010). *Cyber Risks for Business Professionals*. Ely: IT Governance Publishing.

Lee, Y-I. (2009). Strategic transformational management in the context of inter-organizational and intra-organizational partnership development, pp. 181–196. In P.R.J. Trim and J. Caravelli (Eds.), *Strategizing Resilience and Reducing Vulnerability*. New York: Nova Science Publishers.

Samani, R. (2011). Is it possible to control security in any cloud service? *Second International Secure Systems Development Conference: Designing in Security*, Hilton London Olympia Hotel, London (18th–19th May).

Simmons, S. (2012a). *Governance and Consumerisation Positioning Paper.* London: Information Assurance Advisory Council.

Simmons, S. (2012b). Governance requirements for addressing consumerisation. *Governance and Consumerisation Workshop. Who Should do What?* BCS, The Chartered Institute for Technology, London: Information Assurance Advisory Council (15th February).

Trim, P.R.J., Jones, N.A., and Brear, K. (2009). Building organisational resilience through a designed-in security management approach. *Journal of Business Continuity & Emergency Planning,* 3 (4): 345–355.

Trim, P.R.J., and Lee, Y-I. (2014). *Cyber Security Management: A Governance, Risk and Compliance Framework.* Farnham: Gower Publishing.

Website Address

McAfee https://www.mcafee.com/enterprise/en-gb/security-awareness/ransomware/what-is-stuxnet.html#stuxnet-worm (accessed on 26th November, 2021).

11.10 Further Reading

Sallos, M.P., Garcia-Perez, A., Bedford, D., and Orlando, B. (2019). Strategy and organizational cybersecurity: A knowledge-problem perspective. *Journal of Intellectual Capital,* 20 (4): 581–597. https://doi.org/10.1108/JIC-03-2019-0041.

Trim, P. (2009). Placing disaster management policies and practices within a stakeholder security architecture, pp. 213–227. In P.R.J. Trim and J. Caravelli (Eds.), *Strategizing Resilience and Reducing Vulnerability.* New York: Nova Science Publishers.

Trim, P.R.J., Jones, N.A., and Brear, K. (2009). Building organisational resilience through a designed-in security management approach. *Journal of Business Continuity & Emergency Planning,* 3 (4): 345–355.

11.11 Bank of Questions

Question 1: Provide a definition of cyber security and explain why you have defined it in that way.

Question 2: How should the cyber security manager distinguish between intra-organizational relationships and inter-organizational relationships?

Question 3: How important is it for senior managers to liaise with government representatives and participate in cyber security knowledge transfer?

Question 4: What measures/sanctions need to be put in place regarding Bring Your Own Device to work?

Question 5: Which factors need to be taken into consideration as regards a cyber insurance policy?

Question 6: Reflecting on the link between cyber security and resilience, explain why the cyber security manager needs to link the two bodies of knowledge.

12 A Cyber Security Awareness Programme

12.1 Introduction

There is no doubt that the cyber security manager is at the heart of the process of identifying cyber threats and works with various managers, both in-house and those based in partner organizations, to reduce the possibility of a cyber attack penetrating the organization's defences. Developing a robust security umbrella with staff based in partner organizations will ensure that there is a collectivist approach to security. Furthermore, through the process of liaising with staff employed by government and law enforcement agencies, senior management will receive relevant cyber security threat information, which will be used to maintain a high level of cyber security awareness delivered through internal marketing seminars and training programmes.

Maintaining cyber security awareness requires that risk management is undertaken and the risk management communication process is open and viewed as a shared responsibility with various stakeholders (internal and external to the organization) adopting a responsible attitude towards identifying and dealing with known and perceived cyber threats. In order to ensure that the cyber security manager is pro-active in terms of cyber security management, it is essential that security and intelligence are integrated and placed within the business continuity management planning process, and security is viewed as everyone's responsibility.

The chapter is structured in the following way. First, attention is given to the learning objectives (Section 12.2) and this is followed by establishing a collectivist approach to cyber security (Section 12.3). The communication of risk (Section 12.4) is followed by communication, trustworthy behaviour and cultural differences (Section 12.5) and preventing cyber attacks (Section 12.6). Attention is then given to cyber security awareness (Section 12.7), which is then followed by a learning summary (Section 12.8) and a conclusion (Section 12.9). A mini case (Section 12.10) is followed by an extended case (Section 12.11), and a set of references (Section 12.12). Further reading (Section 12.13) is followed by a bank of questions (Section 12.14).

12.2 Learning Objectives

The reader will be able to:

- establish what a cyber security awareness programme involves;
- establish who is involved in producing a cyber security awareness programme; and
- evaluate a cyber security awareness programme.

DOI: 10.4324/9781003244295-12

12.3 Establishing a Collectivist Approach to Cyber Security

A cyber risk report in Management Today (2014) made clear that insider crime was a major issue confronting managers and that they needed to be aware of how hackers launched DDos attacks by deploying viruses and malware. Because senior management did not undertake investigations into computer and Internet use on a regular basis and coupled with the fact that the organization's security policy was not reviewed on a regular basis either, it meant that the organization was more vulnerable than management perceived. Part of the problem seems to be attributed to a general lack of cyber security awareness among organizational staff and staff based in partner organizations. Knowing that a company-owned laptop is used for work but is also available to family members to download and play computer games should be of concern. The risk associated with infected malware being loaded onto a device is high bearing in mind that people consider websites safe and also that they do not always distinguish between a genuine and a fraudulent individual/company, as the latter use sophisticated marketing campaigns (e.g. phishing and competitions) to trap an unsuspecting individual.

Mattern et al. (2014: 705) have stated that:

> Information sources for cyber intelligence are as broad as for any other intelligence target field. Multiple sources are usually needed to get a complete picture of the threat landscape. Relevant data may come from specific network activity, global cyber activity, organizational policy and action, or from geographical events. The data can be open source, proprietary, or classified. What matters most is that the information is timely, actionable, and relevant, helping to reduce uncertainly for decisionmakers. When analyzed and contextualized, information becomes intelligence. Intelligence is what reduces uncertainty and enables timelier, more cost effective, and more informed decisions about policy, operations, and resource allocation.

The cyber security manager, working with the risk manager, can adopt a view that security is an investment as opposed to a cost. This message can be promoted throughout the organization and discussions with the head of finance, and other senior managers can result in a security budget being established that provides those charged with security with adequate resources so that the cyber security risks identified are ranked and prioritized, and the necessary investments are made in computer systems and networks, and staff, for example.

Working with the risk manager, and also the risk managers and assistant risk managers in partner organizations, the cyber security manager can devise an up-to-date risk register/set of registers and update them as and when necessary. Each risk register will contain the risks identified and listed in a ranked order of importance (5 being the highest level of risk and 1 being the lowest level of risk), and also the possible impacts associated with a known vulnerability, and who in the organization is responsible for managing the risk in association with the vulnerability identified. For example, a customer database may be a shared responsibility between the marketing function and IT, but the security issues identified will involve the risk manager and the business continuity manager. So the individuals cited will have responsibility for monitoring the threats relating to the risk identified but the cyber security manager will have equal responsibility (shared with the risk manager) for maintaining the risk register(s). Specific individuals can be nominated to evaluate the risk and update the risk rating and change the risk ranking, but there must be supporting evidence upon which the assumptions and recommendation are made. This is because some risks may be perceived as less threatening than previously due to security systems being improved through time. The advantage of this approach is that the necessary organizational structure(s) are put in place and these will be amended as the business model configuration changes (e.g. as a result of business moving online and/or new network partners being admitted to the partnership arrangement), thus ensuring that the key individuals concerned are associated with the appropriate reporting systems and are assigned appropriate accountability and are held responsible for their actions. These are important points as Mattern et al. (2014: 704) have recognized:

> Cyber Intelligence seeks to not only understand network operations and activities, but also who is doing them, why, and what might be next ... . Cyber Intelligence should drive the cybersecurity mission. Intelligence-led operations require (a) a proactive security posture, (b) a thorough, accurate, timely understanding of the threat environment, and (c) a commitment to decisions based on data.

This means that management need to integrate information sources so that the capabilities of the organization are utilized in order to deal with potential network threats.

The advantage of such an approach is that it allows security to be integrated into the business model, thus ensuring that security is viewed as relevant, holistic, manageable and a shared responsibility. This should result in security embracing all the business functions, including design and development, human resource management, finance, procurement, manufacturing and marketing. Most importantly, it will allow risk and risk communication to be managed by a group of managers and not a single manager or department. The emphasis is, therefore, on managers being able to understand and develop an awareness of how organized criminal syndicates and state sponsored agencies, target data and information. By being aware of how targets are selected, the cyber security manager can better understand what advanced persistent threat(s) (APTs) involve and how they should be dealt with.

12.4 The Communication of Risk

ENISA (2011) purport that an organization's risk management strategy encompasses a communication policy that is viewed as being embedded in the risk management approach. The advantage of this is that senior managers, such as the cyber security manager and the risk manager, can cooperate in developing the organization's communication policy and work alongside marketing staff that deal with promotional activity. Logically crafted messages can be devised that are integrated into internal marketing activities (e.g. company newsletters, and in-house seminars and training programmes), with the intention of communicating cyber security awareness as widely as possible so that it creates a ripple effect and leads to word-of-mouth across business functions. By ensuring that external risk communication is given priority, those in the industry can make sure the risk communication process is flexible and is updated through time, and can hold training sessions also with suppliers, wholesalers, retailers and specialist dealers/providers. ENISA (2011: 3) have provided some relevant advice about this and state:

External communication and consulting by specialized consultants, as well as exchange of information and cooperation with other organizations should also be planned and implemented on a regular basis. The exchange of this knowledge and experience can prove extremely helpful for addressing issues related to both the risks and the process to manage these risks, leading thus to a view on risks that is free from subjective estimations. Furthermore, involving external personnel in such activities contributes towards the renewal of available know-how and risk perception.

Reflecting on the above makes clear that two aspects are in tandem: the need for an appropriate risk management process that is viewed as a shared responsibility; and the need for a risk communication process that is also viewed as a shared responsibility. Focusing on the external environment, the cyber security manager can think in terms of the local market, the business itself, the competitors and their actions, the broader financial and political environment; the law and regulatory environment; the social and cultural conditions that prevail; and the external stakeholders (ENISA, 2011: 4). The cyber security manager needs to focus on how an impact can affect the organization's reputation and result in reputational damage, and it is for this reason that cyber security management needs to be viewed as a shared responsibility and placed within a collectivist, stakeholder framework.

As regards the internal environment, ENISA (2011: 5) suggest that a number of areas need attention: key business drivers (market indicators, competitive advances and product attractiveness, for example); the organization's strengths and weaknesses, and also the opportunities and threats; the internal stakeholders; the organization's culture and structure; the assets of the organization(s) as from the perspective of resources (people, systems, processes and capital, for example); and the goals and objectives and the strategies that are in place to assist management to achieve the goals and objectives. Placing this in perspective, the risk manager can, in unison with other senior managers, decide what form communication will take with external stakeholders, and managers that engage in risk management/protection of a risk asset, need to prioritize information sharing with staff in partner organizations and establish reporting systems. By assigning responsibility for the management of risk to individual managers and holding them accountable for their actions during specific outcomes, the risk analysis process in place can be evaluated by auditors. To be effective, there should be a two-step process of auditing: (i) an internal audit that is undertaken by an appointed committee of informed managers; and (ii) an externally conducted audit that is undertaken by an approved and recognized organization, which has an established record and approved certification.

The complexity involved is now apparent. The type of leadership style/model in place and the level of responsibility and control need to stand up to outside scrutiny. If the auditing process is thorough, incremental change will occur but revolutionary change can be embraced if necessary (Greiner, 1967). This is because:

A transformational leader places a high emphasis on trust and trust-based relationships, and considers that employees need to be in harmony with the organization's objectives. This can be interpreted as an individual employee having the same value system as their peers (and other employees) and that there is a match between the employee's value system and the organization's value system, hence internal mutuality.

(Trim and Upton, 2013: 53)

This makes clear the need for internal marketing and the role that is played by the cyber security manager. By helping staff to understand and relate to top management's vision, and ensure that cyber security is viewed as an essential component of security, it should be possible to establish a security culture that is reinforced through appropriate cyber security training programmes and staff development programmes. Because cyber attacks are viewed as debilitating, a transformational style of leadership can be adopted to manage the cyber security process as it allows innovatory processes to be put in place. Kakabadse (2000: 6) suggests that a transformational leader is a good listener and is well able to empower people to manage change, which are key in terms of devising and implementing cyber security initiatives. The transparent working practices that result and which are promoted through open communication benefit from increased interaction between individuals and a hardening of the security culture.

12.5 Communication, Trustworthy Behaviour and Cultural Differences

Bearing in mind that organizations have overseas partners and staff communicate with them in different languages and work in different time zones, the emphasis on developing trustworthy relationships takes precedence as staff deal with different stakeholder organizations that possess different organizational cultures. The cyber security manager has as a consequence to establish a network of reliable informants and responders that operate across borders, who are culturally sensitive and aware of legal issues and possible legal challenges. While people with an individualistic value system are known to be self-sufficient and less dependent on others, those from a collectivist society are considered to be highly influenced by the norms and duties emanating from the in-group (Usunier and Lee, 2009: 43–44). Through the process of understanding how people from a different culture view risk and how a risk manager in a different cultural setting operates, it should be possible for the cyber security manager to understand how people from a different culture evaluate an organization's vulnerability, how they share threat information, how they undertake risk management, how they implement a risk mitigation strategy and how they engage in risk communication. This is important in terms of devising a coordinated risk management strategy based on an organization's risk appetite. What the cyber security manager needs to note is that the business continuity management planning system is linked with and embraces corporate and marketing intelligence, security and legal affairs (e.g. corporate law department) (Trim and Lee, 2019a: 30).

During a cyber attack on an organization, should the attack get through the defences, it is likely that the impact will not only cause a disruption in terms of a loss of power resulting in lost production or the loss of data and a suspension of trading, but also reputational damage and the renegotiating of deals with certain customers. For example, in 2001 a man was sentenced to two years in prison for releasing a large amount of waste into public parks and creeks throughout Queensland, Australia (Verton, 2003: 27). The man carrying out the attack used the Internet and stolen control software to inflict the damage. The person responsible had worked as a consultant on a water project and had initiated the attack after he had been refused a full-time job with the company that installed vital equipment relating to the project. It became known later that the man had tried a number of times to break in and carry out the attack before he eventually succeeded.

By having a cyber security contingency communication plan in place, stakeholders can implement contingency plans to bring a disruption to a close. In order to do this, the dependencies relevant to the restoration process (including suppliers and outsource partners) need to be outlined in advance (ENISA, 2009). Hence,

> A risk communication strategy must therefore be grounded in the business continuity management planning framework and if an impact does occur, the recovery process can be as rapid as possible owing to the fact that the procedures are adequately documented and those in charge or associated with the recovery process are competent to ensure that it goes ahead as planned.
>
> (Trim and Lee, 2014: 80–81)

On reflection, the cyber security manager needs to be competent to undertake, on a regular basis, a situation(al) analysis and a business impact analysis that feed into the business continuity management planning process. The best way to achieve this is to ensure that cyber security management incorporates cyber security awareness and a distinction is made between cyber security training and cyber security education, and a robust cyber security approach is developed that incorporates cooperation between industry, government and academia.

12.6 Preventing Cyber Attacks

Trim and Lee (2011, 2014: 159) indicate that there are six main factors that the cyber security manager needs to take into account in order to prevent cyber attacks on the organization; they are as follows: (1) Action to Protect Against Cyber Attack(s), which requires a foresight risk policy (operational and strategic) to be in place; a defined BYOD policy; an in-house security awareness programme (education and training) and effective contingency responses. (2) Cyber Security Issues to be Addressed, which include an integrated information system to protect personal, private and company data from an information breach; a set of programmes to deal with social engineering, advanced persistent threats, state espionage, compliance and regulatory action; and consumerization and new market offerings. (3) Effectiveness of Existing Risk Management Models, which involve the need to better understand the organization's risk appetite and the consequences of risk from both a quantitative and qualitative perspective; a need to understand human factors and more effective coordination between different organizations (e.g. government and business). (4) Cyber Security Management Framework to Counter Cyber Attacks, which includes industry standards and increased cooperation; efficient deployment of controls and countermeasures; and organizational strategy underpinned by the concept of resilience. (5) An Effective Organizational Knowledge Base that Embraces Risk, Compliance and Governance, which includes a monitoring system to be in place; strategic (external) intelligence; and the sharing of knowledge with competitors and government agencies. (6) Government, Industry and Academia and an Adequate Pool of Skills to Counter Cyber Attacks, which includes a set of broad based education and training programmes; situational awareness to be incorporated in a range of courses and programmes; executive courses and programmes of study for senior and junior managers; and a common strategic intelligence forum covering all aspects.

The pressure on companies and government to keep the public informed cannot be under stated. South Korea has embraced technology and it can be noted that in excess of 95% of the homes have permanent access to the Internet, which has left people open to cyber attack, one of which affected 35 million accounts on a social network (British Embassy Seoul, 2012: 46). There was also an attack on a government-backed bank and this reiterates the fact that cyber security needs to be viewed from a stakeholder perspective.

12.7 Cyber Security Awareness

In order to reduce the possibility of a data breach through cyber security awareness, it is necessary for senior management to increase threat awareness by developing a behavioural awareness programme. Trim and Lee (2019b) take cognizance of the fact that there is a wide literature relating to information systems management, marketing, communication and motivational research (social psychology) that can be drawn on and utilized, and that the cyber security manager can use persuasive communication theory in conjunction with motivation theory, to explain how to create an awareness programme that influences behavioural change. All types of sensitive and confidential data (e.g. product specifications, sales figures and profit margins) and information (e.g. sales territory agreements) and contracts needs to be safeguarded. A collectivist approach to security should result in an appropriate cyber security awareness programme being developed that ensures the organization is resilient enough to withstand an attack (Shillair et al., 2015).

Safa et al. (2015) and Esteves et al. (2017) outline a number of issues relating to security behaviour and it is clear that the cyber security manager needs to be aware of the different types of cyber attack that hackers are known to carry out, if, i.e., the knowledge is to be translated in terms of a cyber security awareness programme. This can only be achieved, however, if top management create a new vision for the organization, which manifests in the implementation of a coordinated information security policy at various levels within the organization. Safa et al. (2015) indicate that managers need to be aware of conscious care behaviour and this means that they are responsive to the way in which employees think through the consequences of their actions before they work online. Sharing information across business functions and organizations is linked with trustworthy behaviour and as it is relatively easy to transfer data and information via the Internet. Walters (2008) suggests that managers need to be aware of two points: trust and reliability. Through trust-based relationships, the cyber security manager can, working with the training manager and the head of internal marketing/marketing manager, develop a cyber security behavioural awareness programme that makes staff aware of the actual and possible cyber threats confronting the organization and its partners.

In order to devise a cyber security awareness programme that can be utilized by the cyber security manager to create sustainable, behavioural change, Trim and Lee (2019b) draw on persuasive communication theory (Petty and Cacioppo, 1984, 1986) in conjunction with motivational and attitudinal theory (Katz, 1960; Fishbein and Ajzen, 1975; Herek, 1987; Ajzen, 1991). Communication can be harnessed through feedback gained relating to the effectiveness of the message and the overall awareness campaign, during specific monitoring points. The cyber security manager needs to note that attitude functional theory (Katz, 1960; Herek, 1987; Shavitt, 1989; Eagly and Chaiken, 1993) highlights the fact that individuals have different levels of knowledge and have different motivations and because of this, fear appeals may be needed to influence behavioural intention (Johnston and Warkentin, 2010). By having an appreciation of what individual behaviour gives rise to, the cyber security manager can formulate a cyber security awareness programme that overcomes resistance and inertia (Tsohou et al., 2015).

12.7.1 Motivation and Communication

To understand better the psychological aspects of human behaviour, the cyber security manager needs to know what constitutes "normative beliefs" and "self-efficacy" (Bulgurcu et al., 2010; Safa et al., 2015; Tsai et al., 2016), because by doing so, they will be aware of what the theory of planned behaviour constitutes. According to Trim and Lee (2019b: 226):

> 'normative beliefs' refers to an employee's understanding of the organization's policies and their perceived social pressure regarding compliance and expected behavioural change; and as regards 'self-efficacy', this is an employee's assessment of their own level of knowledge and skills to complete tasks.

Hence, a cyber security awareness programme needs to take into account and be based on an individual's view of compliance (Bulgurcu et al., 2010) and how senior staff within the organization hold staff accountable for their actions.

Camp (2009) argues that there is more than one method of risk communication and Bada and Sasse (2014) suggest that a security awareness programme may not result in people acting responsibly. Messages need to be interpreted in a meaningful way by the user and because of this, security awareness warnings should be non-technical and authoritative in nature (Modic and Anderson, 2014). Persuasive communication theory, (the Elaboration Likelihood Model (ELM)) (Petty and Cacioppo, 1984, 1986) can be used to formulate a systematic information processing strategy (De Meulenaer et al., 2015). This is because persuasive communication is used to get employees to adopt an inward-directed approach that results in their commitment to increasing organizational effectiveness (Williams, 2005). What the cyber security manager needs to realize, however, is that in order that information is communicated effectively among different audiences, the different levels of knowledge and motivation of individuals need to be taken into account. Daft and Lengel (1984, 1986) suggest that messages are transferred and absorbed in different ways (direct and indirect means) and Borup et al. (2015) found that text was the most preferred source of feedback.

In order that the cyber security manager can establish, prior to the launch of a cyber security awareness programme, how it is likely to be received, they need to understand the motivational level of individuals. Hence, functional theories of attitudes have proved helpful in terms of predicting how certain types of individual will respond to a situation/event in terms of their level of motivation. As regards the knowledge function, it

> helps people to organize information and better understand their operating environment; the utilitarian function, relates to how people obtain rewards or

minimize punishment; the ego-defensive function, works to protect the 'self' from unpleasant situations or threats and maintain self-esteem; and the value-expressive function (self-expressive, which is one of the social functions), revolves around an individual expressing their central values and beliefs to other people through their behaviour. It is also worth noting that people adhere to self-presentation (eg., social-adjustive function, which is another social function). Therefore, behaviour is related to an individual gaining social approval and maintaining relationships with their peer group.

(Trim and Lee, 2019b: 227–228)

Bearing in mind that the "knowledge function" is responsible for an individual's attitude and their behaviour, and is interconnected with other functions of attitudes, the cyber security manager can establish how the knowledge function can influence an individual's attitude and shape their behaviour, and gauge how behavioural change manifests in an organization's cyber security policy. A key point to note is that an employee is expected to conform to the organization's policy (normative beliefs) and their behaviour is expected to be compliant (Bulgurcu et al., 2010).

The cyber security manager, working with other managers within the partnership arrangement, will need to look for inappropriate behaviour and develop their knowledge of trends in online crime (Esteves et al., 2017). This is so that a potential problem can be recognized and dealt with in advance of it becoming a major concern/incident. When dealing with matters of a human resource management nature, it is important that both ethical issues and legal issues are kept in mind, and that the rights of individuals are protected. Employees that are known not to implement company policy can be sent on a cyber security refresher course and by acknowledging the role that security plays in safeguarding the firm's operational capability, it should be possible for senior management to establish a security culture that ensures that staff place security at the top of their agenda. Cyber security training courses can be introduced to help remind staff that they need to change their behaviour and information/messages can be produced on a regular basis that reinforces the aims and objectives of the cyber security awareness programme.

12.7.2 *An Approach to Behavioural Change*

A key area that needs attention in terms of cyber security behaviour is intelligence and the cyber security manager should view this from the perspective of strategic cyber intelligence. Strategic cyber intelligence should be linked with organizational resilience and involve the sharing of information with relevant government organizations/agencies. This requires that staff use competitive intelligence tools and engage in forecasting, and embrace the relationship management approach when working with in-house security and intelligence specialists. This is due to various security experts joining the decision-making process at different times and for different reasons. Furthermore, the cyber security manager needs to use a pro-active approach as regards encouraging interaction between functions (e.g. intra-company and inter-company). This is because in a number of cases, highly sensitive data and information are discussed and exchanged. Inter-functional cooperation and decision-making allows security policy to be integrated into the strategic planning process and the use of communications technology should be managed and monitored by IT (Information Technology) staff through the company's compliance policy and information/cyber security policy (Ifinedo, 2014).

By recognizing that individuals have certain likes and dislikes, and acknowledging that they possess different levels of knowledge and motivation, and relate to cyber threats differently, the cyber security manager, working with human resource specialists and the training manager, can identify what needs to be done in order to bring everyone up to the required level of cyber security behavioural awareness. In order that an inclusive cyber security awareness policy is adopted throughout the partnership arrangement, Trim and Lee (2019b: 232–233) identified the factors that influence attitude/behavioural change of six different types of people, in terms of knowledge and cyber security awareness: Star (high level of knowledge and highly motivated in cyber security awareness issues); Adaptor (low level of knowledge and highly motivated in cyber security awareness issues); Leader (high level of knowledge and moderately motivated in cyber security awareness issues); Semi-adaptor (low level of knowledge and are moderately motivated in cyber security awareness issues); Satisfier (high level of knowledge and low motivation in cyber security awareness issues); and Reformer (low level of knowledge and low motivation in cyber security awareness issues). The segmentation of people proves relevant in terms of grouping individuals so that they can undergo specifically designed training programmes and be subject to different but reinforcing cyber security awareness information.

By differentiating the groups in the way outlined, the cyber security manager can identify the knowledge gaps that exist and specify the rewards/punishments that are to be invoked so that those that need to develop their knowledge and become more cyber security aware undergo the appropriate training. What needs to be recognized is that cyber security training provision needs to be current and delivered at an acceptable level so that those undergoing the training acquire the appropriate skills in a timely manner and are not overwhelmed by the process. Careful attention needs to be given to the way the information/message is perceived (Acquisti and Grossklags, 2007) and the way in which a change in behaviour is related to the perceived threats identified (Venkatesh and Bala, 2008; Tsai et al., 2016). It is important, therefore, to note that attention needs to be given to the supporting arguments and also, the authenticity/reliability of the information source (e.g. the person delivering the message) (Petty et al., 2004).

This suggests that in order for a training programme to be effective, it is necessary to take into consideration the different levels of cyber security training required in terms of the needs of each group with regard to their level of knowledge, their motivation, their skill set, the type of support required and the future role that they will play. There are four points to consider:

> (i) the quality of the information received; (ii) the additional information needed but which staff do not have access to; (iii) the ability of the group members to integrate the information; and (iv) the ability of the group members to engage in critical appreciation.
>
> (Trim and Lee, 2019b: 233)

The various training and support programmes developed can help individuals to reduce the gap between "self-efficacy" and raise their confidence level so that they perform their tasks appropriately (Ajzen, 2002; Bulgurcu et al., 2010) and are rewarded for it.

In order that behavioural awareness and attitudinal change occur through time, the cyber security manager needs to work with senior management and produce a cyber security behavioural awareness programme framework (Trim and Lee, 2019b: 222–234), which details the link between security and cyber security (persuasive communication (*correctness*)); the processing of information (issue-relevant information (*the elaboration continuum*)); key variables that influence attitudes towards cyber security (variable and elaboration process (*multiple-roles*)); evidence that cyber attacks are harmful (the truth of a message (*objective-processing*)); arguments and discussion, and clarification of the organization's risk appetite (counteracting arguments (*biased-processing*)); attitudes relating to cyber attacks (examining information for merit (*trade-off*)) and people understand why it is important to invest in security (message processing (*attitude strength*)). What needs to be noted is that the messages devised and used are influential in terms of influencing behavioural change, but behavioural change is a process and continuous in orientation.

Barker (2021) reinforces the view that cyber security awareness is a continuous process and needs to be supported by the appointment of cyber security champions/ambassadors who are charged with ensuring that staff identify with the organization's security culture, which is reinforced by the organization's value system. The cyber security champions/ambassadors provide both inspiration and guidance, and can direct staff that are working remotely, to help points so that they can receive help to solve cyber related work-based problems. It can be noted that the interactions between individuals result in explicit knowledge being turned into tacit knowledge, and vice versa (Nonaka et al., 1996). The objective of a cyber security behavioural awareness programme framework is to build a collectivist mentality throughout the partnership arrangement and to ensure that the relationship building process revolves around structural bonding (Han et al., 2008). By harnessing the commitment of staff in this way it should result in an increase in operational effectiveness (Slater and Narver, 1995) as staff will be more aware of the nature of cyber attacks and how they are evolving, and how countermeasures can be implemented. By embracing the learning organization approach, the organization should be less vulnerable to a cyber attack, which are in fact becoming more sophisticated and more persistent (HM Government, 2016).

12.8 Learning Summary

As has been made clear throughout, strategic intelligence is at the heart of cyber security and although risk management is central to cyber security provision, and reinforced through risk communication and training, it has to be acknowledged that a transformational leadership model, which advocates the transformational management approach, is central to the cyber security awareness process. The cyber security awareness programme can be implemented throughout a partnership arrangement and can be used to support existing staff and newly appointed staff, and make sure that they are compliant. By acknowledging that business continuity management planning is pivotal, the cyber security manager can gain the support of top management and ensure that the organization's value system is communicated to staff and staff, in turn, relate to it and exercise security oriented judgement. Figure 12.1 outlines the process involved and highlights the importance of senior management establishing trust-based relationships with staff, which are influential in terms of behavioural change.

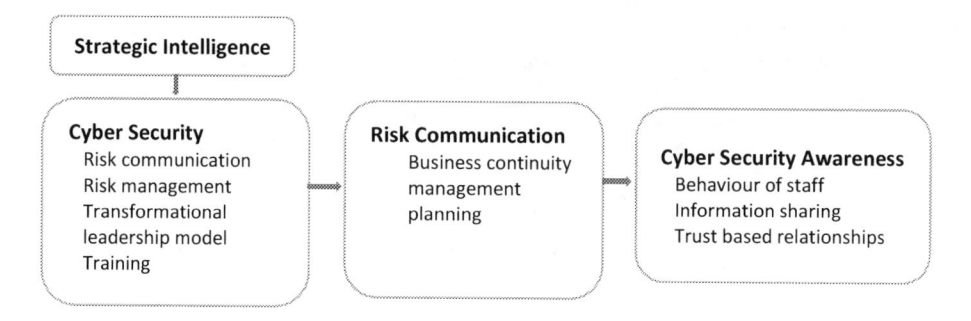

Figure 12.1 Cyber security awareness in context.

The reader will be able to:

- devise a cyber security awareness programme in the context of a security culture;
- implement a cyber security awareness programme in the context of a security culture; and
- evaluate a cyber security awareness programme in the context of a security culture

12.9 Conclusion

The cyber security manager, assisted by other managers but mainly by the risk manager, the training manager and the internal marketing/marketing manager, can harness in-house and external knowledge in order to devise an effective cyber security awareness programme that meets the needs of staff operating at different levels of complexity and who have different levels of exposure to cyber attacks. By knowing how to mitigate cyber risks, and drawing on relevant management theory, the cyber security manager is well placed to provide guidance with respect to assisting senior management to establish a security culture that reinforces the fact that cyber security is central to a partnership arrangement remaining resilient.

12.10 Mini Case: Increasing Cyber Security Awareness

The cyber security training programme had been organized at short notice and staff were unhappy because it replaced a planned company excursion to the coast. The person in charge of the training session had been brought in from an external training company that specialized in security training and providing security based solutions, and had a strict view as to what security was.

"Good morning everybody", said Mrs. Gilbert. "How are you today?"

Silence prevailed. Those present looked at each other and one even shook his head. Eventually, people started to respond and some even smiled.

"Well, I know, you have given up a day out to be here but let me tell you, it will be worth it". Mrs. Gilbert started the session by getting people to introduce themselves to each other. The ice breaker was not that well received because those present had all been with the company for three years plus. They knew each other by sight if not by name.

"Good, now it seems that we have to address a key concern, which is, how can people be made aware of the different types of cyber threat that exist".

"We know all that", said Mr. Thomas, who had been with the company for over six years and was known to be a no-nonsense person.

"Do you now", replied Mrs. Gilbert, "We shall soon find out".

Those present warmed to Mrs. Gilbert and the training programme gained momentum. Mrs. Gilbert drew on various statistics and presented a strong case built around, cyber security awareness being crucial to organizational change and responding to crises. She made it clear that people do group together if they feel threatened and also, coping with image and identity is all about cultural change and group identity. Within a short period of time, the group had covered social identity theory and had discussed in detail aspects of personality and motivation. External image was covered in the context of reputational damage and the need to establish why identity threats occur was given adequate coverage. Drawing on the work of Piening et al. (2020), Mrs. Gilbert explained that organizational identity threats are events that call into question people's perception and personal identity and social identity, and how people within the organization relate to people from different business functions.

A key issue to be addressed later in the day was how organizational members respond to an event, a cyber attack, and how they deal with the crisis so that it does not escalate out of control. By understanding that a data breach can result in adverse publicity, a fine and indeed a loss of business, drew the group's attention because a story had just surfaced in the news relating to a scam that had seen a company send out false invoices to a number of companies. Mrs. Gilbert was aware of the case and informed those present that she used to work for a company that normally over paid on invoices. Indeed, it is so much of a problem for some large companies that they employ a full-time member of staff to check through "duplicate" or spurious invoices and check that over payments are corrected (e.g. money is recovered). Mrs. Gilbert also told the audience that she had experience of flying to a European capital and returning by another airline, only to be double charged for the trip when in fact it was as shared route and she should only have been charged for a return trip. Sorting it out took many months and also, it was problematic because one of the airlines kept changing the dates of the trip on the invoice. The airline had only agreed to investigate the claim further when she had threatened to report the airlines to the appropriate authorities.

Reflecting on the importance of organizational identity, Piening et al. (2020: 332) suggest that organizational identity threat response includes three aspects: threat recognition; threat attribution and threat response. What managers need to recognize is that to deal with a cyber threat effectively, there has to be a flexible and adaptive culture in place that allows people from different business functions to come together and share information so that there is complete transparency. This means that staff from information communications and technology (ICT) need to be approachable and both provide non-IT specialists with information and respond to enquiries and provide support when necessary.

The last session of the day focused more intensely on motivation and how managers can keep their subordinates focused on maintaining awareness and an interest in cyber related occurrences. A pro-active approach was recommended and also, it was suggested that cyber security training and cyber security refresher courses should be provided at fixed intervals as this was the best way of keeping people informed and also ensure that they developed the necessary skill base to counteract cyber attacks.

During the question and answer session at the end of the day, several ideas were put forward for dealing with business to business situations because several employees were involved in buyer-supplier relations. It was decided that group identity was a major factor and open communication was more appropriate than closed or infrequent communication. Furthermore, by being open to information sharing and adopting a joint approach to problem solving, it was possible to have an integrated cyber security policy in place that benefitted all the parties concerned.

Questions

Question 1: Why is it important to keep staff motivated in terms of cyber threats?

Question 2: What cyber security related information should be shared by managers in partner organizations?

Question 3: How can a collectivist approach to cyber security be developed?

Case Source

Piening, E.P., Salge, T.O., Antons, D., and Kreiner, G.E. (2020). Standing together or falling apart? Understanding employees' responses to organizational identity threats. *Academy of Management Review*, 45 (2): 325–351. https://doi.org/10.5465/amr.2016.0457.

12.11 Extended Case: A Cyber Security Awareness Programme

When using the various standards that exist to assess risk, the cyber security manager needs to take into account confidentiality, integrity and availability (collectively known as CIA) and use an appropriate risk analysis tool. This is so that the level of risk can be interpreted by taking into account the interdependencies and establishing how multiple impacts will affect the organization and raise its level of vulnerability. Such intelligence will allow the cyber security manager to devise and implement organizational structures that contain countermeasures and at the same time, allow the workforce to be better informed about dealing with cyber attacks.

As regards a business impact assessment, the cyber security manager can look at the risk assessment policy and establish the possible impact on the business in terms of lost income due to the cancellation of contracts. Risk assessment needs to be as transparent as possible so that staff know the necessary steps that are gone through (risk assessment details, CIA (confidentiality, integrity and availability), identification of threats and various threats (cracking keys and passwords), and the available countermeasures to reduce the risk of an asset (Trim and Lee, 2014: 154). Risk can be denoted on a scale of 1–5 or denoted as low risk, medium risk and high risk.

Business continuity and policy management require the cyber security manager to review the organization's policy in terms of compliance and review policy against ISO standards, and the various controls, governance and audit points (department or site) can be selected for attention if, i.e., problems have been known to occur (e.g. staff logging into databases they do not have access to). The latter refers to the security of data and the link to the organization's risk register and the role that the cyber security manager plays in reporting security matters to senior management. With regard to enterprise risk management, individual managers are provided with specific risk assessments and both the cyber security manager and the risk manager are held accountable for how the risks are prioritized and how they report matters in terms of making the organization compliant.

The cyber security manager needs to keep a record of all the internal and external factors that senior management need to know and monitor as regards an organization's vulnerabilities, and this is done in isolation of the risk manager, who also compiles a separate record of events. This is so that if an internal enquiry is conducted into a data breach, for example, both the cyber security manager and the risk manager can provide information that outlines how each has conformed to company policy. There will of course be commonalties but also differences.

The various policies, which come under the heading Consumerization of IT, relate to BYOD and as well as the vulnerabilities, there is also the risk associated with tracking devices (Wilson, 2012). As regards the use of devices, the transfer of data between points highlights the issue of industrial espionage (Wilson, 2012), and the need to prevent hackers from breaking into a device and accessing data and information that is inadequately safeguarded or provides access to data held in the cloud (Wilson, 2012). There are issues in terms of the vulnerability and interconnectedness of platforms (system network) (Wilson, 2012) and whether the manufacturer/vendor of a device complies with recognized standards so that the device is considered safe to use (Wilson, 2012).

The role of social media is becoming more important in terms of an organization's marketing capability, and the corporate/user interface may constitute a potential vulnerability, hence an emergency response team needs to be in place to deal with all types of incidents (ranging from technical expertise to media expertise) and needs also to be able to deal with the public (Wilson, 2012).

Taking cognizance of changes in online human behaviour in terms of the usage of a platform is important (Collins, 2012) and the cyber security manager needs to be aware of the importance of information assurance. The cyber security manager, working with the digital marketing manager, needs to consider the use of integrated, multi-media channels and make use of multi-media tools if an attack is launched. If an attack has been successful and impacted the organization, senior managers need to (Mehringer, 2012) (i) investigate and confirm the incident; (ii) prepare a communication response and (iii) notify the media, subscribers and the public.

A number of recommendations can be provided that help to shape a cyber security awareness programme. These include reducing the problems associated with software vulnerability (Mehringer, 2012), which can be done through improving the quality of software in the context of private-public partnerships (Bryant, 2012). A more integrated approach can be adopted as regards how companies calculate the risk associated with interdependencies (Panzieri, 2012). Tracking and tracing cyber attacks allow senior managers to better understand the vulnerabilities evident (Panzieri, 2012) and what attackers are focusing on. Risk management needs to be enhanced through information sharing and collaborative working arrangements, the objective being to identify probable impacts and the role of the emergency team needs to be thought through so that the necessary support is provided in real time (Panzieri, 2012).

Bearing in mind that cyber attacks are asymmetric, anonymous and anarchic, the cyber security manager needs to be aware that those carrying out cyber attacks will continue and try a different attack vector (Roehrig, 2012) until they gain access to the target/asset. Because of this, information and intelligence sharing is necessary and this includes forensics (Roehrig, 2012). Cooperation between the military and civilian sectors, at both the national level and international level, will help to build a common culture of cyber defence based on education and training that incorporates networking and interoperability (Roehrig, 2012).

By engaging in risk management assessment and prioritizing investments in cyber defence, trusted security operations will be put in place that includes a realistic impact analysis (e.g. economic impacts and organizational and operational impacts) (Pevtschin, 2012). The cyber security manager needs to remain vigilant however and ensure that social engineering techniques and the deployment of malware (e.g. to carry out industrial espionage) is covered in a cyber security awareness programme. Staff need to be informed of how to prevent sensitive data that can be used for sophisticated social engineering attacks (Thon, 2012) from being given out. When weighing up the possible impacts in terms of the investment needed in countermeasures, and the balance between technology and the role of management in terms of low and high intensities (Vernez, 2012), the cyber security manager needs to help devise an awareness programme that includes continual monitoring (Vernez, 2012) and is underpinned by the collectivist approach.

Questions

Question 1: Which factors should the cyber security manager take into account when formulating a cyber security awareness programme?

Question 2: Why is it important to have a unified and co-owned cyber security awareness programme in place?

Question 3: Explain how staff employed by partner organizations can contribute to a shared cyber security awareness programme.

Case Sources

Bryant, I. (2012). Improving cyberspace trustability through software. *SMi Cyber Deference Conference*, Copthore Hotel, London (18th June).

Collins, B. (2012). Environmental impacts on IA. *IAAC Research Workshop. Consumerism: Same Old IA Issues... or Not?* BCS, The Chartered Institute for IT, London (19th June).

Mehringer, S. (2012). Cyber attacks: NATO takes a direct hit. *SMi Cyber Deference Conference*, Copthore Hotel, London (18th June).

Panzieri, S. (2012). The Italian national cyber security approach. *SMi Cyber Deference Conference*, Copthore Hotel, London (18th June).

Pevtschin, V. (2012). The EOS cyber security working group white paper update. *SMi Cyber Deference Conference*, Copthore Hotel, London (18th June).

Roehrig, W. (2012). Cyber defence: The role of EDA. *SMi Cyber Deference Conference*, Copthore Hotel, London (18th June).

Thon, R. (2012). Social media and the Norwegian National Security Authority (NOR NSM). *SMi Cyber Deference Conference*, Copthore Hotel, London (19th June).

Trim, P.R.J., and Lee, Y-I. (2014). Cyber Security Management: A Governance, Risk and Compliance Framework. Farnham: Gower Publishing.

Vernez, G. (2012). Cyber security awareness campaigns. *SMi Cyber Deference Conference*, Copthore Hotel, London (19th June).

Wilson, P. (2012). Embedded into the company's structure? Or an add on? *IAAC Research Workshop. Consumerism: Same Old IA Issues... or Not?* BCS, The Chartered Institute for IT, London.

12.12 References

Acquisti, A., and Grossklags, J. (2007) What can behavioral economics teach us about privacy? pp. 363–380. In A. Acquisti, S. Gritzalis, C. Lambrinoudakis, and S. di Vimercati (Eds.), *Digital Privacy: Theory, Technologies and Practices.* New York and London: Auerback Publications/Taylor & Francis.

Ajzen, I. (1991). The theory of planned behaviour. *Organizational Behaviour and Human Decision Processes*, 50 (2): 179–211. https://doi.org/10.1016/0749-5978(91)90020-T.

Ajzen, I. (2002). Perceived behavioural control, self-efficacy, locus of control, and the theory of planned behavior. *Journal of Applied Social Psychology*, 32 (4): 665–683. https://doi.org/10.1111/j.1559-1816.2002.tb00236.x.

Bada, M., and Sasse, A. (2014). *Cyber Security Awareness Campaigns. Why Do They Fail to Change Behaviour?* Global Cyber Security Capacity Centre: Draft Working Paper. Oxford: Oxford University (July).

Barker, J. (2021). Cyber culture and awareness. IAAC (Information Assurance Advisory Council) webinar 24th November (12.30pm to 1pm).

Borup, J., West, R.E., and Thomas, R. (2015). The impact of text versus video communication on instructor feedback in blended courses. *Education Technology Research Development*, 63 (2): 161–184. https://doi.org/10.1007/s11423-015-9367-8.

British Embassy Seoul. (2012). *Republic of Korea Homeland Security Market.* Seoul: DSO, Defence and Security Section, British Embassy (April).

Bulgurcu, B., Cavusoglu, H., and Benbasat, I. (2010). Information security policy compliance: An empirical study of rationality-based beliefs and information security awareness. *MIS Quarterly*, 34 (3): 523–548.

Camp, L.J. (2009). Mental models of privacy and security. *IEEE Technology and Society Magazine* (Fall): 37–46. https://doi.org/10.1109/MTS.2009934142.

Daft, R.L., and Lengel, R.H. (1984). The nature and use of formal control systems for management control and strategy implantation. *Journal of Management*, 10 (1): 43–66. https://doi.org/10.1177/014920638401000105.

Daft, R.L., and Lengel, R.H. (1986). Organizational information requirements, media richness and structural design. *Management Science*, 32 (5): 554–571. https://doi.org/10.1287/mnsc.32.5.554.

De Meulenaer, S., Dens, N., and De Pelsmacker, P. (2015). Which cues cause consumers to perceive brands as more global? A conjoint analysis. *International Marketing Review*, 32 (6): 606–626. https://doi.org/10.1108/IMR-04-2014-0144.

Eagly, A.H., and Chaiken, S. (1993). *The Psychology of Attitudes* (1st ed.). Fort Worth, TX: Harcout Brace.

ENISA. (2009). *Cloud Computing: Information Assurance Framework*, European Network and Information Security Agency, pp. 1–24 (November).

ENISA. (2011). *Risk Management*. European Network and Information Security Agency, pp. 1–108. http://www.enisa.europa.eu/act/rm/cr/risk-management-inventory/rm-process (accessed on 27th February, 2011).

Esteves, J., Ramalho, E., and De Haro, G. (2017). To improve cybersecurity, think like a hacker. *Sloan Management Review*, 58 (3): 71–77. http://mitsmr.com/2mXYJdD.

Fishbein, M., and Ajzen, I. (1975). *Belief, Attitude, Intention and Behaviour: An Introduction to Theory and Research*. Reading, MA: Addison-Wesley.

Greiner, L. (1967). Patterns of organization change. *Harvard Business Review*, 45 (3): 119–130.

Han, S-L., Kim, Y.T., Oh, C.Y., and Chung, J.M. (2008). Business relationships and structural bonding: A study of American metal industry. *Journal of Global Academy of Marketing Science*, 18 (3): 115–132. https://doi.org/10.1080/12297119.2008.9707520.

Herek, G. M. (1987). Can functions be measured? A new perspective on the functional approach to attitudes. *Social Psychology Quarterly*, 50 (4): 285–303. http://www.jstor.org/stable/2786814.

HM Government (2016). *National Cyber Security Strategy 2016–2021*. London: HM Government.

Ifinedo, P. (2014). Information systems security policy compliance: An empirical study of the effects of socialisation, influence, and cognition. *Information & Management*, 51 (1): 69–79. https://dx.doi.org/10.1016/j.im.2013.10.001.

Johnston, A.C., and Warkentin, M. (2010). Fear appeals and information security behaviors: An empirical study. *MIS Quarterly*, 34 (3): 549–566.

Kakabadse, A. (2000). From individual to team to cadre: Tracking leadership for the third millennium. *Strategic Change*, 9 (1): 5–16.

Katz, D. (1960). The functional approach to the study of attitudes. *Public Opinion Quarterly*, 24 (2): 163–204. https://doi.org/10.1086/266945.

Management Today (2014). Are you ready for a cyber attack? *Management Today* (September): 28–29.

Mattern, T., Felker, J., Borum, R., and Bamford, G. (2014). Operational levels of cyber intelligence. *International Journal of Intelligence and CounterIntelligence*, 27 (4): 702–719.

Modic, D., and Anderson, R. (2014). Reading this may harm your computer: The psychology of malware warnings. *Computers in Human Behavior*, 41 (December): 71–79. http://dx.doi.org./10.1016/j.chb.2014.09.014.

Nonaka, I., Takeuchi, H., and Umemoto, K. (1996). A theory of organizational knowledge creation. *Unlearning and Learning for Technological Innovation*, (Special Issue) 11 (7/8): 833–845. https://doi.org/10.1504/IJTM.1996.025472.

Petty, R.E., and Cacioppo, J.T. (1984). The effects of involvement on responses to argument quantity and quality: Central and peripheral routes to persuasion. *Journal of Personality and Social Psychology*, 46 (1): 69–81. http://dx.doi.org/10.1037/0022-3514.46.1.69.

Petty, R.E., and Cacioppo, J.T. (1986). The elaboration likelihood model of persuasion, pp. 123–205. In L. Berkowitz (Ed.), *Advances in Experimental Social Psychology*, Volume 19. New York: Academic Press. https://doi.org/10.1016/S0065-2601(08)60214-2.

Petty, R.E., Rucker, D.D., Bizer, G.Y., and Cacioppo, J.T. (2004). The elaboration likelihood model of persuasion, pp. 65–89. In J.S. Seiter and R.H. Gass (Eds.), *Perspectives on Persuasion, Social Influence, and Compliance Gaining*. Boston, MA: Pearson.

Safa, N.S., Sookhak, M., von Solms, R., Furnell, S., Ghani, N.A., and Herawan, T. (2015). Information security conscious care behavior formation in organizations, *Computers & Security*, 53 (September): 65–78. https://dx.doi.org/10.1016/j.cose.2015.05.012.

Shavitt, S. (1989). Products, personalities and situations in attitude functions: Implications for consumer behaviour, pp. 300–305. In T.K. Srull (Ed.), *Advances in Consumer Research*, Volume 16. Provo, UT: Association for Consumer Research.

Shillair, R., Cotten, S.R., Tsai, H-Y., Alhabash, S., LaRose, R., and Rifon, N.J. (2015). Online safety begins with you and me: Convincing Internet users to protect themselves. *Computers in Human Behavior*, 48 (July): 199–207. http://dx.doi.org./10.1016/j.chb.2015.01.046.

Slater, S.F., and Narver, J.C. (1995). Market orientation and the learning organization. *Journal of Marketing*, 59 (3): 63–74. http://www.jstor.org/stable/1252120.

Trim, P.R.J., and Lee, Y-I. (2011). A pro-active approach to managing cyber security threats. *The CAMIS Integrated Governance, Risk and Compliance Conference and Knowledge Sharing Event, Incorporating the iGRC Consortium Demonstration and Network Sensor Devices*, Birkbeck, University of London (15th December).

Trim, P.R.J., and Lee, Y-I. (2014). *Cyber Security Management: A Governance, Risk and Compliance Framework*. Farnham: Gower Publishing.

Trim, P.R.J., and Lee, Y-I. (2019a). Cyber security: Communication and risk management. *Sécurité & Stratégie*, 32 (April/June): 26–31.

Trim, P.R.J., and Lee, Y-I. (2019b). The role of B2B marketers in increasing cyber security awareness and influencing behavioural change. *Industrial Marketing Management*, 83: 224–238. http://dx.doi.org./10.1016/j.indmarman.2019.04.003.

Trim, P.R.J., and Upton, D. (2013). *Cyber Security Culture: Counteracting Cyber Threats through Organizational Learning and Training*. Farnham: Gower Publishing.

Tsai, H.-Y.S., Jiang, M., Alhabash, S., LaRose, R., Rifon, N.J., and Cotton, S.R. (2016). Understanding online safety behaviours: A protection motivation theory perspective. *Computers & Security*, 59 (June): 138–150. https://dx.doi.org/10.1016/j.cose.2016.02.009.

Tsohou, A., Karyda, M., Kokolakis, S., and Kiountouzis, E. (2015). Managing the introduction of information security awareness programmes in organisations. *European Journal of Information Systems*, 24 (1): 38–58. http://dx.doi.org./10.1057/ejis.2013.27.

Usunier, J-C., and Lee, J.A. (2009). *Marketing Across Cultures*. Harlow: Pearson Education Limited.

Venkatesh, V. and Bala, H. (2008). Technology acceptance model 3 and a research agenda on interventions. *Decision Sciences*, 39 (2): 273–315. https://doi.org/10.1111/j.1540-5912.2008.00192.x.

Verton, D. (2003). *Black Ice: The Invisible Threat of Cyber –Terrorism*. Emeryville, CA: McGraw Hill/Osborne.

Walters, P.G.P. (2008). Adding value in global B2B supply chains: Strategic directions and the role of the Internet as a driver of competitive advantage. *Industrial Marketing Management*, 37 (1): 59–68. https://doi.org/10.1016/j.indmarman.2007.06.010.

Williams, C.C. (2005). Trust diffusion: The effect of interpersonal trust on structure, function, and organizational transparency. *Business and Society*, 44 (3): 357–368. https://doi.org/10.1177/0007650305275299.

12.13 Further Reading

Li, L., He, W., Xu, L., Ash, I., Anwar, M., and Yuan, X. (2019). Investigating the impact of cybersecurity policy awareness on employees' cyber security behavior. *International Journal of Information Management*, 45: 13–24. https://doi.org/10.1016/j.ijinfomgt.2018.10.017.

Trim, P.R.J., and Lee, Y-I. (2019). The role of B2B marketers in increasing cyber security awareness and influencing behavioural change. *Industrial Marketing Management*, 83: 224–238. https://doi.org/10.1016/j.indmarman.2019.04.003.

12.14 Bank of Questions

Question 1: Provide a definition of cyber intelligence and explain your understanding of the subject matter.

Question 2: How can strategic intelligence be integrated into the company's business model? Provide examples to reinforce your arguments.

Question 3: How can the risk communication policy be integrated into the organization's risk management strategy?

Question 4: Why must the cyber security manager understand the importance associated with cultural value systems when formulating a cyber security awareness strategy?

Question 5: What is a cyber security contingency plan composed of?

Question 6: How logical is it to devise a cyber security awareness programme that takes into account the cyber security knowledge and skills of different groups of people?

Index

Printed in the United States
by Baker & Taylor Publisher Services